Home Visiting

Home Visiting

Promoting Healthy Parent and Child Development

by

Carol S. Klass, Ph.D.

·P A U L·H·
BROOKES
PUBLISHING C?

Baltimore · London · Toronto · Sydney

Paul H. Brookes Publishing Co.
Post Office Box 10624
Baltimore, Maryland 21285-0624
www.brookespublishing.com

Third printing, September 2000.

Typeset by AeroType, Inc., Amherst, New Hampshire.
Manufactured in the United States of America by
Thomson-Shore, Inc., Dexter, Michigan.

The names of the family members described in the vignettes and interviews recorded in this book have been changed to protect their identities.

Permission to reprint the following quotations is gratefully ackowledged:

Page 11:   Quotation from Martin Buber reprinted with the permission of Scribner, a Division of Simon & Schuster, from I AND THOU by Martin Buber, Translated by Ronald Gregory Smith, Copyright © 1958 by Charles Scribner's Sons, Copyright Under the Berne Convention.

Page 221:   Quotation from Rabindranath Tagore reprinted with the permission of Simon & Schuster from THE COLLECTED POEMS AND PLAYS OF RABINDRANATH TAGORE (New York: Macmillan, 1937).

Library of Congress Cataloging-in-Publication Data

Klass, Carol Speekman.
    Home visiting : promoting healthy parent and child development /
Carol S. Klass.
        p.   cm.
    Includes bibliographical references (p.   ) and index.
    ISBN 1-55766-261-4 (alk. paper)
        1. Parenting—Study and teaching.   2. Child development—Study and teaching.   3. Home-based family services.   4. Social case work.
    I. Title.
HQ755.7.K59   1996
649'.1'07—dc20   96-26512
                                                                                       CIP

British Cataloguing in Publication data are available from the British Library.

Contents

About the Author ix

Foreword   *Jeree Pawl* xi

Preface xv

Acknowledgments xix

Introduction 1

   Approach 4

   Overview of Topics 6

I   Home Visiting: The New Profession

   1   The Relationship Between Parents and the Home Visitor 11

      Forming the Parent–Home Visitor Relationship 12

      Progression of the Parent–Home Visitor Relationship 20

      Establishing Reciprocal, Positive Feelings Between
         Parents and Home Visitors: A Personal Relationship 25

      Shared Delight in the Child 28

      Home Visitors' Relationship with Teenage Parents 29

      Difficulties and Dilemmas 34

      Conclusions 37

   2   The Home Visitor's Approach 39

      Communication and Interpersonal Skills 40

      Additional Knowledge and Skills 59

      Culturally Diverse Families:
         Beliefs, Values, and Practices 71

      Difficulties and Dilemmas 78

      Conclusions 83

   3   Home Visitors' Professional Development 85

      Education 87

      Supervision 102

      Difficulties and Dilemmas 105

      Conclusions 106

II   Promoting Healthy Parent and Child Development

   4   Developing a Sense of Self: The Foundation of
      Social and Emotional Development 111

      Developing Sense of Self: Birth–6 Months 113

Developing Sense of Self: Ages 7–18 Months 119
Developing Sense of Self: Ages 19 Months–3 Years 124
Developing Sense of Self: Ages 3–5 Years 130
Difficulties and Dilemmas 134
Conclusions 137

5   Guidance and Discipline 141

Guidance and Discipline Defined 142
A Developmental Approach 143
Guidance and Discipline in Early Infancy:
   Birth–8 Months 144
Guidance and Discipline: Ages 8–17 Months 147
Guidance and Discipline: Ages 18–36 Months 151
Guidance and Discipline: Ages 3–5 Years 157
Difficulties and Dilemmas 160
Conclusions 162

6   Communication and Language 165

Communication and Language 166
Prespeech: Birth–10 Months 167
Emergence of First Words and Jargon Talk:
   Ages 10–15 Months 171
Word Combinations: Ages 16–24 Months 174
Language and Communication: Ages 2–5 Years 177
Emerging Literacy 181
Difficulties and Dilemmas 184
Conclusions 186

7   Routines, Rituals, and Celebrations 189

Everyday Rituals 190
Childhood Illnesses 209
Family Celebrations and Traditions 212
Difficulties and Dilemmas 215
Conclusions 218

8   Play, Learning, and Development 221

Infant Play: Birth–12 Months 222
Toddler Play: Ages 12–30 Months 227
Preschool Play: Ages 30 Months–5 Years 235
Difficulties and Dilemmas 239
Conclusions 244

9   Siblings 245

Preparation for the New Infant 246
Birth of the Additional Baby 248
Parent Expectations and Comparisons 250
Valuing Each Child as Special 252
Sibling Relationships 254
Parents and Siblings: Balancing the Home Visitor's Interaction . . . 256

Difficulties and Dilemmas 259
Conclusions 261

III Person and Profession

   10 Personal History and Professional Competence 265
       Janice Discusses Her Home Visiting Work 267
       Janice's Personal and Professional History 273
       Cynthia Discusses Her Home Visiting Work 279
       Cynthia's Personal and Professional History 285
       Childhood Pain to Professional Competence 298
       Conclusions 301

Appendix: Resources for Home Visitors 305
Endnotes 311
References 329

Index 339

About the Author

Carol S. Klass, Ph.D., has had a long career in helping parents and teachers of young children improve their caregiving skills. She now works as an early intervention specialist with parents and teachers of young children having behavior problems. Earlier she founded and directed a prevention/intervention family child care program for infants and young children at risk of abuse and neglect. She has been Coordinator of Research at the Parents as Teachers National Center. As a vehicle to improve professional practice for home visitors, family and child care teachers, and supervisors of early educators, Dr. Klass has organized several ethnographic action research programs. She now coordinates the Greater St. Louis Action Research Collaborative (ARC), a learning community of leaders, administrators, and teacher educators. ARC is a Danforth Foundation program. Her first book, *The Autonomous Child: Day Care and the Transmission of Values,* reported a case study of how teachers reproduced larger social values in their everyday interaction patterns with children. Dr. Klass and her husband have two grown sons.

Foreword

Anyone who has ever entered a family's home and attempted to offer support, do treatment, provide developmental information, help with being a parent, educate, or explain and demonstrate useful exercises or holding techniques will recognize the dilemmas, delights, and challenges that are explicated in this book. In an extremely thoughtful, sophisticated, yet very practical manner, Carol Klass gives us a much-needed basic primer that will be of great value to anyone attempting to work with parents and their young children in a home visiting framework. The book is equally relevant to people with a wide range of backgrounds and expertise. Whether the reader is an occupational therapist, a childhood educator, or a psychotherapist practicing in this setting, this book, overall and in specific chapters, makes significant contributions to understanding home visiting and to what the reader needs to know to do successful home visiting work. The book is a serious and successful attempt to capture the unique processes of home visiting. The book presents a beautifully conceived and useful developmental framework that is crucial but often missing from the training of many who work with parents and children.

Carol Klass's book comes into the field at a signally propitious time. We are in an era in which, increasingly, support for single-parent families, those who have newly immigrated, and new parents in general is primarily home based. In addition, those families being served include those whose very young children are exposed to drugs and at risk of abuse and neglect, among other things, and are developing in stressful, unresponsive, understimulating, or violent environments. The number of children trapped in such costly environments grows ever more numerous while there is shrinking economic support for the services they need.

Since the early 1970s, it has become increasingly clear that the experiences infants and toddlers have within their close, caregiving relationships and within the social context in which families are embedded are crucial contributors to the young child's developing sense of self and sense of others, to their ultimate beliefs and values, to their sense of possibility, and to their general competencies. It is equally clear that offering needed services competently can enhance their relationships and positively shift aspects of their surrounding context. These services are a desperately needed response to the infants', toddlers', and parents' personal needs, a community need, a national need, and an overarching human need.

A promising and central attempt to meet this need has been the proliferation of home visiting programs designed to nurture, educate, treat, support, and care about young families. Healthy Start, Even Start, Fair Start, and Early Start programs of all kinds and foci, as well as family preservation and family support centers(the new settlement houses),are reaching into communities. As a result, home visitors with a range of motivation, skills, supports, training, and knowledge are providing these services. Whatever their goals, and they are myriad, all are devoted to working with parents to make positive differences for these parents and their small children to create something that is better than it was when the visitor first stepped over the threshold.

What Klass has done is to produce a book that speaks to all of these practitioners. Both in overall concept and in revealing, detailed vignettes, Klass has something useful, insightful, or practical to say. Whether she is focusing on the complexities of parent–child–visitor relationships or on child development, the book is clear and useful. Her chapters on child development are models. They manage to present the developmental progression from the point of view of the child and the parent. That is, she shows what each emerging level of development in an area means to the child's skills, understanding, and sense of self, and what each emerging developmental level might mean, demand, or engage in the parent.

As she describes aspects of the mutual experience of parent, child, and visitor, Klass thoughtfully describes the repeated dilemmas posed to the home visitor. She understands the simultaneous and conflicting needs of all parties involved. How can the home visitor modulate attention effectively between mother and child, and how can the home visitor support the efforts of the mother to do the same between the visitor and the child? Klass's insights and understanding capture the dilemma well, and these insights are complemented by practical ideas on how to solve the dilemmas. This happens throughout the book.

Klass's book stems from her 20 years of experience with young children and their various caregivers, from her supervision in a variety of programs, and from her ability to make keen observations. It stems as well from her splendid knowledge of infant-toddler development and infant–parent interaction; from her thoughtful understanding and articulation of the experiences of doing this work; and from her careful analysis of the complex relationships between the parent(s), the child, and the home visitor. She uses this understanding of the relationship context to portray in vivid and useful ways the many aspects of the parent–visitor relationship. She does this skillfully enough that the book is relevant both to the untrained and to those professionally trained in some or all of the required skills. The vignettes alone could teach any practitioner not only something about the complex experience of doing the work but also how to convey useful, dynamic information both in ways and in moments when it is welcome, helpful, and natural.

The book is coherent and flows from the author's mastery of a well-researched body of knowledge. It represents a splendid and useful distillation of a wide range of thinking about supportive therapy, interpretive therapy, therapeutic intervention, and a host of distinctions that we have watched coalesce into something more closely resembling a single, responsive approach. The same useful distillation is true for the book's developmental material.

Klass offers an opportunity for many practitioners to understand more about what they do, how they can do it better, and why, in a wholly engaging and available form. Her presentation also takes a strong position regarding the need for clarification of the limits and possibilities of what a particular home visitor may feel reasonably responsible for and competent to provide in terms of skills, training, and goals. She makes an equally proper, strong, and convincing argument for the need for appropriate and knowledgeable supervision on behalf of everyone involved.

I believe Klass's book offers a timely, rich, and thoughtful source of understanding, knowledge, and support to home visitors. At the same time, it offers a model for how seriously and carefully the role of the home visitor must be conceptualized, delimited, and supported. It is only by being as thorough and as careful about home visiting as Klass has been that these efforts can be of as much benefit as possible and do no harm.

I trust this book will not only prove useful to individual practitioners but also generate useful and needed discussion in the field. It should be a strong impetus to provide proper, thorough training; a sound knowledge base; and the necessary supervising support for the home visitor who works with children and their families. Out of this should flow a new respect for this cadre of dedicated home visitors who forge relationships with families that result in new strengths, new hopes, and new possibilities. The book and the task could not be more important.

Jeree Pawl, Ph.D.
Director, Infant-Parent Program
San Francisco General Hospital
Department of Psychiatry
University of California at San Francisco
San Francisco, California

Preface

The summer after our wedding, my husband and I worked at a lodge in Colorado. The guests were primarily people on bus tours. Next to the lodge entrance where people got off the bus were horses tied to hitching rails and Cotton, the wrangler. Often a tourist would say to Cotton, "I'd like to ride, but I'm a little afraid. I've never been on a horse." Cotton would bellow, "That's okay, lady, this horse ain't never been rode. You just get on, and the two of you can learn together."

As I began to listen to home visitors tell me about their work, I remembered Cotton's words to the tourists. Home visiting is a new profession in which both the home visitor and parent are learning to do their respective tasks. Home visitors tell me how different each home is, how they are never quite sure what will happen during the visits, in spite of their prior planning. Over time, visitors and parents develop close personal relationships, and visitors often make a difference. But home visiting can be messy and unpredictable. I wrote this book to try to make sense of the ever-changing, complex nature of the home visitor's work.

A developmental frame of reference guides the discussion in this book. Three themes are central to home visiting. The pivotal premise is that development occurs within and through relationship. Infants and young children develop within their relationship with their parents. When home visitors make an impact, parent development occurs within the relationship with their home visitor. A second premise is that all relationship involves mutuality. As parents influence their young child, so too their child influences parents. As home visitors influence parents, so too parents influence home visitors. A mother's soft voice and rocking soothe her infant, and her infant's smile and cooing stimulate her to sing softly. A home visitor's support and guidance may stimulate a parent to begin to give her toddler some clear limits, and the parent's action may give the home visitor confidence to initiate new topics. A third premise is that child and parent development are intertwined with their social environment.[1] Friends and relatives, neighborhood and workplace, local community resources, and national economy and policy all have an impact on the everyday life of families. Thus, an effective home visitor's perspective includes not only the specific family visited but also the family's informal and formal support systems.

As I was writing this book, I realized how much of my own professional history was coming into play. Since the mid-1970s, I have helped adults in their work with infants and young children in several roles and programs. Working with parents, teachers, family child care providers, and home visitors, I have had the opportunity to observe the subtleties and complexities of adults' everyday interactions with young children. As I reflected on what I observed, I began to understand the meanings of these ever-changing interactions. As I have observed adults working with young children in school and at home, I have seen wide differences; but, along with these differences, there are commonalities in patterns of adult–child interactions across contexts.

Since the late 1970s, I have combined work with parents, teachers, and caregivers with qualitative research, much of which has focused on adult–child interaction. When I conducted a participant observation case study of child care programs, I found that patterns of child care teachers' interactions with young children emphasized individual as opposed to social learning and, on a small scale, reproduced individualism, the macrovalue of the larger society.[2] In an early intervention program for the Illinois Department of Children and Family Services, I hired and provided ongoing training in rural counties and factory towns to women who, in their homes, cared for infants and young children at risk of maltreatment. In this project, I found that I could understand how the life history of talented family child care staff intersected with their skill in relating to young children.[3]

In 1988, as research coordinator for the Parents as Teachers (PAT) National Center, I began observing several PAT home visitors conduct home visits and wrote a case study on the parent educator's role.[4] That was the beginning of the work that led directly to this book. In my present position as an early intervention specialist at a children's hospital, I help child care program teachers and parents of young children who are having behavioral difficulties at home and in the classroom. In my work with parents and other adult caregivers, the taken-for-granted daily routines and adult–child interactions are examined, and together we develop adaptations so that the young children can succeed. In clinical work, I try to help adults to look carefully at their everyday interactions with young children and to think about the meaning and purpose of how they relate to their children.

In all these positions, I have shuttled back and forth between scholarly literature and my own clinical experience and research.[5] Core themes have been themes of relationship, child and parent development, and the complex interconnections between child and parent development and the social environment. As I read scholarly work, I could see the ideas being worked out in the nitty-gritty reality of parenting and early education. Problems that perplexed parents and teachers were being addressed in scholarly literature, but I found that the scholarly information usually was not easily accessible to the people in the field.

Beginning with Urie Bronfenbrenner's landmark work in 1979,[6] developmentalists have asked how social context promotes or inhibits normal development. Developmental research and theory have moved from concentrating on disorders that are in the individual to looking at interpersonal issues and disturbances within relationships. Relationship has become central to understanding development throughout the life span. I have used this new developmental perspective successfully to understand my own clinical and research experience and thus have made it the basic model for child–parent–visitor development in this book.

In this book, the term *parent development* is parallel to *child development*. Home visiting promotes parent development, not just by teaching parenting skills but also by helping parents grow in ways that affect parents' relationship with their child. I also use the term *paraprofessional* to identify the home visitors who do not have professional education. A significant number of home visiting programs employ paraprofessionals.

I have tried to integrate my clinical and research experience, developmental theory and research, and the everyday nitty-gritty encounters between home visitors and parents. Cotton was not quite telling the truth when he said that the horse had "never been rode." But he was right when he said that we can get on and learn together.

Acknowledgments

I wrote this book with the emotional and cognitive support of my family and friends, who read and critiqued the initial drafts. Each offered a different viewpoint to help me clarify my points. My husband, Dennis, read the first and last draft of each chapter. He helped me by catching my habitual phrasings, and he warned me when I was being too directive. Our son Greg pointed out places where the text was not based on clearly formulated logic. He also found implicit assumptions that I had missed.

Close friends and colleagues provided additional viewpoints to strengthen each chapter. Marion Wilson helped me recognize that I needed to describe more fully the struggles involved in home visiting and to acknowledge that home visiting is an ongoing process. Joy Royce and Louis Smith helped me speak more directly to home visitors. Joy repeatedly called attention to places where my language missed my intended audience, and Louis challenged me to use my voice and the home visitors' voices and to keep the literature a separate component in endnotes.

Parents as Teachers (PAT) home visitors allowed me to accompany them on the home visits that are described in the interviews and vignettes in this book. This book was possible because parents across social class and ethnicity graciously and generously allowed me to accompany their PAT home visitors into their homes. I felt very privileged to be welcomed into these young families' homes.

The final suggestions of Elaine Niefeld, my editor at Paul H. Brookes Publishing Co., had a refreshing developmental frame and helped me structure the book to reach a wider audience.

As I worked on this book, I often felt the spirit of my dear friend, colleague, and mentor, the late Dorothea Gray Pflug, to whom this book is dedicated.

In memory of Dorothea Gray Pflug,
dear friend, colleague, and mentor

Home Visiting

Introduction

Marquisha: *The home visiting program has made a wonderful difference in how I feel about myself. Talking to Cynthia, she treats you like a bigger sister, more or less, like your friend. She's just like the big sister I never had. Talking to her, I can talk about my problems if I'm going through any problems. I know Cynthia respects me and cares a lot. I told her, "You know something, I needed somebody a long time ago that cared about me the way you care about me. Care enough to boost me up instead of letting me down." Cynthia is a person you can talk to because she's looking at you. You can see that she is understanding your feelings from the expression that she shows, that she really cares. A person that you can look straight in the face and talk to. You know, when I talk to people, I don't hold my head down. Cynthia is a person you can look at, talk to because she's looking at you. You can see that she understanding your feelings from the expression that she shows, that she really cares. I had never really met nobody that cares about me. Other than my mother. I knew my mother loved me and everything else. I knew she loved me with all her heart. But a person that I can talk to and tell my problems to. They know how to answer me. Maybe it's not everything I want to hear, but I know what Cynthia's saying is true.*

Before this program, I mean, I had little reason to live. I was just like in my bed all the time, just grogging around. Then I signed up for this program with Cynthia. If it wasn't for Cynthia, I'm telling you, I wouldn't have a business. The day Cynthia walked in that door, I still think about it. I mean, even when I'm laying down sometimes at night, I think if Cynthia had never come, I would never be where I'm at right now. I look at Cynthia sometimes and say, "Boy, that is a woman!" Made a big difference in my life, and for my kids, for every last one of them. I love the way my kids love to play with Cynthia. I learn something about my kids every time she comes over. And my 3-year-old says, "Come on, Mom, let's play like Cynthia did." I'm learning every day.

1

Marquisha is a 39-year-old mother of six children ages 3–21 years. I interviewed Marquisha after she had completed 2 years in Even Start. During these 2 years, her home visitor, Cynthia, visited her and her children twice a month. Later I told Cynthia that Marquisha had said Cynthia has been an important person in her life and in her children's lives. "Yes," Cynthia replied, "She often tells me that. And I know that Marquisha is probably one of two people in my life that I have truly influenced in a way that allowed them to make dramatic changes." Cynthia knows that very few of her families will respond as dramatically as did Marquisha. She said that it is harder to know what her visits mean to some people. But she knows that she is making a difference.

This is a book about home visiting, a new profession in which adults strive to assist other adults in improving their everyday family life. Modern home visiting began in the 1960s as one part of the War on Poverty. In the early 1960s, child development research gave evidence that the first 5 years of life are the years of most rapid intellectual development and that what happens during these years has consequences for later development. Developmental literature moved from a unidimensional focus on the child's development to a bidirectional focus on parent(s) and child. At the same time, literature on cultural deprivation claimed that the poverty cycle could be broken by compensatory education, which would allow poor children to be better prepared for schooling. This social sciences literature coincided with the civil rights movement and with President Johnson's antipoverty political agenda. Federal assistance became available for impoverished families with young children in the form of federal grants to states for child care programs, Head Start, and early intervention programs.[1] Home visiting became a central program component of early intervention programs such as the Child and Family Resource Program sponsored by the Administration for Children, Youth and Families; Ira Gordon's Home Learning Center Approach to Early Stimulation in Gainesville, Florida; and David Weikart's Ypsilanti Perry Preschool Project in Ypsilanti, Michigan.

The 1970s brought a marked increase in single-parent homes, teenage parenting, and employed mothers of children under age 6. As a response to qualitative changes in social values, economic realities, and changes in the traditional family, family support programs began to grow across the United States.[2] Home visiting became a primary means of service delivery in many of these programs. Most home visiting programs have the child as their main focus and have prevention and intervention goals such as preventing low birth weight births, preventing child abuse and neglect, promoting healthy child development, and improving school readiness.

Although home visiting is a new profession, it was a part of earlier U.S. history. The latter half of the 19th century saw increasing industrialization, massive European immigration to the new world, and rapid urbanization. As a response to immigration and urbanization, settlement houses emerged and developed programs to support the family. Settlement houses were one of the first movements of the Progressive Era. Through these settlement houses, wealthy women regularly visited children's homes, raised funds for day nurseries, supervised matrons who maintained these nurseries, and taught night classes in English, homemaking skills, and child care. The settlement house programs were the beginning of the U.S. family support movement, dedicated to socializing recent immigrants to normative American values of middle-class family life.

By the beginning of the 20th century, the hallmark of the Progressive Era was social reform. The first White House Conference on Children in 1909 was part of this movement toward social reform. G. Stanley Hall began the child study movement, and Hall's ideas were integrated into the newly begun Parent Teacher Associations (PTAs). When they began, PTAs primarily focused on parent education.[3] In the 1920s, with the popularization of the progressive education theory of Dewey and the psychological theories of Freud, Gesell, and Watson, parent education flourished. As parent education expanded, family support for immigrants declined. The 1920s also were the decade when nursery schools, which embraced parent education, were begun for middle-class children. Until the 1970s, parent education focused on the social scientific theory of the time; parent educators were experts teaching parents what parents needed to know if they were to raise successful children.

Today our theory is different. We recognize that the *parent* is the expert about her or his own child and that effective home visiting is a partnership between professional and parent, not the "expert" teaching the parent.

This book attempts to portray the complexity and the developmental possibilities in home visiting. Home visiting programs vary according to the population served, the program agenda, the strategies used to implement the agenda, intensity and duration of service, and the types of people who conduct the home visits.[4] The vast majority of home visiting programs are primarily prevention-oriented and serve families with children, from pregnancy through age 5 years. The home visiting this book discusses has as its goals to help parents, first, to understand child development and, second, to develop appropriate parenting skills.

APPROACH

Since 1988, I have observed and consulted with parent educators employed by the Parents as Teachers (PAT) program in Missouri. I shared my observations with home visitors who, in turn, responded to my observations. Then we met together to reflect on what was happening in their visits and on the meanings that each of us found in the visit. This self-reflection combined with collaborative reflection is called *action research.* Such reflection on everyday practice is the hallmark of action research. Through this process, the researcher tells the story of practice from the perspective of the people engaged in the action. In the research process, participants and researcher gain new insights that lead to improved practice. I have used action research data to provide vignettes to illustrate principles and practices of home visiting and to have home visitors explain their understanding of the process.

The book is designed for home visitors and those adults who do supervision, preservice, and in-service professional development of home visitors. I have tried to write in a manner in which home visitors can see themselves in the home visiting vignettes and conversations with home visitors that illustrate developmental issues, parenting practices, and home visitors' work.[5] As readers understand the home visitors whose work is described in the book, they may understand themselves better. Most vignettes of home visitors or conversations with home visitors are from extended study of one home visitor named Janice. Between 1988 and 1990, I observed Janice as she completed monthly home visits with two working-class families. Then, between 1992 and 1994, I observed her home visits with three additional families.

Having been engaged in professional development of adults since the mid-1970s, I have learned that people learn best when they can watch highly skilled models. Janice is an exemplary home visitor who can make the home visiting process most clear. I also observed many other home visitors. Not all home visitors are as skilled and experienced as Janice. But everyone can learn to improve his or her understanding and skill. In fact, Janice and I saw how our work together improved Janice's own skill.

Some vignettes in the book depict additional home visitors, and some vignettes depict child care staff or family caregivers. As I began writing this book, I also began working with Cynthia, the director of an Even Start program. Cynthia also is an exceptionally skilled and insightful home visitor, and I have included vignettes from my work with Cynthia, primarily in the first two chapters.

Home visiting can be unpredictable, messy, difficult work. Some families do not seem to relate to friendly home visitors. Janice and Cynthia have had families in their caseload who refused home visits, and each has experienced an array of struggles with families who remained in their program. Success is not guaranteed, even for experienced, talented home visitors. Although I did not witness these struggles or failures directly, Janice's and Cynthia's descriptions of some of these difficulties are discussed in several chapters. In addition, each chapter ends with descriptions of the difficulties and dilemmas that home visitors may encounter in their work.

PAT is a partnership between home and school that is based on the belief that experiences in the early years are critical in laying the foundation for later school success. PAT aims to support parents in their role as their child's first and most influential teacher. The Missouri legislature has mandated and appropriated funds for each of the 543 school districts to serve 40% of district families with children from birth to age 3 years. PAT is a universally accessible nondeficit program. The program entails regularly scheduled home visits by trained parent educators, group meetings with other parents, periodic monitoring, and formal developmental screening of children from birth to age 36 months.

Even Start is a federally funded family literacy program administered by each state through Title 1. The Even Start program that Cynthia directs serves 35 families and has three components: 1) adult education, 2) early childhood education, and 3) parent education. Families in which one or both parents did not finish high school and have a child between birth and age 7 years are enrolled in the program. Transportation and half-day on-site child care are provided for all families during the time that parents are enrolled in Adult Basic Education. Family educators trained in the PAT model visit each family two times per month. Family educators also serve as service coordinators for participating families by coordinating community services for them.

In the United States, a large proportion of home visiting programs serve families at risk such as low-income families and teenager-parented families. This book primarily discusses home visiting for all types of families; the basic assumption is that the primary principles and approaches of home visiting are the same for everyone, regardless of social class, age, ethnicity, or any other distinguishing characteristic. For example, effective home visitors show respect, develop rapport, empathically listen to, and support every family with which they work. The home visitor's task often becomes more complex and challenging when working with families having multiple complex problems, a pattern that occurs with greater frequency in low-income, teenager-parented, and ethnically diverse families.[6] These complexities are addressed in the first chapter on the parent–home visitor relationship and the second chapter on home visiting approaches. In addition, each chapter in Parts I and II ends with a discussion of difficulties and dilemmas that home visitors experience. Home visitors can experience these difficulties and dilemmas with any family; however, not surprisingly, they confront many of these challenges more often with families at risk.

A developmental frame of reference guides the discussion in this book. The most central assumptions underlying this approach to home visiting are that *development occurs within and through relationships,* that *all relationships involve mutuality,* and that *child and parent development are intertwined with their social environment.*

OVERVIEW OF TOPICS

Part I focuses on the complexities of the home visitor role. The first chapter discusses the relationship between the parent and the home visitor. This relationship is the scaffolding that makes it possible for parents to gain new understanding of their child and to strengthen their parenting practices through their home visiting experience. Chapter 2 discusses two levels of skills needed for effective home visiting: 1) communication and interpersonal skills that encourage, maintain, and promote the parent–home visitor relationship and 2) a collection of knowledge and skills that are less process-oriented but essential to the home visiting process. Chapter 2 also examines the complexities and difficulties of working with families at greatest risk in our society. Home visiting programs can support families of all populations. Because of the target population with which I have worked, the people discussed in this book are primarily urban and suburban families; however, home visiting also is needed in rural areas.[7] Chapter 3 discusses ways in which home visitors can gain greater knowledge, understanding, and skill. Professional education and supervision are discussed as contexts for gaining new knowledge, understanding, and reflection on one's practice, individually and through sharing with peers, mentors, and supervisors.

Part II covers the topics that home visitors find most important for effective home visiting to occur. The discussion has a developmental thrust because, regardless of program agenda, every home visitor of families with young children needs a strong developmental knowledge base. This book does not attempt, however, to detail all areas of development; there are many excellent child development texts available.

Each chapter in Part II is organized in three tiers. First, the chapters trace child development from birth to age 5 years; second, the chapters discuss appropriate understanding and parenting skills; and third, the chapters suggest ways by which home visitors can promote parents' understanding of their child and develop appropriate parenting practices. Chapter 4 discusses the foundation of all development, the developing sense of self, which encompasses social and emotional development and affects all other developmental areas.

Once their infant becomes a toddler, young parents often are most interested in talking about guidance and discipline, which is the topic of Chapter 5. Chapter 6 explains how infants and toddlers communicate and how their language and communication develop. Chapter 7 focuses on routines and rituals. It is the mundane, everyday routines that usually are the setting for many parents' difficulties in guidance and discipline, yet these everyday routines are often taken for granted and unexamined. Chapter 8 focuses on play as the primary way in which infants and young children learn. Part II closes with a discussion of sibling relationships.

Part III discusses the relationship of person and profession. Chapter 10 looks at the personal experiences, past and present, of two exemplar home visitors, Janice and Cynthia, and explores how these women's personal lives are intertwined with their home visiting work. In my professional work, I consistently have found that dominant themes of childhood history often show up in skilled professionals' work lives. Furthermore, these professionals experience their work as being very meaningful and express themselves creatively in their work. In Chapter 10, I share the life histories of Janice and Cynthia; then I hypothesize as to how themes in these women's life histories intersect with their home visiting work. I conducted life history interviews of Janice and Cynthia because they are the two exemplar home visitors whose work is portrayed throughout this book. Prior to interviewing Janice and Cynthia, I had no knowledge of their childhood histories. I discovered that each woman had parents with strong values about family life; in fact, their childhood family lives were strong and healthy. Chapter 10 ends with a discussion of the professional competence of home visitors who had troubled childhoods.

This book represents a synthesis of 1) the lived experiences of home visitors and these visitors' discussion of their work; 2) my understanding of the meaning and purpose of their work with families in terms of visitors helping parents understand their child and their own parenting; 3) scholarly literature on child development, parenting, and family support; and 4) my own professional experience in child development, early education, and early prevention and intervention.

Currently, professionals from disciplines such as nursing, education, social work, and psychology, as well as paraprofessionals, engage in home visiting. Thus, home visitors may find different portions of this book useful. For example, child care teachers and Head Start teachers, who do home visits once or twice a year, may find the first two chapters on home visiting most helpful. Mental health workers new to the field of family support also may find the first two chapters helpful. Paraprofessionals, or professionals with little background in early childhood development, can get an overview of developmental progression of young children in each chapter in Part II.

Working with caregivers of infants and young children has helped me better understand the subtle, ever-changing nature of early development and the caregiving process. Throughout this book, I have tried to be mindful of how young children, parents, and home visitors develop and, in turn, how each can influence the other's development. I designed this book to be useful to home visitors, their supervisors, and teachers. I know that this discussion is not complete; however, I hope it can be a useful step in the growth of a new and worthwhile profession in our society.

I
Home Visiting
The New Profession

1

The Relationship Between Parents and the Home Visitor

The true community does not arise through peoples having feelings for one another (though indeed not without it), but through first, their taking their stand in living in mutual relations with a living Center, and second, their being in living mutual relation with one another.
Martin Buber (1923/1958, p. 45)

At the core of home visiting is the relationship between parents and the home visitor. This chapter examines components of the parent–home visitor relationship that maximize the chances for promoting parent development. In turn, the parents' development enhances the parents' relationship with the child, which is the foundation of the child's development. A basic premise of this book is that development occurs both through and within the relationship—which consists of patterns of interaction over time. Just as the everyday patterns of parent–child interaction are the most powerful influences on infant and child development, so too the parent–home visitor relationship is pivotal to parent development.

A central characteristic within the parent–child relationship and the parent–home visitor relationship is that each person influences the other at every moment and in important ways over time. The central characteristic of these relationships is *mutuality*, also termed *reciprocity*.[1]

What *A* does influences *B*, and what *B* does influences *A*. For example, when a young infant is very irritable and difficult to soothe, the child's behavior affects the parents' feelings of competency, which in turn can decrease the parents' ability to provide calm, warm, loving care. Then the infant feels the parents' tension and the child becomes more irritable, and so the cycle continues.

The parent–home visitor relationship is dynamic; it varies both in nature and in effect as a result of the personal characteristics of the parents, the personal characteristics of the home visitor, and the dynamics of the larger environment. The personality, values, and attitudes of the parents and the home visitor affect their relationship. Furthermore, the parent–home visitor relationship is influenced by characteristics of larger social systems, such as the parents' neighborhood and the race, ethnicity, schooling, and social class of the parents and the home visitor.[2] All these factors are at work as the parents and home visitor cocreate their relationship.

This chapter first discusses key elements in forming the parent–home visitor relationship. Second, the chapter examines the progression of the relationship. Third, it discusses the meaning and significance of the personal relationship for the parents. Finally, it explores dimensions of home visitors' relationships with teenage parents.

FORMING THE PARENT–HOME VISITOR RELATIONSHIP

In the home visitor's work with a family, four elements are central; in good home visiting, these elements are made explicit in initial contacts with a family:

1. *Expectations:* In forming a relationship, home visitors discuss with parents their expectations and the parents' expectations.
2. *Agenda:* Home visitors describe what they want to do with the parents and the child.
3. *Roles:* In the initial phase of home visiting, home visitors and parents clarify their roles—those behaviors associated with the specific roles of parent and home visitor and their relationship.
4. *Setting:* The setting of home visitors' work in the parents' personal space raises issues different from other work settings such as office, classroom, or clinic.

Expectations: Parent and Home Visitor

All relationships involve expectations of ourselves and of other people. At the outset, it is important for home visitors to state clearly their expectations and to invite parents to share theirs. The home visitor role is new in our society, so what people expect to happen during and after the visit can be ambiguous; thus, it is helpful for the home visitor and the parents to say explicitly what each expects. Expectations are multiple. The home visitor asks, "What do I expect of myself, what do I expect of the parents, and what do I think the parents expect of me?" And the parents ask, "What do I expect of myself, what do I expect of the home visitor, and what do I think the home visitor expects of me?" Intertwined with these expectations are the parents' and home visitor's expectation of the child and what will happen to the child as a result of their work together.

A big area of a person's expectation in this type of relationship is expertise and authority. Sometimes home visitors and parents may have different ideas about where the authority lies. In family support programs described in this book, the home visitor assumes that parents are the experts in their child's development and aims to support, affirm, and promote the parents' relationship with their child. Some parents, however, may assume that the home visitor is the expert and is coming into their home to teach them the right way to parent. In other words, parents may give total authority to their home visitor as a teacher and put themselves in a subordinate role. This expectation violates the kind of relationship that makes the parent–home visitor partnership work. In these situations, it is not the task of home visitors to challenge the parents' expectation; but, at the same time, home visitors need not accept the authority that the parents project onto them. Rather, home visitors may need to adjust their approach—for example, by being very specific about goals and the approach to be taken and trusting that, over time, the parents' experiences in working together with the home visitor will influence the parents' original expectations.

During the initial phase of home visiting, the home visitor can encourage parents to express their expectations for their infant or child and talk about their priorities regarding their child's behavior and skills. It also can be helpful to ask specifically how parents would like to use their time with their home visitor. The home visitor can use what the parents say to establish rapport and build a partnership with the parents. Some parents' goals or priorities may seem developmentally unrealistic, and home visitors can discuss these issues with the parents in an open and respectful manner as they share developmental information. Within these discussions, the home visitor can communicate clearly that the parents are always the decision makers in matters about their child.

Because the home visitor role is ambiguous, many parents enter the relationship with uncertainties. Some parents have little experience in opening their home to others. They may worry about their privacy being violated or about the adequacy of their home being judged. Sally is a young mother with learning disabilities who joined a Family Support Program when her son was 3 months old. She shared her concerns about her adequacy as a parent with her home visitor.

> It's hard to explain. I was a first-time mother, and I was real nervous. I mean, I babysat and stuff like that, but I never had a baby for 24 hours a day. I didn't know if I'd do things right. I used to think I was bad and couldn't do it. I could never raise a child. But just being in the program, I think I am as good as any parent, maybe even better than some.

Sally was in and out of juvenile detention centers as an adolescent and quit school in the eighth grade. Given her troubled background in her family of origin and adolescence, she had misgivings about being visited at her home.

Rob, a parent in the Missouri Parents as Teachers Program, expressed his initial wariness of the home visiting program.

> I was just skeptical. I don't know. Probably because I work with the fire department, and it is involved with school districts. And I'm just skeptical about your tax dollar. . . . Is this just another program to get more employment for the school district staff? And I'd have to schedule being home during the visits, and I thought that might be a pain to do.

Being aware that parents initially may have uncertainties, home visitors' clear statements of their own purposes and expectations for their work with parents, as well as their invitation to parents to share their expectations, can help parents gain confidence in themselves and in this new experience. Knowing that parents may be expecting a report card, home visitors can look for opportunities to praise the parents and child.

Experienced home visitors are confident themselves. They trust the power of the process of the developing relationship. When beginning in this role, however, home visitors also may have uncertainties. The comments of two home visitors in the Missouri Parents as Teachers program, Janice and Lynette, illustrate initial discomforts and developing skills.

> It is always difficult to begin a relationship, no matter how long you have been doing this, no matter how comfortable you feel with all the families you have been serving over the years. Your heart beats a little faster when you walk into someone's home for the first time, because you want to be accepted by them, and you are never sure what it is going to take to have that happen. When I first began, I was a motor mouth. But in the past couple of years I've learned that it is okay to have quiet time when no conversation is going on between the parent and me, or between the child and me. And this helps the parent feel a sense of calm. And when they feel

that you are calm with whatever is going on in their family, they will feel more calm about what is going on—for example, being calm when the baby starts crying or the toddler starts being negative. If we act like this is something we expect kids to do, that it's no big deal, then the parent doesn't feel embarrassed and nervous about it. I think a lot of the changes we have felt is basically one of comfort with what we are doing—our own self-confidence.

Before the birth of Janice's children, she had taught third grade. Given the newness to her of the home visitor role, Janice's own expectations were not very clear. She did not have the self-confidence that she had in her teaching, where she knew what she was supposed to do. With experience, she began to understand her relationships with parents and to trust her skill. Then she could maintain a slower, calmer pace during her home visits.

Lynette also changed with experience.

Since I had been a kindergarten teacher, I knew I was comfortable with the kids. So, at first, I would fill the time in play activities with the child. And I know that sometimes we feel like we are expected to go in there and tell the answers. And, at first, I thought I needed to have the answers, since that was expected of me.

Home visitors bring their prior work experiences into their new role as home visitor, and this influences their interactions with parents. All adults experience uncertainty in new occupations, and home visiting is no exception. Having a clear understanding of the program agenda and the tasks involved assists the home visitor's transition into this new role.

The Agenda: What Is My Job?

Among the first tasks of home visitors is to understand clearly the agenda of the program in which they work. The program agenda varies with the population being served and within the overall agenda of the agency or institution overseeing the program, and also with regard to whether professionals or paraprofessionals do the home visiting.[3] Is the program universally accessible? Is it for teenage parents only? Is it for at-risk, low-income parents? Is it for families with low birth weight infants? Is the agenda primarily to lessen existing difficulties or to prevent the occurrence of problems? Possible agendas might be to promote the health of infants and young children, to promote the cognitive skills of at-risk children in low-income families, to help parents develop an understanding of child development and appropriate parenting skills, and to work toward prevention of child abuse and neglect. Still, regardless of the agenda, nothing can be accomplished until first a trusting relationship is formed.

Within program agendas, the home visitor chooses activities determined by a continuum of priorities ranging from giving information, to understanding how a family is doing, to deciding what resources can be brought to bear, to being a surrogate parent to a teenage mother. Competent home visitors know their agenda when they are in the home. It is impossible to pay attention to everything. Home visitor Janice explains her goals and the agenda that she sees as basic to her work.

> I think parents appreciate someone coming in who sees lots of children the age of theirs and who can help them be objective, but who also helps them appreciate that these are really great kids. And even though they are great, I think parents want to be sure that they are great. Parents also appreciate the screening we do and knowing appropriate kinds of things for themselves and their children to do—things that will maintain their children's interest, things that will nurture their development without pushing. I think they really are looking for appropriate ways to nurture their child.

In the preceding discussion, Janice describes her basic tasks: helping parents to learn appropriate activities and appropriate parenting strategies to nurture their child. Janice understands that parents can take in information when they are affirmed, and the strongest affirmation for them is taking pleasure in their child.

Respective Roles: Who Is Responsible for What?

In forming a relationship with parents, home visitors try to ensure that parents understand behaviors associated with the roles of home visitor and parent. The most important dynamic of family support programs is developing mutual respect and partnership between parents and home visitors. Historically, parent education put the parent educator in the role of an expert directing the parent. In contrast, the home visitor in family support programs is an empathic listener, consultant, resource, guide, advocate, and partner. For example, in the traditional parent education model, the professional chooses a topic such as sleeping and then lectures on appropriate parenting practices to promote healthy sleep patterns in the child.[4] The modern home visitor first learns how the infant or young child is sleeping and how the parents assist the child's sleep. Then the home visitor shares developmental information and possible parenting strategies as related to the lived experience of the parents and child. The topic may be the home visitor's or the parents' choice. The directives of traditional parent education are replaced by joint problem solving—a working alliance in home visiting. Parents are the experts in their child's development, active participants in the home visit, and the final decision makers with regard to nurturing their child. Home visiting is a helping relationship defined by collaboration between the home visitor and the parents.

Effective home visitors are able to work on two levels at the same time. They are completely engaged in interactions with the parents and child while they track the process; that is, they observe the interactions during the visit and are aware of their own reactions and feelings. Sometimes unpredictable intrusions within a visit can be very difficult to manage. When home visitors can relate to the family and simultaneously be aware of their own feelings and make decisions based on these feelings, they are more likely to be successful. Cynthia illustrates this ability to work on two levels at the same time.

For over 2 years, I have been working with Marquisha and her large family, her sister, and [between them] their 12 children, between 2 and 22 years old. I was sitting on the couch with Marquisha. Her 18-year-old daughter stood next to us with several envelopes in her hand. She took the envelopes and held them up to the light and read the dollar amounts. Well, then it occurred to me, they were welfare checks, and she was looking at hers and reading the amount—and her mother's and her aunt's and her cousin's. Her mother knew I was there to visit and was very embarrassed. She said, "Rashonda, stop doing that. Quit reading other people's mail." But Rashonda kept doing it.

By that time, I was aware of my own feelings. I was irritated with the 18-year-old. It's like, "Why are you doing this? Why are you embarrassing your mother? Rashonda, go in the back of the room, and just leave us alone." And she kept doing it, and then she'd look at me and say, "I'm not opening the mail, am I, Cynthia?"

Well, at this point, I was aware of feeling baited. "Okay, Cynthia, what are you going to do about it? How are you going to handle this?" In my head, I knew I had to decide, "What am I going to do?" I know I have a good relationship with this family, a decent relationship; but it's not the strongest in the world. I was being challenged by the 18-year-old. Her mother is embarrassed. So what do I do?

I just stuck with what I know best, which is to be myself. And I answered honestly, but I was conscious of "Don't let your anger show. Just be honest." So what I said to Rashonda was, "Nope. You are not opening up the envelopes, but you still are invading people's privacy." And that is all I said. Then I turned back to her mom, and we continued our conversation. Rashonda put the envelopes down. She didn't leave the room. She sat down and just kind of listened and played with her baby. By the time I left, it was okay. We were back on track.

Cynthia feels secure in her relationship with this family. As a professional with 20 years of experience in work with low-income families of diverse ethnicity, she has developed confidence in trusting her judgment, even when everything seems to be falling apart. Had she scolded Rashonda, Rashonda probably would have fled the room, enraged. Her honest, respectful reply not only ended Rashonda's behavior but also gave Rashonda permission to remain and be in a position of possible learning. This two-level process using internal as well as external dialogue is a skill that develops over time with experience and ongoing supervision.

The Setting: Working in the Parents' Space

Home visitors enter into a family's private space, a space that many families experience as protective. Not only do home visitors venture into the parents' private space, but parents may not understand why their home visitor is there; thus, parents may not feel safe. Given their uneasiness, parents carefully watch their home visitor from the moment she or he gets out of the car. Given parents' uneasiness, home visitors can help parents feel comfortable when they themselves are relaxed, genuine, and able to find a common ground on which to make their first contact. Once the adults are able to have a relaxed exchange, home visitors can describe their role and begin to learn what the parents would like from their visits. Home visitors understand that they cannot accomplish anything until they know the family, the family knows them, and a relationship is established. They also know this process takes time.

As a guest in parents' homes, effective home visitors take cues from parents, for example, asking the parents' permission before touching or picking up their baby. Similarly, it would be inappropriate to enter other rooms in the home unless invited to do so. Janice explained how she tries to follow the parents' lead.

I try to come in as the guest in the home, not as somebody that is in charge of this hour. I always try to keep in mind that it is the parent's home; thus, as much as possible, I try to follow the parent's lead. If the parent sits on the floor first, I sit on the floor. Wherever she sits first is where I sit first. Once I introduce an activity, usually we both sit on the floor with the child. But, if the parent initially is most comfortable remaining on the chair, I'll respect that decision. Then, in a few minutes, I'll invite the parent to join the child and me.

But just as important as my own agenda and planned activity, I invite parents to share observations of their child, happenings within the family, concerns, or questions. The visit always is for the family, and I try and keep foremost that I am interested in how parents would like to use our time together.

Over the years, Janice has developed an initial pattern when first visiting parents. Her behavior communicates to the parents respect and genuine interest. Janice knows that the language of her behavior as well as what she says will communicate to parents who she is and what these visits are going to involve.

When home visiting is not sought out by a family, a first visit can be very difficult. Cynthia described her first visit with a family with whom she had worked for 2 years.

I have been working with two sisters in their late 30s and their children, who range in age from 19 years to, when I first met them, a newborn. So, there are 12 children between the sisters who live in this household, and the older children of these sisters also have children. So, at any given moment, there are up to 20 people in and out of this household.

On my first visit, I knocked on the door. This was a referral from the child protection agency. They did not want to see me. They did not want me in their home. They did let me in. It was dark in the home. There was a couch and a loveseat in this fairly large room, a small TV on the shelf. One of the moms let me in, and I introduced myself. I did my spiel about how I am from Parents as Teachers, and this is what we do. I'll bring these games, and we are going to talk about development—the whole spiel.

She kind of looked at me, and turned about, and walked away. And she didn't come back for 5 minutes. You know, you are just kind of standing there. [I was] like, "Well, now what do I do?"

So, pretty soon she comes back with her other sister, and I had to go through this spiel again. She wanted her sister to know about this, but she really wanted somebody there with her while I was there.

It did not take long for Cynthia to realize that this was not going to be a normal visit, and her spiel and planned agenda had to be disregarded. Although she felt awful, she persevered.

And no one asked me to sit down. I had been told to take my cue from the parent. They just left me standing there. So, I finally thought, "That's not going to work. I'm not going to be able to take my cue here. Either I leave or I ask to sit down, which is what I did. "Would it be okay if I sat down?" They replied, "Oh well, all right, go ahead."

Well, then they brought the kids out, and they sat on one side of the room. And I was over on the other side with the children. The TV was blaring. I didn't have the nerve to ask them to turn it down, because I thought, "You know, I'm just getting started with this. I'm not going to ask them to do that." So, I kind of sat there and played with the children, a 3- and a 4-year-old. We talked, and I got some books out and read some books. The parents sat on the other side of the room, and they watched me.

Then someone knocked at the door. A third adult came in, and the three of them sat over there and had their own conversation and said things I couldn't quite hear. They would laugh. And I thought, "I'm not paranoid, but I know they're talking about me, and they don't want me here. I'm going to leave and never come back." And so I read stories, played with the children, and watched a little TV.

Cynthia described this family's life as being on the edge of chaos, yet she knew she was making a difference.

Now the family has moved from Parents as Teachers into Even Start. Neither mom had finished high school. They are in adult education; they bring their children to the child care center, and I make two visits a month.

At the end of my second year working with this family, the evaluator asked one of these parents, "Why are you in this program?" And she said, "Because Cynthia just won't go away." And I think there is some truth in that. I just wouldn't give up. There were a lot of times I wanted to, but I saw that spark of interest. I know they wanted to do something for themselves and for their kids. I just kept coming back. Last year they only attended the adult education center 1 out of 4 days. This year Marquisha has been attending 3 out of 4 days and has even gotten several attendance awards for perfect weekly attendance.

Over time, Cynthia has communicated to Marquisha and her sister that she cares and that they and their children are important. Cynthia knows that each parent, regardless of how problematic her behavior may seem, wants the best for her children and herself. This knowledge gives Cynthia the commitment and courage to persevere. In turn, Marquisha and her sister have learned that they have a friend who truly cares. They have experienced what Pawl stated is "one of life's greatest privileges—the experience of being held in someone's mind."[5]

PROGRESSION OF THE PARENT–HOME VISITOR RELATIONSHIP

Establishing Appropriate Boundaries

Each home visiting program has its own goals, an agenda, and time limitations. Regardless of the program agenda, the process of implementing an agenda is through patterns of interaction over time, through an *extended* relationship. Because home visiting is relatively new in our society, there can be a blurring of the appropriate boundaries of parent–home visitor interaction.

Working in a family's home adds to the role ambiguity. Once parents feel they have a trusting relationship with their home visitor within the privacy of their own home, parents may extend the discussion beyond the explicit goals and tasks of the home visiting program to include personal problems that preoccupy them.[6] These topics may involve family conflict such as with spouse or parents, internal stresses such as depression, or external problems such as housing or inadequate income or employment.

Some home visitors have a hard time distinguishing what they can do and what they are unprepared to handle, as well as a hard time knowing how to maintain carefully their boundaries of involvement with families. Some home visitors try to solve others' problems when they do not have the expertise; doing this would violate the family support program goal of empowering parents. When parents discuss highly personal matters or external problems beyond the home visiting agenda, home visitors can listen empathetically and, when appropriate, strive to help the parent seek other services in the community to meet their needs. When home visitors work with a parent who shares his or her personal troubles with them, they can seek advice or help from peers or supervisors, a sign of a mature professional aware of his or her professional limitations. Multiple, complicated family problems can be so great that they interfere with parents' attention to their child and often are beyond a home visiting program that does not include broader social services.[7] (See Chapter 2 for a discussion of networking with community resources and working with at-risk families.)

Cynthia discussed how she strives to maintain boundaries.

> *I see myself in a helping relationship without taking over. I listen because if the parent brings something up, it is foremost on the parent's mind. So, you at least listen to it. A lot of times home visitors get hooked up trying to solve everything. But most people don't want you to tell them what to do anyway. So, I'll listen to the parent. And sometimes you can tell they just needed to get that off their chest, and then they can go on. And sometimes you need to let them talk about it more and explore options with them. When you are working with families, you are there to help them problem-solve, not do things for them.*

Cynthia understands that one of her most effective approaches is listening to parents, even when they go beyond the planned agenda of discussing their child and their parenting. At the same time, she understands that her role is not to rescue parents who are immersed in problems. The author, acting as interviewer, explored further the issue of boundaries.

> *Carol: In those families where there are substantial problems, like serious emotional problems or external problems like housing, do you find that you also are making decisions when it is time to get a professional with expertise that you don't have?*

Cynthia: Oh sure! But I still listen. I make the decision that this is not my realm of expertise and I need to help this family get other resources. I'll say to the parent, "You know, I am not really experienced with this kind of thing. I am not a counselor. I don't feel I really can help you with this, but I know someone who can." Then I offer possible services. I'll tell them that if they would like to talk more about this, because it really seems to be bothering them, here is the number of someone who can help. For the most part, I give them the information and let them self-refer. On a few occasions, I thought the situation was really bad, and I called the psychologist who works with families in our district, and he then called the parent.

Cynthia knows specifically what her agenda is and what her areas of expertise are. As a parent shares a problem beyond the scope of the family support program, Cynthia is able to think on two levels, talking with the parent while thinking through whether the parent's problem is a situation requiring just listening and support, listening and help with problem solving, or listening and networking with community resources. Having built trust into her relationships with parents, Cynthia actively listens to whatever the parent chooses to share, yet she is able to let parents know when they have entered areas beyond her expertise. In turn, parents appreciate Cynthia's honest statements regarding her own limitations, for this acknowledgment communicates genuineness and respect for the parent.

Janice, who has been a home visitor with working-class families since 1986, shared her perspective.

When a parent puts out something that I don't feel equipped to discuss, I have to remember sometimes all she wants me to do is listen and that I can provide an important service to her by just listening very empathetically and not offering anything other than my ears really, and a friendly gesture, and a suggestion of whom she might contact.

We have to be real honest with parents and let them know where we are good and where we are not. And that the things I know, I know pretty well. I really know child development and understand parenting, but I don't know anything about housing. And if they have a housing issue, they need to call Mrs. Smith at such and such bureau because I know she is good and can help them. I think when parents hear that we are real honest, on that they will trust us more on the issues where we do have expertise.

Like Cynthia, Janice understands that when a parent is troubled, listening empathetically can be all the support needed. At the same time, she is quick to recognize when a parent's problem is beyond her expertise; then she explains who can be of assistance to the parent.

Building on Strengths

Home visitors recognize parents as experts regarding their own children. In their interactions, home visitors can recognize the important job of parenting and can acknowledge this parental expertise. From the outset, home visitors can identify parents' strengths, affirm them, and strive to use these strengths as the building blocks for their relationship and for the parents' development. Janice described her approach.

> Especially in early parts of my relationship, I make sure I can praise things the parent does. And that makes them realize right up front that not only do I enjoy their baby, but I think they are doing a good job. Even if there are some things they are not doing, I really praise the things they are. And at the end of my visit, when I give them our handouts, I'll say, "You probably are doing this already." In as many subtle ways as possible, I try to find the strength of the parent and build on that.
>
> My goal is for parents to trust themselves, to trust what they know, to trust their judgment because they have a foundation of child development information, parenting information that our program provides for them so that they feel strong in what they do. And you know, interestingly, when parents feel strong in what they do, they are more likely to ask for help when they need it.

Karyn, a first-time mother of a 24-month-old, described what Janice's home visits meant to her.

> She never left the house without telling me, "You are doing an important job. It is very hard work, and you are doing it well." I always waited for her to say that.

When working with troubled families, home visitors can feel uneasy, even overwhelmed, with the many difficulties of a family and find it difficult to spot the positive and build on that. In these situations, home visitors may need to give themselves and the parents time to get to know one another and build a relationship. The child often can serve as a common ground on which to begin a conversation. At first, maybe the only common ground will be a television show or an event within the community. When home visitors can be genuine and interested, over time, they can develop a relationship such that they can see, acknowledge, and affirm parents' interests and strengths.

Sharing One's Own Family Life

Just as home visitors learn to develop boundaries for areas they can address and for areas beyond their expertise, so too do home visitors develop sensitivities with regard to determining when sharing their own family life is appropriate. The parent–home visitor relationship involves balancing professional neutrality with the parent–home visitor alliance. Initiating descriptions of one's own family life that are unrelated to the family one is visiting are *not* appropriate. However, when a parent expresses a concern or asks a question, home visitors' brief vignettes from their own family life can communicate understanding, support, and validation of the parent. The effective home visitor tries to keep the child's and parents' development as the focus; thus, any personal sharing must be integral with ongoing concerns, questions, or happenings within the family being visited. Janice's discussion with Shelly, the mother of a 24-month-old, is illustrative.

Shelly: *Erin loves the playground at the park. She's getting better with the slides. She holds on pretty good. But on the swing, she doesn't have the concept to wait until the swing stops to get off.*

Janice: *I remember it was hard for me when my boys were small. I used to find myself saying, "Be careful," again and again and again. It's hard because I also wanted them to try and to be competent.*

Shelly: *I try and remember to say to Erin, "Pay attention to what you are doing."*

Once Janice shared this personal vignette, Shelly then elaborated on her concern. The two adults brainstormed together about how Shelly could ensure Erin's safety while encouraging her to climb and swing competently. Janice explained her rationale for sharing her own family life with parents.

I think personal sharing helps rapport. Not that I am always spinning off about my family, but every now and then I am willing to share about my own life or about my own child that matches up with something in their lives. I mean, I don't care what family it is, I try to pull something out of my life. For example, this week, with one really low-income family, the mother was working as a nurse's aide part-time in a nursing home. And I didn't have anything in common with this woman except that my husband's aunt is in a nursing home. And I was able to say to her how important the people are to our family that do the kind of work that she does. And just pulling together that nursing home experience, validating her importance to my life, did something for us. It made her see me as a person, which is what I think I need to be to parents for them to pay attention. I heard a phrase at one of our staff meetings that I really believe—that parents need to know that we care before they care what we know.

Janice wants the parents to know that she cares and respects them. When something in a parent's and child's life together triggers Janice's thoughts of her own family, her sharing is another way she communicates the meaningfulness of this family's life. Janice aims to have mutuality in her relationship with parents, a mutuality in which parents' comments have meaning to her in the same way that she hopes her comments are meaningful to them.

Parents are disclosing so much of their private life to me that if I don't disclose something about me to them, they are going to think it is too one-sided. I am in their home, asking about their baby, asking about their opinions, and if I don't share something, if I don't let them at least part way into my life, it seems like there is too much distance. And that's not fair to them. I don't go overboard and talk a lot about my kids, but I want them to know that I am a mother, and that I have experienced some of these things. And as I get the sense that there is some closeness developing between us, then I feel more comfortable discussing some touchy issues. I am not as comfortable getting into problem areas with somebody I do not know very well. And I don't think it works either.

Janice accepts and trusts her own family experience. She is sensitive to balancing the parents' levels of disclosure with her own sensitive disclosure of selfhood, a disclosure of *only* that which matches what the parents are sharing. As she shares her own experience, she is assisting parents in accepting and trusting their experience.

ESTABLISHING RECIPROCAL, POSITIVE FEELINGS BETWEEN PARENTS AND HOME VISITORS: A PERSONAL RELATIONSHIP

Whether or not they know it, parents make decisions every moment they interact with their infants and young children. Home visitors are in the home only an hour per week or per month, but the parents spend a great deal more time with the child. So, it is not what home visitors tell the parents or the decisions they think are best for the child that in the end will make a difference. The child is affected by the decisions the parents make in the morning, at bedtime, when the television is on, at the store, when the new baby is born, and so on. When parents are making decisions that help the child's development, then the program is successful. Regardless of a home visiting program's agenda, parents are the final decision makers in their child-rearing practices. When home visiting programs are successful, parents' new understanding and skills allow them to be informed decision makers when making deliberate decisions such as what kind of toys to buy for their child, and everyday decisions become habitual and are taken for granted, such as what to say while diapering and feeding an infant.

Parents' informed decision making emerges from their extended interactions with their home visitor, from their personal relationship.[8] In personal relationships, each person influences the other continuously over time. Just as the toddler learns to say "please" and "thank you" because she has learned from her parents over time, so too, as a result of their relationship with their parent educator, the parents become comfortable talking to their 4-month-old son as they change and feed him. Shelly talked about the home visitor's continued influence.

We always look forward to Janice coming. . . . What is she going to tell us this month, and what is going to be going on [in the visit]? And I can't wait to show her what we can do. And, you know, Janice will say something and then leave. And, in a few days, Erin would be doing it, and I will think, "Oh, I knew she was going to do this."

Janice has been visiting Shelly, Rob, and their daughter Erin for 2 years, since Shelly's third trimester of pregnancy. Patterns have developed in Shelly's and Rob's relationship with Janice. They look forward to her visit when they can share Erin's new skills. They sense that Janice truly enjoys relating to them and their child. They remember Janice's descriptions of the new developmental strides they can expect in their child. In her discussions with Janice, Shelly sometimes describes an experience she and Erin have had and then tells Janice how she remembered what Janice had told her during a prior home visit—sometimes as long ago as the previous year.

How does this personal relationship between parents and home visitors develop? The relationship evolves from extended interactions over time. Several home visitors in the Missouri Parents as Teachers program identified key themes in forming their relationship with parents. Lela described her work with working-class and low-income mothers and fathers.

First, parents have to trust you, and that takes time. I try and build a rapport so that they can talk to me about things they are concerned about, topics like sleep problems, discipline, or toilet training, with comfort, and not feeling like they are being failures as parents. And they need to know that I am not there to judge them, that I'm there as a support person. And if there is any information I can get them that they need, I'll be glad to do that. And sometimes I even bring in personal experiences in my own life so that they'll know that, hey, a lot of other parents experienced this problem, too.

Several themes emerge in Lela's description. Parents need to feel comfortable enough to talk about whatever is going on in their lives. They can do this in the example given if Lela has developed rapport with them so that they can trust her. Like Janice, Lela feels that occasional sharing of her personal experience supports parents in the knowledge that they are not alone in their concerns.

Ernestine also works with working-class and low-income families. Ernestine explained her relationships with parents as follows:

> I think I give genuine concern and even sometimes state, "I am concerned" or "I care." And what we focus on often depends on the family. What is going on in that family? And I try to be available to listen to whatever is going on in that family's life that the parent chooses to tell me. As I listen, I make sure I give them eye contact, and sometimes even restate what they have said to help them know I understand.

Ernestine sees *genuineness, concern, caring,* and *active listening* as central to her relationships with parents. The parents with whom she works feel her genuine concern and caring, for often they share "whatever is going on" in their family life—a clear sign of their trust. Although she always enters a home with activities and ideas to discuss with parents, she is quick to adjust her agenda when parents want to share their concerns. Mutuality is a part of these relationships; both parent and home visitor control the agenda of the visit.

Janice discussed how she tries to praise what she sees parents and their child doing as she strives to help them trust themselves and "feel strong in what they do." Extended observations of Janice's home visits illustrate her approach.

> Greg (age 19 months) is playing with a large tub of beans and assorted spoons and cups. As he puts a spoon into a cup, he says, "Spoon in cup." His mother, Karyn, repeats his statement. Janice remarks to Karyn, "You are so good at saying his words. And he then hears the correct pronunciation. He knows you understand him, and you are encouraging him to talk."

As she praises Karyn, Janice provides developmental information and developmental interpretation: "He then hears the correct pronunciation. He knows you understand him, and you are encouraging him to talk." Greg's parents explained how they would describe Janice to a friend who knew nothing about the family home visiting program.

> Karyn: She is the best, like a surrogate mother to me. She is warm, and I always feel comfortable with her. She is so encouraging. And I feel free to call her when I need her helpful knowledge, even though we have moved out of the district. I don't have enough words for her. She is very warm—like a friend. And she gives information in a way that you can accept or reject it.

Don: *And she has a genuine interest in Greg. She doesn't lecture. She tells you what she thinks, not go do this or that. And when playing with Greg, I used to take the lead. Now Greg takes the lead, for Janice taught me that he could feel more connected and accepted if he took the lead.*

Karyn and Don describe Janice as warm and comfortable, easy to talk to, someone whom they see as a friend who has a genuine interest in their child and upon whom they can call when needing help. They acknowledge that Janice shares a wealth of information, yet it is *they* who choose what they think is relevant for their family. Although they are aware that Janice has influenced their parenting, they also are aware that they are the decision makers.

From this discussion of home visiting and comments from parents and home visitors, several themes arise that are basic to forming personal relationships between parents and home visitors:

- Parents feel the home visitor's genuine concern and caring.
- The home visitor enjoys the parents' child.
- The home visitor is warm, and the parents feel comfortable—as if they are relating to a friend.
- The home visitor actively listens to whatever the parents choose to discuss.
- The home visitor is nonjudgmental and validating, praising the parents' actions when appropriate.
- The parents are the decision makers.

For further information on the parent–home visitor personal relationship, see Chapter 2.

SHARED DELIGHT IN THE CHILD

When home visitors show they enjoy playing with a child or when they delight in a child's new skill, parents experience this enjoyment as affirmation of themselves. Janice consistently expresses her delight in an infant's or young child's achievement. As Erin easily puts together a puzzle, Janice tells Erin's mother and father, "I can't tell you how exciting it is to see how she just does it, with such ease, for her young age!" After this visit, the author remarked to Janice how delighted Janice seems to be in Erin's play. Janice unhesitantly replied, "But it is fun!" Erin's father, Rob, shared his experiences with Janice as follows:

She always is so enthused about what Erin is doing. It's not like a job to her, I don't think. I think it's just something she really enjoys doing, and she gets paid for it. The last time you both were here. And Erin [age 25 months] started jumping rope. And the surprise that came over both of your faces when she started jumping. When you left, we were like, "Did you see their faces?" Like it was no big deal to us.

In meetings with the author, Janice spoke of how important it is that parents know that she enjoys their child as much as they do, and she sees this enjoyment as helping them feel closer to her. When she has her final visit with each family, Janice shares her pleasure and appreciation with parents. On this last visit, she gives parents a summary sheet that highlights one thing from each of her visits. She explained this process as follows:

On the summary sheet, I write, "Thank you for sharing this special time in your life with me," and then some little blurb about their child, and that they are doing a good job as a parent. I'm really sincere in saying that. I enjoy going and seeing them. And it is a special time in their lives. And they have every right to keep it private, but they have shared it with me. And I appreciate that.

Janice understands that she can connect most readily with young parents through her genuine enjoyment of their children. As she celebrates an infant's or young child's accomplishment with parents, she also is encouraging parents' skill in observing their child's development.

When parents consistently experience a home visitor's enjoyment and delight in their child, they often enjoy telling their home visitor stories of happenings between visits. This sharing and joint pleasure is reminiscent of grandparents' and parents' shared joy in their children. Several parents reported that they always are eager to tell Janice stories about their child because they never feel like they are bragging. As Erin's mother stated, "If I tell somebody else, they'll just think I'm trying to show off my child. But I know Janice really cares and really enjoys Erin in the same way as I do." Given the close bond Rob and Shelly feel toward Janice, they eagerly tell her about family happenings—a trip to their uncle's farm, a family birthday party, a parent's illness—in a manner reminiscent of sharing with a relative who has stopped by for a visit. As they describe these events, they often invite Erin to tell Janice about some specific aspect of the event, and Erin usually does so, in a simple manner, typical of toddlers.

HOME VISITORS' RELATIONSHIP WITH TEENAGE PARENTS

Teenage parents often share the characteristics of low-income families—for example, difficulties of accessibility and multiple external and internal problems. In fact, children of unmarried teenage parents are very likely to be poor.[9] Many home visiting approaches with teenagers are similar to those used when working with low-income families. Like low-income families, teenager-parented families are not all alike, and some can manage better than others.

Teenage parents are in the midst of characteristic adolescent issues, such as striving for independence from their families and longing for peer companionship while being a parent to their infant or young child. As with parents experiencing multiple stresses, teenage parents' immaturity and needs may be so great that they may not recognize their child's needs. The home visitor role often expands to include counselor, referral source to community resources, and surrogate parent. Carrie described her home visiting work with teenage parents as follows.

We wear two hats—surrogate parents and parent educators—aiming to provide developmental guidance. We have a dual approach, but both are one. Our teens always have their own agenda. They mostly are interested in meeting their own needs, which can be gigantic. One of our most difficult challenges is to move from parent need to focus on the parent's child. We understand that as we move mother along, we bring her baby along. As we help moms feel their feelings, they can recognize their baby's feelings—that the best way to understand their toddler's fear is to understand their own fear. And whenever a teen is in crisis, we are their referral source. Recently, a pregnant girl was badly malnourished, her hair was coming out, and she had massive headaches. Six months ago she had an abortion. Addressing this child's mother's immediate needs took me 2 hours. These crises make our work very episodic.

Carrie has learned that teenage parents cannot see their infants' needs or respond to their infants' feelings, unless they first feel that they themselves have been heard. Carrie knows that her work can be astonishingly draining, and she appreciates having another teen-parent home visitor, Diane, with whom she can share problems, strategies, and successes. Carrie and Diane also gain assistance and support in their weekly 2-hour staff meetings. Providing support and professional development to teen-parent home visitors is essential for providing quality service.

In many teen-parented families, the teenage mother and child live in the teenage mother's home. Although home visitors strive to focus their work on the teenage mother, it is important that they also relate to the grandparent whose home they are visiting and who often is centrally involved in child rearing. This process involves difficult balancing for the home visitor between a focus on strengthening the young mother's role while respecting and affirming the grandparent's role. Cynthia discussed how she approaches these families.

When you have a teen parent and her mother at odds, in conflict over how to raise that baby, that gets real sticky, and you have to be very careful. One of my rules of thumb is always talk to the parent of the child, the teen. I will direct my talking to the teen parent. If the grandmother is there and offers things, I will interact with the grandmother. But I always try to come back to the parent of the baby and reinforce that role. A lot of times teenagers really don't want to be the parent of that baby, and it is easier to let grandmother take over; and grandma takes over, and sometimes that causes tension. Yet there are some extended families where everyone works pretty well together to raise that child.

Teenage parents are not a unified group in our society. As director of her district's Even Start program, some of the families Cynthia sees are headed by teenage parents. Cynthia sees the fact that the parent joined Even Start as indicative of some maturity, for Even Start focuses on gaining a high school diploma in addition to parenting a young child. Cynthia explained:

The teens I am working with are ready to leave, and are trying to get out of their childhood home. They are 17 or 18, for the most part. Many of the teens we have in Even Start are not living with their parents; rather, they are bouncing from house to house. In these instances, they are in control and are assuming the role of parent, in the sense of making a decision of where that child is going to be. But what they tend to do is drop their child off at different places, a friend watches the child for a day, an aunt watches the baby for a day, or a boyfriend, which is difficult for the child as well as the teen parent. Yet it is hard to generalize. We have another teen mom who moved out of her home because her mother is an alcoholic and abusive. So she took her two kids and left. She is 18 years old. She tried living in shelters for a short period of time, got a part-time job, and now has her own apartment.

As previously discussed, Cynthia knows that if she is going to help a teenage parent, she must have a personal relationship with that parent.

In working with these teen families, the key is time and number of contacts, because the more you are there, and the more you get to know that parent, and the more you can connect with the parent as a person in her own right, not as the mother of a child, the more you can have a personal relationship. The relationship is the key. And once you can establish that you see them as a person and one of their roles as a human being is to be a mother of this child, but that they have other things that they do that you care about, that helps.

The task becomes even more difficult when the home visitor's views contradict those of the grandparents. Home visitors do not want the teenage mother to feel caught in the middle or the grandparents to feel threatened. There is no ready solution in these situations. Expressing respect and genuine interest and actively listening to all family members is helpful. Janice shared her approach in these situations.

I try and help parents recognize and value the grandparents' perspective. Because many times young parents will talk with you about the frustration they feel about the grandparent spoiling their baby, or being overly intrusive, or any number of things. What I always try to do is to frame it in terms of the grandparents' love and interest, and that if there is a way the parent can think about it in terms of a loving relationship, even if it is an uncomfortable loving relationship, if they can think about it as love. And yes, it is still their baby, and they still have the power to do things their own way, but acknowledge the grandparent's perspective.

I remember one teen mom where the child was getting to the age of wanting to touch and explore, and the grandmother was determined that this coffee table was going to stay where it was with the artificial flowers on top, and the child would learn not to touch it. I empathized with the mother, and as it played out over several months, the mom would say to me, "When I am here by myself with the baby, I move all that stuff up. When my mom is here, we have to have it down. But those are the times that I try to take the baby somewhere else to play, or try to stay closer to her." Then after several months, I went back and everything was gone. The grandmother just joked about it, "Yeah, we just sort of got rid of the whole thing." How they worked that out internally in their family, I don't know. But I felt my role was to try to encourage the mom to talk continually with her parent and make this a mutual decision allowing for the child's safety and exploration in whatever way they could work it out in that family.

Janice knows that the infant's grandmother usually is significantly involved in the baby's care and needs to be recognized and valued. Janice described how she has given this teenage mother support and developmental information and encouraged the teen to discuss her infant's needs with her mother when there is a disagreement between them. With Janice's help, the teenage mother is able to be the decision maker regarding her infant.

Because problems of overcrowding and the many extended family members interrupting a home visit can be common within teen-parented families, it may be more effective to have individual visits out of the teen's home. In these situations, often the most productive work with the teenage parent is in more neutral territory, such as the teen's high school or the home visiting program's office. At the same time, effective home visiting programs also try to reach the extended family members. Grandparent support groups can be useful in giving grandparents a setting in which to meet each other, express their frustrations, and gain support and possible ideas to improve their relations with their teenage child-parent. One parent support program has monthly meetings for teens and their entire extended family. Transportation, a dinner, and child care are provided. Then adults attend three 20-minute sessions offered by a variety of social services and health professionals in the community—for example, one session on health resources in the community, one session on guidance and discipline of young children, and one session on sibling rivalry.

In many situations, the home visitor becomes a surrogate parent to the teenage parent. Carrie and Diane are home visitors of teen-parented families. Beyond home visiting, they meet weekly in small groups with the teens at their school. They described their work with teens as follows.

Carrie: *They have a real difficult time expressing themselves and usually are not sure what the problem is. So, one of our jobs often is just to observe behaviors. For example, a mother who normally talks all of a sudden seems very quiet and is kind of off by herself, away from her friends. That usually indicates she is dealing with a pretty heavy problem. So, we might approach her and ask an open-ended question. And then she shares with us her problem.*

You usually can tell that they are trying to express themselves. But often there is so much anger in their family that they start screaming at each other. The mother, the daughter, and the baby's daddy will start hollering, and then they get real depressed because they never have been able to convey what they needed to express. So, in group, we talk a lot about "What did you really want to say?" And we talk about the different ways of being able to say it.

Diane: *And with many of our mothers, we try to get them counseling. Social skills play a big part in what we do—what is the appropriate way to act? You know, a lot of our teen mothers feel like they don't have a family. The majority of these kids sort of have been left on their own to raise themselves. And it is amazing! When you talk to them about how they want to raise their babies differently, their ideas often are more structured than the home life they came from.*

Most of the teenage parents with whom Diane and Carrie work come from troubled families. Not only are they very young, but their childhood homes often have characteristics of troubled families, such as disorganization, family conflict, poverty, and substance abuse. Given their immaturity and social and emotional problems, many of these teens have difficulty paying attention to their babies' needs. Diane and Carrie know that they themselves must hear the mothers' needs and address some of these needs before the mothers will be able to see the needs of their babies. The home visitors' role rotates among being a counselor, a surrogate mother, a friend, and a role model.

Many home visiting programs have teenage parents as part of their caseload. Home visitors provide a very important supportive role to teens who are caught in the middle, having normal adolescent strivings yet simultaneous responsibilities of parenting and often still living with their own parents. Some programs have worked with school districts to have their programs integrated with the junior high and high schools so that teenage parents can more easily finish their schooling. Terry and her mother, Sarah, who also was a teenage parent, explained to the author how home visiting has helped them.

> Terry: *They understand you. At first, you think you are just the bad kid, and everyone is looking down on you. But they support you and tell you you still are normal.*

> Carol: *Has [the program] made a difference in your feelings about Nicholas [age 24 months]?*

> Terry: *Yes, because now when I think he has done something wrong, I just know that it is to be expected and that he is not a mean kid or trying to be rotten. That's what they say he is supposed to be doing.*

> Sarah: *When I was young, forget it! You got pregnant. You left school. It was an embarrassment. You couldn't go to school. I think Weston High has outdone themselves on this, because they want the girls to finish; they want them to go ahead and do something with their lives.*

Terry's comments are in stark contrast to those teenage mothers who see their children as intrusions and often infer intentionality in their actions—parenting patterns that are seen among parents who abuse and neglect their young children. Sarah joins Terry during Terry's home visits. She enjoys telling Terry's home visitor about Nicholas's new skills; however, her role is primarily that of an observer.

DIFFICULTIES AND DILEMMAS

Home visitors encounter some parents with whom it is very difficult to develop a meaningful relationship and thereby assist them. Two types of parents with whom it is challenging to work are 1) parents who are unmotivated and minimally involved with their child and 2) parents who are substance abusers.

When parents are unmotivated and minimally involved with their child, they also probably will not remain in the room during a home visit. Working with these parents can be very demoralizing to a home visitor, who has to be ingenious to capture such parents' attention. In reality, these often are parents who themselves were reared in a troubled family with minimal parenting and probably are somewhat depressed or in some other way overwhelmed by their ongoing problems. For these parents, their young toddler may be viewed as intrusive; they get little joy from parenting.

With unmotivated, minimally involved parents, forming a trusting personal relationship takes extended time and repeated visits. Without a personal relationship, the home visitor never will gain the parents' trust or involvement in the home visit. Cynthia's experience with unmotivated, minimally involved parents provides some guidelines in working with this type of family.

You may have a parent who sees the child as a burden and wants nothing to do with the child. I have worked with some moms, especially younger moms, who have that attitude, but not so much that at some point I can't get them to interact with their child. The key is time and number of contacts because the more you are there and the more you get to know that parent, and the more you can connect with the parent as a person in her own right, not as a mother of the child, the more you can get her involved in your visit.

The relationship with parents is the key. And once you have that established, once parents understand that you see them as a person, and one of their roles as a human being happens to be a parent of this child, but they have other roles and other things that they do that you are interested in, then you can begin to get them involved with their child. As I get to know the parent and establish the relationship, and as trust builds, I sometimes get real directive. If they walk out of the room, I just yell, "I need you in here, help"—that kind of thing. I may say, "This child is driving me nuts, you need to come help me," something that is kind of funny. And they'll come back and not leave me.

Last year I worked with a mom who saw her child as a pain in the rear, an imposition. It was a real challenge to work with her. Often I had to say, "I need you to come back in here with me. This is for you, too, and not just for your child." I would have to be directive. Once I got her back in, I would find a way to relate to her, not necessarily as a mother, but, "How is your job?" I have found that when both child and parent are together, the child usually is trying to relate to the parent, whether the parent is connecting or not. And I can use that—"Did you see the way she looked at you? Look at that. Look, she wants you to see what she is doing." Most parents can't resist that. And sometimes I speak for the child; for example, this mother would deliberately hurt the child. When the child put her hand down to feel the xylophone, the mother took the stick and hit the child's hand with it. And I said, "Oh, Mom, that hurt me, I was just trying to feel what this was like." And the mom looked at me and said, "That tap didn't hurt her." But what it did was stop the child's play. So I talked about that a little. I said, "It may not have hurt her, but, you know, she is not interested in it any more." You have to be careful and not say, "What did you do that for?" or "Look at what you did." At the same time, you have to help parents see how their actions and interactions with their child make a difference. It is difficult, but you have to keep working at it.

Cynthia understands that when she works with unmotivated, uninvolved parents, she first must connect with the parent as a person, not as a parent. She lets the parent know that she knows the parent does other things and has other interests and other problems and that she is interested in relating to the parent as a person. Once she develops a personal relationship, she uses several strategies to work with the parent. At times, she is directive; at other times, she speaks for the child because she knows that some parents do not understand that their behavior has an effect on their child. Often she points out when the child is approaching the parent. In many cases, these parents are so concerned with their own problems that they are not aware when their child seeks their attention. Most important, Cynthia is persistent and confident that, with time, she can develop a personal relationship with most parents and thereby begin to help the parent. At the same time, Cynthia recognizes that some parents never will be open to working with a home visitor. In spite of her extensive experience, Cynthia finds accepting this reality to be very difficult.

A second challenge involves working with parents who are substance abusers.[10] Regardless of parents' social class, education, or income level, home visitors may encounter substance abuse among the parents with whom they are working. Parents who are overwhelmed with feelings such as anxiety, depression, loss, or bouts of panic may use alcohol and other drugs to relieve their pain. Substance abuse has a significant impact on the lives of the entire family and on the home visiting process. Addiction prevents parents from responding to their infant's or young child's needs.

Experts believe approximately one in six or eight children has an alcoholic parent.[11] Given the illegality of drug use in America, the true level of drug use is not known. Prenatal exposure to alcohol can cause fetal alcohol syndrome (FAS), prematurity, and low birth weight.[12] Babies born with FAS often are small and usually do not catch up in size as they grow older. In most cases, these babies have small eyes, a short, upturned nose, and flat cheeks. They may have organ malfunctions, especially with the heart. Most have some degree of mental retardation.

The effects of prenatal exposure to crack and cocaine are on a continuum of injury from minimum symptoms to severe impairment in all areas of a child's development. Characteristic behaviors include increased sensitivity, irritability, hyperactivity, tremors, speech and language delays, processing difficulties, motor delays, and poor social skills. Plasticity in development is greatest in the first 18 months to 2 years of life; thus, early detection and accompanying intervention have the potential for compensating for difficulties due to prenatal exposure.

Alcoholism or drug abuse is not always obvious. If parents repeatedly seem confused, do not remember having arranged an appointment, or give evidence of mood swings, inability to concentrate, or insomnia, they may be abusing alcohol and other drugs. Once home visitors suspect that a parent is abusing a substance, they try to openly discuss the issue and offer support. Parents can hear their home visitor only if they have a personal relationship with their home visitor. Substance abuse is not within the expertise of home visiting; however, home visitors can offer assistance for parents to gain access to professional services. When substance abuse is endangering the safety of young children, a call to child protective services is warranted. Once home visitors recognize substance abuse, they also need to assess whether it is safe for them to continue making home visits with this family. Chapter 2 discusses this issue in further detail.

CONCLUSIONS

This chapter discusses the formation and progression of parent–home visitor relationships. Two very skilled home visitors, Janice and Cynthia, shared their experiences in establishing and developing relationships with parents, and several parents shared how they view these women. These parents spoke of Janice and Cynthia as their friend, their surrogate mother, and their confidante. Janice and Cynthia related that, in their work, it is the *parents* who are the experts about their child and who are the decision makers regarding how they parent their child. These home visitors explained that they can assist parents' decision making only if they have a personal relationship with them. Parent development occurs through and within parents' relationship with their home visitor, just as child development occurs through and within the child's relationship with his or her parents.

The process of developing relationships is different for different people. The chapter points out some common themes across people, such as the importance of a trusting relationship between parent and home visitor; discussing expectations, tasks, and roles; and maintaining boundaries of involvement. Also discussed is working with families who are parented by a teenage mother. Beyond developing a personal relationship, home visitors use many different approaches to promote parenting. Chapter 2 discusses approaches to effective home visiting and explores those approaches that assist in working with parents who are members of cultural backgrounds different from that of the home visitor.

2

The Home
Visitor's Approach

In our endeavor to understand reality we are somewhat like a man trying to understand the mechanism of a closed watch. He sees the face and the moving hands, even hears its ticking, but he has no way of opening the case. If he is ingenious he may form some picture of a mechanism which could be responsible for all the things he observes, but he may never be quite sure his picture is the only one which could explain his observations.

> Albert Einstein and Leopold Infeld (1938/1966, p. 31)

Once parents and home visitors have developed the personal relationship described in Chapter 1, home visitors can address program objectives. The primary purpose of home visiting is to help parents to understand their child's development and to improve their parenting skills. When home visiting is effective, parents see themselves and their child from a whole new perspective and interact with their child in new ways.

This chapter discusses approaches that promote effective home visiting, which can be performed using many approaches, some of which overlap with one another. This chapter examines these approaches in four parts. Part I explores 12 communication and interpersonal skills that encourage, maintain, and promote the parent–home visitor relationship:

1. Individualizing across families
2. Establishing respect and rapport

3. Providing empathic listening and support
4. Engaging in observation and offering descriptive affirmation
5. Modeling
6. Sharing developmental information
7. Making developmental interpretations
8. Offering suggestions
9. Questioning
10. Problem solving
11. Promoting active parent involvement
12. Achieving streams of interaction: balancing and initiating

Part II discusses five additional skill areas that are essential to effective home visiting:

1. Promoting informal support through social networks
2. Networking with community agencies, institutions, and organizations
3. Promoting the program agenda
4. Maintaining efficient organization and management
5. Being aware of legal and ethical issues

Part III discusses issues in home visiting with families of diverse cultural backgrounds, especially those who are disproportionately at risk. Finally, Part IV discusses difficulties and dilemmas involved in working with parents who are concrete thinkers and with those families who live in chaotic conditions.

I. COMMUNICATION AND INTERPERSONAL SKILLS

This section is divided into 12 aspects of communication; however, in reality, each approach works together with the others to form the whole. For example, home visitors do not listen empathically unless they respect parents. They cannot give helpful developmental interpretation of a child's action unless they are keen observers and are knowledgeable in child development. Furthermore, communication is more than just language. In order for infants and young children to learn to communicate, they must have experienced repetitive daily give-and-take exchanges with their parent and caregiver. In order for parents and home visitors to communicate, they must have a relationship grounded in mutual respect and trust, and their conversations must express such mutuality.

The approaches discussed here are skills that cannot be taught. The home visiting process involves the organic unfolding of a relationship. Recipes do not work. Even for experienced home visitors, the home visiting process is unique to each family and can be known only as it develops over time. Home visitors can improve their skills through experience in home visiting; through thinking about their experience; and through gaining constructive feedback from peers, mentors, and supervisors. Thus, underlying this discussion is a paradox. Some of these communication and interpersonal skills are essential to forming the parent–home visitor relationship, yet a relationship takes time to develop. More paradoxically, the parents and home visitor need to know one another and have a trusting relationship before some of these approaches can be effective.

Individualizing Across Families

Because each family is unique, effective home visiting means individualizing the approach to address each family's distinctive patterns, and it necessitates different approaches with different families. When home visitors assume that each of the families with which they work is unique, they use their observation skills and extended conversations with parents to guide their work. They understand that each family has its own routines, problems, values, standards of behavior, and priorities. Different kinds of communication are suited to different families. For example, once a home visitor becomes aware of a mother's unique style of interaction with her infant and the activities that the mother most enjoys with her infant, then the home visitor can support the mother's participation in these activities with her child.

In order to individualize, home visitors also look beyond the everyday patterns of the family to understand the family's connection with extended family members, neighborhood, workplace, and so forth. For example, when a grandmother is very close to the infant's mother and regularly provides child care, the home visitor encourages the grandmother to participate in the visits or includes discussion of the grandmother in her or his conversations with the infant's mother. When an infant is enrolled in a child care program, the home visitor invites parents to talk about their experiences and feelings about the program. Not only do home visitors make adaptations in their approach with different families, they must also make accommodations in their approach with individual families as families change and need different approaches at different times. Janice spoke with the author about her perspective on individualizing across families.

Janice: *You have to know that when you step through the door, you may find something that is totally different than what you anticipated. It could even be a family that you have visited for 2 years, and you can walk in, and the mom may look different, she talks different, she may simply be different from what she has ever been before. The child may be behaving differently and you know that something is going on with her. I have to change. I have to step back and listen, listen to what it is that is happening in this home right now.*

The cues usually come from the parents. You must be able to read their signal. You also must be able to read what the child's needs are at the time. Development may be entirely different than what you anticipated when you came through the door. This is especially true when you are working with a family that has had a premature baby because those babies really are on a different time schedule. You may think that they are going to be developmentally at such a stage because [the child was age] 3 a month ago, and that is what you expect. And they may be far more advanced than you had expected. There is an incredible call for flexibility.

If you haven't been able to blend the parent's agenda with your agenda, you might as well not be there. There are certain things that you want the parent to have access to, such as what are appropriate expectations for a child at this stage of development. But if that's not what is high on her agenda, pick out the one or two key points you want to get through and forget the rest, and spend most of your time addressing what are her issues for that day, and do the best you can with it. That's why it is incredibly important to be prepared and to know the range of things that are likely to come up with parents and their whole family, really.

Carol: *As I listen to you, I sense the ever-expanding lens that you have from your extended experience with a large range of parents and your understanding of the range of parent development and not just child development.*

Janice: *That's true; but on the other hand, you can pretty quickly pull in the range of things likely to come up. Because it is just not that much. You know, if I think about what it takes to work with families that have 2-year-olds, there are likely to be only so many issues that they are going to be facing. I may go to a visit thinking that I am going to talk about toilet training, and the issue the parent wants to discuss is that child's night-mares. Well, I'll put my issue aside for the next visit, for we are going to talk about nightmares. And I know that this is an appropriate topic within that 2-year-old time frame; so I shift topics.*

Although Janice enters each home with a planned agenda, she is quick to shift her agenda when either the child is behaving differently from what she had anticipated or the parents have issues they want to discuss. Janice understands the mutuality of her relationship with parents and knows that parent-initiated agendas always come first. In this way, Janice communicates respect, affirmation, and support. She also knows that parents integrate knowledge into their decision making most readily when parents raise the issue themselves. Being experienced and knowledgeable in child development, she knows the range of behavior and potentially problematic issues for each period of development. When parents initiate a concern separate from her initial plan, she understands that concern within a developmental frame and can assist the parent spontaneously. At the same time, however, Janice understands that when parents initiate discussion of a concern with which she does not feel equipped to deal, she listens, supports, and, when appropriate, suggests another professional with expertise in the area of the parents' concern. This issue of professional boundaries is discussed in Chapter 1.

Establishing Respect and Rapport

When home visitors communicate that they value and accept parents, parents feel they are respected. When parents feel some mutual understanding, agreement, and connectedness with their home visitor, the home visitor has established rapport. A home visitor's first task is to find a common ground with the parent and thereby begin to develop rapport. Cynthia described the various topics she discusses in a first visit: commenting on something she sees in the home, something the parent or child is wearing, even television or movies. As home visitors have informal conversations with parents, they are helping parents feel at ease and connected with them. In this process, home visitors are conveying respect and genuine interest in parents.

When a home visitor has been working with a family for some time, the first few minutes of conversation often are a continuation of a topic discussed in a previous session. For example, Cynthia knows that Sally's mother-in-law, in whose home Sally lives, just began a new job. Upon arrival, Cynthia asked Sally, "How does your mother-in-law, Donna, like her new job?" Her question sparked a brief conversation about Donna's new job. Then Sally told Cynthia about how Willy's child care teachers are trying to address the problem of his biting the other children. Cynthia first renews her bond with Sally, who then shares what is on her mind—her son's biting problem. Cynthia then can proceed to discuss Sally's concern.

When Cynthia enters a home, she strives to let the parents know she understands she is a guest in their home.

When I first walk in, it's a little awkward because the parents are not sure what to do with me, or where to put me. I'm aware that this is their home. I want to be invited to sit down or be told where to sit down. Usually, I'll introduce myself and tell the parents why I'm there. And then I'll say, "Where would you like me to sit?" Then I am saying, "This is your home, you make the choice of where you want us to meet." I'm somewhat direct. Then I talk to them about some common ground like the weather, or, if the child is there, we talk about the child.

Cynthia communicates respect and genuineness in her own way to the parents with whom she works. She is skilled at removing emotional distance between herself and the parents and thereby develops trust and rapport with them.

Providing Empathic Listening and Support

Empathic listening and support are intertwined in home visitors' interactions with parents throughout their home visits. As they carefully listen, home visitors try to see things from the parents' perspective and recognize the parents' feelings. When Sally tells Cynthia that her 20-month-old son Willy had a 104-degree fever over the weekend, Cynthia comments, "That's scary." When Karyn tells Janice that she took Greg (age 9 months) to the eye specialist because he had been scratching his eyes, but the specialist could discover no cause, Janice comments, "All kinds of medical things occur this first year. And when you're concerned, it's good to trust yourself and call the doctor." Janice and Cynthia's empathic responses give support to these mothers and communicate that they understand and value what the parent is sharing.

Once a personal relationship is formed, parents share their frustrations, ambivalence, or anxiety about their child or their parenting. As they listen, home visitors suspend judgment. Sometimes they can help parents understand that these are normal feelings experienced by many parents. Parents then feel accepted and can be more at ease knowing that their feelings are universal. Sharing one's own personal life experiences is another way of showing empathy and support. Visiting Karyn 5 weeks after her baby Greg was born, Janice had the following conversation:

Janice: *How was your delivery?*

Karyn: *It was a c-section. He was so big. They didn't give me realistic expectations of my recovery.*

Janice: *That was one of my big surprises! I was told what to expect of my baby, but nobody told me what my body would feel like.*

Karyn: *My husband, Don, took off work for 3 weeks, and that helped.*

Janice: *Do you have any relatives nearby?*

Karyn: *No, except for Don's sister, who has a 3-month-old and a 3-year-old.*

Janice: *That's tough, really tough. When my first was born, my mother was with me for 3 weeks. I can still remember when she drove off. Bob and I looked at each other. I almost can feel that now because my feelings were so strong.*

Janice expressed to Karyn that she hears her and understands her feelings. This conversation occurred during her second visit with Karyn. Janice's empathic support and personal sharing are significant threads in establishing the rapport that is essential to her effectiveness.

When home visitors value listening, they allow *ample time* for parents to talk about what is concerning them, to share what has happened since the last visit, to respond to the home visitor's questions, or to ask questions themselves. Home visiting demands *total focus.* The home visitor's attentiveness and body language communicate support and interest just as words do. As parents talk, home visitors sort through what is being said so that they can respond appropriately. Sometimes what the parent leaves unsaid is just as important as what is said.

Much of our talking involves telling stories. In the telling of stories, we give meaning to our lives.[1] That is, as we talk, we are thinking about our experiences and weaving our experiences into the meanings we make of our lives. When parents and home visitors have developed a personal relationship, parents talk about their child, experiences they have had with their child, and family life in general. The home visitor's ability to listen actively and empathically to what is being said not only affirms parents but also contributes to parents' understanding of themselves and their family. Sometimes it is even helpful to ask parents to explain a word they have used or to invite the parent to say more, and, in this manner, both support and assist the parents' thinking. For example, a mother says her new baby is well behaved. When asked to say more, the mother describes how helpful it is that her baby can sleep through the night and is not colicky, as was her first child. As she talks, she realizes the issue is not her baby's behavior, but rather that her second baby's calmness allows her to sleep more and be more relaxed.

Engaging in Observation and Offering Descriptive Affirmation

Keen observation of both parent and child actions serves three purposes. First, by observing, the home visitor can identify positive parenting behaviors and build on these positive strengths. In recognizing and supporting the parents' strengths, home visitors support the parents' self-confidence and lessen any feelings of discomfort. Second, home visitors observe to assess the developmental level of the child and adjust their interactions and activities to this developmental level. Being in the home provides an opportunity to be aware of the family's neighborhood and physical resources in the home, such as amount of space or amount and quality of toys. Third, home visitors can use their observations to describe verbally positive parent and child actions and in this way affirm the parent. This is a more powerful and specific form of praise than using evaluative words such as *good* and *nice job.* Drawing attention to specific positive behavior helps parents understand their successes rather than merely recognizing that they are pleasing the home visitor. This use of observation is termed *descriptive affirmation.* Descriptive affirmation also models an effective parenting strategy for parents—verbally recognizing the child's positive behaviors and thereby fostering the child's sense of self-worth. In other words, the home visitor builds on parents' strengths in the same manner that the home visitor strives to help parents build on their child's strengths.

Within each home visit, Janice describes the positive behavior of both parent and child as she interacts with them.

> *Erin (age 31 months) is hammering golf tees into a square of styrofoam. Her mother, Shelly, comments, "You did a good job hammering that one in."*
>
> Janice: *That's a good way you have praised her, telling her what you are pleased about. You are hooking a little description onto your praise so that she can develop her own concept of what she did. What we want is for her to develop her own sense of pride—helping her recognize her successes.*
>
> *[Later in the session Erin picks up her toy phone and gives it to her mother as she says, "Call Robbie."]*
>
> Shelly: *You want me to call Robbie.*
>
> Janice: *You are so good at automatically repeating and expanding Erin's speech. You probably are not even aware you are doing it. But Erin knows she is being heard and you understand her.*
>
> Shelly: *I remember last year when Erin began talking, you suggested I repeat but not correct her.*
>
> Janice: *That's it. You are encouraging her speech and at the same time she hears the correct way.*

Janice has visited Shelly, Rob, and their daughter Erin monthly since Shelly's third trimester of pregnancy. Her relationship with Shelly is continuous over time, even when she is not present. Although Shelly no longer is aware of repeating and expanding her daughter's speech, she does remember that she had learned the skill from Janice the previous year. As Erin plays, Shelly positively describes her action. In turn, Janice is quick to affirm Shelly's parenting. When Shelly repeats and expands Erin's speech, Janice again affirms Shelly's action. With her affirmation, Janice interprets the meaning of Shelly's action in terms of Erin's development. During one home visit, written observations by the author documented that Janice had provided positive descriptions of the child's action 12 times and had given 4 examples of positive descriptions of the parent's actions. Janice explained:

> It comes naturally now. I don't even realize I am doing it a lot of the time. To me, it is a combination of parallel descriptive talk to support the child's action or language, but it also helps the child recognize her accomplishment. I always try to point out strong points of the parent and build on that. They are more likely to hear and remember my developmental information when I "hook it" to what they are doing.

Beyond affirming both parent and child by describing positively their actions, Janice frequently provides developmental information, suggestions, or interpretation of the developmental meaning of the observed actions. The following sections discuss these additional approaches.

Modeling

Modeling refers to the home visitor's interactions with the child that the parents may imitate, for example, the way the home visitor plays with the child, speaks to the child, asks the child questions, or reads to the child. Modeling can help parents feel safe to try out new ways of relating to their child. Modeling is most effective when it is spontaneous rather than an explicit demonstration. Demonstrations implicitly place the home visitor in the expert role, thereby leaving parents feeling less than adequate. As home visitors interact with a child, they can talk about what they see happening with the parents. They can explain the meaning of the child's actions developmentally or comment positively on the child's involvement. In this way, the parents are involved and are not just observing passively.

During each visit, Janice provides a developmentally appropriate play activity for the young child. Janice actively participates in play with the child and, at the same time, maintains a dialogue with the child's parent as to the developmental meaning of the child's actions.

Janice sits on the floor with Mia (age 20 months). Janice gives Mia a cloth bag, and Mia dumps out toy kitchen items—cups, plates, utensils, pots, and pans. Mia hands Janice a plastic cup and a metal lid. Janice remarks, "This lid doesn't fit on the cup. There's a pan. I wonder if it'll fit on the pan." Mia puts the lid on the pan. Janice exclaims, "The lid does fit on the pan!"

Mia picks up a fork as she says "fork." Janice says, "A fork, you can take a bite." Mia puts the fork to her mouth as Janice says, "It tastes pretty good." Mia picks up the knife also, but puts only the fork to her mouth. Janice comments to Tracy (Mia's mother), "It's interesting to note that Mia puts only the fork to her mouth." Tracy answers, "We usually don't let her have knives." Janice explains, "Mia remembers that."

Janice lifts a cup as she suggests to Mia, "We can pretend to pour juice into my cup" (Mia does so) "and drink it. Can you give Mommy some juice too?" Janice pretends to drink from the cup as Mia pretends to pour juice into a cup for her mother.

Janice comments to Tracy, "A lot of imitating goes on at this age. Children love to role-play family activities like cooking. It's a time when they can be in charge. Pretend-play is a natural way small children learn. When she gets a little older, she'll love to dress up in grown-up clothes."

Mia says, "juice," and Janice says, "You are pouring juice into the cup." She asks Mia, "May I have some in my glass, please?" Mia pretends to pour into Janice's glass. Janice smiles and says, "It tastes good." Mia pretends to pour juice into her cup and drink from it, and Janice comments, "You're having some, too. Let's give some to Mommy." Mia pretends to pour into her mother's cup. Janice then suggests that Mia cook her mother some eggs for breakfast, and the role-play continues.

Throughout Janice's play with Mia, she models ways to promote Mia's emerging language, repeating Mia's words and extending them into complete sentences. She also models positive reinforcement. She describes Mia's actions and thereby affirms her competence. As they play, she explains to Tracy the developmental importance of pretend-play. She makes certain that Tracy also is involved in the play. When Janice writes notes on this visit, she reminds herself to continue discussing Mia's spontaneous pretend-play with Tracy.

Sharing Developmental Information

One of the home visitor's central tasks is providing information about child development and appropriate parenting practices. Parents hear and remember this information when it relates to ongoing conversations or activities, such as when home visitors provide information as part of a conversation initiated by the parents or as part of the home visitor's observation of parent or child actions. Developmental information helps parents understand their child's current behavior and anticipate the next steps in their child's development.[2] Tracy, the young mother in the previous example, explained:

> Now I know the things that are going on. And things that aren't happening shouldn't be happening yet. Like, for instance, when I was worried about Mia with potty training and that she wasn't doing good, Janice reassured me that they go through stages like that. Things that I don't know, she kinda helps clear up. And it's reassuring with Mia, who now is going through bad times with her temper. And Janice reassures me that they go through stages. And you will have bad times and good times. That kind of stuff reassures me.

Many parents experience concern when their child is behaving in bothersome ways or is not progressing as fast as the parents expected. When Janice explains that children go through stages that can be hard on parents, but that do not last forever, parents like Tracy are reassured.

Janice frequently provides developmental information as she is positively commenting on a child's or parent's action.

> Janice has just arrived at Marta's home. As she and Marta chat about Thanksgiving, Brianna (age 7 months) crawls about the living room. Marta shares that Brianna began crawling 2 weeks ago. Janice gives Brianna an infant toy, and Brianna sits on the living room floor and begins exploring the toy.
>
> Janice comments, "Brianna sits up so smoothly from that position. 'Miss motor.' Her motor skills are just wonderful! One of the things that makes crawling challenging when it begins this early is that Brianna's memory is not up to her motor skills. You tell her not to touch, and she won't remember. You will need to have quite a repertoire of distraction tools to redirect her when she moves at this young age."

Janice observes Brianna's skill in moving from a crawling to a sitting position. She delights in Brianna's early motor development, and her delight communicates that she cares about and enjoys this infant. Within these comments, she shares developmental information—that Brianna's memory is not as advanced as her motor development, so she will not remember her mother's directives. She also makes a simple suggestion: Marta can use distraction to redirect Brianna.

Making Developmental Interpretations

Within the activities and conversations of a visit, home visitors can interpret the meaning of a parent's or child's action as another way of promoting parents' understanding. When a parent describes her toddler's new constant climbing, the home visitor can explain the developmental significance of this climbing—how the toddler's exploration is a sign of healthy curiosity and a primary way she learns about the world. Similarly, when a home visitor observes a parent's interaction with her child, the visitor can explain the significance of this interaction. When she hears a parent repeatedly state rules, she can explain how the parent's consistent guidance is giving her toddler security so that he will be able to explore and develop increasing independence. Providing developmental interpretations within the context of home visit happenings is a skill that develops with experience and supervision. Janice is very skilled in making interpretive comments, as she does in her home visit with Natalie and her daughter Jene (age 5 months).

Natalie: *Jene puts her lips out and pouts when upset.*

Janice: *Jene is saying, "I'm learning how to communicate. I can let you know when I'm unhappy. I don't have lots of tools yet, but I'm good with my mouth."*

[Jene is lying on her back, holding a toy ring that she has in her mouth.]

Janice: *Everything in her mouth. It's so good. She is curious and first learns about items through mouthing them. And there is a connection between mouthing toys and eating later on. She is getting used to different things in her mouth. It will be easier to have different kinds of table foods. Babies who are not used to lots of toys in their mouths may want only milk and mush.*

Janice's interpretations of Jene's actions helps her mother understand the developmental significance of these actions. Parents' understanding of the developmental meaning of their child's behavior can guide their child-rearing interactions and deepen their enjoyment of the child. When there is more than one child in the home, making interpretive comments to the children about their siblings often helps them understand each other's feelings and actions. Beyond helping the children's understanding, the home visitor is modeling effective parenting.

Offering Suggestions

Different ways of offering suggestions communicate different messages. How parents hear a message influences their relationship with the home visitor and the effectiveness of the process. When a person gives a direct suggestion, the listener may hear authority and expertise. When a suggestion is given that does not relate to ongoing events, the listener may feel a lack of connectedness. When home visitors want to respect, support, and ensure that parents understand that they always are the final decision makers in their child rearing, they should be very sensitive to the manner in which they give suggestions. Janice discussed her method as follows.

I try not to make a lot of suggestions, especially direct suggestions. Rather, I try to point out strong points of the parents and build on that. They are more likely to use these comments rather than a suggestion. If I were to give a lot of suggestions, I doubt if they would be remembered. My primary task is empowerment. I might frame a suggestion as, "Some parents have found that it helps if. . . ." I don't want them to think I am coming in as the expert; rather, I am coming in to support them. I am under, supporting, not on top or next to you.

Janice strives to relate to parents as a partner, not as an expert. She often discusses a variety of methods other parents have used in similar situations. When Janice does give a suggestion, she either is answering a parent's question or concern or the suggestion is part of her observation and descriptive affirmation. As Janice watches Greg (age 7 months) roll over and then get into a sitting position, she comments:

He has excellent motor coordination, the way he went from rolling to sitting. You really no longer can leave him. Have you purchased a gate?

As their relationship develops, Karyn, Greg's mother, feels comfortable sharing her concerns about Greg (now age 27 months) with Janice.

Karyn: *Greg loves to dump things into the trash, like my cookbooks. He broke one of my $30 frying pans.*

Janice: *It's a difficult age. He will get through this. You will get through this. He doesn't have inner controls. He's into "I want it my way."*

Karyn: *It's driving me crazy.*

Janice: *Give him his own trash can. He's at the age where he loves to put things in containers.*

Janice gives Karyn support and offers a suggestion with developmental information to help Karyn understand Greg's actions. Janice described her growth in this area as follows.

Initially, especially in my first year, when a parent would ask, "What should I do about this?," I would be quick to tell them what I thought they ought to do. I don't do that anymore. I have found it's much more effective to ask, "What have you tried?," using a whole series of questions, and then, "What else have you tried?" And very often one of the things they have tried is something that I can say, "Well that's really a good idea. I hope you take that one up." And then we talk about it. It makes them feel better if they can have ownership of the idea, if I can reinforce something that they have tried. It has more power than if I would say, "I think you should do. . . ." And another method I use is I speak in terms of children in general: "Some children usually benefit from this, others benefit from that, and so on." Then parents can pick out what they want without feeling threatened or without seeing me as the expert. On the other hand, if there is an issue of the child's safety, such as wearing a seatbelt in the car, I will be very direct.

In asking parents to share prior methods, Janice is letting parents know that she thinks they know many good ways to handle situations. When she speaks of how children benefit from different kinds of experiences, she trusts that it is the parents who are the decision makers and that they merely need some information to assist their decision making.

Questioning

Questions are a natural part of conversation. In home visiting, open-ended questions encourage parents to talk more. Questions are open-ended when more than one answer is possible, for example, "What are some of the things you enjoy doing with your baby?" When a parent makes a statement, home visitors can ask a question to make sure they understand the parent, such as asking the parent to give an example or asking the meaning of a word used. Sometimes a question can help a parent focus on specific issues that are a concern. For example, when a parent says, "He's bad all the time," the home visitor can ask the parent to give an example of the child's behavior that she or he sees as bad. The parent hears that the home visitor is listening and wants to understand. Once examples are given, the parent and home visitor can discuss the issue.

   Especially during an infant's first year, Janice asks questions that track the infant's development. Her first few visits with Marta and her infant Brianna illustrate this pattern.

On Janice's first visit with Marta and Brianna, Brianna was 4 weeks old. On her second visit, Brianna was 4 months old. Janice asked Marta, "How is her sleeping? Does Brianna turn over? How does she react to books?" On the third visit, Brianna was 5 1/2 months old. Janice asked, "What sounds is she making? How is her sleeping? What is her feeding schedule?" On the fourth visit, Brianna was 7 months old. Janice asked Marta, "What is her favorite thing to do? How is her eating? How does she fall asleep?"

As Janice asks these questions, she is assessing the infant's developmental strides. Often one of these questions leads to an extended conversation, for example, discussing how the infant's nighttime awakenings cause the parents' drowsiness and impatience during the day or how the family has needed to adapt to the infant's need for regular feedings.

Problem Solving

When parents ask the home visitor a question, they often put the home visitor in the expert role and expect a quick answer. Rather than accept the expert role, home visitors can use the parents' questions or concerns as the first step in joint problem solving.[3] Not only does this joint problem solving help parents address their concern or question, but their participation also increases the likelihood that they will remember the information discussed. When a parent shares a concern with Janice, she uses the situation for joint problem solving.

Shelly tells Janice that Erin (age 31 months) recently had been very negative, always saying "No" when Shelly asked her to do something. Interspersed with play and conversations with Erin, the adults discuss her new pattern of negativism around toileting and hair washing.

Janice: *How do you respond to Erin?*

Shelly: *I started the star routine on the calendar and that's helping a little bit. Sometimes I'm real patient, but other days. . . . I finally said to Rob, "When she wants to go, she'll go." Now I hold a star and say, "Do you want a star?," and she'll say "Yes" and go to the bathroom.*

Janice: *That's real smart.*

[Shelly then describes the battle she and Erin had over washing Erin's hair.]

Shelly: *I don't want to fight with her, but I want to keep the discipline.*

Janice: *I think you have handled both situations positively. Kids need to understand that their parents understand their feelings, but rules are rules. The trick is to know when to ease up and when to stay firm. Are there enough situations where you can give her some space?*

When parents share a concern, Janice always asks the parents how they deal with the issue. In this way, Janice has some time to think, and she gains information. Furthermore, being involved in the problem solving means that parents have ownership of the solution. Janice explained:

I always begin with "What have you tried?" And sometimes the question may change the direction of the discussion. The first issue may not be the most important issue for the parent.

Often some of the parents' actions are appropriate, and Janice can affirm them. As they talk, she provides developmental information and gives suggestions.

When both parents are present, home visitors can invite each parent to share her or his understanding of the problem. Sometimes a few questions help the parents look at the problem from a larger perspective. For example, if a parent complains that her son does not remain at the table during dinner, the home visitor can ask questions to frame the discussion around the family's patterns of eating dinner. The home visitor can ask parents what they would like to have happen. When focusing on desired solutions to the problem, the conversation becomes positive. During a discussion, the home visitor can help parents understand that there usually are several ways to handle every situation. Sharing how other parents have handled a similar situation can be helpful and reassuring. As possible solutions are discussed, both short- and long-term benefits and liabilities can be identified.

Promoting Active Parent Involvement

One of the challenges of home visiting is balancing involvement with both parents and children. Active involvement increases the likelihood that parents will learn and remember child development information and child-rearing strategies that have been a part of the visit. Janice discussed her approach as follows.

Parents will learn best through their own and their home visitor's interactions with the child and through their observations of their child engaged in activities during the visit. They will understand child development best by having it related to what their child is doing at any given moment.

I initiate the activity with the child to provide an opportunity for modeling. Then usually I invite the parent to join us, unless the activity is built around the child exploring something. But even then, I always end my visits with a book, and, in these situations, I'll invite the parent to read the book. I want parents to feel that they are a real integral part of the visit. And also I want to see how they interact with their child. And if a parent is very immature, or developmentally slow, I take her down the path a little more slowly and with much smaller steps.

Janice does not implement parent education in the abstract; rather, she informs parents as she interacts with the child and parents. The central focus of her visits are play activities that she initiates with the child, activities in which she is an active participant. Then she invites the parents to join the activity.[4] Janice understands that the parents' learning is promoted when they are doing an activity with her and their child. The process reinforces the mutuality of the relationship Janice strives to maintain. Parents usually enjoy their child's delight in having two or three adult playmates, and positive feelings promote learning.

> Janice takes toy musical instruments out of a bag and says to Mia (age 36 months), "Now we're going to hear a song, and then after the song, we'll play the instruments." Janice has a small tape recorder on her lap. She helps Mia's little sister, Maggie (age 18 months), push the button, and the "itsy-bitsy spider" song plays. As the song plays, Janice and the children's mother, Tracy, sing. Mia and the adults do the hand motions with the song. During the second song, Janice gives Mia cymbals, Maggie maracas, and Tracy a tambourine. She does the hand motions to the song as Tracy and the children play the instruments. The two adults and children continue the activity for about 15 minutes. As the children play their instruments, Janice comments, "Anything that promotes a sense of rhythm is really valuable. Children love this kind of activity."

Janice understands that it is important for the play activities to be simple and inviting. Yet having parents as active play participants during a home visit is not a simple matter. First, a trusting, personal relationship with the home visitor must be in place in order for parents to feel comfortable playing, and this relationship takes time to develop. Second, parents do not expect to be playing during a home visit and may feel a little awkward at first. In fact, some parents never play, in spite of their home visitor's skill at promoting parent involvement, because their definition of parenting does not include play. Promoting active involvement of the parent is another skill that takes experience to develop.

Achieving Streams of Interaction: Balancing and Initiating

A consistent challenge for home visitors is balancing their interaction with the parents and their interactions with the children. Home visiting involves multiple tasks, such as discussing developmental characteristics and emerging skills of the child, discussing parenting practices and issues, initiating activities with the child, and involving parents in these activities. For each visit, home visitors have a specific activity and a developmental topic related to that activity. At the same time, however, parents or children may initiate a topic or activity unrelated to the home visitor's plan. Home visitors then must adjust their plans to integrate what the parent or child has initiated.

Interaction with Parents Janice described a situation in which the mother's agenda became the theme of her visit. Her planned activity was to invite the toddler's exploration of a bag filled with assorted items and to discuss the child's curiosity and intellectual development with the mother.

> This was the fifth home visit with a 2-year-old child, and his language . . . well, he just wasn't talking very much at all. And all year long I had been very frustrated because I felt like the mother never was involved in really hearing what I was saying. Finally, yesterday his language was something she brought up, and I was thinking, "Thank goodness."
>
> Language didn't quite fit my intent of the activities I brought, but I shifted gears to make the activity a language activity. Because now this was something she finally was ready to discuss, and listen, and try things out. And it was great! It was wonderful! I had started out using the bag of items to explore and had intended to talk about intellectual development and the values of exploration.
>
> Well, my original intent to talk about curiosity and intellectual development became a very minor piece. I emphasized instead the adult's parallel talk and naming for the child, naming what he was pulling out of the bag. And describing what he was doing with what he pulled out. I demonstrated naming and parallel talk and then got her to try it. She was a mom who was very much into asking her child questions and giving directives. Just an incredible number of questions. She couldn't even make a statement without putting it in the tone of a question.
>
> This is not an activity I ever used in this way. But I thought, I don't care. I'm going to have a language emphasis because finally she is ready to talk about language. She finally is ready to look at herself and see how she can encourage language development with her little boy who really needs to be talking more.

Janice was able to be flexible and shift her original plan in order to use the mother's expressed interest as the basis of the visit's activity and discussion. Because Janice knows child development, she could immediately shift her topic to helping this mother learn how she could facilitate her son's language development. As the toddler pulled items out of the bag, Janice modeled methods to stimulate language; for example, she described what the child was doing as he played and encouraged the child to name the items. Given the interest and concern this mother had expressed, Janice was able to encourage her to try some new parenting approaches. Janice has a goal that her work will involve a partnership between parents and herself. If parents are to benefit from her work, she must be ready to work with them to deal with the concerns they are expressing at the moment.

> When I go into a visit, I will have a generalized plan for what I hope will happen; but I always think that it has to fit in terms also of the parents' agenda. I really don't come in with lots of details about what I am going to

do in a visit, and my reason is that I want to have some control in the visit, but only an element. I want a lot of control to be with the parents. If I've got it in my head that I've got to talk about their toddler sharing, that might not exactly fit. I would rather talk about sharing when the mother brings up that the child cannot share with other children. I like to respond to rather than initiate these issues.

I can click off developmental information, but I don't think that's nearly as meaningful as pointing it out when I see it, as talking about it when the mother sees it, and letting her really believe, as is the case many times, that she is seeing something first and then we get to talking about it. However, there is also this tricky balance between having the parent bring up an issue and my letting them know in advance that a particular development is likely to occur. The difference is the scope: I mention in advance developments the parents can anticipate. We discuss it in depth when they see it and bring up the issue themselves.

Janice is steeped in developmental knowledge and appropriate parenting strategies. She knows what topics need to be covered for each developmental period. She understands that she can be an effective promoter of parents' understanding and skills only when the parents' lived experience gives them reason to be interested in the topic. (Part II discusses developmental progression, birth to 5 years, in five central areas of home visitors' focus.)

Interaction with Children In addition to their involvement with parents, home visitors also are relating to young children. Beyond the activities and discussions that the home visitor and parents initiate, children also initiate activities. Child-initiated activities most often occur either at the outset of a visit or after the child is finished with the activity that the home visitor has introduced. When Janice enters a home, a child may be playing with a toy. Janice then frequently engages in playing with these toys with the child. On other occasions, a child might go get a toy specifically to share with Janice.

Erin (age 20 months) comes into the living room with a large plastic beach ball that she throws to Janice, who is seated on the floor. As she rolls the ball to Erin, Janice suggests, "Let's roll it." After a few exchanges with the ball, Janice asks Shelly if she has a laundry basket.

Shelly returns with a circular laundry basket that Janice places in front of her. Standing a few feet from the basket, Erin throws the ball into the basket several times. Each time she is successful, Erin jumps up and down as she says, "I got it! I got it!" Her mother hugs her as she says, "I'm so proud of you."

Janice then suggests, "Let's give Mommy a turn." Shelly first playfully bounces the ball as she says, "I have to dribble a bit." Then she shoots a few baskets.

Janice holds the basket high as she says to Erin, "Do you want it high or low?" Erin replies "low" and then successfully throws the ball into the basket. As Janice raises the basket, she says to Shelly, "It's a totally different game when I put it on the floor and then lift it higher."

Janice now puts the basket on its side as she suggests to Erin, "How about rolling it like when Mommy goes bowling?" Erin does as Janice has suggested, and when the ball goes into the basket, she again jumps up and down saying, "I did it! I did it!" Janice then asks Erin to get a little ball, which Erin does. Erin throws it into the basket and then suggests, "Mommy's turn."

In this last sequence, Janice improvises to extend the activity with new ideas—introducing the basket, utilizing the basket in several ways, suggesting a different-size ball. She encourages Erin's mother to join the play, and both mother and child express delight in the activity. Janice explained her rationale for utilizing children's toys during home visits.

One of the reasons that I like to use the children's toys is that I think I sometimes can expand on what the child does with that toy in ways that the parent might not have thought about—give them new ideas for stuff that has been around for a while. The other thing it does is it helps parents to further believe that they have made good choices in the toys they have bought for their child. Further, it lets the family realize that the things they want to be a part of the home visit are certainly as important as the things I choose. All along, we are trying to promote the idea of following the child's lead, of paying attention to the child's cues.[5] Thus, if I ignore what the child brings in, I am not practicing what I preach, so to speak.

Even the most disadvantaged family has something that their child has been playing with before I arrive. If I can, I'll use it in some way, or observe the child playing with it. In cases where the toys are not appropriate, I use safe household objects that the parent probably has but hasn't designated as toys.

Achieving a balance in interacting with parents and their children is a progressively developed skill. Often a child's initiative or a parent's question can be felt as interrupting the flow. After observing how Janice was able to maintain a discussion with Tracy while having several sequences of exchanges with Tracy's 20-month-old baby, Mia, the author asked her to explain what was going on in her mind during her discussion with Tracy.

Well, I do this deliberately, for I want the parent to see that you can acknowledge the child's desire to be a part of it, and still get your point across, without telling the child, "Be quiet, wait a minute until I am finished," and so forth, that you really can juggle both roles—an adult role and interacting with the child as well. And it is a way to help the child feel a sense of being included. Because if you tell the child, "Wait a minute," the child is going to keep bugging you and bugging you and bugging you, and they're coming out looking bad instead of coming out looking good. You play with her doll for a couple minutes. They are satisfied, having been included, and then you go on with your adult conversation.

Janice knows that each moment that she is relating to parent and child she is modeling for the parent. Often parents have difficulty with their young child's persistent interruptions. In modeling, Janice exposes parents to a way of dealing with a child's interruptions. As parents watch, they see how their child responds. Then the parents can decide whether what they are observing is something they would like to try.

II. ADDITIONAL KNOWLEDGE AND SKILLS

Part II discusses a collection of knowledge and skills that are essential for promoting the home visiting process. Unlike communication and interpersonal skills, these skills do not occur or interact together; therefore, each area is discussed separately.

Social Networks: Promoting Informal Supports

Social ties among parents become networks that are powerful influences motivating behavior, beliefs, and development. Parents' social networks can provide information, emotional and material assistance, and support and encouragement of certain child-rearing attitudes and behavior, as well as role models. In order for infants or young children to flourish, their parents need access to support, encouragement, and assistance, all of which can be provided through social networks.[6] In other words, in order for parents to fulfill optimally their child's developmental needs, they need the support of not only family members within the household but also people in their larger network of social relations. In these relations, parents learn that they are not alone in their child-rearing responsibilities.

As they work with families, home visitors become sensitive to the differences in social networks of these families and the varied influences that these networks have in a family's functioning.[7] Social networks can include extended family, neighbors, peers in the workplace, and peers with whom parents associate socially. Both relatives and friends can offer informal support to young parents.[8] Extended family and friends are relationships that can provide companionship and support. The size of parents' personal networks may vary greatly. A parent who is a full-time homemaker with very small children may experience isolation and accompanying loneliness. Many young parents in our society are quite mobile and may be relatively new to the community and therefore have minimal personal networks. In these situations, home visitors often can assist parents in developing relationships, for example, informing parents of neighborhood play-group possibilities, community play groups, or "parent's day out" programs. Some home visiting programs also offer parent group meetings or parent–child sessions, both of which are excellent settings for parents to develop peer relationships. Janice described a method she has used to promote parents' social networking.

> I have done a small-group meeting about infancy, and mothers have come together in somebody's home, and we would talk about babies. And we would plan, maybe or maybe not, another similar meeting for this group. But what is more likely to happen is they make it happen for themselves. The kids in one of these groups are 8 or 9 years old now. I had no idea they would continue as a group. Their parents continue to get together as couples for a card club, and that was strictly through their contacts in these infant groups.

The family's social network can expand to include the child care staff. When the infant or toddler is enrolled in a child care program, the connections between parents and child care staff become central to the child's healthy development. Young children feel secure when they hear similar messages from parents and their child care teachers. When home visitors value families' social networks, they can sensitively respond to parents' discussion of these experiences. For example, when a parent is having difficulty relating to her infant's child care teacher, the home visitor can listen empathically and engage in joint problem solving with the parent to discover possible strategies to resolve the parent's difficulty.

Extended Family and Social Support   Often home visitors work with young parents living with their extended family in the same house, next door, or within the same neighborhood. Extended families can offer young children multiple strong emotional attachments with adults committed to their well-being.[9] For families at risk, extended families often can buffer parents and their young children from the impact of stress, for example, availability of child care and pooling of money for food and housing. When home visitors work with several extended families, they recognize that there are considerable differences in the way extended families are organized and relate to each other. The home visitor's task becomes more complex when the home visit includes extended family members. Cynthia discussed her experience.

When parents are living with extended family members, sometimes I go on a home visit and I'll have the grandmother there or an aunt or sister there. What I usually do is leave it to the parent to decide whether or not that person stays, and it also is up to the other person who is there if she or he wants to stay. Sometimes they elect to leave. But what I find is if someone is there, especially if it is the grandmother or the aunt who is helping to raise the child, they'll stay. One of my rules of thumb is always to talk to the parent of the child. When the grandmother is there and offers things, I'll interact with the grandmother, but I always try to come back to the parent of the baby and reinforce that role. Or if it is the father, sometimes the father will be in the bathroom listening but won't come out because he doesn't want to participate actively. . . . And I respect his decision.

As she relates to young parents, Cynthia remembers that her role is to strengthen the parents' role as decision makers. Thus, Cynthia invites the parents to decide whether extended family members participate in the home visit. She also respects how family members may choose to be involved, whether actively or passively. When extended family members do participate, Cynthia accepts this extension yet maintains her primary focus on the parents. She communicates her valuing of all family members' role in rearing the child and at the same time communicates that she understands that the primary responsibility belongs to the actual parents.

Sometimes parents disagree with other family members over their child-rearing practices and share these disagreements with their home visitor. Cynthia discussed her approach in these situations.

I have encountered families where everyone has a different approach. As I am working with the family and getting to know the people, I get a better sense of where they are coming from and what they consider important in child rearing. Anytime the family has a conflict and I am working with people who have opposing views on something, I try to find a common ground. And if they are coming from the same family, there usually is a common ground. They have shared experiences, and so there is something that they both believe in when it comes to raising that child, and I try to use that as the beginning point.

Cynthia begins with the assumption that all family members have shared experiences that give them a common ground on which they all can agree. Once Cynthia and the parents identify this common ground, Cynthia is able to assist family members in working through their differences. As she discusses differences with family members, Cynthia also helps them understand that young children feel secure when hearing similar messages from their family caregivers.

Janice also confronts these situations, and she shared her approach as follows.

Parents are very likely to talk about grandparents somewhere along the line. Some do it much more often than others. Some will do it in a positive mode; some will do it feeling frustrated about their experiences.

Regardless of the parent's approach to the grandparent, I try to lay the groundwork of the grandparent's perspective. I even did that before I became a grandparent myself because I think it is important to establish that we really honor the whole family and that we understand that grandparents have a different perspective and show their love in a different way. But it doesn't mean that they should be ignored just because you have a home visitor coming in with different ideas. I try to help pull it all together, instead of pulling it apart. You can affirm the parents' role but also help them understand where the grandparents are coming from.

Janice tries to avoid making parents feel caught in the middle between their interest in the home visiting program philosophy and the rest of the family's beliefs, although she may be providing new information and new suggestions that may be contrary to the family's beliefs.

I try to back out of that whenever and as much as is possible and let that be the parents' decision as to how to deal with the information. I might sympathize with the parent when she is going through this. . . . As far as discipline is concerned, parents can feel caught in the middle when dad does not agree with what mom is doing, and grandmother certainly doesn't agree with what mom is doing. And mom thinks she is trying to do something that she has learned through our program. It is easier when a parent can learn a new technique and practice that new technique on her own, before dad is home or when grandma is not around, and get pretty good at it. And then when dad sees it, mom feels very confident in passing along that suggestion because it has become her suggestion. It is not her home visitor's suggestion. It is something she has seen work with the baby, and she now wants to convince dad.

Janice strives to help parents respect their own parents' perspective, even when it is different from their own. Sorting through differences in disciplinary approaches is not an academic exercise, and there is not a hierarchical value to different people's perspectives. Like Cynthia, Janice always strives to build on the parents' strengths. She knows that parents can approach differences best when speaking in their own voice, based on their own successful experience.

Social Supports in the Neighborhood and Workplace

There are settings, such as the family's neighborhood and parents' workplace, in which the child does not participate directly, but that are significant to the parents and thus have an effect on the child. When parents have neighbors who offer companionship, support, nurturance, feedback, and connectedness, parents then have social resources upon which to draw. With this support, parents are more able to feel confidence and strength to meet the needs of their infants and toddlers. With a strong neighborhood connectedness, parents feel a sense of security, belonging, and peace of mind that gets translated in the ease with which they relate to their young children.

When parents experience support and affirmation at their workplace, they are able to return home and give full attention to their family. When they experience tension or vulnerability at work, they are not as well equipped to relate spontaneously to the day-to-day patterns of life with their spouse and young child. In other words, social networks can spark stress as well as support. When parents have limited access to employment and safe neighborhoods, they also have limited opportunities for social networking. When parents' stress is increased, this stress influences their child's development. The cultural diversity section of this chapter discusses this dilemma further.

Networking with Community Agencies, Institutions, and Organizations

Informal social networks such as extended family, friends, and neighbors provide young families with many different services. At the same time, however, families sometimes need services from more formal support systems, such as out-of-home child care, mental and physical health services, public aid and housing, juvenile justice, shelters for homeless families or battered women, and so forth. These resources are formal services offered by government agencies (e.g., the Women, Infants, and Children [WIC] program), private nonprofits (e.g., Alcoholics Anonymous), and private for-profits (e.g., a child care center run as a for-profit business).

Chapter 1 examines home visitors' need to know what they can do and what they are unprepared to handle; in other words, recognizing the boundaries of the program's agenda and the home visitor's expertise. When parents initiate discussion about personal troubles or external difficulties beyond the home visiting agenda and the home visitor's expertise, the home visitor can listen empathically and assist the parent to gain help from resources within the community. Before home visitors can connect parents with the appropriate community resources, they must be familiar with community resources. Becoming familiar with these resources extends the tasks of home visitors.

When the administration of a home visiting program is committed to community networking, the home visitor has available needed information and resources. One home visiting program in a suburban, multicultural, multi-income district illustrates integrating community resources into a home visiting program. Mariam Skoten, Director of Early Education, discussed her program's use of community human services.

I believe our district's early childhood programs are simply part of a big pie. Therefore, we often become a hub of referrals. Sitting on my staff now is a social worker [Jill] who has an adjunct position with the county department of mental health, who offers this free of charge to school districts. And this social worker is housed at the well-baby clinic in our area. Thus, she serves as an intermediary to the health care provider that many of our families utilize.

It's neat because when a home visitor discovers some health concerns, either vocalized by the family or a concern of the home visitor, they immediately call Jill. And Jill can network expediency of health care, for example. She can break through the bureaucratic system of public health provisions.

Also, we have used on our staff, in adjunct positions, our Division of Family Services [DFS]. When a family identifies for us that they have a case worker in this agency, we alert the case worker that we now also are involved. And the family gives us permission in writing to do this. And then the case worker and home visitor work together. We have had some situations where our families have been under abuse or neglect with court orders. And again, with the family's written permission, we have become involved in providing alternatives to discipline. We have had DFS workers that actually have transported parents to parent education seminars.

Another tangent that has been real interesting to us is for our teen parents to work in tandem with the public health nurse, who has been identified through the county's department of health to see teen parents judged at high risk. We work in tandem with them.

We also have connections with our local day care centers and nursery schools. We have gotten some scholarships for our [program recipients]. There are very few [special programs] in our area that offer day care for infants, but we have gotten some scholarships.

Coordination with businesses in the community is an area where we need to experience growth. Kiwanis has supported us by financial contributions and increasing the community's awareness of our program. They bought our first VCR. Because we are so involved in the total community, when we have a need, we just express that need to our community. And it is often filled through church contributions or donations from civic organizations such as the Kiwanis.

In order to get known, I and our staff did a lot of workshops. For example, I did a workshop on [our program] for all day care center directors and their guests to alert the community to what we were about. And we've sent letters to all the ministers, to all the physicians, in the community. In staff meetings, we keep emphasizing that awareness must be comprehensive, intensive, and ongoing—the community's awareness of us and our awareness of the community.

Mariam sees her district's home visiting program as an integral part of the community and as a hub of referrals to local human services agencies. She and her staff have developed relationships with professionals in an array of agencies that potentially can serve their young families. Given her close relationships with many agencies, she is able to hire professionals from these agencies as consultants to serve as a bridge between families and the agencies. Just as an agency can provide services to promote the home visiting program (e.g., providing transportation so that a parent can attend group meetings), so too the program staff can promote an agency's goals (e.g., by helping parents learn positive discipline strategies). When community resources are integral to a home visiting program, the home visitor gains needed information and support in her or his work.

Promoting the Program Agenda

The agenda of home visiting programs is different for different program sponsors and different populations being served.[10] For example, the agenda of the Patrick O'Hearn Elementary School home visiting program in Boston, implemented by parents, is to increase parent involvement.[11] Programs with a primary health focus such as the Prenatal/ Early Infancy Project utilize nurses to serve young at-risk mothers. Some programs focus on promoting the parents' role as teacher of their child, such as the Head Start home visiting program.

Home visiting programs vary in their method of helping home visitors know clearly what their tasks and goals for home visits are. Effective programs have some explicit structuring of services, ongoing supervision, and professional development meetings. Parents as Teachers (PAT) and the Portage Project provide home visitors with very concrete lesson plans and home visiting observation record forms.[12] In these two projects, home visitors have a lesson plan for each developmental period from birth through 60 months. When home visitors are just beginning their work, these lesson plans can be helpful guides, as they were for home visitor Lela.

When I first began, the lesson plans were my bible. And I kept them right on my desk beside the families' folders. Every time I planned a visit, I used them almost to the letter. Now that I have worked a few years, I may go back to them, especially with young babies, to check to see that I didn't miss anything. Now I have a developmental framework and know what is appropriate for the different ages of the children.

Experienced skilled visitors always have an agenda based on a developmental framework. Janice explained:

I like an overall structure of the things I would like to cover, the major issues of each developmental phase. For example, in Phase IV (8–14 months), the major issues are parallel talk and independence. I always try to hook the developmental information to something the baby is doing. I always have a play activity and spend time playing with the child and then inviting the parent to join the play. I believe that the mom gains the most information through the child as we are doing something with that child. But my focus always is interaction.

Lesson plans initially are important tools with which to assist home visitors. With time, their primary tool is their developmental framework. Highly experienced home visitors such as Janice understand that their primary tool and focus always is interaction in the context of a strong personal relationship with parents and their young children. A primary premise of this book is that no home visiting agenda can be successfully implemented without a strong personal relationship between parent and home visitor.

Maintaining Efficient Organization and Management

Home visitors work with a wide range of people and a wide range of settings. Given the complexity of their work, careful organization of use of time, materials, and record keeping becomes an essential skill.

Use of Time   Home visitors coordinate home visits with schedules of individual families while allowing time for their other responsibilities, such as completion of home visit reports, supervision and staff meetings, and community networking. Given these multiple tasks and different daily schedules of parents, home visitors benefit from careful time management. This scheduling needs to allow time for travel and record keeping. Documentation of a home visit is most accurate if it is done soon after the visit. At the same time, a schedule needs built-in flexibility to adapt to needed cancellations, such as when an infant is ill.

Janice explained the rationale for limiting the number of consecutive home visits on the same day.

Doing home visiting is a very intensive thing to do. . . . I can do four [consecutive visits] as an experienced home visitor. But beyond that I do not believe I am giving a high-quality visit to the last family. In fact, I don't even feel that I am giving as good a quality to the fourth family as I did to the first. You cannot retool your own head to go from one family to another, because this is intense work. Even when there are no problems brought forward, it is intense work.

The thing about a home visit—you are essentially on stage every minute you are on the visit. In the classroom, you even get little children occupied for a few moments, and you can turn around and take a deep breath. In home visits with a parent and child, you have no time to take a deep breath. You must be ready to answer, ready to respond, to observe, and to interact.

Janice understands that the total focus demanded during 1 hour of interaction with parents and their young children is a focus that cannot be maintained indefinitely. Over years of experience, she has discovered that four is the maximum number of visits she can effectively complete within one day.

Organization of Materials   In order to give a family total focus, home visitors need to organize and prepare all materials in advance of their visits. Materials can include toys for different developmental periods, parent handouts, and individual family folders. Given the different materials for different families, as well as materials for their use within the agency, home visitors need a very clear organizational system. Not surprisingly, car trunks often provide an easy-access file, especially for toys and family folders. Janice explained her system.

I spend a lot of time at the beginning of my program year doing initial organization that will make my day-to-day work flow more smoothly. For example, I organize my individual folders for the year for each family that I am going to see. If the child is 6 months old at the beginning of a program year, I will put in not just the handouts I want to use for my very next visit but also the standard handouts I know I will be giving that family for at least 6 months, maybe 10 months. I want to get a whole set of materials in one place so that I don't have to search for handouts each time.

I know there are certain handouts I am going to use time and time again. And also, I will put in key information such as the mother's first name—readily accessible. I don't want to drive up to the house and say, "Ooh, oh, what is her first name?" I make certain I know the child's name, the family's name, young siblings' names, and the mom's first name. I take a glance at the outside of the folder and there it is, along with their telephone number and directions to the house, right on the front.

I also put on the outside of the folder the dates that the child will enter a different developmental phase, so that I will know the key changes in development I can expect. I color-code with dots on the folder different ages of the children. I also keep certain key handouts addressing certain issues. I would put all my good discipline handouts in, say, an orange folder and all my good language handouts in a blue folder, so that when I want it fast, I can get it. Issues like sleeping, eating, setting limits, toilet training, key issues that appear again and again across families.

Home visitors figure out their own system of organizing their materials. As long as they have some system that allows them to enter the home unencumbered with a mind full of details, they can give total focus to their interactions with parents and their young children.

Record Keeping   Home visitors can save time if they can give time shortly after each home visit to write notes on what they did specifically during the home visits, any parent concerns, their observations of parents and child, and reminders for the next visit. For example, they might ask themselves, "What information do I need to give the parent next time? What topic did we leave unfinished?" This write-up needs to occur after the home visit because it would be distracting to write during the home visit itself. If the home visitor is writing during the visit, parents most likely will think about what is being written and lose their focus on the ongoing activity or discussion. Similarly, as they are writing, home visitors are missing subtleties of behavior and are not able to respond promptly to either parent or child. Visitors can use these written records as a guide for evaluating one's relationship with a family and planning for the next visit and as a resource during supervision and staff's professional development meetings. In some situations, the written descriptions of the child's developmental progress can be invaluable assistance when a referral is needed, for example, for an evaluation for possible special education services.

Being Aware of Legal and Ethical Issues

Confidentiality   As previously discussed, the new role of home visiting can be ambiguous to parents. Meeting in the parents' home invites the parents to relate on a more personal level than meeting in public settings. The combination of role ambiguity and the personal nature of the parent–home visitor relationship sometimes invites parents to share personal information that is outside the boundaries of the home visiting program agenda. Personal sharing introduces issues of confidentiality. No doubt each home visiting program has its own policy regarding confidentiality. However, several guidelines cross over all program agendas.

Confidentiality is an ethical obligation in all home visiting. At the outset, home visitors can tell parents that personal information discussed during a visit will remain confidential unless a child or parent is in danger, such as indications of child or spouse maltreatment or a parent's suicidal thinking. Home visitors never should discuss clients in settings separate from supervision or team meetings. Some home visiting programs are part of a larger social services delivery system that includes other professionals such as physicians, nurses, and therapists. In these situations, home visitors need to share appropriate family information; yet they can offer only that information needed by the other services professional and can do so in a confidential manner. Knowing what is appropriate information to share sometimes can be difficult. Before home visitors contact community agencies to link families with their services, they need parents' written permission. Confidentiality issues often confront home visitors with dilemmas such as how much confidential information is necessary for a specific referral.

In order for parents to trust their home visitor, they need to feel confident that the home visitor will not discuss their child or their parenting with other people. When home visitors do illustrate how other parents handle a parenting issue or how a child has learned a specific skill, they speak in general terms so that no parent could recognize the people described. In this manner, home visitors demonstrate by their actions and words that they honor confidentiality with all their families.

Maintaining confidentiality also extends to any written materials about a family. Janice explained her approach.

When parents share personal information, I do not include it in my written records. I may put in a key phrase related to the discussion to trigger my memory in future visits. But I never add any details or subjective interpretations about what they talked about. My written records are public records that can be subpoenaed; thus, I try and keep them as objective as possible. I believe every home visitor needs to do her or his written records with the assumption that every single piece of paper could be subpoenaed for a child custody battle, for example.

Janice is rigorous in maintaining written observations of what she did in each visit, child and parent actions, any parent concerns, and reminders to herself for her next visit. She maintains these records as objectively as possible and excludes any personal family data or her own subjective interpretation. In this manner, she maintains confidentiality.

Child Maltreatment   Child abuse and neglect are not protected by the ethical obligation of confidentiality, because the home visitor's duty to the welfare of the child comes before the duty to the child's parents. Home visitors are mandated to report evidence of child abuse and neglect. Each home visiting program has its own procedure for reporting child maltreatment. When home visiting programs have a primary intent to develop a partnership with parents, home visitors need to inform parents of their forthcoming report to the child protection agency. Although it is difficult for the first few times, experienced home visitors with strong personal relationships with parents find it most helpful to make the reporting call while they are in the parents' home and with the parents present. In this manner, home visitors make certain that parents know there are no secrets, and the call is based on their striving to assist the family. These situations never are easy, and feelings of parents and home visitors often are in turmoil. Knowing that they have the strong support of their administrators can give home visitors the courage to relate openly to parents about the child maltreatment report. When this is possible, the home visitor often becomes part of the child protection agency's team in offering help to the family. Home visitors may encounter other family situations in which they do not have a strong personal relationship and, in fact, suspect that making a hotline call could put themselves in danger. In these situations, administrators usually make the call. Each state allows hotline calls to be anonymous. When safety is a question, anonymous calls may be appropriate.

It can be harder for a home visitor to report child maltreatment than for a teacher to do so, because home visitors have developed a trusting, personal relationship with the parents and know that their report probably will be devastating to them. Often the most difficult situations are in the gray areas when there is no concrete physical evidence of maltreatment such as neglect in supervision or emotional abuse. Cynthia described an example.

> We had a situation this year where there were many, entirely too many, people living in a home. The water was shut off for a period of time. And I reported it as a situation that had implications of health hazards. The child protection agency then was aware of it and began working with the family to try to get the water turned back on. This home is not the best place for these kids. It is chaos. I really struggle going in there. It's not like I see someone get hit with a belt, or I see a black eye or big bruise; it's just that I know that every day, this home is not a good environment for that child. I struggle with that on each visit. And then when something happens like the water getting turned off, and the adults in the home don't seem to be doing anything about it, I report it. Because, in my mind, maybe now someone will do something about this situation.

Twice a month Cynthia visited this family. On each visit, she left knowing that the children were living in a dysfunctional home environment, with too many people coming and going. Once Cynthia had a concrete basis on which to call the child protection agency, that is, no running water in the home, she was able to help this family gain resources to improve their daily life.

III. CULTURALLY DIVERSE FAMILIES: BELIEFS, VALUES, AND PRACTICES

Each family has patterns of beliefs, values, practices, role expectations, and rituals that reflect the family's ethnic, racial, religious, or national membership, that is, that reflect the family's culture. America is a culturally diverse society, and the diversity increases as we move into the 21st century. Respecting and accepting a family's culture makes effective home visiting possible. This section discusses working with families of diverse backgrounds, especially those that are disproportionately at risk.[13]

When home visitors work with families of cultural backgrounds different from their own, the skills of respect, rapport building, empathic listening, and support are especially important. We all have assumptions about other cultures, which could lead to stereotyping. To provide effective service when working with families of different cultures, the home visitor is flexible and open-minded and rigorously avoids stereotyping. At the same time, the home visitor recognizes and respects cultural characteristics and values.

What people see, hear, and understand is filtered through their own cultural heritage. Home visitors' sensitivity to how their own behavior, attitudes, and values reflect their age, gender, ethnicity, and social class is the first step in their ability to relate to families of a different culture. In other words, competent home visitors are dual-minded—aware of their own actions, thoughts, and feelings as well as the actions, thoughts, and feelings of the families with which they work. This dual-mindedness is an especially important skill in working with families of diverse backgrounds.

When home visitors work with families who are members of a culture different from their own, they try to do several important tasks at the same time. First, home visitors work at understanding and respecting each family's cultural patterns. Second, home visitors try to recognize differences within, not just between, different family cultures. Third, home visitors see the uniqueness of each family, regardless of their culture. For example, the home visitor understands that the disciplinary values and practices of the Yamamoto family represent their Japanese American heritage; however, the Yamamotos also have developed patterns of relating to their children that are uniquely their own and not just typically Japanese American.

Working with culturally diverse families requires balancing: balancing awareness of the family's cultural patterns with awareness of one's own and using that awareness to track what is happening within home visits. For example, a home visitor knows his strong preference for children sleeping in their own beds, yet is working with a family where the toddler sleeps with her parents. As the toddler's mother discusses her child's nighttime sleep patterns, the home visitor monitors his own comments to make certain that he does not unwittingly share his bias.

Diverse Cultural Backgrounds

When home visitors are working with families of cultural backgrounds different from their own, they recognize that some parenting values and practices may be strange to them. Effective home visitors recognize and respect these differences and strive to work with the family within the framework of a family's beliefs and practices. The effective home visitor knows that what is happening within a home visit can be interpreted in different ways. For example, the home visitor may interpret the parents' description of their toddler's behavior as active exploration, whereas the parents may see the behavior as a sign of the child's hyperactivity, of the child's attempt to get them mad, or of the child's "badness." When a home visitor recognizes differences, it is helpful first to ask questions to understand better what a specific belief or practice means to a parent. What does "spoiling" her 4-month-old baby mean to a young African American mother? Does *spoiling* mean something different to a Vietnamese American mother? Being spoiled may be the label that this mother's extended family has given her baby, or "spoiling my baby" may be the mother's way of telling the home visitor that she thinks her baby cries because he knows she always picks him up when he cries. Once the home visitor understands and shows respect for this mother's interpretation of the meaning of her baby's behavior, then she can explore alternative meanings with her.

When parents' ethnicity is different from that of the home visitor, home visitors' understanding and respect of the behaviors, attitudes, and values of parents make a personal relationship possible. The issue is complex, for within each race, nationality, or religion, there are many differences. Janice discussed her experience.

> It is different to work with families of a different race. But it depends on the family as to how different it is. Some families will accept you very warmly, and you can't feel very much difference at all. Others, you can sense a difference even when you are accepted. And then it is important for you to figure out what is the difference so that you can adapt to their differences.

Working with some families of a different race, Janice experienced no cultural barriers. In other families, she needed to be sensitive to and respectful of their differences so that she could communicate effectively with them.

Cynthia worked for many years with ethnically diverse families in a center-based Head Start program. The author interviewed Cynthia after her first year as director of an Even Start program where she made twice-a-month home visits. Cynthia discussed her home visiting experience with families from various cultural backgrounds.

> I think I have worked with maybe one or two families where a wariness stayed there the whole time. But I don't blame people for that. It's a scary thing to have people come into your home, especially if you have had to deal with social workers and that kind of thing. I am not naive enough to think that I am everybody's best friend. People take from me what they want, and that's okay.

Over the years, Cynthia has had many positive relationships with parents. However, she knows that not all families accept her. She understands that many people have had problematic relationships with representatives of public agencies and that opening one's home to strangers is a new and scary experience for some people. At the same time, Cynthia understands the unique contributions that home visiting can offer to both professionals and parents.

> This program has taught me so much about working with families in general and in particular about working with families of color. I have had a lot of experience with that, but not in the same context. This is the first time I have had the opportunity to visit homes as well as see parents at the center, for we are doing a home-based and a center-based model. Before I just worked at a center-based program and never saw people's homes and didn't go there all the time and get involved in what's going on with the family as intimately as I do in home visiting.
>
> I think the home visit is the key to the relationship. Because when I am accepted in the home, I am privy to a whole different environment. I see the environment the family lives in and know what they are up against and what kinds of things happen to them, good or bad. I know when they have lost their couch or when they got a new one—those kinds of things make a difference in building a relationship.

In visiting homes, Cynthia has a new and more intimate understanding of the families with which she works. Although she worked for many years with similar families in a center-based program, she did not understand the unique particularities of each family's daily life until she regularly visited their home. Cynthia also understands that if she is successful, she must meet each parent where he or she is.

You can't [know] everything . . . about how to build relationships, because, first of all, people are people, and they all are different. Basically, people develop; they never stop developing. So what you have to be able to do is identify their developmental level. The key is to learn where the person is and work from there.

Cynthia acknowledges the wide range of differences among and within cultural groups, and she does not always expect every parent to readily accept her. She realistically acknowledges that she does not develop a personal relationship with each parent. Cynthia is sensitive to this reality but does not let it hamper her work. Visiting homes has given her an in-depth understanding of the complex problems that families at risk confront daily. Within this understanding, she respects parents and understands that, regardless of their level of maturity or the complexity of their problems, all parents have hopes and dreams, and most want the best for their child. In turn, parents feel Cynthia's respect and can be open to learning from Cynthia. Latoya and Ann, two mothers participating in the program, described their feelings toward Cynthia.

Latoya: *Cynthia cares about everyone. She's helped me have more patience, play more, know how to relate more without yelling and without feeling like I gotta pop them.*

Ann: *Now I'm more prone to keep busy instead of slouching around the house. It's built my self-esteem, and I have a more positive outlook. I have a different perspective on things. I'm a different person as far as doing frivolous things. Now I read, go to the library. Before, I would rent action-packed movies. Now I read something I could learn from.*

Social Class Differences

Families of all social classes face challenges; however, the difficulties faced by families with low incomes are more likely to be multiple and complex. Poverty increases the likelihood of the presence of risk factors such as employment problems, poor housing, violent neighborhoods, and accompanying social and emotional problems.[14] At the same time, even though low-income families are at risk for difficulties, these families are not, as is often assumed, inherently weak, disorganized, or unhealthy. Home visitors working with low-income families have a complex, difficult job requiring great flexibility and sensitivity. They need to believe that, in spite of their difficult circumstances, people with low incomes are worthy of respect and dignity and have their own hopes and dreams. Cynthia described how to look for common ground when working with these families.

I think I use the same approach. It's just that what you use or what things you talk about may be different. But the approach is the same. And that is, I look for a common ground. I look for something to make that first contact with. It might be a hairdo; it might be the clothing they are wearing. "Oh, that is a pretty color; it really suits you." It might be something in the home that decorates the home. And that wouldn't make any difference whether it is a middle-income or low-income home.

For me, I think the thing that makes the difference is that it has to be genuine, and you really have to like the hairdo or like the knick-knacks on the shelf. Or it doesn't ring true. From the time you get out of your car, you are being assessed. And the look on your face makes a big difference in how that person is going to receive you when he or she opens the door. I usually try to find something that I can talk about that is not stuffy so that I can be natural, but not forcing, such as, "What a pretty shirt," or "It's a pretty day out"—a comment that will get me going.

Many middle-income homes have different things in them than low-income homes. But it is just the material things that are different. Although most families have TVs and a VCR. So that is always a good topic of conversation. "Seen anything good on TV lately?," or, "Have you watched any good movies?" People feel comfortable talking about that.

And it doesn't matter what kind of family, what age, race, or income level. The child is the common ground, and there always are lots and lots of things you can say about that child: "Oh, look at all that hair, look at the way he smiles." How much a family makes or where they live, that shouldn't matter, because you are trying to serve that family and help them do the best that they can do.

Cynthia knows that, from the moment she steps out of the car, she is communicating with parents. Body gestures such as her facial expression communicate as much as words. She also knows that the first step in building a relationship is being genuine. Whatever she says, she honestly believes or feels. Cynthia begins her interaction on a common ground with parents. She is able to do this because she deeply believes that people are more similar than they are different. She establishes mutuality at the outset in a conversation about some aspect of the parents that she likes. Because the program's purpose is fostering the child's development, there is always a child present. Cynthia also can find something wonderful about each child to talk about with his or her parents. Her primary focus is the child's parents, though, because she understands that it is her relationship with the parents that allows her to promote the parents' relationship with their child.

When home visitors work with low-income families, potential problems may include 1) difficulties regarding the accessibility of families,

2) difficulties in recruitment of families, 3) increased external and personal problems, and 4) safety issues.[15]

Accessibility   Low-income families tend to be very mobile, and often they do not inform their home visitor of their impending move. Thus, home visitors may spend a great deal of time tracking down those families who have moved. Even when low-income families are not mobile, it may be difficult for a home visitor to have minimal distraction and adequate space to conduct a home visit, given the crowded conditions of some low-income families' homes. Low-income families also often live in poor neighborhoods with limited resources, such as parks or libraries where a visit can be conducted.

A common dilemma is that parents with low incomes may not keep their appointments; that is, they may not be home at the scheduled time for home visiting. When low-income families relate to an array of agencies, such as public aid, emergency rooms, and WIC, they are accustomed to long periods of waiting and assume that professionals think that their time is of no value. Furthermore, some never have had trusting relationships with adults, so they see no reason for taking seriously a time commitment. As a result, some low-income parents do not take responsibility for being present for their home visiting appointment.

Home visitors who work with these families learn that frequent reminders make possible more completed home visits. If a parent has a telephone, a call before a home visit can be effective. If parents have no home telephone, a reminder via postcard can be helpful. Once home visitors have established a trusting relationship, an impromptu visit is most helpful; that is, the home visitor drops by the home, explains that she or he is in the area and merely wants to remind the parent of the visit the next day.

Recruitment   Home visiting programs that serve low-income families cannot depend on written brochures, newspaper releases, and word of mouth—strategies that are often adequate for other families. If a home visiting program serves low-income families, staff probably need to be very assertive in recruiting them. Smith and Well's case study of a program serving low-income urban families described successful strategies.[16] Their suggestions include setting up tables at grocery stores, meeting parents at bus stops, meeting parents at homeless shelters, and networking with public aid and WIC staff so that they give parents the needed information.

Increased External and Personal Problems   Low-income families are disproportionately at risk for having personal social and emotional problems and health problems, as well as external problems such as unemployment, inadequate housing, or inadequate neighborhoods. When families are experiencing multiple problems, they often cannot focus on their parenting or on their young child's needs until basic family needs are addressed. When home visitors first address the concerns uppermost in the parents' minds, such as the threat of the heat being turned off, parents can develop trust in their relationship with their home visitor over time and begin to pay greater attention to the needs of their child. In these situations, the home visitor's agenda cannot be the initial focus.

Maintaining one's professional boundary can be an essential skill when working with families experiencing multiple problems. Often these families need services that are more comprehensive than those available in the home visiting program. Weiss argued convincingly that home visiting is a "necessary but not sufficient" service for families with multiple, complex problems.[17] When home visiting is a stand-alone program, home visitors gain knowledge of available community resources so that they can assist families in seeking additional help.

Given the stressors that accompany poverty, home visitors regularly experience unexpected complications. Flexibility, patience, and a strong commitment to service become requirements when working with families experiencing multiple complex problems. As with all families, establishing a personal relationship is the first task before other issues can be addressed. It may take more time to develop trust and rapport and for parents to feel their home visitor's genuine concern and caring. It may take persistence, returning again and again, calling again and again, before a parent can feel trusting enough to maintain appointments. The home visitor knows that most parents want the best for their child, regardless of how the parenting may seem to be compromised. Although it may be more difficult, finding a common ground to talk about and parent action to praise are essential. Supervision and team meetings in which home visitors can share their difficulties and successes are important supports for working with families having multiple complex problems.

Safety Maintaining personal safety is basic to effective home visiting. Safety concerns differ across communities. In isolated rural areas, inadequate roads may require that the home visitor's car be in good condition for rough use. Inner-city communities with high rates of violence may demand that two home visitors rather than one conduct visits. At all times, home visitors make certain that another responsible staff person knows their visiting schedule, which includes the family's name, the date, and the time of visit and their expected time of return. Some home visitors who work in dangerous communities use a two-way radio communication system. Others call when their visit is complete. When neighborhoods are potentially dangerous, it is important to know the neighborhood well in order to avoid getting lost. Once families and neighbors become familiar with the home visitor, often they can look out for the visitor, for example, watch for their car and greet them outdoors. When safe parking is a question, some home visiting programs hire drivers to transport home visitors to and from the homes. When working with parents addicted to alcohol and other drugs, assessing potential danger is needed for each visit.

If, upon arrival, home visitors discover that they have entered in the middle of a domestic dispute, they leave. Personal safety is always the first necessity when working with troubled families. Cynthia described her work with families living in chaos.

> More often what happens is you get to a home, and something is going on, either the electricity is going to be shut off or mom has had a fight with her boyfriend or something unexpectedly has happened to upset the parent. I take the cue from the parent. Generally, they will tell me what is going on. My first response is to say, "Do you want me to stay, or do you want me to come back at a different time?" It is a respect issue. This is not my chaos; this is someone else's chaos. People, generally, when they are in flux like that, don't want someone watching their chaos. So I respect that, and I'll just say, "Do you want me to come back later?" Sometimes they will say yes, and I'll reschedule our appointment. If it is a situation where someone is in danger, if I feel the mother is at danger of hurting herself or the child, then I may not leave without making sure that the mom has the hotline number or some other support. Then there is the scenario where I'll go in and they'll want me to stay, because they need help or someone to talk to; and then I stay.

Table 1 lists some safety precautions for home visitors to consider.

IV. DIFFICULTIES AND DILEMMAS

Two types of families with which it is predictably difficult to work are, first, those parents who think concretely and have difficulty generalizing, and, second, those living in chaotic conditions. Lela described her frustrations in working with the four parents in her caseload who are concrete thinkers.

> A frustrating thing I am feeling right now is how to deal with the parent who doesn't grasp things, thinking like a child. Lori and Cherry's mom, Toby, and Sandy, just off the top of my head. I share information with them on one visit, and the very next visit they ask the same thing. Sometimes I am at a loss as to how do you get through?

Lela made these comments during a weekly staff meeting, and her co-workers were able to offer several helpful suggestions. Cynthia finds that it is helpful to be concrete and directive when working with this

Table 1.   Safety precautions for home visitors

- Make certain your car is in good working condition.
- Post a sign in your car that identifies the program.
- Call the office before and after a visit that could involve danger.
- Make a home visit with a colleague rather than being alone.
- In dangerous neighborhoods, make home visits in the morning.
- Call the parents just before a home visit so they can watch for you.
- Carry a cellular phone.
- Be respectful and professional.
- If a situation does not feel right, do not leave your car.
- Be organized with materials that are beside you so that you do not have to hunt for them.
- When you leave the home visited, have your car keys in hand.

type of parent. Cynthia visits Sally twice a month. Sally has difficulty managing her very active 18-month-old. Cynthia used a sensory activity as the setting in which to guide Sally.

> Cynthia places a large plastic tub filled with birdseed, assorted spoons, and plastic tubs in front of Willy. As Cynthia removes the lid, she says to Sally, "I brought this for a couple reasons. You know last time you told me Willy was doing so well with spoons. And you and I have been talking about setting limits. You know how he loves to throw things. Plus, it feels good and is fun to play in."
>
> [Willy immediately picks up some seed and tosses it out of the box.]
>
> Sally: In the box, baby.
>
> [Willy begins putting seed into a small tub with his hands as his mother softly says, "Good boy! You are so smart! You are taking the seed and putting it in the tub."]
>
> Cynthia: That describing what he is doing is wonderful! That's what he needs to learn language.

Cynthia knows that the parents who think very concretely learn best from their own experience. In her twice-monthly visits, she frequently has described Willy's actions and then has told Sally how important these descriptions are for Willy's developing language as well as his self-esteem. In other words, she models parenting behavior that she is trying to promote in Sally. When Sally spontaneously describes her child's actions, Cynthia reinforces this important skill as it happens.

> [Willy throws a small amount of seed.]
>
> Cynthia: He's still throwing, right?
>
> Sally: You can tell! Yeah.

Cynthia: *We have to set limits for him. When he throws things, what do you do?*

[Sally shrugs. Cynthia suggests it might help if Cynthia put Willy on her side of the tub so that it would be easier for her to guide him.]

Cynthia: *It'll be easier to catch his hand if you don't want him to throw the seed. And when you are with him, you are helping him keep calm. You can take his hand to show him how to use the spoon, too.*

Cynthia gives a specific directive with a simple explanation that Sally can understand. After this visit, Cynthia explained to the author that Sally usually does not remember Cynthia's specific guidance. Cynthia knows that it will take time and repetition for Sally to show her son spontaneously what she wants him to do.

As Sally is watching her son play in the seed, Cynthia explains how this play is a calming activity that helps his eye–hand and small-muscle coordination as he dumps and fills. The experience of the moment becomes the teaching moment. Cynthia further described how she works with parents who are concrete thinkers.

> *Basically, what I do is work at two different levels. I work with the parents at whatever level the parents are. When they are at very concrete levels, I do a lot of demonstration hands-on activity where the parents are practicing in order to help them understand a concept or skill.*
>
> *After I have known the parent for a while, I get better at knowing how the parent learns, whether they need to be told to watch it or to do it themselves, or whether they do better watching a videotape. Usually, I'll have the parent watch me, and I coach them through it with their child. I'll demonstrate and then have them try it and then coach them through. I talk about what the parent is doing and how the child reacts, and how that relates to the child's learning. Because that is what they often have trouble understanding—how their actions help their child learn. A lot of them really don't understand that, but not just low-functioning parents; lots of parents don't understand that what they do affects how their child learns—not what their child learns, but how their child learns.*
>
> *And in group meetings, we have to have something the parents can hold and touch to understand. So when we are working with self-concept for kids, and how words and negative interactions impact a child, we take a paper doll. And each negative statement becomes a bruise or a tear in the doll. We told them things that they might say to their child. Then they had to judge whether or not that was something that supports the child's self-esteem. And they actually made a tear in the paper doll. The statement was damaging to self-esteem. In this concrete way, they begin to understand how to work with their child.*

I think the low-functioning parents have to experience for themselves before they are able to provide that kind of activity for their child, let alone relate that to child development. Some of them never really quite get it. Most of the people we serve do not live by themselves; they live within an extended family. And that extended family helps to raise that child. So we don't limit ourselves to just working with the parent during a home visit. We work with the father, the aunt, the grandmother, or grandfather, whoever is home and helps with the child rearing.

Cynthia understands that, in order for some of her parents to understand a concept or a skill, they must have direct experience, and, in that experience, the home visitor talks about the meaning of that experience. Cynthia often models for parents and then invites the parents to participate in an activity. As the parents play with their child, Cynthia coaches them, as illustrated by her work with Sally. Effective home visitors know that some parents need more time than others, as well as repeated concrete experiences, and home visitors realize that they need to exercise patience and persistence. Nothing will happen if the parent and home visitor do not have a trusting personal relationship.

It is very difficult to work with families that seem to be on the edge of chaos, for example, families with large extended families coming and going throughout the day or families with multiple, complex external problems and little ability to cope with them. Given Cynthia's respect for each family, once she arrives, she invites the parents to decide whether they wish her to enter into their chaotic world. The author asked her how she relates to those families who seem to live in perpetual chaos.

Cynthia: I went to a home with 12 children ranging in age from 18 months to 9 years, two mothers, and three adult men who were visiting the women. The men didn't want me there. And they tried to intimidate me by singing nasty songs. I know these moms well enough that I thought, "Nope, I am not going to leave. These moms don't want me to leave. They don't think this was not a good time for a visit," so I stayed. And finally, one man in particular finally gave up and went and sat outside.

Carol: But what happens when you can't get the moms' focused attention because of so many kids?

Cynthia: Then I hang out and play with the kids. It doesn't matter if I have mom's attention. I mean, it does matter in the long run, but I will stay. I know I am the only constant in these women's lives. With this family, I spent the first 6 months playing with the kids, and neither mom would talk to me. Often they would enter into another room and kind of half-listen. [This went on] for 3 months before they would sit with me. And then they couldn't sit with me the whole 50 minutes. They would get up and go have a cigarette or make a phone call.

Cynthia's persistence is nonwavering; eventually, the parents understand that, yes, she does want and expect them to be with her and their children. But first they need to experience Cynthia's care and commitment by her persistent visiting, active play with their children, and consistent invitation for them to join her, even when they do not do so for many months. For these two young mothers, Cynthia is the first adult who has been absolutely predictable.

I know they want me to come. Their friends in Even Start were teasing them, for they only come 1 in 4 days most weeks. They replied, "We don't need to come, but Cynthia is always visiting us at home!" It's now so different than when I first started visiting them. They screen all their phone calls, but when it's me they come to the phone.

People see you in a certain light and expect you to do the same thing. One of the things that I do for these chaotic families is that I provide a routine within the time frame that I am in their home. I come and stay a certain amount of time and always have things to do. They know we are going to play some kind of game, do some kind of activity. I'm going to read a story, and then I'm going to ask them to read. And the longer I have been there, the more successes I have had in getting them on the floor to play with their kid. Not every time, but it is much better than last year.

Cynthia is secure in her competence and the parents' desire to give their babies the best they can. Thus, she is willing to try new strategies, even though she does not know whether they will work. What she does know is that she cares and that the parents eventually will learn that she cares; then, with her guidance, they will be able to move forward. Cynthia described a poignant example of her creative initiative.

One of the moms seemed so depressed that I changed my mode of operation one day. These are not women who would tell me about personal problems such as having a fight with their boyfriend. But I went to their home and decided to change what I normally do. When I got to this mom's home, I said, "I don't want to see the kids. Do you have someone who can watch them while you and I go to McDonald's?" We went to McDonald's, and I bought her a soda. And I just talked to her like a person and said, "You really have been down. Is there some way I can help?"

And she cried, and talked about how she has to do everything for these two families. And everyone else is in and out of this house, and how the teenagers and boyfriends of the girls come in and eat all the food she has bought for the little kids. And she goes to bed at night wondering if they will have food in the morning, and often they don't. And this happens almost every night. There are a lot of people in this house, up to 20 people, and she is tired. She is tired of trying to swim upriver when there is this current the other way.

That was the only time she talked to me like that. And what I did for her was try to hook her up with the child abuse network because they do in-home counseling. I don't know if she will do it. But on the positive side, this mom tested on the sixth- or seventh-grade level last fall. And after 1 year, she now is in the 11th-grade level. She only comes to Adult Basic Education 1 day instead of 4 days a week. But this is a parent who told me, "The reason I am still here is because you won't leave me alone." But it is hard. I feel like I have been in a washing machine being pulled in all directions. I went there once and the 3-year-old was fingerpainting the baby's head. And the mom was screaming at him, and we couldn't find anything in the house to wipe the paint off with—no rags, tissues, nothing.

What I try to do is, for the time I am with this family, to bring order, the only order this family experiences. In that living room, for 10 minutes, if I can get everyone around me listening to that book, I have brought order for a piece of time. And that to me is powerful because I show that it can be done. And the parents aren't stupid. They experience this, and they remember, and the next time, maybe they will pick up the book and sit down to bring that order.

Cynthia believes that parents can give their child improved parenting, if the parents themselves can experience a personal relationship with a caring adult who can give them support and guidance. She understands that some of the parents had troubled childhoods and live in extreme chaos with no support. Although she feels like she is being pulled in too many different directions when visiting these families, she knows the parents feel that they are overwhelmed with responsibilities with very little support. Her persistence and predictable, unswerving respect and care allow these parents to know that their struggles to take care of their children are valued and make a difference in their young children's lives.

CONCLUSIONS

This chapter examined two levels of home visiting skills. First, the chapter identified 12 communication–interpersonal skills. These are high-level skills that improve through experience over an extended time through self-reflection on that experience and through constructive feedback from professional peers and supervisors. These 12 skills encourage, maintain, and promote the parent–home visitor relationship. Second, the chapter identified five areas of knowledge and skill also essential to the home visiting process. Unlike the first 12 skills, these areas do not overlap or occur together. They are more like a collection that can be taught at least partially, for example, knowledge of available community resources, child maltreatment laws, and areas of confidentiality. This is knowledge involving societal rules and resources. To illustrate these two levels of skills, two exemplary home visitors, Janice and Cynthia, shared their experiences with families and their understanding of these experiences. To gain clarity, the chapter discussed different approaches separately, even though experts agree that home visiting is an organic, unfolding process in which visitors use several approaches simultaneously. The chapter also presented home visiting approaches to use when working with families of a background culturally different from that of the home visitor. The chapter concluded with a discussion of the difficulties and dilemmas involved in working with parents who are concrete thinkers and those families who live in chaotic conditions.

3

Home Visitors' Professional Development

The starting point of any process of thinking is something going on, something which just as it stands is incomplete or unfulfilled. Its point, its meaning lies literally in what it is going to be, in how it is going to turn out.

John Dewey (1916, pp. 146–147)

The quality of the relationship between the home visitor and the parents determines the likelihood of parents' gaining an understanding of child development and effective parenting skills. Previous chapters discuss skills that enable home visitors to be effective in helping parents understand their child's development and develop appropriate parenting approaches. This chapter explores ways to help home visitors improve their understanding and skills. Just as the home visitor enables parents in the practice of parenting, so too do team members, mentors, and supervisors help home visitors in the practice of home visiting.

Home visitors are artisans in the same sense that teachers, musicians, and athletes are artisans. As artisans, much of home visitors' craft is learned on the job. Home visiting can be understood only as it evolves in each visitor's practice, which takes place in many unpredictable and unique situations.[1] Much of home visitors' knowledge is tacit in that the knowing is in the action; thinking and doing are interwoven. Home visitors know their job in the same way baseball players know batting or musicians know playing music–they know it in the doing. Both the athlete and the musician improve their skills by reflecting on what they do. Athletes and musicians have coaches to help them think about how they are playing, develop their own strengths, and recognize their weaknesses. This chapter explores the kinds of coaching home visitors need to improve their reflection and practice. In home visiting, coaches are peers, mentors, and supervisors.

The continued professional growth of home visitors is a process parallel to the dynamics of parent development occurring within home visits. As in parenting, professional development is an unfolding process learned on the job. There are no recipes or formulas. Often the job seems untidy and unpredictable. Like parenting, the home visitor's work involves both feeling and thinking–emotion and intellect.[2] The relationship between home visitors and their professional peers, mentors, and supervisors is the key to continued growth. Just as home visitors are respectful partners with parents, mutual respect and collaboration between the home visitor and in-service consultants, peer mentors, and administrators promote home visitors' continued development.

Three powerful ways of learning for home visitors involve 1) education to gain new knowledge and understanding of how that knowledge can be applied to one's practice, 2) reflection on action, and 3) learning by doing–practicing over time. Reflection on action means that home visitors stop and think about how they understand their work. They know that each home visit is new, that parents have their own way of thinking and their own goals for their child. With practice, visitors learn to think about what they are doing while they are doing it. They become more aware of both the uniqueness of each family and common themes across families. As their relationship with a family evolves, home visitors develop a series of expectations of the parents, child, and their own actions and reactions. They become more aware of both the successful and the problematic approaches they are using.

As they reflect on their experience, home visitors learn to focus in concrete ways on the key struggles that parents and young children have. Home visitors' experience is complex. They often go into a home where there is a great deal of activity. It is reflection on that complex experience that allows home visitors to focus on what is important in the moment. With experience, they develop practical "how do you get the job done" parenting skills such as getting young children to sleep, toilet training, and so forth. For example, Janice has learned to assist parents in problem solving when they express a concern. When Janice first started doing home visits, she aimed to have all possible answers to give to a parent who shared a concern or asked a question. Initially, she would feel relieved that she knew the answer to share. Over time, Janice learned that the parents' role would be strengthened if they could develop skills in thinking through possible approaches rather than merely getting an answer to one specific problem. With time, Janice slowly developed this skill through practice and reflection on this practice.

One of the difficulties involved in clarifying the process of home visiting is that home visiting is implemented across several disciplines, most commonly social work, education, and nursing. In addition, some community-based home visiting programs hire home visitors without related professional training.[3] Program developers believe that when home visitors have a cultural background similar to that of the parents, they can understand and more readily develop personal relationships with parents than can professionals. Because home visiting is a new professional role, effective professional development for home visitors may involve learning processes that may not be a part of the disciplines in which the home visitor was educated.

This chapter describes education and supervision from a perspective that sees both as settings for relationships for learning. This approach to professional development is fundamentally different from much of in-service education that offers unconnected workshops or courses of instruction. The supervision described here, in which supervisor and supervisee have shared power, with mutual expectations and shared evaluation, is very different from a model of supervision adopted in some disciplines, which is based on monitoring and evaluating against a set of standard competencies.

EDUCATION

The only map of education most people have is their own schooling, which, for most people, consisted of didactic teaching; that is, memorizing and rote learning of information, habits, and skills. This chapter promotes an educational approach that is different from traditional teaching and follows the educational style of Carl Rogers, John Dewey, and Jerome Bruner.[4] This educational approach takes place in a climate of inquiry in which learners actively think about their lived experience and integrate new information in a way such that learners discover new meaning in their experience.

The aim of continuing education is to assist home visitors to be reflective practitioners and to recognize the meaning of their actions and experience. New information can help home visitors look at their actions and relationships in a new way and thereby reconstruct their experiences. This approach is not linear; that is, teaching and learning do not occur in a straight line (e.g., first addition, then subtraction, then multiplication and division). In contrast to linear thinking, home visitors' learning is experiential. They take new understanding and apply this understanding to their everyday practice.

Janice explained how discussions with occupational therapists in her program's weekly staff meetings assisted her, not just in learning something new, but in opening new ways of working with families.

> Occupational therapists have been very helpful. They can break down motor development in a way you don't see, for example, how a child gets in and out of a sitting position, how they reach for things—the detail that makes a difference in how a child functions. I didn't have a clue about these details until occupational therapists came to staff meetings on a regular basis.

> In a program . . . with a strong focus on language and cognition, we can let motor development happen rather than pay attention to it. Paying attention to motor development makes a difference, especially if visiting a child whose development takes a different twist, for example, a child with low muscle tone or one really slow in walking. I have learned what are the very small signs of progress. I can help the parent see these signs and encourage ways to promote the development.

Janice was able to integrate information from occupational therapists directly so that she could see more in a child's movement and provide additional information and guidance to the child's parents. Janice uses this sensitivity to movement often in her work with families. For example, as Erin (age 18 months) watches Janice take toys out of her bag, she backs up and sits on her mother's lap. Janice comments to Erin's mother, "It's interesting to see how she backs up into you. She has a good sense of body space." Janice's education involved content (new information from occupational therapists) and reflective action (her application of this information to her work with families).

Home visitors' work is planned but not predictable. Each day teachers go to work in a classroom with a set of textbooks with which to teach a given set of specific subjects, with a principal available who can help in a crisis. Nurses work in a hospital with a predictable set of work procedures such as medicines, medical records, and rounds and with physicians who are in charge. In contrast, home visitors carry a small bag with materials they have chosen themselves into the homes of young families, each of which is different, with their own patterns and problems.

Home visitors make minute-by-minute decisions in ever-changing unique settings. Because home visiting is so personal, it is inescapably individual. Individual home visitors' personal histories influence how they understand and value their work. At the same time, everyone is inescapably social in the sense that we not only can be a subject creating but also can take the role of the other and look back at ourselves from the perspective of the other.[5] What the home visitor does is deeply rooted in learned ways of seeing, thinking, and acting, ways learned through relations with others beginning in infancy. The complexity of self as both an individual and a social being sets up provocative challenges for educating home visitors. Effective in-service education involves a dual process: Every individual's way of working needs to be valued and nurtured, and the individual's growth needs to be within a social setting. So, the *process* of professional development opportunities is as important as the *content*. Just as the relationship between the home visitor and parent is as important as the play activity, so too the relationships between the home visitor and her or his peers, mentors, and supervisors are as important as the educational curriculum.

Structure and Process of Continuing Education

Continuing education is an integral part of a home visitor's professional life when active, reflective learning is a central part of the home visiting program. Administrators of a program can structure this active learning within their team meetings. Cynthia, director of an Even Start program, discussed this need.

> The program is a place for growth, not just for our children and our parents, but for ourselves. Everyone needs to know that this is a place for growth. When home visitors are hired, we tell them they are expected to actively learn new knowledge and skills. For this to happen, it takes a leader who is able to forge relationships of respect and support in working together. The art is to know how to help people become active, reflective learners.
>
> Last month I gave everyone a reading I thought was very helpful because it clearly described effective approaches with families. No one touched it. Then, last week, I shared this material in terms of concrete happenings with everyone's families. I made it come alive—in the context of people's work with their families. There has to be engagement. And people need to learn to reflect on how new knowledge relates directly to work with their families.

Cynthia provides clear administrative expectations of professional development in a community of respect and support in working together.

Program Philosophy and Principles   Effective administrators provide a clear program philosophy and principles to help guide their home visitors. Home visitors work in many different home settings, but key principles and a consistent philosophy guide their minute-by-minute decision making as they relate to families. The following comments from the author's individual conversations about key principles and philosophies with three professionals in three different positions of a home visiting program in one school district illustrate this program's overarching principles and philosophy. As Director of Early Education, Margaret has been in charge of her district's home visiting program for 14 years. Janice has been a home visitor for 9 years. Having been a home visitor for 4 years, Cynthia is directing the district's Even Start program.

> Margaret: *You integrate the principles and philosophy in the totality of your program, coming back to it in a lot of ways, in what you say in all the different contexts of working with the staff. First is empowering the parents. And that's not possible without having rapport with parents and supporting them. And at the core is the home visitor's strong foundation in child development.*

> Janice: *We always are striving to empower parents. In as many subtle ways as possible, I find the strength of the parent and build on that. When I use handouts, I'll say, "You probably are doing this already." If you have a mindset that you'll fix parents, they'll know it. If you go in with the attitude that parents know a lot, and together we'll be working for the benefit of the child, they'll sense the respect you have for them. Respect is essential. And the home visitor must be secure in the basics of child development.*

> Cynthia: *The key is respect of parents and understanding the notion of reciprocity. You are a partner, not doing something for parents, but everyone is learning together. And you must be knowledgeable about what you are talking about. Basic child development is a must, but so are several other disciplines, too, like nutrition and health. And you have to be introspective, for we learn by reflecting on our experience.*

The author interviewed Margaret, Janice, and Cynthia on separate days in different settings. Yet parallel themes emerge through the portrayals of these three professionals, themes that are central to their home visiting program.

Team Meetings   To ensure active, reflective learning, administrators should structure regularly scheduled team meetings. These meetings can take place in an informal setting where home visitors can learn new content and then directly apply that content to their everyday work with families. Whenever content is provided, actively processing the meaning of this content in terms of home visitors' everyday work not only has an impact on their work but also promotes their ability to be reflective.

It takes time for colleagues to know and trust each other so that they can feel safe both to share their own experiences and to respond to what others are saying and doing. Furthermore, it is not a given that all home visitors are introspective. Some need team meetings to promote this ability. When team meetings become a safe setting in which home visitors can openly share their work with one another, each person learns about the others' styles, and their styles can be compared with one's own style. Exploring differences can increase home visitors' sensitivity to the particularities of their own way of working and can provoke questions about what may have been taken-for-granted practices or beliefs. Home visitors have unique styles, personalities, interests, beliefs, biases, and distortions. Any new changes or approaches are personal and are made to address her or his pattern of knowing, interacting with, and understanding the families being served.

Given the individual, solitary work of home visiting, team meetings can provide opportunities for support and encouragement.[6] Home visitors are bonded together by shared commitments and experience. Janice described the importance of sharing with colleagues.

Colleagues who do the same kind of work that I do, other home visitors, are important to me because we share similar experiences. So that when I run into a problem, I know that I can talk with one of my colleagues, that the conversation will be maintained as confidential. With them, I can sort of brainstorm and process things that I need to work on to help a family. We can share how each of us has dealt with similar situations with different families, and what the outcomes have been. In reality, there are few problems that are really unique to a family. That is the nice thing about having a fairly large staff, the sharing among team members. You need to have a way among your colleagues in a protected environment that you can work through some of the difficulties that you confront.

Janice describes team meetings as a setting for home visitors to reflect on their own actions and those of the families they serve. Together home visitors can collaborate in solving problems—in expanding notions of what is possible. This mutuality of interest, respect, and support provides encouragement for individuals to take risks and attempt new approaches.

Ernestine, an experienced home visitor, discusses a problem she is having with her team members in the following example.

Ernestine describes her frustration in working with a directive mother, Kamera, who seems to be interested only in promoting academic learning of her 26-month-old son. Regardless of the play activity or Ernestine's interactions, Kamera focuses on color, shape, or number. Ernestine told the group, "I'm out of control. It seems no matter what I do or say, Kamera remains directive." Individual home visitors shared similar frustrations and then brainstormed together on possible strategies. They suggested that Ernestine could choose only very open-ended activities, such as sensory play in birdseed or sculpting with playdough. In fact, introducing sensory play with birdseed did provide a setting for Kamera to interact in a new way with her son. Over extended additional visits, with Ernestine's support and assistance, Kamera learned to value her son's actions as a 26-month-old toddler and to encourage developmentally appropriate play. Ernestine gave brief reports in team meetings, and together the team explored both the meaning of ongoing happenings and additional possible approaches with this family.

When Ernestine stepped back from her involvement with Kamera and shared her concerns with her peers, she gained new perspectives of what might be possible. As she heard individual home visitors share similar frustrations, she gained support and encouragement. Ernestine had felt out of control during her visit with Kamera. After discussing this visit with her colleagues, she returned feeling hopeful that she had a new possibility of making contact with this mother.

When a team has more than 10–12 members, the total group is too large to have meaningful mutual, reflective sharing. For large staffs, structuring part of each team meeting into small groups, pairs, or triplets is necessary to ensure open sharing of practice, exploration of the possible meaning of this practice, and brainstorming of possible additional approaches. There always is some need for total-group presentations or use of videotapes. These total-group activities can be most productive if home visitors can reflect on how the topic relates to their own practice in small groups. Afterward, a total-group wrap-up is an effective closure to such meetings.

Most programs have home visitors of different ages and with different lengths of experience. Increased experience gives greater understanding of the meaning of the home visiting process. Informal team meetings with regular, open sharing allows the more experienced home visitors to share insights and discuss their own changes. They can be models of learning how to learn and can expand the perspectives of the less experienced. When less experienced home visitors feel support and safety, they can actively question their practice and gain assistance from their experienced colleagues. In this way, a climate of inquiry develops.

Seminars, Workshops, and Conferences   Other structures for learning are seminars, workshops, and conferences sponsored by other organizations and agencies. When home visitors can meet people in related professions and can learn from these professionals, their own knowledge and understanding are expanded. This multidisciplinary experience is especially important for home visitors because their work can encompass education, health, and social services. Janice explained why attending conferences has been one of the most influential ways for her to develop new knowledge and skill.

I like conferences because they give me the opportunity to hear people from other fields, such as a physician or child protection worker. It broadens my perspective. It also is stimulating to meet other conferees who are in related fields. And I get ideas for reading. For I also like to read—to dig into books for new perspectives or depth of understanding.

Janice understands that her work cuts across disciplines. Thus, she actively seeks new learning opportunities from professionals in other related disciplines, with support from her home visiting program, which has funds to support this form of continuing education.

Programs can create an educational structure and process that promote sharing of experience and support, both giving and receiving, so that home visitors can pursue their craft with confidence and enthusiasm. Learning is a continual, fluid, and individual as well as collaborative process, and it can be a natural part of the culture of a home visiting program.

Content of Continuing Education

Home visiting is a complex, dynamic process. Home visitors' actions arise from an interaction of their personal abilities, style, and experience with their professional education and the requirements of a particular program. In addition, each family is unique; thus, visitors use different approaches with different families. For example, when Erin is 24 months old, Janice initiates a game in which Erin makes a parade by matching similar toy vehicles and people, for example, a fire truck and a police car. Then Erin matches cards depicting mother and baby animals. That same day Janice initiates the same vehicle-matching game with Molly, who also is 24 months old. Janice knows that Molly is intellectually not as quick as Erin, so she omits the second, more abstract game.

In examining the continuing education of home visitors, it is important to recognize that the different domains of knowledge and skill overlap and often are interdependent.[7] For example, home visitors have skill in understanding the vulnerabilities unique to low-income families when they understand how neighborhood, welfare, housing, employment, health, and education can have an impact on a family's functioning. Given this complexity, arranging for the content of home visitors' continued professional development involves the challenge of providing education across disciplines in many areas of knowledge and skill.

Child Development   Regardless of whether home visitors are nurses, social workers, or educators, when they work with families with young children, a solid foundation in child development is the first priority of professional education. As home visitors learn about development in the areas of cognition and language, as well as biological or physical, sociocultural, and psychological–emotional development, the emphasis needs to be holistic, that is, on the intertwining of all these developmental realms. For example, when discussing cognitive development, Janice can relate how she needed to provide different activities for Erin than for Molly, children of the same age with different abilities. Cynthia can describe how she structured a toddler's play with birdseed so that his mother, Sally, who is a concrete learner, could have simple concrete experiences in managing her child's behavior. When in-service sessions combine child development content with process, that is, home visitors talking about their work with families, learning becomes more active and reflective. Then there is a higher probability that the home visitors will be able to use this learning in their everyday work with families.

Education to Broaden One's Perspective   Education for home visitors cuts across many disciplines beyond child development, disciplines such as health and nutrition, language and communication, occupational and physical therapy, special education, and social services. Given this complexity, regular use of outside consultants for staff in-service can assist home visitors in gaining new tools beyond their personal and professional experience.

Margaret is Director of Early Education in a large district that has had a home visiting program for 14 years. In Margaret's program, outside consultants across disciplines regularly lead the weekly staff meetings. A child psychologist who has a family therapy practice leads two sessions each month: one group supervision session for staff to discuss difficulties they are having with specific families, and one session to share child development or family systems information. Consultants representing other disciplines such as health and nutrition, occupational therapy, pediatrics, and community agencies such as the child protection bureau and the substance abuse clinic also lead sessions.

Margaret discussed the purpose of these staff meetings.

We need to bring in people with different lenses, different expertise, to broaden the staff's knowledge—people such as social workers, child psychologists, pediatricians, occupational therapists, people knowledge-

able in drug and alcohol abuse, children's learning problems, and people representing community agencies. But we also need a balance. Sessions also need to involve the staff in issues directly related to their tasks, such as parenting skills for helping your baby go to sleep, baby massage, movement and music, even nitty-gritty kinds of things like toy making.

Home visitors gain a deeper, broader, richer understanding of what they do as consultants, providing them with multiple perspectives on the home visiting process. At the same time, in a significant number of meetings, staff can work together to improve their skills in tasks basic to the home visiting process. In these sessions, staff think aloud about their work and build on their own expertise and the expertise of their professional peers. Colleagues become a source of not only new information and insight but also new ways of working with families— expanding ideas of what is possible. The process is interactive and involves self- and collaborative reflection.

To reemphasize the point, beyond child development knowledge, home visitors' best resource is their own experience and active reflection on this experience. Thus, active learning is enhanced by close connections between educational topics and the professional concerns and experiences of home visitors. At the same time, professional education involves home visitors' moving beyond their unique individual experience and perspective and expanding their lens so that they can understand the complexities of their work, take in multiple points of view, and be open to new perspectives. The following are five areas of knowledge and skill that are useful in helping to be open to new tools beyond one's own personal and professional experience:

1. An ecological approach, or an understanding of social systems
2. Knowledge and skill in working with at-risk families and families of other cultures
3. Understanding family systems, adult development, and the family life cycle
4. Working with divorced, single-parent, or blended families
5. Knowledge of available community agency resources

Ecological Approach Discussion of home visiting often focuses on parent–child relationships and the home visitor's striving to enhance this relationship. When home visitors take an ecological approach, they also consider young children in their total family environment and the interplay of the family with other social systems, such as neighborhood, church, and workplace.[8] They understand that the quality of a family's life is interconnected with the quality of their social environment. Taking an ecological perspective, home visitors look inside to the everyday patterns of parent–child interactions and outside to those social systems and settings that support or constrain these everyday patterns. There is a give-and-take mutuality between these external social systems and the child and family. For example, the manner in which child care teachers and parents greet each other as the young child arrives influences not only the parents' feeling of trust in this caregiver but also the caregiver's feelings of support and affirmation. In turn, the child feels secure in the similarity between home and child care program or feels insecure because of mixed messages or tension between parents and child care staff.

When home visitors take an ecological, social systems approach, they locate each family in its social environment in terms of ethnicity, race, religion, education, and occupation. With this perspective, they are sensitive to a family's access to resources, to personal–social networks, and to potential constraints, all of which influence the family's everyday lifestyle. With this knowledge and sensitivity, home visitors can then individualize their approach so that they communicate respect, support, and affirmation to each family they serve.

Given our individualistic culture, it is not a given that the average home visitor will take an ecological approach. Thus, staff development sessions can expand perspectives by providing informational sessions on the notions of ecology, social systems, and how home visitors can take an approach that includes the family's environment. Having this understanding, home visitors are sensitive to the messages parents receive from various parts of their environment, that is, their neighborhood, church, elementary school, workplace, and the media. They know that, sometimes, parents receive mixed or contradictory messages from different parts of their environment. In team meetings, staff members can share how the social environment affects families and, in this sharing, gain new understanding.

Culturally Diverse and At-Risk Families   In paying attention to children's and families' social environment, home visitors develop sensitivities and accompanying skills in recognizing and relating to cultural diversity and the differing individual and social patterns of different cultures. They know that relationships and understanding can have different meanings for people of a different race, ethnicity, religion, educational status, or social class. For example, they expect families from different cultures to have different informal networks – people outside the home with whom the family participates in activities. Social networks can be helpful in providing information and support, or they can be stressful. Knowing that some families have fewer support networks helps home visitors to see where they can provide assistance. Knowing that some families may be very close to extended family members who give young parents strong child-rearing messages helps home visitors recognize the potential conflicting messages that the parents may be receiving from their family and from the home visitor. A first step in education for working with diverse cultures is helping home visitors recognize how their own behavior, attitudes, and values reflect their own culture. Then, when relating to families of a different culture, home visitors can be alert to keeping their own biases from blocking communication with a family. Second, staff in-service can assist home visitors in gaining specific knowledge of the cultures of the families they serve. This is another topic in which consultants who represent different cultures can broaden a program's perspective.

Professional development of home visitors working with families at risk entails additional content and process. When home visitors work with families at risk, they encounter an increase both in personal problems families face (e.g., family conflict, depression, anxiety) and external problems (e.g., housing, jobs). Given these problems, it is not unusual for these parents to have difficulty in focusing on their young children's needs. Just as home visitors make more visits with families at risk, so, too, they need additional professional guidance. It is not uncommon for home visitors who work with troubled families to see the needs of young children being unmet and to feel frustrated, angry, discouraged, and overwhelmed. At-risk families are more likely to have group behavior patterns that conflict with the home visitor's traditional purposes. Often there may be no quiet place to meet with parents, or there may be repeated interruptions during a home visit. Home visitors may provide a safe target toward which parents can vent their frustrations and be angry and hostile. Given this work context, staff meetings that focus on patterns of at-risk, troubled families and adaptations in working with these families provide an invaluable resource for home visitors.

Adult Development, Family Systems, and Family Life Cycle A third area of continuing knowledge and skill involves adult development, family systems, and family life cycle. Social scientists have developed theories of adult development to aid in our understanding of both individual adults and differences among adults as a group. Developmental theories describe predictable sequences of growth and adaptation throughout life.[9] Changes in development include changes in a complex interwoven fabric of interpersonal behavior, moral and ethical behavior, cognitive complexity, and preoccupations. Different periods in life involve different age-related tasks and life issues. For example, middle-class parents in their early 20s with very young children often are preoccupied with issues different from those of middle-class parents who are between ages 30 and 40 and just starting a family. The younger parents may be just beginning a career. In contrast, in our culture, the period between ages 30 and 40 is typically a time of rapid career advancement; thus, career issues may preoccupy parents at this age. Just as home visitors individualize their approach with families of different cultures, so, too, knowledge of adult development helps them relate effectively to individual differences among parents.

Family systems theory posits that the behavior of each family member is interdependent with that of every other family member. Each family member has an expectation that involves what is expected of him or her and how each member's role fits into the total family structure. A gifted child may have the role of strengthening his or her parents' feelings of competence and thus feels compelled to succeed in all tasks. Alternatively, a father may have the role of unquestionable control and power; thus, in his family interactions, he feels obligated to reward and reprimand each family member.

Family systems theory explains that families go through a developmental process, a family life cycle, that involves shifts in family organization and functioning. It is helpful for home visitors to learn how a family is organized and to understand that this organization is different in different life cycles of a family. Family life cycles include issues of marriage, childbirth, and separation (e.g., entering child care or school, a mother or father returning to work), school age and adolescence, the empty nest, and retirement. Home visitors most often work with families within the same life cycle; however, these families may be intimately related to extended families in different phases of the family life cycle. Thus, an understanding of the family life cycle can assist home visitors in their ecological approach to families.

Divorced, Single-Parent, and Blended Families Home visitors can expect to work with families who experience the problems and possibilities in divorced, single-parent, or blended families. Professional education can provide understanding of these increasingly common family patterns. Divorce is a transitional process, not a legal relationship, and children are an integral part of the process. Every divorce involves a challenge for parents and children to reorganize. Daily routines change, separation issues become dominant, and issues of marital responsibility versus parental responsibility need to be clarified. As parents go through the divorce process, they redefine themselves. In this process, home visitors can assist parents in helping their young children to understand these substantive changes and at the same time to feel secure in their parents' love.

Once a separation is finalized and the young child lives with only one parent, patterns of single parenting emerge. It is important for home visitors to acknowledge that single parents, mothers as well as fathers, can manage the economic, physical, and psychosocial tasks of family life. Home visitors can learn the many strengths of single parenting, such as increased flexibility, children's increased understanding of their parent's work, and increased expectation that every family member contributes to the maintenance of the whole family. Understanding the potential strengths of single parenting assists home visitors in relating to single parents in a respectful, supportive, and affirming manner.

Blended families also can involve challenges for parents. Each family has developed unique daily routines and brings unique patterns of family celebrations to the blended family. Some patterns have been taken for granted for young children and/or their parents; thus, it can be an unexpected adjustment to encounter different daily routines or different ways of celebrating. Creating new routines and rituals together can be a very important step in a blended family's life together. Home visitors can offer support and encouragement to parents experiencing these new challenges.

Networking with Community Agencies A fourth area of knowledge and skill involves networking with community agencies. As discussed in Chapter 2, home visitors know what they can do and what is beyond their expertise. With visits in a family's home, it is not uncommon for parents to initiate discussion of personal difficulties, such as conflicts with their spouse or parent, or external difficulties, such as child care or housing. As a result, familiarity with community resources becomes knowledge upon which home visitors often rely. When home visitors work with families with multiple problems, networking with community agencies is a recurrent part of their work. Cynthia described some of her experiences.

One of the successes and also frustrations we have had in our work with different community agencies that serve our families is discovering how difficult it can be to get services. For example, I called a rape crisis line at 10:00 in the morning because a mom had come in and told us she had been raped by her boyfriend and needed to talk to someone. We had never handled this kind of situation before, so we called the rape crisis line. The machine said to call back at 10:30.

Just the phone systems we have now can be problematic for our families. You call a number and are told to press 1 for this, 2 for this, 3 for this, 4 for this. A lot of people get lost and don't know which button to press. And they'll hang up and won't try. Just the way the system is set up sometimes thwarts people's attempts to get help.

Then we have situations where counseling is available with a sliding fee. But again, child care and transportation are not available. And most counseling centers will not do home visits. On the other hand, once we work with our local medical clinics, we often can expedite getting appointments for the kids when we call the clinic and tell them this is one of our families. We have a contact person there. In fact, we have a case now in which the child had been seen at one of the bigger hospitals in town. Because mom missed two appointments and had no transportation for a 30-mile round trip, the hospital said they would not work with this family anymore. I called our local clinic, which got the family into a different hospital that does provide transportation. And now the child is being served.

Cynthia and her staff know the individuals who work in different community agencies. Given their relationships with these individuals, the staff can gain personalized help for parents who cannot successfully use the agency.

That kind of coordination makes a world of difference. We try to put our people into job training and vocational rehabilitation programs. Through networking, knowing someone who works there and will take our calls, we can get our parents access. The parent doesn't have to deal with number 1, number 2, and so forth. Once you have a person who knows who you are and knows your program, then you are much more likely to get something done.

The other day we had a parent who wants to go to the community college and was having difficulty getting a transcript. I called my contact at the community college, who went to admissions and was able to troubleshoot for the parent. That's the way things can happen. All too often people get lost in the system and have trouble getting services; they get frustrated and give up.

What we are able to do is walk them through the process and thereby keep their spirits up. "Yes, it's a pain. Yes, it's a bummer. But yes, you can do it. Here's the number. Call now. Here is what you need to say." And the next time our parents will know how to do that, will know how to ask that question.

Staff meetings can be a setting for joint exploration of community resources: governmental agencies, such as public welfare; Women, Infants, and Children programs; the child protection agency; mental and physical health agencies; as well as private agencies, such as recovery programs, shelters for battered women, and out-of-home child care. This is an area where outside consultants can broaden the staff's knowledge. In some situations, home visitors may have the knowledge of available community resources, but lack the skill in helping parents gain access to these resources. Skillful approaches to networking with community agencies can be discussed at a staff meeting and often are an important topic for the individual's supervision (see last section of this chapter).

Education for Effective Skill Building

Knowledge and skill are mutually interdependent. Team meetings can focus specifically on skill building, especially communication and relationship-building skills—the building blocks of home visiting. When staff meet regularly and discuss their work in small groups, these meetings can become a setting for reflecting together about their hands-on work. The skills discussed in Chapter 2 can be addressed, either by home visitors sharing concretely their experience or by sharing videos of their work. Given the intensity of home visitors' work, these group discussions might involve some of the following recurrent themes:

- Forming and maintaining relationships of trust and support
- Learning to take the perspective of the parent
- Expressing strong feelings, negative and positive, and having these feelings reflected back
- Understanding the developmental potential of individual children and individual parents
- Understanding the program's limits of responsibility

Working collaboratively to learn and reflect upon practice is a slow process. This process is possible when all staff members strive to support, affirm, and guide one another's personal and professional growth in a climate of openness and inquiry.

Continuing Education Across Large Geographical Areas

A significant proportion of the United States is rural; thus, some home visiting programs cover large geographical areas. In these situations, administrators can initiate innovative forms of continuing professional education. Use of the telephone, telecommunication, and the mail are useful avenues of collaboration between home visitors and their mentors. Programs can develop a videotape library as an integral part of ongoing education. Videos can illustrate exemplary home visiting and can demonstrate and discuss the use of supervision and mentorship processes. A user's guide provides additional assistance. Similarly, technology such as faxing, voice mail, and electronic mail systems on the Internet can offer a means of continual collaboration with both peers and mentors. Networks among professionals formed across large distances also provide support and opportunities for continued growth. The Foxfire Teacher Networks provide a model of professionals collaborating across wide geographical distances. Foxfire offers summer workshops for educators, and these workshops evolve into networks—support systems in which Foxfire graduates engage in continued collaboration in the interest of promoting professional development.[10]

SUPERVISION

Home visitors' work is intense and is based on trusting relationships. Forming and maintaining these parent–home visitor relationships involve emotions as well as the intellect. Self-knowledge is necessary for professional competence, and the core of continuing education is home visitors' active reflection on their experience. This reflection helps them recognize the meaning of their actions and experience. Regular collaborative supervision provides a relationship through which to promote this continued professional development. A supervisory relationship offers a safe setting in which home visitors can discuss their experiences, both successes and failures, and gain feedback from an experienced practitioner. This discussion of supervision is guided by the work of ZERO TO THREE/National Center for Infants, Toddlers, and Families.[11] ZERO TO THREE has taken the lead in addressing the need for supervision in home visiting and other programs supporting the development of infants, toddlers, and their families. ZERO TO THREE discusses how reflection, collaboration, and consistency are key features of effective supervision.

Effective supervision parallels home visitors' relationship with the families that they serve because it is likewise a relationship of respect, support, collaboration, and mutuality. Ideally, the supervisor's expertise includes having been a front-line worker conducting home visits. Within supervision, home visitors become increasingly skilled in focusing on the nuts and bolts of their experiences; reporting these experiences; and gaining feedback, knowledge, and suggestions.

Dan is an outside consultant who provides group supervision for Cynthia's home visiting program. Cynthia described her early work with Dan.

It was my first year doing home visiting. I was working with two small kids, mom, and dad. I had completed a developmental screen with each child and was explaining it to their mom and dad. Out of nowhere, when I asked the question, "Is the child learning to help in the house or imitating helping?," mom commented, "I wish I could get him [the dad] to help," as she looked at her husband. The dad replied, and they began arguing back and forth. Dad walked out of the room, angry. Mom sat there and began crying. I just sat there like a bump on the log. I finally said, "Would you like me to leave?" She replied no. And dad was within earshot. Everyone felt uncomfortable. I finished explaining the Denver [developmental screen] and left as soon as I could.

That week when we met with Dan [the team's supervisor], I explained the situation—how I felt ill at ease and didn't know what to do. Through talking it over, Dan helped me understand that I'm not there to be a marriage counselor or help them talk it through. That's not necessarily what I'm there for. It's obvious they are having marriage difficulty. And they let me see that. Dan's suggestion was when you find yourself in that situation, instead of getting pulled in or doing nothing, you could say, "You both seem to be having difficulty, would you like to talk to someone? Would you like me to recommend someone for you?" Or you can say, "This seems to be a difficult time. Would you like me to leave and come back later?" Dan affirmed my response, which was the same as his second suggestion. And when I went back to their home, I suggested someone for them to talk to.

In this visit, Cynthia had responded in an appropriate manner to these parents' fighting. Her response was intuitive. As a new home visitor, she had not thought through issues of maintaining boundaries, and she did not have a clear understanding of the options she had in situations like this. Being able to share this experience with the team and the team supervisor provided Cynthia with a deeper understanding of her work and at the same time affirmed her response to these parents.

Within supervision, the focus is primarily on process and on interaction. Supervision offers a setting in which to feel secure enough to reflect on emotional reactions to one's practice.[12] The setting is safe enough to expose one's insecurities, mistakes, and questions. In turn, the supervisor reflects back to the home visitor the home visitor's thoughts and feelings and offers support. Collaboratively, the home visitor and supervisor interpret and gain understanding of both the troublesome aspects of work and the successes. In these experiences, home visitors often gain improved understanding of their thoughts, feelings, and actions as well as support, guidance, and encouragement to move forward in their work. Cynthia described a supervisor who helped her better understand herself and her experiences at work.

One of the persons who influenced my work life was Lee Samuels. Lee was my supervisor when I worked for the Head Start program in Oregon. Lee was extremely bright. What Lee did for me was to help me look at myself and look at my strengths and my weaknesses and learn to understand myself better. He was able to do that in a supervisory role. He's probably the only supervisor I ever had who would sit me down on a regular basis and process what was going on in the program, what was happening, why it was happening, and how we could take it somewhere else. Lee helped me look at my own personality traits, where they were effective and where they weren't.

Lee helped me realize I don't have to have all the answers. Performance has been very important in my family, and I've always felt like I have to know everything. He helped me realize I don't—that true power lies in knowing what you don't know, in being able to admit it, and then seeking help.

Lee taught me a lot about being a supervisor, how to help people grow. He was never afraid of his female side. In that respect, he taught me something about men, too. He would talk to me about being a man, and I never had a man do that. If I'd be upset with my husband or something, Lee would say, "Well, Cynthia, this is the way men look at it." That really helped me, too, on a personal note. No one had ever done that for me.

For Cynthia, Lee helped her reflect on her personal style and her work experiences. Their relationship had the same kind of mutuality that effective home visitors have with the parents with whom they work.

When home visitors work with families with multiple problems, supervision is even more important. Working with such families sparks powerful feelings in the visitor. Some of the feelings are problematic, such as the sense of futility, vulnerability, and hopelessness. At these times, visitors need to be self-aware. Self-monitoring is essential, as are support, affirmation, and guidance from peers and supervisors.

Introducing the topic of supervision may spark multiple dilemmas. The term *supervision* is understood differently in different disciplines. For some disciplines, supervision means overseeing, monitoring, and evaluating. This description of supervision envisions an alternative, process-oriented approach. A further problem is the many structural barriers within home visiting programs, such as limited (or nonexistent) funding resources to have individuals providing one-on-one supervision for all staff members. Notwithstanding these dilemmas, for all program administrators, the first step in moving toward a supervision model is awareness of the need. Once administrators understand supervision, they can work toward lessening or removing structural barriers.

Once administrators are committed to a supervision model, they can adapt the structure of their program to provide features of this model. Commitment is the first step because demands of direct service can obscure supervision needs. As previously discussed, self- and collaborative reflection can be a central feature in the shared culture of staff meetings, a culture that is valued and protected by administrators. Time, structure, and clear expectations make the occurrence of these processes possible. Sharing successes and problems of work with families can be incorporated into staff meetings as a framework for staff to share their work and gain feedback and suggestions for their practice. As previously discussed, small-group meetings of staff are a safe setting in which peers can share and reflect on one another's home visiting experiences. Peer supervision also can be a powerful force for improved self- and collaborative reflection. Home visitors can attend one another's sessions, take written notes or videotape these sessions, and then meet to reflect collaboratively on both the happenings and the home visitors' thoughts and feelings. Often home visitors learn as much from observing their peers as from being observed. Outside consultants can provide supervisory expertise to support and guide this type of collaborative reflection.

DIFFICULTIES AND DILEMMAS

The professional development discussed in this chapter may seem new and offer challenges to both home visitors and their administrators. Some home visitors may have difficulty with the professional development principles and suggested approaches discussed in this chapter. They may not be introspective, or they may not have had prior experiences that promote self-knowledge. Individuals may have a very private personal and professional life and be offended with the expectation that they openly share their home visiting experiences with others. If individuals' prior professional experience has involved hierarchical communicating and relating, promoting partnerships with parents characterized by mutuality may be frightening. Change can be frightening for everyone. Change involves unpredictability and accompanied uncertainty. Each person enters a field with a distinct personal and professional biography. When an individual's biography is very different from the demands of the current position, uncertainty can be expected. By recognizing these obstacles when administrators change the form of professional development, they can provide time and support for home visitors to adapt to change.

Administrators also have professional development needs, but their needs may not be addressed by program policy, structure, and finances. In many programs, administrators work independently and may feel the same kind of isolation as do home visitors. Administrators may have been promoted from direct service, and they may not have the benefit of preservice education directly related to their new role. As a result, administrators often have to create innovative ways of ensuring their own professional growth. Seminars at national conferences such as the ZERO TO THREE Training Institutes can offer a setting for shared learning and gaining new insights, similar to good continuing education of home visitors. The administrators within a geographical region can meet regularly. These meetings can provide the kind of peer supervision and guidance discussed in this chapter. An outside consultant with supervision expertise can assist in facilitating these regional meetings and can help expand members' notions of what is possible. The Erikson Institute, for example, has taken leadership in offering an in-session supervision seminar for administrators and supervisors of programs serving infants, toddlers, and their families in the Chicago area.[13] Development of videotapes on supervision also can be an invaluable resource, especially for those living in rural areas. When programs cover large distances, possibilities of telecommunication and Internet exploration and communication can offer professional support, information, encouragement, and guidance.

CONCLUSIONS

This chapter discusses how home visitors, like artisans, learn best through practice over time. This learning through practice is possible if home visitors reflect on their practice and, in this reflection, gain new understanding of the meaning and purpose of their practice. The skills of reflection on practice can be promoted when a program's staff development is interactive. Team meetings provide a setting in which home visitors can tell stories to one another in a climate of mutual inquiry. They can share successes—a directive mother now engages in spontaneous play; they can express frustration—repeatedly the family is not home at the scheduled time; they can share dilemmas—experiencing conflicting concerns between grandmother and teen mother; and sometimes they can share failure—a family's withdrawal from the program. These meetings can become settings for shared delight as well as shared frustrations, dilemmas, challenges, and failures. When team meetings are small enough to develop relationships of trust, these home visitors' stories can be the springboard for them to practice reflection and gain support, feedback, encouragement, and new ideas. Learning from one another is the given expectation. Just as the personal relationship between home visitor and parent can strengthen a parent's role, so, too, when home visitors work together with shared goals and common bonds, the experience can be strengthening, deepening the home visitor's understanding and enabling her or him to move forward with renewed commitment.

A solid foundation in child development is the first step in home visitors' continuing education. Home visitors' work cuts across disciplines beyond child development; thus, staff meetings can provide the setting for outside consultants to broaden home visitors' knowledge base. When process is intertwined with content, that is, when home visitors can talk together about how their work relates to this content, then they can apply this new learning to their everyday work.

In addition, regular collaborative supervision gives home visitors a trusting relationship in which to discuss their work and gain feedback and guidance from an experienced practitioner. Supervision offers a safe setting in which to reflect on one's emotional reactions and to expose mistakes, insecurities, and questions. Together supervisors and home visitors reflect on and interpret both the difficulties and the successes. Supervision is an especially important resource for those who work with families with multiple problems. There are indeed many structural barriers with home visiting programs that may make individual supervision an impossibility. Given this reality, administrators can adapt their program structure to provide features of the supervision model.

In sum, professional development is a lifelong process in which home visitors actively reflect on their practice, individually and with peers. Program participants meet together in a climate of inquiry. Team meetings are a place to share stories, grow, and learn and to give and accept feedback, new perspectives, and new strategies. This mutual, respectful collaboration cuts into the individualistic nature of home visitors' everyday work and provides support, encouragement, and guidance to return to the field.

II

Promoting Healthy Parent and Child Development

4

Developing
a Sense of Self

The Foundation of Social
and Emotional Development

"I do like a mother's love," said Tottles, hitting Nibs with a pillow. *"Do you like a mother's love, Nibs?"*

"I do just," said Nibs, hitting back.

"You see," Wendy said complacently, *"Our heroine knew that the mother would always leave the window open for her children to fly back by; so they stayed away for years and had a lovely time."*

J.M. Barrie, *Peter Pan* (1911, p. 128)

This chapter uses the terms *self* and *sense of self* to reflect the perspective of current infant research and theory.[1] Initially, the infant has no awareness of self. But the components of sense of self are observable; they are inner experiences inferable through observed infant behavior. Sense of self is an inclusive concept that comprises social and emotional development and influences all other developmental areas, such as physical and sensorimotor, language, communication, and cognition. *Self* in this meaning comes before there is self-reflection.

The sense of self appears to develop within a paradox: We develop our own individual sense of self only within our interactions with others. The sense of selfhood is a social achievement and is learned from living with others. Infants and young children develop a sense of self within parents' taken-for-granted day-to-day child-rearing interactions. These child-rearing interactions are mutually created; that is, parents shape their infant's actions at the same time that infants are shaping their parents' actions. This sense of self begins at the moment of birth and remains with us throughout our lives.

The infant's emerging sense of self is the organization of feelings, actions, and expectations underlying behavior.[2] The sense of oneself is extremely complex; it is the core of what it means to be human. Adults can talk about their inner lives, but the components of the infant's sense of self are inner experiences inferable only through observed behavior. For example, when a 3-month-old engages in social smiles and coos at others, we can infer an emerging sense of self in relation to others—a social self. Young infants experience a sense of self long before they experience self-awareness. Explaining sense of self is difficult because the concept seems so abstract and nonobservable. Yet the developing sense of self is the scaffolding, the anchor, and the foundation of development.

Since the mid-1980s, infant research using film and videotaping of newborns, young infants, and their parents has revolutionized our understanding of the infant's developing sense of self. For example, infant researchers now know that infants are born with specific emotions and abilities to relate socially. Changes in sense of self do not happen because of changes in the infant alone; rather, they are the result of the infant's physiological and mental capabilities *and* their experience with significant others. From the beginning, the newborn is experiencing both self and other. As Winnicott stated, "There is no such thing as a baby";[3] that is, there is no such thing as a baby *without its primary caregiver.* The capacity to experience oneself as an infant occurs only as the infant relates to another.

The infant's and young child's sense of self takes place in developmental leaps.[4] Every few months, significant changes occur in the infant's and young child's sense of self. Major shifts in the infant's social experiences result from these gains; in turn, these shifts in social experience have an impact on the infant's sense of self. This chapter tracks these developmental changes. The discussion encompasses both infants' and young children's behavior and parents' behavior, as changes in children's sense of self are intertwined with their relations with their parents. As the chapter tracks the infant's and young child's developing sense of self in relation to significant people in the child's life, it explores how home visitors can support, affirm, and promote parents' understanding and relationships with their infants and young children.[5]

DEVELOPING SENSE OF SELF: BIRTH–6 MONTHS

Parents' interactions with their newborn primarily center around physiological regulation. As parents hold, caress, rock, and talk to their newborn, they learn to adjust their behavior to their infant's behavior; for example, parents gently rock their infant after the infant begins to fuss or talk to their infant during feeding. In the same way that the infant's behavior triggers a response from the parent, the parent's behavior triggers a response from the infant. For example, the infant becomes quiet as the parent rocks, or the infant looks intently into the eyes of the talking parent while nursing. A pattern of mutually influencing behavior begins and continues in their everyday interactions. Some infants may have sensory systems that are over- or underreactive, and thus the infant may not readily respond to the parents' efforts or may be fussy. In turn, some parents themselves may have shortcomings in their ability to be responsive to their infants. The difficulties and dilemmas section of this chapter discusses these problems further.

Parents of newborns experience both delight and uneasiness. Their uneasiness arises from the awesomeness of their task as a parent. Home visitors can help parents feel more at ease by providing helpful developmental information so that parents can have *predictable expectations* of their newborn. Home visitors can explain to parents of newborns that an infant has a built-in cycle of six states of consciousness: deep sleep, light sleep, semi-alert, wide-awake alert, fussing, and crying. Knowing that the infant experiences this predictable cycle allows parents to be more in control of their caregiving. One parent's comments are illustrative.

> I tell people that don't know anything about the program that home visitors will give you ideas of what to look for, what to expect next in the development of the child, and things you can do that can help that development to go along. And I just tell them that we wouldn't be without it. . . . We waited a long time before having children, and not knowing what to do after having the baby, we were like, well, you know. I guess I was kinda iffy about some things and not knowing how to do other things.

Self-Calming

The newborn's first task is to achieve calmness (i.e., to be regulated inside) and to be interested in the surrounding world. One of parents' first areas of guidance is assisting their new infant to self-calm. When infants can self-calm, they can stop crying or fussing and settle down without help from anyone else. Self-calming is the first form of independence and self-control that an infant learns. Usually by age 8–10 weeks, infants learn to calm themselves. Sammons identified ways in which infants self-calm: by sucking; by movement of their hands, arms, or legs; by taking a certain body position; or by using their vision.[6] Self-calming is a mutual achievement of parent and infant and is achieved through their communication. Parents learn the meaning of different cries, for example, learning when they can let their infant calm herself and thereby put herself back to sleep, as opposed to when their infant needs to be fed. Discussing self-calming during home visitors' first visit after an infant's birth can be very helpful because many parents are aware of neither the occurrence nor the importance of self-calming.

Infants and toddlers prenatally exposed to drug and alcohol abuse are likely to be fussy and irritable and to have difficulty calming themselves. Villarreal, McKinney, and Quackenbush have developed a series of suggestions for caring for such infants and toddlers and helping them self-calm (see Table 1).[7]

Table 1.   Suggestions for helping infants with prenatal exposure to drug or alcohol abuse to self-calm

- Hold and swaddle the infant. Wrapping the infant tightly in a soft, snug blanket can give the infant a sense of security. These infants usually like to be held fairly tightly. Softly speaking to, gently touching, or massaging the infant while holding him or her can assist in calming. Using the same routine helps the infant become accustomed to the process.
- The infant may be sensitive to stimulation. Thus, bright lights, fast movements, or loud noises should be avoided.
- Keep the infant in a position so that he or she is facing the caregiver directly. It may take a few weeks of practice before the infant naturally makes eye contact with the caregiver.
- The infant often enjoys soothing by sucking, even when not feeding.
- A gentle foot, ankle, or back massage can help tense infants relax.
- Because diaper changing can be stressful, use of diapers with tape is easier. It is easiest for the infant if diapers are changed when he or she is sleepy. Speaking softly and massaging helps ease this process.
- Infants prenatally exposed to drug or alcohol abuse may have uncoordinated suck and swallow reflexes. They may have difficulty keeping food down. Given these difficulties, caregivers need to take ample time for feeding and be as relaxed as possible. Several short meals may be easier for the infant than only a few longer meals. These infants need their caregiver to hold their bottle.
- Solid foods need to be introduced gradually in small amounts.
- Sleep can be very problematic for infants prenatally exposed to drug or alcohol abuse. They may not be able to wake up gradually, and they often move quickly from a deep sleep to intense crying and screaming. Because most infants feel sleepy after feeding, feeding just before bedtime can help promote sleep. Infants with prenatal exposure normally cry before they sleep. Speaking softly, giving soft massages, and using a night light can be reassuring.

(continued)

Table 1. *(continued)*

- Infants ages 6–9 months can have a predictable bedtime. A bedtime ritual can assist in calming the infant before sleep.
- Infants prenatally exposed to drugs and alcohol sleep more restlessly and wake more than other infants. When such infants awaken in the night, caregivers can speak softly to them. Bottles or food should not be given during the night.
- The infant needs help in being comfortable with touch. Caregivers should gently touch the infant frequently for brief periods.
- Caregivers should speak frequently throughout the day to the infant.
- In some cases, nothing a caregiver does stops the infant from crying. Infants prenatally exposed to drug or alcohol abuse can experience discomforts that cannot be relieved. In these situations, caregivers need a helper to provide them with a break.

Adapted from Villarreal, McKinney, & Quackenbush (1992). ©ETR Associates. All Rights Reserved. Excerpted and adapted with permission from *Handle with Care*, ETR Associates, Santa Cruz, CA. For information about this and other related materials, call 1-800-321-4407.

Temperament

Home visitors also can help parents understand the wide differences in a baby's responsiveness to people and the environment, in the infant's activity level, and in how quickly the infant becomes upset. These differences reflect inborn patterns that are collectively termed *temperament*.[8] Temperament differences are seen in movement, ease of soothing, degree of alertness, and manner of sleeping. The infant's temperament affects the way he or she responds to his or her parents. In turn, the parents need to learn to adapt their response to their infant's unique temperament. The following discussion between Karyn and Janice is illustrative.

Karyn: One day he screamed all day. I called the pediatrician, and he said to put him on the dryer and turn it on. I let go and got angry, and then he said to bring in the baby. He said that Greg was okay and that he is going to be a difficult baby.

Janice: He still cries, but now you feel better because you know it is not a health problem. [Karyn nods yes.] There's so much learning that goes on. The baby needs to learn your signals; you need to learn his signals. And the baby needs to learn your husband's signals, and [your husband] needs to learn those of the baby. You don't know each other very well yet. It's really tricky.

Karyn: He's jumpy. Like, when the nipple on his bottle makes a sound, he jumps. Even when he's sleeping, he's jumpy.

Janice: Swaddling—wrapping him snuggly in his blanket and cuddling him—often helps, keeping him closed in. My third baby was colicky. Even when it's the third baby, it's tough when they cry a lot. Have you tried massage?

Karyn: No.

Janice: Try rubbing his shoulders. Babies carry tension in their shoulders, like we do. And put him on his back, stretch and bend his legs one at a time, and massage them, and rub his tummy.

Janice commented that the pediatrician's suggestion of calming Greg by using the hum and vibration of the dryer is the physician's way of telling Karyn, in everyday language, that her infant's temperament is difficult—that Greg is difficult to soothe and comfort. As she rephrased Karyn's description, Janice let Karyn know that she understands her feelings. She supported Karyn by sharing her own parenting experiences. She used everyday language to provide developmental information regarding the mutuality of parent–infant relationships. She provided a suggestion directly related to Karyn's concerns. In this conversation, no doubt Karyn felt understood and affirmed.

Newborns are designed to seek stimulation, to respond selectively to their environment, and to participate in social interaction. Newborns have some voluntary muscle control and can turn their heads, suck, and look. They choose to look at faces, suck to soothe themselves, and turn away from unpleasant sounds or sights. These behaviors indicate that the newborn is capable of purposeful actions.[9]

The newborn's sense of being is integrated. Different experiences can be joined if they share the same quality of feeling.[10] For example, a mother may comfort her infant in different ways—for example, speaking quietly, stroking softly, or holding the baby while walking calmly. The infant experiences these different occurrences as the same form of comfort. A sense of organization thus is created.

The young infant's experience is controlled by what is pleasurable and unpleasurable; in other words, emotions are the organizing basis for guiding behavior.[11] Initially, very young infants have little ability to manage their feelings and are dependent upon their parents for this regulation. As they interact with their young infant, parents respond empathically and help their infant avoid too much excitement or discomfort. Infant theorists term regulation of infants' feelings *affect regulation*.[12] Brazelton and Cramer explained how parents regulate their infants' behavior:

A mother will lean over her baby, reach for a flailing extremity, hold the baby by the buttocks, enclose him or her in an envelope made up of her intense gaze and her soft vocalization. Out of this cluster of five behaviors, she will heighten one of them, her voice, to elicit a response. As her voice increases gently, the infant responds with a cluster of behaviors— relaxation of the whole body, softening of facial features, intense looking at her, then a soft "coo." The mother's clustering of behaviors around each vocalization is as important in producing the response as her voice alone. A baby must be "contained" in order to attend to her. The mother also must learn her baby's system of clusters. The capacity of a mother to form a behavioral envelope to contain the baby, to maintain the baby's alert state, and to allow the necessary rhythms of attention–withdrawal becomes critical to her ability to communicate.[13]

Holding, touching, caressing, and rocking are central ways parents regulate their infants' feelings. In these everyday child-rearing interactions, infants experience love and comfort through physical affection.

When infants are about 2 months of age, a developmental leap brings new behaviors that promote sociability. Cycles of wakefulness are extended, eye-to-eye contact is increased, and the infant enjoys frequent spontaneous social vocalizing and social smiling. Young infants have excellent motor memories. Memory allows young infants to have a sense of continuity with their previous experiences. For example, infants have memories of past interactions with their parents that provide them with expectations guiding their behavior.[14] These memories recall the affect and sensations of past experiences and provide a guide for their present experiences. The memories include a wide array of social behavior between infant and caregiver, for example, simple interactive games that most parents invent with their infants.

Bonding and Attachment

It is within everyday, taken-for-granted child-rearing relationships that young infants develop the qualities of sense of self. Infant theorists use the terms *bonding* and *attachment* to explain this relationship.[15] Most parents form a strong initial bond with their infant at birth or in the hours and days immediately following. A variety of parent behaviors are automatic and seem to be specieswide, for example, exaggerated greeting responses, body-touching games, and imitation of the infant's facial and vocal expressions. Home visitors must understand, however, that not all parents have positive feelings after their infant's birth and not all parents quickly bond with their infant. When parents do not immediately feel bonded, they think that something is wrong with them and may feel guilty. Home visitors can assist these parents in recognizing that, in reality, this new infant brings a giant change in the parents' lives, that their ambivalent feelings are a normal part of being a parent, and that it may take time to learn how to feel comfortable in their new role as parent. Furthermore, some parents experience difficulty bonding with their second child, feelings that surprise and trouble them. Again, home visitors can assist parents to understand that their feelings are normal.

As the infant spontaneously smiles and coos or fusses and cries, these behaviors become signals for their parents to respond.[16] Home visitors can help parents recognize these early forms of communication and understand how the parents' responsiveness fosters their infant's sense of connectedness and security. Janice's observations of Natalie's responses to her baby Jene (age 3½ months) are illustrative.

> *Janice puts Jene on an infant blanket and gives her a three-ringed rattle. Jene begins to fuss once again. Her mother, Natalie, picks her up and softly bounces her as she gently rubs her back. Janice uses the baby's voice to affirm Natalie's responsiveness, explaining, "I know how to communicate with my Mommy, and she understands me."*
>
> *Natalie prepares a bottle for Jene and holds her in her lap as she continues to chat with Janice. Jene falls asleep. Janice affirms Natalie's parenting skills by saying, "It's important to pay attention to a baby's signals. We could have continued on the floor, but we followed Jene's signals. She became fussy. Kids at all ages need to know that adults respect their feelings. 'It's time for Mommy to pick me up.'"*

Janice supports and affirms Natalie's responsiveness to her infant's signals. She helps this young mother understand that her responsiveness is communicating respect to even such a small infant.

By age 3 months, infants favor those who regularly care for them. By age 5 months, infants' everyday experience and their development of an internal working model of their attachment figures allow the infant to have firm attachments. Not all babies have a single attachment figure. Infants show strong attachments to both parents or to parents and another caregiver, such as their child care teacher.

Parents and their infants develop a natural pattern of attachment behaviors. Infants signal their needs by crying or smiling, and their parent responds; thus, the two-person dance begins.[17] Essential for a healthy attachment to form is the opportunity to develop real mutuality—partners smoothly following each other's lead. As home visitors observe attachment behaviors, they can help parents recognize the significance of these behaviors, as illustrated by the following example.

> *Maggie has awakened from her nap, and her mother, Tracy, has just brought her into the living room. Maggie smiles as Janice softly says, "I'm so glad to see you." Maggie then begins crying as she nestles her head into her mother's shoulder. Janice says, "It's so typical of babies this age to switch emotions. Two things are happening: First, they can be happy, then sad, and vice versa so quickly, and, more importantly, Maggie knows the difference between Mom and other people."*

Tracy: *That's true even between Mom and Gramma.*

Janice: *You're so wise to comfort her when she's feeling that way. She knows Mom is here. [Maggie is now smiling at Janice.] And with Mom here, it's okay to smile at others. It's also nice to be having people in your own home. There is security here and a gradual way for Maggie to deal with a couple of new people.*

Janice's observations of Maggie's behavior and Tracy's appropriate response supports and affirms Tracy. Maggie is learning that her actions can trigger a response from her mother. As she observes, Janice interprets the developmental significance of Maggie's behavior and gives Tracy the simple suggestion to invite to her home people with whom Maggie can learn to interact.

DEVELOPING SENSE OF SELF: AGES 7–18 MONTHS

Infants between the ages of 7 and 9 months have a history, a memory, of relating to their parents, and they have increased experience in communicating by facial expressions, body movements, and posture.[18] Infant specialist Robert Emde described the developmental leap in this period as "the onset of focused attachment."[19] A new form of experiencing connectedness emerges. Infants can initiate and respond to social gestures. Infants enjoy simple interactive games such as pat-a-cake and peek-a-boo, giving evidence of *shared joint attention*. Now infants begin pointing and can follow their parents' pointing. By age 9 months, infants make requests by pointing at a bottle or pointing to go outdoors. Developmentalists say the infant is giving evidence of *shared intention*. By age 9 months, infants are crawling about to explore their surroundings. In order to resolve uncertainty, infants pause and look from their desired goal to their parent in order to gain assurance from the parent, providing evidence that the infant can understand the parent's expression of feeling. These new skills allow infants to begin to understand that their inner experiences can be shared with someone else.

Parents' Responsiveness

In their interactions with their infants, parents often understand the feelings behind their infant's behavior and respond in a way that matches their infant's feeling. Parents' behavior is *not* a strict behavioral imitation. Often the match is a similar expression made by a different action; for example, the infant's stretching movement is matched by the parent's stretching voice tone and tempo. As parents reflect their infant's feelings back to the infant, the infant feels connected and gains understanding of her or his own feeling, and thus her or his own sense of self. Stern described how infants and their parents share feelings states as follows:

A 9-month-old girl becomes very excited about a toy and reaches for it. As she grabs it, she lets out a exuberant "aaaah!" and looks at her mother. Her mother looks back, squinches up her shoulders, and performs a terrific shimmy of her upper body—like a go-go dancer. The shimmy lasts only about as long as her daughter's "aaaah!" but is equally excited, joyful, and intense.[20]

Parents experience the feeling qualities of their infant's experience. When parents' behavior reflects the same quality of feeling, young infants experience their parents' empathic responsiveness and communication.

Trust

As infants become mobile, they actively explore the world around them. When they are securely attached, infants use their parents as a safe base from which to explore. Erikson described infants' first developmental task as achieving basic trust as opposed to mistrust.[21] Infants learn to trust others to meet their needs and in turn to trust themselves to make things happen. A trusting infant sees the world as a good, stable place in which to be. Trust emerges when infants have their needs met, including the physical needs of nourishment, sleep, and warmth as well as the psychological needs of cuddling, talk, and play. When infants experience consistency in having their needs met, they are confident that they can give cues to let someone know what they need, that they can influence others.

Home visitors can help parents recognize what their infant is learning when they respond to their infant.

Greg, age 9 months, begins to cry. His mother, Karyn, picks him up, and his crying ends. Janice speaks as if she is in Greg's voice to affirm Karyn's responsiveness: "That's so reassuring to me. Mom really understands what I mean, and she is helping me."

As Karyn spontaneously interacts with Greg, Janice helps her understand how important her actions are for her young infant's understanding of self and the world around him. As Karyn consistently responds to her son's behavior, her son develops an understanding that he influences another; through these experiences, he develops a sense of personal control.[22] That is, when the infant succeeds in gaining a positive response from her or his parent, the infant gains a sense of effectiveness.

When home visitors sense that a parent is not responding to the infant, they can model spontaneous gestural and verbal responses to the infant. In these interactions with the infant, the home visitor can help the parent to see the infant's pleasure in the interaction and understand the developmental importance of this process. Some home visitors may be working with parents whose own concerns prevent them from tuning in to their infant. The difficulties and dilemmas section of this chapter discusses this issue further.

"Loveys"

Often an object connected to their parents' warmth and love can provide security for young infants and toddlers, especially during transition times, such as from waking to sleeping.[23] Such objects, sometimes called "loveys," allow young children to comfort themselves in the same manner as thumb sucking comforts them. A single beloved object taken to bed may become part of a young toddler's self-comforting routine. Maggie's sister Mia's "aw" is illustrative.

Mia (age 17 months) asks her mother, Tracy, "Where is aw?" Tracy explains to Janice that "aw" is Mia's name for her special pillow. Tracy explains that the pillow was a fancy pillow that she had received as a shower present. She and her husband would say "aw" as they would put Mia to bed. One night she asked for her "aw," and ever since it has been her special pillow. Janice remarks, "Aw has a real warm sound. The message is comfort and security."

Loveys are a normal part of development and provide an important way for young children to comfort themselves. Home visitors can help parents understand how loveys play an important role in young children's learning to comfort themselves.

Stranger Anxiety

A sign of strong attachment occurs at around 8 months of age, when infants protest being separated from their parents and show fear of strangers and strange places. The intensity of these fearful reactions varies widely from one infant to another. This pattern often is referred to as stranger anxiety. There seems to be no clear basis for this typical fearful pattern. It seems to occur as infants become more aware of new places and of new people. After about a month or so, most infants learn how to handle new experiences.

Because stranger anxiety is quite predictable at around 8 months of age, home visitors can give parents needed information so that parents can expect this first sign of fear in their infant and know that their infant's behavior is normal. When visiting infants during this phase, home visitors can respect the infant's fear and help the family feel at ease.

Janice arrives at Tracy's home, and Maggie (age 8 months), Mia's little sister, is crawling about the living room. When Janice begins to speak, Maggie stops crawling and begins to cry. Her mother picks her up as Janice comments, "Someone strange is in my house."

> *Janice then sits on the rug, several feet from Maggie and her mother,
> and says, "I'll stay away and won't rush her. When Janice and Carol
> come, Maggie is not sure yet. We are not Mia, Mommy, or Daddy. She
> knows she loves Mia, Mommy, and Daddy. She's not sure of these new
> people, and needs some time to get used to them."*
>
> *As Janice speaks, Tracy returns Maggie to the floor. However, Maggie
> begins crying again. As soon as Tracy picks her up and holds her, Maggie
> stops crying. Janice comments, "That's so wonderful, the way you just
> pick her up and love her when she is unhappy. She can feel secure
> knowing you are there." Maggie coos as she nestles in her mother's arms.*

In her prior visit with the family, Janice had discussed stranger anxiety
with Tracy. As Maggie expressed fear of Janice, Janice respected Maggie's discomfort and moved away from her. As she observes Maggie,
Janice interprets to Tracy the meaning of Maggie's fear response. As
Tracy comforts her infant, Janice affirms her responsiveness.

Independence and Autonomy

Developing independence and autonomy is an integral part of the
healthy development of sense of self and begins at birth. A newborn
gives evidence of purposeful action when she sucks her fist and calms
herself. As mentioned earlier, this self-calming is the newborn's first
achievement of independence. Infants ages 5 and 6 months both initiate
and turn away from interaction with their parent—another sign of
autonomy. Once infants and toddlers become mobile, this mobility
sparks new explorations and feelings of independence and autonomy,
accompanied by feelings of ambivalence. These young children are
testing new feelings of separateness, yet they continue to be pulled
toward their parent. Dependence and independence are a part of toddlers' daily explorations. Within a few moments, the toddler will both
push away Mommy and cling to her. "No" becomes a favorite word,
though often the toddler desires that which is negated. As toddlers test
both their parents' limits and their own growing independent actions,
this negativism is a natural phase of the developing sense of self.

Home visitors can explain to parents the changing behaviors that
they can expect in the coming weeks and months. When they understand
that their toddler's sudden refusal to cooperate in dressing is a normal
developmental phase, parents can develop accepting responses and at
the same time set boundaries. During her visit with Karyn and Don,
Janice discusses the changes they can expect in their son's behavior.

> *This is about the age that it will seem as if Greg [age 14 months] is saying
> "Oh yeah, I'll show off my autonomy." He'll test your creativity. [Ages]
> 14–24 months is one of the most difficult times with little guys. Another
> challenge—he's not going to want to do something you want him to do.*

This is something that is going on inside him, not like walking. He's testing, not in a nasty way; it is legitimate testing. It'll be important to prioritize what you never are going to let him do. He'll find all kinds of ways to say "No" before he can say the word. He will tell you with his body. It's called negativism. It's one of those things it's nice to know it's coming. There is nothing wrong with my child.

Home visitors have the opportunity to normalize toddler's negativism and strivings for independence and to help parents see these behaviors as central to the developing sense of self.

Parent–Child Play

Initially, everyday interactions between infant and parent are the setting for the infant's developing sense of self. As infants grow older, parents' focus on their infants' physiological regulation decreases. Now that their infant can experience new forms of shared experiences, parents' engagement in interactive games enhances their infant's developing sense of self.[24] From the beginning, parents and their infants engage in playful games: making faces, changing voice tone, tickling, and so forth. As the infant matures, these games are extended from gestures to simply play sequences. In these games, infants experience warmth, shared attention, shared feelings of pleasure, and connectedness; they have a sense of being understood and valued.

During their visits, home visitors can affirm parents' playful interactions with their young children.

Janice has just arrived at Karyn's and Don's home. As Janice, Karyn, and Don chat, Greg (age 13 months) walks about the room with a small toy car in hand. He then goes to his father, who hugs him warmly and asks him, "Where is your nose?" Don and Greg then play a brief game of Greg identifying and then touching his own as well as his father's nose and eyes. Greg goes to his mother, who says, "Teeth." Greg replies, "Teeth," as he touches his mother's teeth, then chuckles. He then returns to his father, who hugs and kisses him.

Janice quietly comments, "You are giving your Daddy lots of love. And he's going to soak it up, too." When hearing Janice, Greg walks toward her for a moment, then, chuckling, returns to his father and then his mother as he babbles with sentence intonation.

Since Greg's birth, Don has been very involved in parenting. Unless he is on vacation, Don usually is at work during Janice's home visits. However, Karyn often discusses with Janice her husband's evening play experiences and sometimes has specific questions from Don, such as suggestions for new play activities. Janice affirms Don's hugging and kissing as important ways of communicating love. Home visitors have innumerable opportunities to reinforce the importance of parents showing love through physical intimacy, for example, holding, hugging, kissing, massaging, and rocking.

During their visits, home visitors can initiate simple play sequences with infants and toddlers and invite parents to enter into this play. As they engage in interactive games, home visitors model healthy infant–adult interactions. As parents play with their child, the visitor can help parents understand the developmental significance of these experiences. (See Chapter 8 for a more detailed discussion of play, learning, and development.)

DEVELOPING SENSE OF SELF: AGES 19 MONTHS–3 YEARS

At about ages 18–24 months, toddlers can speak in two-word sentences such as "Baby cry. Me up." Now toddlers have the ability to refer to themselves as external, objective people (e.g., using verbal labels to refer to themselves, recognizing themselves in the mirror). Increased language means increased shared experience and a sense of togetherness between toddlers and their parents.[25] Independence, autonomy, and negativism continue. Erikson spoke of autonomy as the second developmental task, which, if not achieved, leads to shame and doubt.[26] As memory grows, pretend-play sequences are expanded (e.g., washing baby doll's hair and then feeding her). With multiple-word statements, extended pretend-play, and declarations of autonomy, toddlers have reached another developmental leap.

Parental Regulation

Parental regulation, including physical, behavioral, and emotional regulation, continues to be central to toddlers' developing sense of self. In early infancy, much of parenting involves physiological regulation such as regulation of feeding and sleeping. As toddlers struggle with feelings of independence and negativism, parenting involves increased emotional and behavioral regulation, regulating intense feelings and new behaviors that accompany the young child's exploration of self and others. Regulation involves not only clear limit setting but also clear behavior expectations and recognition, support, and verbalization of toddlers' feelings.

Encouragement

As toddlers begin to take initiative, parents have many opportunities to encourage their child's new strivings. As toddlers try to put on their own shoes and socks, strive to open the door, and climb into their car seat, for example, parents can positively acknowledge their child's effort (e.g., "You put on your shoes all by yourself."). Encouragement helps children recognize their accomplishments and know that they are valued. "Mom wants me to try to dress myself; in fact, I can do it." Encouragement involves specific feedback, describing the child's specific action. Home visitors can assist parents in recognizing that encouragement helps their child recognize success, feel a sense of mastery, know that he or she is valued, and continue to be motivated to take initiative. In contrast, global, evaluative comments, such as "good," "nice," "good job," invite the child to focus on pleasing adults rather than on recognizing the value of the behavior for which the global praise was given.

During the following home visit, Cynthia helps Sally understand how her responses to her son, Willy, can support and encourage his play. This is important for Sally to learn, because she often tells Cynthia that Willy always seems to be running about and getting in trouble.

> Willy (age 19 months) has dumped out the small, colored wooden blocks onto the rug. Willy hands two blocks to his mother, Sally, as Cynthia says to Sally, "He's inviting you to play." Sally says, "I guess so." She then taps the two blocks together, as does Willy, and they both chuckle.
>
> Cynthia remarks, "You brought him right around. He also likes when you imitate him. It lets him know you like what he is doing." As Cynthia speaks, Sally gently hugs her son. Sally and Cynthia then briefly chat about Willy's pattern of throwing things. As the adults chat, Willy begins stacking the blocks. Cynthia says to Willy, "You put them on top of each other. Yeah!" Sally repeats, "Yeah!"
>
> Sally evens the blocks on her son's tower as she says to Cynthia, "He gets so discouraged when they fall." Cynthia says, "And you're helping him so that he doesn't get discouraged."
>
> Sally rolls a block, and her son imitates her. Cynthia affirms, "That was neat. You showed him the roll. And that roll is a way to move the block, not throw it." Willy then puts a block in his mouth and makes a humming sound. Cynthia puts a block in her mouth and imitates his sound. Willy smiles and continues the game. Cynthia explains, "When I imitate his actions, I am telling Willy that what he does is wonderful."

Cynthia understands that Sally is a concrete learner. She describes what Willy is doing and in this way encourages him and models for Sally. Likewise, she describes to Sally what Sally is doing and how her actions are encouraging her son's involvement.

Gender Identity

By age 2, most children can name their own sex correctly. By age 2½–3, most toddlers know whether other people are men or women and boys or girls. This ability to label one's own and others' sex correctly is termed *gender identity*. Accurate labeling does not mean that young children have complete understanding of gender. Until children are 5 or 6 years old, they do not understand that people stay the same gender, even when they wear different clothes.

Sex-Role Identity

Toddlers also are developing sex-role identity. Sex roles are socially defined behaviors, attitudes, rights, and duties associated with being male or female. Sex-role behavior is behavior that corresponds to the culturally defined sex role. Traditional sex-role behaviors include mothers cooking and doing child care and fathers working and cutting lawns. Sex-role stereotyping involves rigidly defining sex-role categories. As more mothers of very young children work outside the home and as more fathers share in household and child-rearing tasks, sex-role expectations are changing. Nevertheless, remnants of sex-role stereotyping continue, for example, in thinking of men as independent, aggressive, logical, and assertive and of women as dependent, gentle, and emotional.

Parents want their children to develop to their fullest potential. Increasingly, occupations are open to both women and men, and both partners in a marriage more frequently work full-time. With these societal changes, young children can develop the behaviors, attitudes, and values that will allow them to be active participants both in the workplace and within the home. Boys can learn to express their feelings and develop caregiving skills, and girls can develop assertiveness and problem-solving skills. In order for children to develop to their fullest potential and take advantage of the full range of options that will be available in the 21st century, it is essential for them to know that both men and women perform a wide variety of jobs and that each gender is able to express a full range of abilities and emotions.

Home visitors can help parents understand that they are their children's primary models for learning how to be male and female. When young children's fathers cook or change diapers, or mothers replace electrical fuses or put oil in the car, these actions counterbalance our traditional cultural sex-role stereotypes. Parents also send messages to their children about how boys and girls should act by the toys they purchase for their children and by the kind of behavior they allow, encourage, or punish. Parents can provide a range of experiences for both their sons and daughters. Boys can be integrated into household tasks such as cooking and folding laundry; girls can assist in raking the lawn and assembling a toy. Both sexes can enjoy blocks, connecting toys, vehicles, dress-up clothing, dishes, and dolls.

Most parents do not think about sex-role stereotyping as part of their child's everyday experiences. However, television programs and commercials for children frequently reflect sex-role stereotyping. Males outnumber females. Women tend to be portrayed in submissive, passive roles. Like television, children's books often reflect sex-role stereotypes; for example, boys are usually main characters, and girls are onlookers. In the mid-1990s, more nonsexist picture books are available than previously. Home visitors can help parents recognize this sex-role stereotyping and sensitively discuss the issues involved.

Topics such as sex-role behaviors are value-laden and become sensitive in times of societal change. Home visitors always must be respectful of parents' values and must recognize that some parents value sex-role stereotyping. There are times when a home visitor's information violates explicit values parents hold, and, as guests, home visitors may choose to refrain from sharing information in respect for parents' values. On other occasions, home visitors may choose to provide information, but they always must honor the parent as decision maker.

Body Image

As toddlers move and explore their everyday environment, they develop new understanding of their bodies. Toddlers love to play games identifying parts of their body, "dance" to music, scoot about on four-wheeled toddler toys, play chase, and catch and throw balls. As they move, they gain an understanding of "my body in space" and "my body in movement." This knowing in movement is termed kinaesthetic understanding. Knowledge of one's body begins at birth. The young infant's mouth is very sensitive and is the first body part used for exploration. Much of the young infant's body awareness occurs within the parents' caregiving—soothing, stroking, holding, rocking, and so forth. Parents continue to be central to their toddler's growing sense of body image because parents provide the indoor and outdoor space for movement, toys, and games and participate as play partners.

Sexual Learning

Closely related to body image is sexual learning. Infants learn about sexuality each time their parents bathe, dress, and diaper them. In these everyday interactions, parents communicate to their child their own attitudes toward their infant's body. In order for infants and toddlers to feel positive about their body and sexuality, it is important for bath time, dressing and undressing, diapering, and toileting to be pleasurable times.

Infants and toddlers are very curious; thus, they want to explore each part of their body from all angles. All babies touch their genital area and discover that this touching is pleasurable. Because the nerve endings of genitalia are quite sensitive, children naturally experience a pleasant sensation. This masturbation is widely accepted as natural and healthy. Toddlers investigate their genital area with the same curiosity that leads them to poke at their nose or ears. Some parents, however, may not realize that the feeling the children have in their genitals is not the same as the intensely excited feeling adults experience in sexual stimulation. Very young children are most likely to fondle their genitals when they are tired, going to sleep, or listening to a story, not when they are excited or are learning about sexual reproduction.

Home visitors can help parents understand their children's sexuality and sexual exploration. Parents cannot prevent these explorations. Home visitors can help parents understand that they can be most effective when they adopt a relaxed attitude and accept the fact that their toddler will outgrow these explorations. If they are uncomfortable with their child's genital play, parents can distract their child with another activity. When parents criticize, punish, frown, or pull their toddler's hand away from the genitals, their child learns that their genitalia and the feelings coming from them are bad and wrong. Similar to the topic of sex-role behavior, the topic of sexuality is value-laden. Home visitors always need to be sensitive to and respectful of parents' values when approaching these value-laden topics.

Play

From birth, infants explore their everyday world and create new meaning from their experiences. From early infancy, the child participates in shared imaginative family games, musical interactions, and stories. During the second year, toddlers enjoy imaginative pretend-play, both alone and with parents. In pretend-play, they try out new roles (e.g., mommy) and create scenarios (e.g., going to work). They act out everyday experiences (e.g., washing the doll's hair). In this acting out, toddlers are in control and gain mastery over their feelings (e.g., about having their own hair washed). When parents join in this pretend-play, they can affirm their toddler's behavior, share in his or her enjoyment, and have opportunities to extend the play.

Social Development

At around age 30 months, toddlers can talk about feelings (e.g., happy, mad) and other internal states (e.g., want, hurt) in themselves and others. This ability reflects the toddler's emergent understanding of self and other that is the foundation of learning social skills. Studies indicate that family discussions about feelings and parental encouragement of their toddlers to share their experiences and feelings are important ways for toddlers to acquire this ability and promote toddlers' feelings of relationship.[27]

As toddlers develop motor and language skills, they enjoy playing with other young children; in this play, important social skills emerge.[28] These social skills are significant new aspects of the young child's sense of self. As they play, toddlers learn from other children's action and get feedback on their own action. Very young children usually play side-by-side, called *parallel play*, during which they learn through imitating each other. Parents play an important role in helping their young children learn to share, to take turns, and to take the perspective of their young friends.

This is a time when many parents form play groups for their young children in their homes. Many community organizations have programs for parents and their toddlers to come together for play (e.g., churches, YMCAs, community centers, some public schools). Home visitors can assist parents in thinking through possible ways of providing peer play for their young child. Often parents seek their home visitor's advice regarding this issue, as shown in the following example.

Shelly: Is it important for Erin [age 24 months] to be with children her own age, or is it okay for her to be with older children, like her cousins?

Janice: Erin could handle preschool, but it's not essential. The way you get a child ready for being 3 is by giving her what she needs at age 2. Most important is the child's secure attachment to her parents. Whenever Erin goes to school, she will be fine because she is securely attached to you and to Rob. You know how to teach her. You're doing a wonderful job. You don't need to force her to go to school. Some children need preschool, either because they don't have exposure with other children or because their parents are not teaching. But you and Rob are excellent teachers. And from what we've discussed in other visits, Erin and her older cousins have great fun together.

Erin plays frequently with her older cousins, and Janice reassures Shelly that this play is wonderful. When families live in areas containing neither neighborhood children nor relatives with young children, Janice informs the parents of the school district's weekly playtime for parents and their 2-year-olds. She also tells parents how some parents form play groups within their home with parents whom they meet at home visiting program meetings.

DEVELOPING SENSE OF
SELF: AGES 3-5 YEARS

Young children experience another developmental leap at around 3 years of age, when they begin telling stories.[29] Usually, these stories are autobiographical. Stories for 3-year-olds are typically family-centered. Stories for 4- and 5-year-olds also include cultural information never experienced, such as television characters, or characters from books, such as wolves and giants. With their new verbal skills and mental abilities of representation, young children see connections concerning time (e.g., what I am doing now, what I did before lunch) and connections in terms of space (e.g., what is next to me, what is in my yard). With this new ability, young children are gaining skills in self-reflection and delight in a new form of shared experience with their parents. Because of their age, young children do not always take the viewpoint of the listener; thus, their stories may have significant omissions.[30]

Once parents and children have developed a personal relationship with their home visitor, both children and parents love to report family experiences. These reports are good opportunities for young children to practice their skill in telling stories, as illustrated by the following example.

> Erin (age 35 months) tells Janice, "My Daddy comes home, but he has to work at the firehouse now." Janice asks, "What does he do at the firehouse?" Erin responds, "He goes out on fire calls. Sometimes he has some parties—when it's dark out." [This home visit is in January, and 2 weeks earlier the fire officers had a holiday party for their families.]
>
> Shelly suggests to her daughter that she tell Janice what happened last night when the fire officers were done with their fire. Erin replies, "Honk-honk-honk." Shelly explains that, before returning to the firehouse, the three fire trucks had passed by their house. All three stopped and honked for Erin and Shelly, who were standing at the window. As Shelly is talking, Erin runs into the bedroom and returns with a small walkie-talkie. Erin tells Janice, "That's where my Daddy talks."

Shelly and her daughter regularly report family happenings to Janice. Erin's comments contain omissions because she is not always skilled in taking the listener's perspective, for example, not understanding that Janice does not know that the fire officers have holiday parties for their families at the firehouse. As Erin tells her story, both her mother and Janice ask questions to assist her ability to add details. As she tells these stories, Erin experiences self-reflection, shared reflection, and enjoyment; and her language and thinking skills are strengthened. These stories are a vivid example of sense of self being socially created because, in her telling, Erin gains an increased sense of connectedness.

Young children sometimes are egocentric—unable to take another person's perspective. Other times they can be sociocentric, able to take another person's perspective. Research provides evidence that very young children often adjust their conversations when speaking to children younger than themselves.[31] For example, 3-year-olds use shorter and simpler phrases when speaking to their 12- or 18-month-old siblings.

Social Development

Infants' and young children's sense of self is based on relationships. As children reach 3 years of age, their relationships expand beyond their immediate family. Important to their developing sense of self are opportunities to play with peers. Up until this point, young children primarily have been relating to parents and siblings. Playing with peers is a young child's first relationship with equals. In this play, young children experience a variety of roles, that is, leading as well as following. They can receive feedback, model other children's actions, try out aggression and experience conflict, learn joint problem solving, and learn giving and taking among equals.

Because peer play is a new experience, difficulties inevitably emerge. Parents need to assist their young child to learn to negotiate—to use words instead of hitting, to take turns, and so forth. Home visitors can assist parents in understanding this process.

[As Erin (age 37 months) completes a puzzle, Shelly quietly tells Janice that recently when Erin's friend Kathy aggravated Erin, Erin pushed her. Shelly states that she is surprised to see her daughter be aggressive.]

Janice: You can help Erin learn how to deal with problems by herself. You can suggest that she use words such as "stop that." She needs to know that she cannot push, but that there is a way that she can deal with the situation. When children this age get together, they are going to have problems. Frame it in a positive way. Tell Erin that, if there is trouble, make sure that you talk about it. However, children this young are not good about negotiating. She also needs to know it's okay to ask for help from you.

Until she was 3 years old, Erin played only with her older cousins. Now Shelly has begun to provide same-age playmates for her daughter, who is her first and only child. Janice helps Shelly understand that Erin's difficulties are normal and that Shelly can assist her daughter in learning basic social skills.

Sex Play Children ages 3–5 years express their curiosity about body differences and functions in their exploratory sex play with peers. Sex play most often involves examining one another's bodies and occurs as children engage in simple role-play themes of family or doctor. Usually, parents can redirect their child's sex play. When sex play seems to stem from children's unanswered questions about body differences, parents can simply discuss these differences or read an appropriate book about the human body to their child.

Prosocial Behaviors Children at this age have new opportunities for prosocial behavior.[32] Prosocial behaviors include sharing, helping, and cooperative behaviors. These behaviors expand young children's experiences of self in relation to others. Home visitors can assist parents in providing opportunities for their young child to assist in family tasks and thereby experience being a valued and responsible member of the family. Young children can assist in household tasks such as cooking, setting and clearing tables, folding laundry, raking leaves, washing cars, and dusting. As the family eats a meal in which a young child assists, the child feels a sense of pride and accomplishment. Repeated household tasks help a young child develop a sense of social responsibility and an ability to respond to others.

As young children play with each other, much of their play offers opportunities not only of shared enjoyment but also of developing skills in sharing and cooperation. As more mothers of young children are employed outside of the home, larger numbers of children experience social interaction with peers in child care programs for longer periods of time. Observations of young children in child care programs provide vivid examples of spontaneous groups of children involved in prosocial behavior. The author's observation of young children's play in child care programs is illustrative.

Lucretia, Demetrius, and Jerry (all 4 years old) have covered most of the rug area in the block center with train tracks that they have snapped together. Over the tracks they build bridges with blocks. Each of the three children then pushes a railcar about the track. Twice they knock down the block structures and rebuild them.

These children have used train tracks and blocks to cooperatively build structures for moving their vehicles about. Their play involves give-and-take decision making and shared enjoyment.

Four girls, each with a hula hoop, have formed a circle. Emma seems to be the leader, for she counts, "1, 2, 3, 4, 5, go!," and then the children twirl their hoops. Emma directs the children where to stand, for example, "Lea, you may go over there. No, Cherise, over there."

Five girls (3 and 4 years old) are sitting in a circle outdoors. The children are playing "Doggie, doggie, where is your bone? Somebody stole it, run back home." Josie is the leader and tells the other girls, "Now lie in the middle" for a turn to be the dog. After about 6 minutes, Suzy suggests,

"Let's play duck-duck-goose," and everyone does so, with Josie again leading.

Jerome beats a rhythm with the palm of his hand on the bottom of a cylindrical container as four children clap and stomp their feet. Occasionally, Jerome calls out "Stop!," and the children do in fact stop. Then, when Jerome signals, the children again begin clapping and stomping to his rhythm.

In these vignettes, the children spontaneously begin a play sequence together. Emma, Josie, and Jerome are developing leadership skills. All of the children involved share in an activity in which they experience feelings of connectedness and delight.

Self-Esteem

Central to a young child's sense of self is judgment of self-worth, often termed *self-esteem*. Self-esteem is the evaluative part of the child's sense of self. Feelings of competence and self-esteem develop when young children experience repeated success in their activities.[33] There also seems to be a close relationship between children's cooperative interaction, prosocial behavior, and positive feelings about self.

Home visitors can encourage parents to provide a wide variety of play activities in which their child can experience mastery and success. Parents' everyday child-rearing interactions also communicate messages to their child that the child is valued and of worth. As discussed previously, parents' responsiveness helps their infant develop self-confidence that he or she can influence others—have a sense of personal control. Similarly, parental encouragement through positive descriptions of their children's behavior and achievements helps children to recognize their success, feel self-esteem, and continue to take initiative (e.g., "You carried your milk so carefully, none spilled," or "You used so many colors in your painting, it looks like a happy picture!").

Baumrind's classic research indicated how different patterns of child rearing lead to significant differences in young children's sense of competence and self-esteem.[34] Baumrind distinguished between authoritative, authoritarian, and permissive parents. Authoritative parents are warm and nurturing and provide consistent limits with explanations, open communication, and realistic expectations for their young children. Authoritative parents have children skilled in task mastery, peer relationships, and sense of self-worth. In contrast, authoritarian parents are low in nurturance, warmth, communication, and responsiveness, but high in levels of demand and control. Permissive parents are high in warmth, nurturing, and communication, but low in control and maturity expectations. Although authoritarian and permissive parents use different child-rearing strategies, their children have similar profiles: They lack initiative; have low self-esteem, little self-reliance, and low self-control; and are likely to be aggressive and less skilled in peer relationships.

DIFFICULTIES AND DILEMMAS

As discussed previously, the behavior of infants signals their parents to respond; in turn, the parents' response invites further infant behavior. Parent–child interaction is mutual and resembles a dance; that is, parent and child learn to respond to each other in the same rhythm. It is within these everyday "dances" that the infant develops a sense of self. Sometimes problems of either parent or infant or surrounding environment can impair healthy development of these mutual interaction patterns, with accompanying difficulties in development of self. If home visitors are keen observers, they can recognize when difficulties are emerging. This section addresses three types of difficulties home visitors encounter that may be beyond their expertise:

1. Personal problems of parents, which can impair their ability to be responsive and attuned to their infants
2. Infants' biologically based disorders that can cause difficulties in parent–infant interaction
3. Community violence, which threatens the safety and security of both parents and their children

Personal Problems of Parents

Sometimes problems in parent–child interaction stem from personal problems of parents, such as single parents feeling overwhelmed, two-career parents feeling overextended and overburdened, and parents experiencing social–emotional problems. Home visitors need to be alert to signs of maternal depression. Signs of maternal depression include low energy, poor appetite, sleep difficulties, and little expression of pleasure. Healthy development of infants is at severe risk if the mother is depressed, for depressed mothers express little positive emotion and much negative emotion. Furthermore, these mothers have low levels of communication and often fail to respond promptly to their infant. When infants are not able to initiate a response from their mother, negative emotions and a sense of helplessness develop. It is estimated that 10%–20% of mothers experience postpartum depression and that as many as 12%–50% of mothers with young children show evidence of depression.[35] When home visitors sense maternal depression, they become aware that the needs of this family are beyond their professional expertise. When the home visitor feels and acknowledges this, he or she can assist mothers in obtaining needed therapeutic help within the community.

Beyond simply conversing with parents, home visitors also interact with the child and observe parent–child interaction. Some parents may be able to talk appropriately with the home visitor, yet have serious shortcomings as they interact with their infant. If a home visitor observes repeated lack of parental attunement and responsiveness to the infant, they are observing serious parenting problems, which can lead to infants defending themselves by becoming apathetic and nonresponsive. Fraiberg explained that unresolved conflicts from the parenting of one's own childhood can be transferred from that old relationship to the new parenting relationship.[36] It is as if one's infant evokes these unresolved (often not remembered) conflicts, which Fraiberg terms *ghosts in the nursery*. Signs of this problem include the infant not responding to the home visitor's attempts to engage the infant and the infant showing little emotional expression (e.g., smiling, frowning). When parent–child interactions indicate potential ghosts in the nursery, home visitors need to assist the family in seeking therapeutic resources in the community.

Regulation Disorders

Home visitors also need to be alert to biologically based problems in the infant. Greenspan has made a major contribution to infant studies in his discussions of biologically based difficulties in infancy, which he terms *regulation disorders*.[37] Some infants' sensory systems are over- or underreactive, causing sensitivities in vision, touch, sight, hearing, or kinaesthetics (movement). Some infants have motor tone problems; for example, they feel very loose and have difficulty holding their heads up. Infants with these regulation disorders may be very fussy. In turn, parents who have difficulties soothing their infant may feel they have failed because they cannot engage in smooth give-and-take exchanges. Problematic infant–parent exchanges escalate the infant's difficulties. Often parents need assistance in adjusting their interaction style to meet their infant's learning style and sensitivities (e.g., varying their voice pitch for an auditory underreactive infant). Evaluation by an occupational therapist may identify specific regulation difficulties. Sensory integration often is a treatment for these difficulties. Study of regulation disorders began in the late 1980s, and many practitioners are not aware of these subtle difficulties in infancy. If home visitors can strive to be sensitive to infants' sensory reactions and motor tone, they can screen these difficulties at a very young age. Once again, identification of such difficulties warrants a community referral. Often the first referral is to an occupational therapist.

Community Violence

Since the 1970s, an increasing number of infants, young children, and their families have experienced continued violence in their urban neighborhoods. The United States has the highest homicide rate of any Western industrialized nation.[38] Community violence is an additional risk factor preventing healthy social–emotional development of both young children and their parents.

When young children live in an environment that has unpredictable, frequent occurrences of violence, they are unable to gain feelings of either safety or security—two essential milestones of early development. Clinicians and researchers give evidence that when young children are witnesses to or victims of violence, these experiences have a significant impact on the children's social–emotional development in the present and in the future. Behaviors associated with young children's exposure to violence include the following:

- Reexperiencing the traumatic event, often in the form of nightmares and repetitive play sequences
- Avoidance
- Numbing of responsiveness
- Increased arousal, involving hypervigilance, exaggerated startle responses, or night terrors
- Sleep disturbances and bed wetting
- Selective inattention
- Lack of curiosity and lack of pleasure in exploring
- Depression and perpetual mourning
- Avoidance of intimacy
- Minimal hope or interest in the future
- Trauma-specific fears, for example, fear of the dark, strangers, being alone, and vehicles
- Low tolerance of frustration, aggression, and impulsivity
- Lack of a sense of trust and security[39]

Parents themselves are traumatized by the experiences of violence surrounding themselves and their young children. It is difficult to be sensitive to a young child's behavior and provide the child with needed support and guidance if the parents themselves are experiencing inner turmoil from these same experiences. Home visitors can acknowledge and affirm the reasons for these parents' turmoil, listen, and empathically respond to them. Most important, home visitors need to be sensitive to boundaries of professional responsibility. When parents and young children are experiencing trauma, the home visitor must be skilled in knowing referral sources in the community that can assist these families.

The discussion of these challenges raises a dilemma frequently faced by home visitors, the dilemma of maintaining a working relationship and at the same time recognizing issues with which the home visitor cannot deal. Recognition of boundaries is central to this dilemma (see Chapter 2). What is important for the home visitor to recognize is that, even when a referral is made, the home visitor must continue to foster the parent–child relationship. After a referral is made, home visitors do not separate themselves from the problem. Rather, they develop the means by which to help the parents understand how their family's problem is having an impact on their relationship with their child and what needs to be developed to counterbalance or compensate for this problem.

CONCLUSIONS

Astonishingly, beginning at birth, the newborn is capable of purposeful action and of expressing feelings and relating to the caregiver. These behaviors point to the newborn's sense of self, the inner organization underlying the newborn's observable behavior. This sense of self develops only within the infant's interactions with her or his parents, interactions that are mutually created, with each partner influencing the other's behavior. With age, emerging patterns of behavior point to the developing sense of self. As the infant develops new behaviors, the infant's parents develop new understanding and new strategies for parenting their child. Table 2 portrays the infant's developing sense of self and the parent behavior that promotes this development. Once a parenting behavior is initiated, it continues to be an important part of the parent–child relationship. For example, the parents' responsiveness and physical affection given to a very young infant continue to be needed throughout the young child's development.

This chapter stresses how the relationship between child and parent is the foundation of the child's developing sense of self. In like manner, the home visitor's relationship with parents is at the core of the home visitor's ability to assist understanding and promote the parenting skills of the mothers and fathers with whom the home visitor spends time. Home visitors' interactions with parents affirm and support parents as well as provide observation and interpretation of child and parent actions. In the same sense that the parent–child relationship is formed by everyday child-rearing interactions, the home visitor's

Table 2.   The child's developing sense of self and the parenting behavior that promotes this development

Infants' and young children's developing sense of self	Parenting: Understanding and behavior
Birth–6 months	
Cycle of six states of consciousness	Mutuality in infant–parent interaction
Self-calming	Predictable expectations regarding
Individual differences—temperament	development
Qualities of sense of self	Physiological regulation
Capable of purposeful action	Assisting infant to self-calm
Experiencing unity	Adapting to infant's temperament
Experiencing feelings	Regulation of feelings
Memory and expectations	Empathic responsiveness
Attachment behavior	Physical affection
	Bonding and attachment
7–18 months	
Intersubjective relatedness	Respect and responsiveness to stranger
Shared attention	anxiety
Shared intention	Accepting child's lovey
Shared feeling states	Expanding child's language
Trust	Boundaries of acceptable behavior
Sense of personal control	Engagement in interactive games
Loveys	
Stranger anxiety	
Emergence of words	
Independence, autonomy, negativism	
Emergence of pretend-play	
19 months–3 years	
Multiple-word sentences	Behavioral expectations and limit setting
Extended pretend-play	Verbalization of child's feelings
Experiencing mastery and competence	Encouragement
Gender identity	Modeling and provisioning for sex-role
Sex-role identity	understanding and identity
Body image	Assisting in child's sexual learning
Sexual learning	Provisions for play
Play with other children	
Emergence of social skills	
3–5 years	
Telling stories	Providing for peer play
Egocentrism and sociocentrism	Extending conversations
Peer relationships	Providing family responsibilities
Prosocial behaviors	
Self-esteem	

interactions—supporting, affirming, and guiding—are the core of the home visitor–parent relationship.

There can be significant difficulties in the child's development and in the home visitor's ability to promote parents' understanding and skill. These challenges stem from three sources: 1) personal problems of the parent, 2) biological problems of the child, and 3) community violence. Clearly, the home visitor's tasks increase in complexity when encountering these challenges. So, too, the need for regular supervision, ongoing training, and access to community resources heightens (see Chapter 3).

5

Guidance and Discipline

The widow she cried over me, and called me a poor lost lamb, and she called me a lot of other names, too, but she never meant no harm by it. She put me in them new clothes again, and I couldn't do nothing but sweat and sweat, and feel all cramped up. Well, then, the old thing commenced again. The widow rung a bell for supper, and you had to come to time. When you got to the table you couldn't go right to eating, but you had to wait for the widow to tuck down her head and grumble a little over the victuals, though there wasn't really anything the matter with them. That is, nothing only everything was cooked by itself. . . . Pretty soon I wanted to smoke, and asked the widow to let me. But she wouldn't. She said it was a mean practice and wasn't clean, and I must try to not do it any more. That is just the way with some people. They get down on a thing when they don't know nothing about it. Here she was a bothering about Moses, which was no kin to her, and no use to anybody, being gone, you see, yet finding a power of fault with me for doing a thing that had some good in it. And she took snuff too; of course that was all right, because she done it herself.

Mark Twain (1855/1947, p. 2)

With so many changes in U.S. society, parents' ambivalence in directing and setting limits with their children is understandable. Across social class and geographical areas, discipline topics draw significantly larger numbers at parent meetings than any other child-rearing topic.

Many parents are experiencing the disappearance of certainties in religious values, in male and female roles, and in predictable income sources. Many families no longer live in homogeneous neighborhoods. Parents and school staff often do not live in the same communities; as a result, many parents may not be sure if they share the same values and attitudes as those their children experience at school. With increased mobility, many young families live long distances from their extended families and the support and guidance the extended families provide. In single-parent families and families in which both parents work outside the home, parents have little time to develop informal social support systems to draw upon for assistance. As they experience these societal changes, parents often feel uncertainty in guiding, teaching, and setting boundaries for their young children.

Some parents are ambivalent because they are strongly motivated to parent differently from the way their own parents did. As these parents try to parent differently, they may not understand young children and developmental principles and thus may be choosing inappropriate parenting methods unintentionally. For example, a young father whose own father had not been available strives to be his son's best pal and thus avoids limit setting, or a mother whose own mother was harsh and critical worries that she will harm her daughter's self-esteem if she is firm and punishes misbehavior.

The problems of violence are also central to problems in discipline. Violence is deeply embedded in our culture; it is the dominant theme in children's television cartoons, political rhetoric about crime and foreign policy, and the everyday lives of many families. There are two parts to the issue of anger and violence in parenting that lead to parents' ambivalence. First, parents do not know what to do and sometimes are frightened when their children are angry and violent. Second, they do not know what to do with their own anger and violence, often expressed in impulsive physical punishment. Although parents hear about nonpunitive, rational means of disciplining their children, the U.S. government permits use of physical punishment in the schools.

This chapter presents three themes:

1. *Parental discipline:* Teaching appropriate cultural and familial norms and setting limits
2. *Parental guidance:* Providing experience and assistance to enable development of understanding and abilities
3. *Child development:* Young children's development of autonomy, self-confidence, competence, and control

This last theme is the goal of parental guidance and discipline.

GUIDANCE AND DISCIPLINE DEFINED

Disciplining is a form of teaching; *discipline* is defined as "to train by instruction and exercise."[1] Parents are the mediators between society and their child. A primary task of parenting is to teach appropriate behaviors, attitudes, and values that will allow the child to develop self-control and relate well with other people.

Two primary purposes of discipline are readily apparent: "first, to stop children from doing something dangerous, hurtful or annoying to themselves and to others, that is, to *control children*; and second, to impart values—that is, to *teach children*."[2] Parents are most effective when they have both short- and long-term goals as they discipline their children. Obedience is the short-term goal and self-control is the long-term goal of discipline. The ultimate goal in discipline is the *child's* self-control. Initially, the young child obeys. Over time, this obedience becomes internalized; that is, parents' rules become a part of the child's conscience and natural way of acting and relating to others.[3]

Brazelton described three stages of self-control or self-discipline: "(1) trying out the limits by exploration, (2) teasing to evoke from others a clear sense of what is okay and what isn't, and (3) internalizing these previously unknown boundaries."[4] For example, first, a crawling infant is fascinated by electrical cords and goes to the electrical outlet. Her parent reacts strongly and negatively to impress upon her that electrical outlets are off-limits. Second, once the infant knows her parent will react, she will look to make certain her parent is watching before she reaches to touch the outlet. She is eager to hear her parent forbid her to touch and thereby is reassured. Third, after several months, when she comes to the outlet, she will shout "No!" to herself. Now the limit is a part of herself—she has internalized it.

Guidance is closely related to discipline. To *guide* is defined as "to assist (a person) to travel through, to reach a destination in, an area in which he does not know the way, as by accompanying him or giving him directions."[5] Infants, toddlers, and preschoolers are new to this Earth, with a very small amount of experience and much to learn. Parental guidance is an essential task in helping these very young children learn how to get along with others and to feel accepted and loved and thereby accept and love themselves.[6] Whether the activity is feeding, dressing, playing, or disciplining, guidance is embedded in parents' everyday interactions with their young children.

A DEVELOPMENTAL APPROACH

This chapter follows a developmental approach in discussing guidance and discipline. This developmental approach assumes that as new developmental accomplishments are achieved, infants and young children need new strategies of parental guidance and discipline to nurture their development. For example, helping the infant to learn how to self-calm is one of the earliest responsibilities of parenting. Once the infant begins to crawl, setting limits becomes a priority. As the young child develops symbolic skills in thinking and speaking, problem-solving skills are a major component of guidance and discipline. Although the need for a specific parenting strategy may emerge at a specific developmental phase, parents need to continue using these strategies as their children continue to develop. For example, children of all ages require assistance in self-calming (although the skill may be termed *frustration tolerance* once the child is a preschooler). Similarly, both children and youth need clear, consistent limits and problem-solving skills—limits so that they know the boundaries of safe and acceptable behavior and problem-solving skills to resolve their difficulties with other people.

GUIDANCE AND DISCIPLINE IN EARLY INFANCY: BIRTH–8 MONTHS

Beginning at the birth of an infant, a positive climate within the home sets the stage for positive parental guidance and discipline. Routines and schedules are central components of a positive home environment. Infants thrive on safe, predictable routines: periods of soft cuddling prior to sleeping, parents' soft talking during feeding and diaper changing, and parents' response to crying. During an infant's first 6–8 weeks, the infant's patterns of sleeping and feeding are not very predictable. After the first 6–8 weeks, parents can begin to adapt their infant's waking and bedtime feeding to their desired schedule.

Balancing the Needs of Infants and Their Parents

Parents of very young infants find that they need to structure their own lives to ensure enough sleep, healthy food, time away from child care, and time with friends and family that is not centered on their child. Then they are able to interact with their infant with patience and understanding. When home visitors are working with parents of very young infants, they can ensure that parents are taking care of themselves. Janice's first home visit after Greg's birth is illustrative.

> *Janice initially inquires about Greg's delivery and his mother Karyn's social support during the first few weeks. In her conversation with Karyn, Janice ensures that Karyn also is caring for herself. This is especially important, for Greg (age 5 weeks) has been very colicky.*
>
> Janice: *My third son was colicky. Even when it's the third baby, it's tough.*
>
> Karyn: *I did get out for 45 minutes to go shopping last night.*

Janice: You need to do that for yourself. It's normal. Also, you are having changes in your hormones.

Karyn: It's a more difficult adjustment not working. It's hard, not getting that feedback that I got when working.

Janice: And your husband wants attention.

Karyn: I told him, "At least you get feedback at work."

Janice: Nobody says, "You're doing a good job. I can tell—you are doing a good job. Have you talked with your sister-in-law?

Karyn: Yes, a little. But it's different for her. She has a good baby, and she is breast feeding.

[Janice tells Karyn about a forthcoming group meeting for mothers and their new infants. She suggests that the group meeting can help Karyn meet people with common experience who can support each other.]

Janice: When you have a baby who cries, no one knows what you're feeling. I know that's how I felt with my third one. I remember calling the doctor and asking if I was doing something wrong. He was wonderful, told me to call him back in a week, and he offered to give me something to help me with my hormones. The information helped me to settle down. Yet I still didn't want to hear [my baby] cry anymore.

In this first visit after Greg's birth, Janice listens empathically to Karyn's comments regarding Greg's colic and her missing feedback. Not only does Janice listen to Karyn, but she also addresses Karyn's need for support. With some parents, home visitors can suggest that the parents visit their own physician for additional help. Janice also shares her own parenting experiences with a colicky newborn. In this sharing, Janice strives to build a sense of connectedness with parents. Just as they share the intimacies of their life, she lets them know that she is a person with similar thoughts and feelings. Chapter 1 discusses this pattern of sharing by parent educators more fully.

Temperament

Some infants are born with temperaments that make self-calming a very difficult achievement. Temperament is the inborn characteristic ways in which infants react to others and to their environment. Temperament includes activity rate, adaptability to new experiences, response intensity, and general mood. Temperament affects not only the way infants respond but also the way others respond to infants. Infants express three distinctive temperaments: easy, difficult, and slow to warm up.[7] Different infant temperaments call for different parent responses. A need exists for a "goodness of fit" between an infant's temperament and the temperaments of his or her parents in order for healthy infant and child development to occur. Goodness of fit "exists when the demands and expectations of the parents and other people important to the child's life are compatible with the child's temperament, abilities, and other characteristics."[8] Parenting an infant labeled as difficult can be very challenging. The difficult infant is slow to develop regular sleeping and eating cycles. Difficult infants respond vigorously and negatively to new things. Difficult babies cry more often. Temperament patterns can persist through preschool years and, occasionally, through adulthood. At the same time, temperament is not fixed, but can be altered by the infant's and young child's relationships and experiences.

How parents react to their difficult infant depends on their own characteristics, expectations, and history of childhood parenting. Parents who are easygoing can adapt to a difficult infant more readily than parents who are intense and somewhat inflexible. Different styles between parents and infants do not automatically lead to problems. When problems do persist, developmental guidance can assist parents. For example, home visitors can clarify innate temperamental differences for parents. This clarification assists parents in understanding their new infant and in helping them have appropriate expectations.

Essential to parental guidance is availability—not only physical but especially *emotional* availability. When parents are emotionally available, they can respond empathically to their infant; thus, an ebb and flow of interactions involving mutual feedback develops. Brazelton and Cramer explained:

> In periods of attention, infants can begin to signal their mothers with smiles or frowns, with vocalizations, with motor displays such as leaning forward, reaching, arching the head coyly, and so on. Mothers respond contingently when they can read the messages conveyed in these signals. As a mother responds, she learns from the success or failure of each of her own responses, as measured by the baby's behavior. In this way, she refines the contingency of her responses and develops a repertoire of "what works" and "what doesn't."[9]

Along with emotional availability, parents need to respond to their infant's cues. That is, infant behaviors such as vocalizations, smiles, and frowns signal to parents to respond. In turn, parents' responses to their infant invite further infant forms of communication; then mutual communication and shared enjoyment take place.

Beginning with their first visit, effective home visitors are keen observers of how parents and their infant interact. Does the parent *respond* to the infant's vocalization (e.g., grimace, smile), and is the response a good *match* to the feeling state being expressed by the infant (e.g., pleasure, curiosity, discomfort)? The match does not have to be a mirror of the infant's behavior; rather, the match needs to speak to the infant's feeling. When the parent coos or cuddles the infant, does the infant respond with a similar emotional expression? Home visitors themselves can observe the infant's behavior and model for the parents responsiveness and reciprocal communication. In this way, they can promote parents' skill. This responsiveness and mutuality is the foundation for healthy attachment that gives infants a sense of trust, both in having their needs met and in their ability to signal their parents' responsiveness.

GUIDANCE AND DISCIPLINE: AGES 8–17 MONTHS

As infants begin to move, their behavior is no longer predictable and new parenting challenges emerge. Infants' mobility means the ability to leave their parents and discover their own independence. Independence may mean that the infant sometimes feels overwhelmed and may seek renewed dependence. Infants need to trust that their parent is available because this availability provides the security for the child to leave the parent. At around age 10 months, when confronting something new or uncertain, infants first look at their parent's face to check for the parent's expression to know whether this new situation or object is going to be fearful or pleasant. Psychologists call this checking with the parent *social referencing.*[10] The parent provides security for the infant to continue to explore.

With the child's mobility, consistent discipline becomes a necessary part of parents' love of their child. Given today's parental ambivalence regarding discipline, this is the time that home visitors need to help parents understand their child's need for *learning limits.* Such learning is dependent on parental discipline and guidance. Between ages 8 and 17 months, toddlers do not have the developmental skills to learn self-control; thus, parents' *external control* of discipline and the child's increasing *obedience* become very important.

During this phase of infant and toddler development, issues of control surface and often dominate parent–child interaction. Home visitors can assist parents in learning how to distract their toddler, which is an effective guidance strategy for children this age. Providing a substitute or alternative activity can refocus the toddler's attention and avoid angry outbursts. Instead of saying, "Don't grab your brother's block," the parent can hand the toddler another toy. The following situation, in which Karyn is talking to Janice about her 15-month-old son, Greg, is illustrative.

Karyn: *Greg throws things in the trash all the time, like my cookbooks. He broke one of my $30 frying pans. It's driving me crazy!*

Janice: *It's a difficult age. He will get through this, and you will get through this. He doesn't have the inner controls. He's into "I want it my way." Give him his own trash can. He's at the age where he loves to put things in containers. Anytime Greg is doing behavior that is frustrating to you, think of an alternative—something that seems similar that he can do, a trash can so he can pitch things into it. Something he can turn around, like knobs on toys. Otherwise, he'll be saying to himself, "Interesting, I can get a reaction from Mom."*

Janice responds to Karyn's concern empathically and gives her developmental information to understand her toddler's actions. She provides a specific suggestion to assist Karyn's skill in guiding her son. With this suggestion, she helps Karyn understand why her son is disobeying her. In turn, Karyn learns that Greg's behavior is normal toddler exploration and can accept it as such, rather than becoming angry at her son's disobedience or feeling guilty at her lack of success in stopping her son's undesirable behavior.

This developmental period often involves a tug and pull between parents and their toddlers. Daily tasks such as diapering, feeding, and dressing can become times of struggle (e.g., the infant's constant movement during diapering and dressing). Central to learning independence is the inevitable "no" response to parental requests. With walking, toddlers want to explore their newly discovered "walking world" nonstop, with no understanding of the danger of electrical cords, hot stoves, stairs, heights, and so on. They initially resist their parents' limits. With the onset of words come demands. These new strides entail ambivalence, which the infant expresses in sending contradictory messages; for example, she does and does not want to sit on mom's lap.

As the child becomes mobile, discussion of safety becomes part of home visiting. Observation and supervision by parents are preconditions of safety. When observing, parents can anticipate potential safety hazards and redirect their children's action. The following interaction between Jean and her 17-month-old son is illustrative.

Jean is folding laundry on the couch as Ricky rides his wooden horse about the living room. Ricky gets off his horse and climbs on its back to stand.

Jean: *Ricky, is that safe?*

[Ricky neither says anything nor gets off his toy horse.]

Jean: *You better get down, Ricky. The horsey might fall over, and you would bump your head on the chair.*

[Ricky gets off the horse and knocks the toy over so that it is lying on its side.]

Jean: *Is the horsey okay? Did the horsey get hurt?*

Ricky: *Check and see.*

Jean: *Check and see if he's okay.*

Ricky: *Horsey ouch.*

Jean: *The horsey has an ouchy. . . . Maybe you'll need to get the doctor's kit.*

Toddlers like Ricky constantly explore and experiment yet do not have the capacity to judge potentially dangerous situations. By being a careful observer, Jean was able to anticipate potential problems, an important guidance skill. When Ricky stood on his horse, Jean positively redirected his potentially dangerous action with an explanation that he could understand. Jean then used Ricky's action (i.e., knocking over his horse) to initiate an alternative activity: role playing that the horse was injured. Once infants begin moving, child-proofing the house becomes very important. Figure 1 provides a checklist for home safety that can be helpful to parents.

- Is the home poison-proof? (Lock up poisonous items or place out of reach of the child.)
- Are emergency phone numbers close by?
- Is bathroom safety-proofed? (Keep bathroom closed.)
- Are all sharp objects (knives, pins, scissors, etc.) out of baby's reach?
- Are all small objects (buttons, beads, hairpins) out of baby's reach?
- Are wall plugs covered?
- How about easily overturned lamps and tables, electric cords, and sharp-edged furniture? (Consider placing padding on sharp corners.)
- Are stairways gated at the top and gated 2 or 3 steps from the bottom?
- Is home safe from suffocation problems (e.g., plastic bags and soft pillows)?
- Are drapery and venetian blind cords, long telephone cords, etc., out of child's reach?
- Are there guards in front of open heaters, fireplaces, furnaces, etc.?
- Are hot liquids, curling irons, toasters, coffee pots out of baby's reach?
- Are baby's toys safe?
- Are all kitchen cabinets (within baby's reach) free from harmful items or safety-locked? Designate one drawer or section of a cupboard for safe items of interest to baby.
- When in an automobile, does your child always ride in a safety-approved infant car seat?
- Are guests' purses (which may contain medications) always put out of child's reach?
- Are smoke detectors with fresh batteries in place?

Figure 1.   Home safety checklist for parents. (From Parents as Teachers National Center. [1993]. *Program planning and implementation guide* [p. 157]. St. Louis, MO: Author; reprinted by permission.)

Another normal part of a toddler's exploration that emerges around age 1 year is biting, hair pulling, scratching, and hitting. The toddler does not initially understand that these actions hurt the other person. Effective parents respond calmly but firmly, telling their toddlers they may not do that; and they stop them until the toddlers can stop themselves. If a parent becomes horrified and overreacts, this overreaction sets the pattern rather than removing it. Biting is especially frightening for parents. Home visitors can help parents recognize that they need to help their toddler understand that under no circumstances do they allow biting. Substitutions such as dolls or teething toys can be given to the child to bite when the child needs to release feelings of anger and frustration. When biting, toddlers do not mean to hurt and are frightened afterward, especially if the victim was another small child who now is screaming. Parental response should include a firm limit and reassurance that they will help their child overcome this incident and that they love the child. Home visitor Janice discussed biting.

Parents need to understand that kids bite because it works. Biting is done out of frustration. Usually biting is to get someone's attention or a way to get a toy. Children bite because they don't have other tools to get what they want. Biting needs to be approached in stages. An infant explores with her mouth through biting. A toddler bites to get what he wants, for he can't talk very well. When an older child bites, the biting often represents a larger problem.

As infants become mobile, a primary task of the home visitor is to help parents recognize that, as soon as their infant begins to move about, parents must set limits (see Table 1) and then help their children follow them. Safety is parents' first guide and distraction their most effective strategy. As mobility increases, accompanied by independence and determination, setting limits becomes much more difficult; and, at this time, home visitors can give parents needed support and guidance.

Table 1.   Positive guidelines for setting limits for toddlers

- Choose the most important issues and limit the number of rules so that they can be enforced consistently.
- Rules should be reasonable for the child's age and developmental level of understanding.
- Tell the toddler in a positive manner what you want him or her to do. Rather than stating rules in the negative (e.g., "No running"), offer a positive alternative (e.g., "Please walk").
- All adults need to consistently enforce the rules at all times and in all places.
- State rules in a simple, brief, specific manner, and be sure that the toddler understands.
- Focus on the behavior. Avoid labeling the child negatively (e.g., "bad," "naughty," "dumb"). Instead, say, "It hurts him when you bite."
- Talk in a calm but firm manner. Avoid shouting.

Clear limits help young children know what is expected of them. Behavioral expectations make children feel secure. When very young children are tired, very hungry, or overwhelmed with stimulation, they are most likely to lose control and need parental limit setting. Parents can offer an alternative activity and divert children of this age. Some parents have difficulty being consistent in their limit setting. Open discussions with home visitors can give these parents the courage to persist even when they feel unsure of themselves.

GUIDANCE AND DISCIPLINE: AGES 18–36 MONTHS

Throughout their waking hours, toddlers continue to use exploration as their primary way of relating to the world. The toddler wavers between bold demands of independence and autonomy and intense periods of clinging and dependency. Toddlers insist on doing tasks without help, such as dressing or getting into the car seat, even when they do not have the necessary skills to do these tasks alone. As toddlers struggle with independence, they frequently respond to their parents with intense negativism. It is as if they are testing both their parents and their own newly discovered independence.

As toddlers explore their everyday home environment from their new vertical, mobile perspective, it is natural for them to be absorbed with feelings of independence and autonomy. Toddlers explore without stopping to remember limits. An adult blocking and thereby frustrating a toddler's exploration most likely will lead to an angry, aggressive outburst from the toddler. Home visitors can help parents understand that negativism is a normal phase of development and should be expected as their toddler navigates between striving for independence, parental obstacles, feelings of dependence, and fears of separation. If parents overreact to their toddler's exploratory or negative behavior, they may be reinforcing, that is, strengthening, this behavior because negative attention is better than no attention at all. Negative behavior that at first is merely exploratory (e.g., testing new limits) can become energized to continue if parents overreact. Often a toddler's "no" does not even signal a negative intention; rather, it is voiced as a declaration of independence. Often a toddler's "no" can be ignored. Sally's response to Jeff (age 27 months), for whom she provides family child care, is illustrative.

Jeff and Suzy (age 4 years) have just finished eating breakfast. As the children get up from their chairs, Sally says to them, "Let's brush our teeth before we go outdoors." Jeff replies emphatically, "No, no, no, no!"

Sally replies in a singing voice, "No, no, no, no." They enter the bathroom, and Jeff sits on Sally's lap as he watches Suzy brush her teeth. Sally tells Jeff, "Let's watch Suzy. While we wait, let's squeeze a little [toothpaste] on your brush." Jeff initially is restless, but as Sally continues speaking softly he calms down. Sally continues, "Now let's get it wet." Jeff takes the toothbrush and puts it in his mouth. Suzy finishes and leaves the bathroom. Jeff immediately goes to the stool in front of the sink and begins brushing his teeth.

Sally consistently expects Jeff to brush his teeth after eating and merely ignores Jeff's negativism. Jeff seems rebellious, frequently saying "no," as he tests Sally's limits and asserts his independence. Understanding toddlers' struggle for independence and their frustration with limits, Sally maintains her consistent expectations. Jeff follows through without resistance. Unlike Jeff, some toddlers do not obey; instead, they may have a temper tantrum.

Temper Tantrums

In this period of ambivalent struggle for independence, toddlers' inner turmoil sometimes erupts into a temper tantrum. Frustrated by not being allowed to do or get what they want, toddlers may roll on the floor, kicking and screaming. When having a tantrum, toddlers are out of control, which can be very frightening for them and difficult for their parents to understand and tolerate. Home visitors can help parents understand that tantrums are another normal part of development and that, even when in a tantrum, their toddler *must* accept their limits. Home visitors can help parents understand that they need to respond to their child's feelings and explain the reason for the tantrum. That is, parents should give their child the words to name how he or she is feeling and at the same time let the child know that they understand what he or she wants, but that now is not the time (e.g., "I know you are angry because you want to go outdoors, but you must take a nap before we go outdoors").

Children respond in a variety of ways to parents' assistance in calming down. Some children need time alone in a quiet room. Others need a parents' soft cuddling. All children need to understand that their parent understands how awful they feel. But a tantrum is not the way to get what is wanted. Once a tantrum has ended, parents can reassure their toddler of their love with a warm hug. As toddlers approach 3 years of age, if their parents have given them consistent limits, they most likely will have achieved inner controls and tantrums will have disappeared.

Parents can be embarrassed when their child has tantrums and may think something is wrong with their child or that something is wrong with the way they are handling their child. They can think that their child's tantrum reflects that they are not a good parent, so they may respond to the tantrum with their own anger and violence. Home visitors can normalize tantrums and help parents understand ways to handle them. Janice explained her approach.

If you say, "Does Joey have temper tantrums?," often parents will be defensive because they might be embarrassed about tantrums. But I still want to talk about tantrums at the appropriate age. Rather, I say, "How is Joey handling his temper?" I want parents to view it as normal and as temporary, and I want them to realize the importance of dealing with the emotion. For example, the child really does feel crazy, and parents need to be supportive: "I know you are mad." And that is different than giving in on the issue: "I'll give you a cookie so you stop crying." I want them to know they can support the child and still maintain their firm limits.

Misbehavior

There are times when no matter what strategy a parent uses, the child refuses to cooperate. Toddler struggles can be very difficult for parents. With growth in mobility and more mature cognitive functioning, toddlers begin to understand themselves as separate from their mother. Ambivalence and conflict emerge when toddlers desire to be separate from their mother yet want her to satisfy their wishes. At the same time, the toddler is a central part of her or his mother's own identity, and, as the todder struggles with independence, the mother is struggling with her own identification and separation from the child.[11]

When toddlers misbehave, parents can use *time-out* to allow both their child and themselves to calm down. Time-out can be an effective way to help an out-of-control child to become calm. In time-out, parents remove their child from all attention for a short period, until the child feels she or he can manage. Tracy's response to Mia provides an example of using time-out.

Mia (age 34 months) begins moving her doll's bed across the living room floor. Her sister, Maggie (age 18 months), tries to assist, but Mia pushes her away. Finally, Mia pushes Maggie so hard that she tumbles down. Tracy then tells Mia that she needs to go to her room if she can't manage. Mia shouts, "No!" Tracy then carries Mia, who is crying loudly, into her room. When Tracy returns, she tells Janice, "She goes crazy in her room, and then suddenly she comes out when she's all done crying. I tell her to stay in there until she's done crying." Janice replies, "It's good that you have followed through. You handled that situation so well. I hope that everyone could do it that well." Mia later returns to the living room and sits on her mother's lap. Tracy comments that usually she might have left Mia in her room a while longer. Janice explains, "The amount of time isn't the important thing. She just needs to have time-out so that she can gain control. You let her come out when she's feeling better; then you can explain to her what's happened. Sometimes when she's screaming, she can't even hear you. She has to first get it all out. Once it's all out, then she'll be fine. It's important that she knows you understand how she feels, but she still cannot push her sister."

Time-out need not be a punishment; rather, it is parents' strategy to help their child calm down. Once the child has calmed down, the parent can talk about feelings to the child. When a child misbehaves but is not out of control, time-out is not an appropriate parent response. Parents can impose consequences that relate to the child's misbehavior. For example, if a child refuses to eat any dinner, the parent can inform the child that there will be no more food until breakfast. Children's misbehavior can be a learning situation. With young children, it often is enough for parents to stop the inappropriate behavior and offer alternative behavior. For example, a parent can suggest to her 3-year-old son that he give his 2-year-old sister a toy to trade, rather than grabbing his sister's toy. What many parents find difficult is their need to be consistent and follow through once they address their child's misbehavior. For example, if a parent warns his 3-year-old that she must stay in the grocery cart or they will leave, the parent must leave when his daughter gets out of the cart, even when this decision is very inconvenient for the parent.

Toddlers gain security in knowing their parents will control their misbehavior. When rules are broken, toddlers need to know that there will be a consequence—a parental response. Consequences can be natural or a logical follow-up of the misbehavior. For example, when playing at dinner, Suzy spills her milk. Suzy then is responsible for cleaning up her milk—a *natural* consequence. Suzy whines throughout her friend's birthday party. Because she cannot manage, her mother takes her home from the party—a *logical* consequence. Often there is no appropriate natural consequence for misbehavior. For example, if a toddler bites, it is not appropriate for his or her parent to bite back. In these situations, parents need to acknowledge their child's angry feelings and at the same time let their child know his or her behavior is not allowed. Parents should then provide an alternative, for example, vigorously punching Play-Doh.

A calm home atmosphere with predictable routines, uninterrupted periods for play, and time for parent–child shared experiences nurture young children's development of self-control. As home visitors help parents understand what to expect of their toddlers and how to positively nurture their development, visitors can emphasize preventive discipline, that is, parenting that prevents the occurrence of misbehavior and prevents parent–child battles. Giving clear behavioral expectations assists young children in controlling their behavior and prevents misbehavior. When changes are to occur in routines, children can be told in advance so that they can be ready for these changes. Anticipating potential problems and providing alternatives can avoid struggles. For example, when a mother knows her son will be overstimulated if she takes him grocery shopping with her, she can choose to take him on errands that do not invite overstimulation, such as to the gas station or to the cleaners. When single parents do not have a ready support system, completing errands without their child may demand careful planning, for example, doing an errand before picking up their child from a child care program or swapping child care with a friend so that each can shop alone.

Giving limited choices respects the child's emerging abilities and encourages independence and autonomy. In the following example, as Mia (age 26 months) and Maggie (age 8 months) are playing, Tracy and Janice discuss preventive discipline strategies.

> Mia has just tossed a wooden square across the floor. Her mother tells her, "Don't throw. It may hurt Maggie." Mia then returns to the shape-sorter truck and places a green triangular shape in the appropriate space. As Mia is playing, Janice comments to Tracy, "When Mia gets ready to throw, it is good to head her off at the pass. That is, tell her what she can do—before she gets herself into trouble." A few moments later Tracy gives Mia a cracker to eat. As Mia sits on her mother's lap, eating her cracker, Tracy says to her, "Crackers all over. We'll need to vacuum."

> Mia: I'll help.

> Janice: It's important for children to realize consequences of what they do—not punishment. If I spill something, "I'll help clean it up."

> Tracy: She's driving me nuts—getting her dressed in the morning. I give her choices, but she'll want something else.

> Janice: You need to choose your battles—what matters. Possibly you could take turns. Yesterday it was your turn [to choose the clothing]. Two-year-olds are beginning to understand taking turns. I'm not saying it'll be a lot easier. But it also can help her understand turns.

> Tracy: She wants to do everything herself.

> Janice: And it's frustrating for you. You are wise to give her limited choices, even if she chooses a third. Limited choices, instead of, for example, "What do you want for breakfast?" It's important if a choice is

offered, you can let her have what she chooses. When we give children choices, we are nurturing their decision-making process. Psychologists talk about it as autonomy. There is an underlying developmental issue in giving choices. Just remember, it's not part of her personality, but part of her development!

In this conversation, Janice achieves a healthy balance as she affirms Tracy's parenting actions, interprets the developmental meaning of 2-year-olds' actions, and gives suggestions related to Tracy's ongoing parenting dilemmas.

Fears

As the sense of self and sense of outside world expand, fears such as fears of strange places, loud noises, Halloween masks, or specific animals may develop. Home visitors can help parents understand that all young children sometimes are fearful. Janice's response to one parent's concern about her daughter's fear illustrates how a home visitor can assist parents in this area.

As Erin (age 30 months) plays, her mother, Shelly, softly tells Janice, "Erin seems to be afraid of men. At the grocery, an elderly man talked to Erin, took her arm, and playfully said, 'Why don't you come home with me?' I thought he was being playful, but Erin seemed frightened."

Janice: *Fears are quite typical for children Erin's age.*

Shelly: *I told Erin, "Did he scare you? He didn't mean to." And I left it at that. Later I told her that if a stranger touches you, you need to get me. But then my brother-in-law, who Erin knows real well, walked into our home, and Erin cried.*

Janice: *This is very typical. Don't try to talk her out of it. Tell her to come to you, just as you did. Let her know that you'll keep her safe. Don't discount her feelings. She really is afraid. It's her age, and it's a piece of development. It's very important never to belittle her feelings.*

Shelly: *I have a tendency to say, "Don't be wimpy."*

Janice: *Her fears are very real. And at this age, fantasy and reality are not separated.*

As Shelly describes her daughter's fears, Janice helps Shelly understand that fears are a normal part of development and that parents need to respect their child's fears. Within the context of a parent's concern, Janice is able to provide developmental information (i.e., "Fears are real at this age") and suggestions (i.e., "Let her know you'll keep her safe").

Home visitors can help parents understand that they cannot eliminate their young children's fears, but they can help them understand and learn how to deal with their fear. For example, parents can respect their son's fear of monsters by explaining to him that monsters are make-believe and that they (i.e., his parents) are in a nearby room and will add a nightlight to his room. It is helpful for parents to know that fears are a normal phase that will pass if they do not overreact. Parents' overreaction can validate and reinforce young children's fear. As a child's world expands, the child experiences new fears, for example, the loud noise of fire engines or the unpredictability of a neighbor's dog. When parents recognize what their young child fears, they often can prepare their child and let their child know they are present to protect him or her. Similarly, parents can limit television viewing and be with their child during potentially scary programs. Young children sometimes have nightmares, which also are a normal phase of development. Home visitors can help parents understand that they can calmly and quietly awaken their child and offer comfort, which usually allows the child to return to sleep. Nightmares most often occur following stressful days.

GUIDANCE AND DISCIPLINE: AGES 3–5 YEARS

Negativism, tantrums, and recurrent parent–child struggles diminish as the child turns 3, and the calmness of early infancy reappears. Given their verbal and intellectual ability, 3-year-olds delight in shared experiences with others. Dinners with 3-year-olds can be an enjoyable, shared family experience. Feelings now have words. Children can carry on internal dialogues, plan their play, use words as substitutes for objects or people in role-play, and begin to control their own behavior. Three-year-olds can tell a story with a dramatic story line and a beginning, middle, and end.[12] Their stories usually are autobiographical.

Beginning at age 3 years, preschoolers have expanded experiences with others their own age. In these experiences, they learn new patterns of behavior from their peers and try out their own actions. Conflict and emerging aggression are common, especially when the preschooler is frustrated by her or his peers. At the same time, preschoolers develop skills in sharing, turn taking, and cooperative play.

Simple Explanations and Alternative Action
With the child's increased verbal skills and beginning reasoning skills, parents can give simple explanations with suggested alternative action as they redirect their child; for example, "Throwing your ball in the

house will break the lamps. Let's go outdoors to throw." In other words, parents should give reasons for their limits. Reasons help children develop standards of right and wrong. Parents can verbalize their child's feelings and thereby help their child recognize his or her feelings, a first step in controlling one's emotions. For example, when her child grabs her sister's doll, the mother can say, "I know you're angry because you want the doll." Parents also can help their child know they will help solve the problem, for example, "When Lucretia is finished, I'll make sure you get the doll."

Sexual Curiosity and Increased Aggression

Parenting 4- and 5-year-olds involves some new challenges. As the sense of self and sense of the outside world expand, sexual curiosity and increased aggression emerge. Four- and five-year-olds are fascinated by aggressive television super heroes, ghosts, and monsters. Given the high proportion of violence on children's commercial television programming, preschoolers benefit from having their television viewing limited and monitored by their parents. Home visitors experience a dilemma when approaching this topic with parents who have their television on all the time whose child frequently watches television alone. In these situations, home visitors need to remember that their role is not to change family patterns, but to support families and provide developmental information.

Whining, stuttering, lying, stealing, swearing, and masturbating emerge at ages 4 and 5 years. These behaviors often are exploratory and temporary. When parents overreact, their child's behavior may become habitual. Four- and five-year-olds have some skills in cooperative play, but possessiveness, conflict, lack of sharing, and name calling also characterize their peer play.

Problem Solving

The ability to solve problems is a powerful skill in maintaining self-control and can be a guiding principle of discipline for preschoolers. The 3-, 4-, and 5-year-olds have the verbal and cognitive skills needed to participate in solving misbehavior problems. As parents include their child in this process, they are respecting and valuing their child's perspective. Children can be encouraged to think of alternative solutions to grabbing, hitting, racing in the house, and so on. Home visitors can assist parents in understanding that, when solving problems, their child can develop a sense of responsibility for her or his actions. Young children need their parents' assistance to think of alternatives.

Just as parents strive toward nurturing problem-solving skills in their young children, so, too, home visitors can strive to approach parents' discipline questions as opportunities to solve problems jointly with them. If a parent's question about discipline can be solved jointly, the parent can own the solutions. The following situation illustrates this approach to home visiting.

Samantha's mother, LeToya, comments to Janice, "We've had problems with Samantha [age 38 months] sleeping in her bed, going to sleep. Last night she lay in her bed and screamed for an hour."

Janice: Do you have a routine?

LeToya: We read a story and get a drink of water before bed. She wants a light on.

Janice: Was there anything different yesterday? What about her food?

LeToya: We had roast, potatoes, and carrots, and she loves roast. Last night we ate later than usual—8:00.

Janice: When do you usually eat?

LeToya: About 6:00. But last night we ran errands before dinner.

Janice: Children this age have no sense of clock time, rather a sense of event time. It sounds like you've figured it out—having such an unusually late dinner. She probably knows that after dinner, she gets to play. Maybe not having play time had something to do with it. Small children are hooked on routines. I would encourage you to stick to routines, of having the same thing happen in the same order every night. Then she'll know that falling asleep is the last step in what is supposed to happen.

Janice strives to support and empower parents and at the same time offer developmentally appropriate strategies. She asks parents what they have tried and does not hesitate to probe the situation so that she can understand what is going on in the family. She explained:

You want to get all the alternatives on the table. And in the discussion, you can intersperse your own ideas. But you want the parent to come up with the solution. I try not to make many suggestions. Rather, I try to point out strong points of the parent and build on that. They are more likely to use these comments of mine than a suggestion. If I were to give a lot of suggestions, I doubt if they would be remembered. But also, our primary task is empowerment. I have learned that parents respond much better if an idea is coming from them rather than from me. For example, when figuring out a problem, I search for a way to say, "That's probably it; you figured it out." I might highlight something on a handout, or I might frame a suggestion as "Some parents have found it helps if. . . ."

Beyond discussions with parents, home visitors can model effective guidance and discipline as they engage in activities with young children. In her interactions, Janice is a skillful model. She frequently anticipates problems and redirects children with alternative actions. If a child does misbehave, she positively redirects the child with a simple explanation. When a child is frustrated or angry, Janice verbalizes the child's feelings and thereby helps the child recognize and accept her or his feelings. Throughout her interactions, she frequently describes the child's actions and thereby affirms the child.

Conscience Development

This discussion of guidance and discipline began by emphasizing that the long-term goal of discipline is children's development of self-control. Children develop self-control as they internalize (i.e., make their own) the limits that parents give them. This process is called conscience development.[13] The young child's understanding of self and others forms the foundation for conscience. The way significant adults relate to young children affects the way these children think of themselves and others. These adults must understand the child's experience from the child's perspective and restructure episodes by stating both feelings and intention. Young children's misbehavior is the perfect setting for adults to help children understand their feelings. If a conflict erupts, the episode can be reconstructed with the child's feelings and intentions stated. For example, a parent can tell her daughter, "I know you are angry because you wanted the truck and it's very hard to wait; but Wanda is playing with it now. I'll make certain you too get a turn." These are the sequences that become the foundation for conscience. Being cared for is the prerequisite for caring for another. Young children know they are cared for when adults verbalize their feelings and intentions.

DILEMMAS AND DIFFICULTIES

Methods of Discipline

Parents most often parent in the manner in which they were parented as young children. Our society has a long history of spanking as the appropriate response to misbehavior: "Spare the rod and spoil the child." When home visitors work with parents who take for granted that spanking is their right and is the most appropriate form of discipline, the visitor is confronted with a challenging task: "How can I empower these young parents and at the same time inform them of alternative methods of discipline?" Many parents do not know methods of discipline other than spanking. Home visitors can suggest that parents can leave the grocery store rather than hit their misbehaving child. Parents can calmly tell their child that he will go to school in his pajamas if he refuses to get dressed, because his dad cannot be late for work. It always is important that first the home visitor find specific parenting that can be affirmed. Second, the visitor must remember that parents are the ultimate decision makers, and the visitor merely can share new information. As they chat with parents, visitors can share some of the negative results of physical punishment (see Table 2).

Rewards

Home visitors often are challenged by those parents who rely on rewards to guide their young child. As with the topic of punishment, visitors can inform parents of the negative consequences of excessive use of rewards. They can emphasize that rewarding a child inhibits self-direction. Rewards can undermine a child's motivation: Children learn to act in order to gain a reward rather than gain pleasure from activities and accomplishments in and of themselves. When a young child repeatedly receives rewards, the absence of reward can feel like punishment. In order for a reward to be an effective way to control a child's behavior, children must be unable to acquire the reward on their own; in other words, they must remain dependent on their parents. In reality, as children grow older, they become increasingly able get their own rewards, for example, earning their own money to go to the movies.

Praise

General evaluative praise responses can have similar negative effects on a young child. Repeating slogans such as "Good boy," "Good job," and "Nice girl" communicate to young children that they are pleasing the adult; thus, they may foster short-term obedience. These comments tell children nothing about themselves, except that they are pleasing

Table 2. Potential problems in use of physical punishment

- Children learn by observation. Parents model aggression and violence when they physically punish their child.
- When they are spanked, children can experience strong underlying messages such as rejection.
- Physical punishment does not guide young children toward behavior their parent considers right.
- Physical punishment works only as long as the parent is present.
- The memory of being hit is remembered more than the misbehavior that triggered the physical punishment.
- Physical punishment is no longer an effective control method once the child is an adolescent.
- A child who behaves only in response to spanking is being set up for problems in school, because many schools do not allow teachers to spank.

the adult. These general praise statements do not contribute to a young child's self-reliance, self-direction, or self-control. One long-term goal is for children to recognize their accomplishments and be pleased with themselves. Home visitors can help parents learn how their specific, positive descriptions of their child's actions not only are rewarding but also are helping their child recognize her or his own accomplishments and feelings of self-worth. Such comments offer encouragement, for example, "You can put on your shoes and socks without any help! I'm proud of you." Young children thrive on their parents' recognition of their good behavior. It is a challenging task for home visitors to emphasize the importance of parents' positive responses to their child's good behavior and at the same time help parents learn ways to be positive without using external rewards or global praise, which foster dependence.

CONCLUSIONS

This chapter began by describing how many parents are ambivalent in directing, redirecting, and setting limits for their young children. Of all possible child-rearing topics, home visitors can be certain that parents will be eager to discuss guidance and discipline. At the same time, home visitors need to recognize that this is an area where parents feel vulnerable. Possibly, parents are disciplining in the manner in which they were parented as a young child. If so, a critique of their methods is a critique of their family heritage. If a child is out of control, parents may see this misbehavior as a reflection of their own incompetence and thus be very sensitive. Home visitors need to approach this topic with sensitivity and respect. If parents do not feel respected, they cannot hear and integrate the home visitor's information and guidance.

Home visitors need to be knowledgeable of the different guidance and discipline strategies needed for different periods of the infant's and young child's development. Table 3 portrays the progression of infant development and accompanying parental guidance and discipline needed to promote this development. It is important to recognize that parenting behaviors continue to be needed as the infant develops. For example, during the infant's first 8 months, parents need to be emotionally available and responsive and to engage in reciprocal communication. These parenting behaviors remain important strategies in promoting toddlers' and young children's development.

The home visitor's task is indeed complex. First, the home visitor needs an understanding of infants', toddlers', and young children's development. Second, the home visitor needs knowledge of appropriate guidance and discipline strategies to promote this development.

Third, the home visitor needs to be able to develop an accepting, nurturing relationship through which the visitor can support, affirm, and guide young parents.

Table 3. Progression of infant development and accompanying parental guidance and discipline

Developmental patterns	Guidance and discipline strategies
Birth–8 months	

Crying as response to discomfort
Vocalizations, gestures, and body
   movements
Expressing different temperaments
	Positive home climate
	Helping infant self-calm
	Emotional availability
	Observation
	Contingent responsiveness
	Reciprocal communication
	Adapting own behavior to infant's
	   temperament

8–17 months	
Mobility Independence and autonomy Social referencing Exploration Dependence Biting, hitting, hair pulling	Home safety precautions Anticipation of potential problems Distraction; alternative suggestions Limit setting: Clear behavioral expectations Consistency
18–36 months	

Independence and autonomy; clinging
   dependency
Exploration
Negativism
Temper tantrums
Simple role-play
Fear
	Verbalization of child's feelings and
	   intentions
	Time-out
	Giving limited choices
	Natural and logical consequences
	Assigning family responsibilities
	Ignoring minor behavior
	Respecting and valuing child's perspective

3–5 years	
Verbal skills Cognitive skills Extended role-play Aggression Whining, lying, swearing, stealing Problem solving	Simple explanations accompanying limits Assisting child in problem solving Monitoring and limiting television viewing Providing experiences with peers Assisting child in conflict resolution

6

Communication
and Language

*I noticed that people would name some object and then turn towards whatever it was
that they had named. I watched them and understood that the sound they made when
they wanted to indicate that particular thing was the name which they gave to it, and
their actions clearly showed what they meant, for there is a kind of universal language,
consisting of expressions of the face and eyes, gestures and tones of voice, which can
show whether a person means to ask for something and get it, or refuse it and have
nothing to do with it. So, by hearing words arranged in various phrases and constantly
repeated, I gradually pieced together what they stood for, and when my tongue had
mastered the pronunciation, I began to express my wishes by means of them. In this way
I made my wants known to my family and they made theirs known to me, and I took a
further step into the stormy life of human society, although I was still subject to the
authority of my parents and the will of my elders.*

St. Augustine (c. 396–397 A.D./
1961, p. 29)

Parent educators know that communication and language are the foundation of a young child's development. The developmental process follows a continuum: Beginning at birth, infants communicate nonverbally
with their parents; then infants develop language, and, as preschoolers,
they become literate. This chapter gives a brief developmental overview

of communication and language and discusses how home visitors can address these developmental areas in their work with young children and their parents.

COMMUNICATION AND LANGUAGE

Communication is sending messages back and forth. We communicate when we let people know what we want and what we are thinking. Communication can be expressed in many ways: a baby's cry or smile, a parent's praise, a singer's style, or a couple dancing.

Language is a shared, rule-governed social system that is capable of symbolically representing thoughts. Language makes it possible for us to express and understand a wide variety of messages. For normally developing children, language emerges spontaneously in social settings as a means of communicating.[1] Language originates from everyday interaction.[2] It can seem like a vocal tennis game, with all of the repetition of words and phrases by child and parents. Language is not restricted to speech, for it also includes sign language and written words. *Emerging literacy* is the young child's understanding of the meaning of written words and increasing ability to use written words to understand and communicate with others.

Communication, language, and literacy focus on meaning. Young children experience meaning through social interaction, as illustrated in the following vignette with Tracy and Mia. Young children develop understanding and skills in communication, language, and emerging literacy through everyday social interactions within their home. Beginning at birth, infants learn to communicate when their parents feed, bathe, diaper, dress, and play with them.

Mia (age 26 months) is placing shapes on a formboard. As she places a triangle onto the formboard, Mia says, "There we go." Mia's mother, Tracy, repeats, "There we go."

Janice: *It's so good you repeat.*

Tracy: *I do it so much that Mia will continue repeating until I do, or she'll say, "Mommy, do it."*

Janice: *It gives her two pieces of feedback: She knows that she is being understood, and she is hearing the way the words are supposed to be pronounced without being corrected.*

PRESPEECH: BIRTH-10 MONTHS

In the prelinguistic phase of language development, from birth to 10 months, infant–parent interaction is the setting within which infants learn to express their needs, wants, and intentions.

Birth-3 Months

The newborn is prewired for interaction; that is, newborns have strong inborn preferences and behavioral tendencies to interact with others. Infants communicate from the first moments of life by giving positive and negative signals. From the beginning, newborns and parents repetitively interact. These interactions take only a second or two. The mother moves her eyes and mouth as her infant looks at her or cries. These repetitive communication patterns are the building blocks of regulation of infants' emotion and behavior.[3]

Infants are born with remarkable abilities to hear differences between speech sounds. Their abilities to hear sounds and voices are a central part of their language learning. Newborns produce sounds that primarily involve crying. Yet infants have several different cries that represent different kinds of discomfort. Beginning at their child's birth, parents are faced with the task of understanding what different cries mean.

Starting at about age 1–2 months, infants show pleasure by laughing and cooing; by age 3 months, they play with speech sounds, especially as they participate in vocal play with their parents. Play and having fun are key ingredients in infant and parent social interaction.[4] This playful interaction often involves imitation within routines such as dressing. It is also the setting in which infants learn what to expect from their parents and in which the parents learn what to expect from their infant.[5] Infants prefer to look at people's faces more than anything else. They love watching their parents' facial expressions change as parents dress, feed, and bathe them. Within these first months, infants learn to read cues from their parents' facial expressions and speech. Similarly, parents learn to read their infants' cues from vocalizations, body movements, and facial expressions. Parents learn that different cries have different sounds and meanings—for example, a soft cry for attention, a steady rhythmic cry for hunger, and a loud shrieking cry for pain.

Beginning with their first visit, even a few weeks after the child's birth, home visitors can help parents understand the meanings of their infant's vocalizations. As parents and home visitor discuss the infant's sounds, the home visitor can encourage parents to respond to their child's vocalizations; thus, the visitor promotes the parent–infant vocal play that is crucial for the infant's development of language and communication. The following conversation between Janice and Karyn about Karyn's 6-week-old son Greg is illustrative:

Karyn: *He makes moaning noises. Is that normal?*

Janice: *Yes. You'll enjoy listening to how his sounds change, changing into vowel sounds and then adding consonants. And he'll get responsive. That's something to watch for. You can make sounds, and he'll respond. He's not using words, but he'll understand taking turns. "I can say something, and she'll respond. She'll say something, and I'll respond." And smiling—waiting for you to respond—all that is reciprocal. Babies look for that. . . . Have you tried sticking out your tongue?*

Karyn: *Yes, and he does that.*

Janice: *That shows how responsive he is to you.*

Janice responds to Karyn's question and in that response provides both developmental information and suggestions to foster Greg's optimal development. Janice's statements are simple and clearly stated within the context of a mother's concern. In these answers, Janice has begun to talk about the most important underpinning of communication and language—namely, the significance of spontaneous give-and-take of infant–mother exchanges.

Ages 4–10 Months

Between ages 4 and 6 months, infants connect vowel and consonant sounds together in a string of sounds called *babbling*.[6] Infants are so delighted with listening to themselves babble that they practice these vocalizations without an audience. On Janice's visit when Greg is 4 months old, his mother tells Janice that now he can say "uh, moo, boo," but mostly "oh." Within the context of this mother's spontaneous sharing, Janice affirms Karyn and provides developmental information and suggestions.

Janice: *He's now stringing vowels and consonants together. [To Greg] You're used to having someone talk to you. I can tell. [To Karyn] It's good to imitate his sounds. It's interesting about language development. Babies babble in their own language. You can hear the difference between babies in Japan and America: The sounds coming out are the sounds of their own language.*

Karyn: *Really!*

Janice: *He's working on the sounds he needs for English. [To Greg] You are a good talker, and that's the best news!*

Janice explains to Karyn that infants change their sounds to sound like their parents' language. This pattern illustrates that hearing and discrimination come before making sounds.

During each visit, Janice and Karyn discuss the progress of Greg's language. When Greg is age 5½ months, his mother tells Janice that Greg now says "Ma," but she knows it does not mean anything. Janice then explains, "You'll change that for him. As you respond differently to different sounds, he'll learn that some of his sounds do mean something." In the winter, Greg has a series of ear infections. Janice explains to Karyn that it is important to keep close track of Greg's hearing, because it has a major impact on his language. When Greg is age 7 months, Karyn and Janice continue discussing Greg's language development.

Karyn: *He doesn't say a lot, primarily "da, da, da."*

Janice: *That's a change from last time. And he is repeating syllables; that is a big step.*

Karyn: *Every once in a while he'll say "Ba."*

Janice: *When you think about it, it makes sense, sounds in the front of his mouth: da, ba, ma. And now he is getting to the age when it is appropriate to begin saying what he is doing.*

When Karyn reports Greg's pattern of making sounds, Janice provides developmental information to help Karyn understand her son's progress. Karyn started the conversation about language. Seeing Karyn's interest, Janice is able to give the simple suggestion that Karyn can begin describing what Greg is doing. When visiting infants and their parents, Janice helps parents to understand how they stimulate their infant's growing skill in language and communication.

Janice's comments to another mother of a 7-month-old illustrate how home visitors can help parents to promote their child's language development.

Jene (age 7 months) begins babbling, and her mother, Natalie, imitates her sounds. Janice comments, "It's important to imitate her sounds like you just did. That is as rewarding to her as it is to you. What fun to get a response and to feel connectedness."

Janice's comments affirm Natalie's spontaneous approach to her infant; at the same time, she provides an interpretation of the developmental importance of her interaction to Jene's babbling. When imitating, parents follow their infant's lead as they match their infant's behavioral style and tempo. This parental response often encourages the infant to respond, and turn-taking sequences begin. Turn taking promotes the infant's developing communication skills.[7]

> Natalie picks up Jene, who smiles at her. Natalie softly chuckles in response. Janice helps Natalie understand how important these brief, spontaneous interactions are for the development of babbling. She says, "Mommy laughs right with you. It's important that you laugh with her. 'I smile. What is Mommy's reaction? I am hurt. What is Mommy's reaction to this?' "

Once again, Janice helps this young mother recognize how her responsiveness is developmentally very important to her infant.

A very large change takes place between ages 6 and 10 months. By age 5–6 months, infants can make consonant sounds. Between ages 6 and 10 months, consonant–vowel sequences produce a kind of syllable, often repeated over and over. This rhythmic babbling often has a sentence-like flow. Now infants often sound like they are making a statement or even asking a question.

Between ages 8 and 10 months, infants can understand single words. Infants understand individual words before they can talk verbally. This ability to understand is termed *receptive language* and lays the foundation for early speech. Now infants can recognize their name and turn toward the speaker. They can understand and respond to "no" when their parents use it forcefully. They can copy nonspeech sounds such as a clicking tongue or smacking lips.

By age 9 months, infants' vocalizations and gestures show that their actions are purposeful. Now the infant's sounds are no longer random; rather, their sounds are those of the infant's specific culture. Using gestures or combinations of gestures and sounds, they begin demanding or asking for things. In addition, infants play gesture games with parents, such as pat-a-cake, and copycat games in which the infant imitates the parent's motor movement, such as in the game "so big."

Within the framework of the infants' and parents' action and interaction, home visitors' conversations with parents help them to understand their child's development and their own pivotal role in this development. During the infant's first months, home visitors discuss how different cries signal different kinds of discomfort and how cooing signifies pleasure. Parents are encouraged to play sound and gesture games with their infant, to talk to their infant about the things they and the infant are doing, to read simple stories, and to recite rhymes as they hold their infant close to them. As the infant becomes older, home visitors point out the baby's rising and falling intonation, which is similar to the intonation of sentences and is a sign that infants are paying attention to the speech around them. Home visitors also call attention to the infant's frequent use of pointing to ask for things—for example, pointing to a desired cookie or pointing to the arm of a doll to show the parent it is broken. When infants are about 10 months old, home visitors make certain that infants can understand simple directions.

Janice's dialogue with Tracy illustrates how home visitors can help parents understand their child's developing language.

> *Maggie (age 10 months) makes repetitive sounds in a rhythmic manner as she crawls about the room. Janice asks Tracy, "Does she like to repeat sounds like that often?" Tracy responds, "Yes, it's one of her favorite activities." As she makes rhythmic sounds, Maggie puts her hand to her mouth. Her mother begins singing softly, "One little, two little, three little Indians . . . ," and Janice sings with her. Janice comments, "Rhythmic babbling is good for language development, for the muscles in the mouth. The occupational therapist who works with our staff says it's really beneficial to help develop those little muscles they need for talking. Your singing is a wonderful way of encouraging Maggie's exploring with sounds."*

In her conversation with Tracy, Janice interprets the significance of Maggie's rhythmic babbling and Tracy's singing, and, in so doing, she assists Tracy in understanding her baby's language development.

EMERGENCE OF FIRST WORDS AND JARGON TALK: AGES 10–15 MONTHS

Around ages 10–12 months, infants make giant strides in all developmental realms—movement, cognition, language, and social-emotional development. Now infants can understand many regularly used words, phrases, and simple directions, such as "Get the ball" and "Don't touch." Understanding language becomes an important underpinning for their emerging speech. Infants learn to wave bye-bye and can appropriately clap their hands and roll their hands in pat-a-cake. They can vocalize along with music and acquire exclamatory speech such as "Ouch," "Pop," and "Uh-oh." In order to resolve uncertainty, when moving toward a new desired goal, infants look back and forth from their desired goal to their parents and, in this way, gain encouragement from their parents. These gestures, termed *social referencing*, indicate significant emotional development.[8]

By age 12 months, infants acquire new skills in the ability to think symbolically, with accompanying gains in communication and language. Toddlers' early words are shaped by their social environment, that is, by the objects and actions associated in their daily activities with important people in their lives. Toddlers differ in the way they develop their first vocabulary. Some toddlers use an expressive style: Their early words are linked to social relationships, such as "Hi," "Want," and "Me." Other toddlers use a referential style: Their early words refer to objects, such as "Keys," "Ball," and "Mommy."[9]

Once infants reach the first-word milestone, vocabulary growth proceeds slowly. It usually takes 3–4 months for the toddler to add the next 10 words. The infant uses single words for many purposes: labeling people and objects (e.g., "Daddy," "Ball"), requesting objects (e.g., "Key"), requesting action (e.g., "Go"), protesting (e.g., "No"), greeting (e.g., "Hi"), and attention seeking (e.g., "See"). Parents delight in sharing with their home visitor their infant's gain in new words.

Karyn: *Can you believe that Greg already can say about 12 words?*

Janice: *Wonderful!*

Karyn: *And our favorite word is "trash." We took him to the botanical gardens, and he pointed out each of the trash cans for us. He also loves fans, but the sound he uses for fan isn't an English word, so we don't count that.*

Janice: *But it is a word if it's spontaneous, consistently used, and you know what it means.*

As Karyn shares her son's growth in vocabulary, Janice shares in her delight. Janice also provides developmental information to help Karyn understand her son's developing language.

When beginning to learn words, toddlers continue to use gestures or their body to communicate, especially when they are frustrated. Janice explains this to Karyn.

Karyn: *Greg [age 14 months] does a little head banging. The doctor said to ignore it.*

Janice: *He wants to communicate, but he sometimes can't and gets frustrated.*

[Karyn then describes how, during his bath, Greg became frustrated and began banging his head against the tub. She figured out he wanted to hold the shampoo bottle. Once she gave it to him, he was fine.]

Janice: *Your analysis is right on target. Babies this age are going to use their bodies when they don't have the words. When he learns to use his arms better, then he'll not use his head. It's like the developmental patterns we talked about when he was a very young infant—development progresses top–down and center–out.*

Head banging can be very worrisome to new parents. Janice helps Karyn understand why her toddler might bang his head. Her explanation sparks Karyn's sharing of a recent example of Greg's head banging and her response. Janice not only affirmed Karyn's response to her infant but also provided developmental information so that Karyn could better understand Greg's behavior.

Between ages 13 and 15 months, infants frequently string sounds together as if they were carrying on a conversation. Child developmentalists term this gibberish *jargon talk.* Home visitors can encourage parents to take advantage of their child's jargon talk by responding to whatever they think their infant might be saying, for example, "I know you like the way Mommy is washing your back." This taking turns talking in pretend-conversation helps infants learn the basics of conversation. Some children, especially those who begin to talk very early, skip this jargon phase. Others continue using jargon along with real words. Jargon usually disappears by age 2½ years.

Another parenting strategy that home visitors can promote is termed *parallel talk.* Parallel talk refers to adults describing what the young child or caregiver is doing as the young child acts.

Janice places on the rug a cylinder filled with small film canisters. The cylinder's top has a hole in the center. She places film canisters on the rug next to the cylinder. Greg (age 14 months) puts a canister into the hole.

Janice says to Greg, "In it goes . . . turning it [another small canister that Greg is manipulating] around." Greg shakes the cylinder. Janice helps him remove the lid, and he dumps out all the film canisters. Janice says, "Now it is empty, all gone." She then puts the top on the cylinder and Greg again begins putting the small film canisters into the hole. Janice remarks, "In it goes. Into the can." As he puts the canisters into the can, Greg looks at his father and babbles, and Janice explains, "Telling Daddy all about it." Greg empties the cylinder once again, and Janice repeats, "Now it's empty, all gone."

Janice then begins talking to Greg's mother and father, Karyn and Don: "When Greg is playing, just describe what he is doing. That helps him know you are interested in what he is doing. As you describe for him what he is doing, that is the way he learns words to think. It builds language connected with experience. Sometimes it might seem kind of boring to you, but developmentally it is very helpful. I also was helping Greg build the concept 'empty' and linking it with 'all gone,' which he knows—building his vocabulary."

Janice is helping Karyn and Don understand that they can foster their child's understanding of language if they describe specifically what their child is doing as he acts. Janice's comments are made as the child plays and are stated as both developmental information and suggestion.

WORD COMBINATIONS: AGES 16–24 MONTHS

From ages 16 to 24 months, toddlers' understanding of new words and simple directions continues to expand. They rely less on gestures and more on words to understand meaning. They absorb new meanings as they experience new words in everyday conversational interactions. Now they can understand simple, short sentences. They continue to understand many more words than they can say. Toddlers now understand and enjoy rhymes and songs. They love picture books, can turn pages, and begin labeling pictures. They can recognize and point to several body parts.

At around age 18 months, there is a rapid increase in vocabulary, which continues through the preschool years. The toddler's and young preschooler's language development follows a predictable sequence. Toddlers combine a word and a gesture, termed a *holophrase* — for example, saying "Cookie" while grabbing mother's hand. Then, between ages 18 and 24 months, they begin using two-word sentences to express an idea, termed *telegraphic speech* — for example, "More milk" or "Daddy go." Toddlers use this telegraphic speech for many purposes — for example, requests ("Stop it"), responses to requests ("Doll mine"), and commenting ("Daddy hat").

Parents have innumerable opportunities to reinforce and extend their toddler's telegraphic speech.

Janice and the author have just arrived at the home of Shelly and her daughter Erin (age 22 months). Erin says to Shelly, "Daddy, firehouse." Shelly affirms, "Yes, Daddy is working at the firehouse today." As Erin and Shelly complete the puzzle they had been doing before their visitors' arrival, Erin tells Janice, "Daddy cut lawn. Erin swing. Mommy push." Shelly responds, "Yes, last night Daddy cut the lawn while Mommy pushed you in the swing."

Shelly has learned from Janice that, when she extends Erin's speech, she is both affirming Erin and promoting her language development. These expansions often remake Erin's sentence with correct grammar. Shelly's response tells Erin she is interested and encourages Erin to continue talking. During this home visit, Shelly describes to Janice a recent errand she and her daughter have taken. Shelly describes how

Erin noticed and named the many items alongside the road as they were driving. She comments, "It's not often that we are in the car that we are not talking. I remember last year, you said how important it is to talk about what we are doing." Shelly has integrated Janice's information and now uses it in her everyday interactions with Erin.

Toddlers between ages 19 and 24 months love to label objects and begin to form categories of objects in their mind, for example, "truck" for all large vehicles, "dog" for all small four-legged animals. Now the child can understand simple phrases when visual cues are not present, for example, "Let's go get Daddy," or "Let's go in the kitchen to eat lunch." When parents read to them, they can follow the sequences within simple stories.

Within the parents' taken-for-granted everyday child-rearing inter-actions, parents often may not notice their young child's developmental gains in language. As home visitors interact with a child and parent, they have many opportunities to call attention to the child's growth in language and thinking. When Mia, at age 25 months, asks her mother for another drink, Janice comments, "Mia continues to express new concepts, doesn't she? Like 'another.' " When, at age 30 months, Erin tells her mother that she "can't" find a toy, Janice tells Erin's mother, "Using the contraction 'I can't' is complex language use for a 2-year-old." As Erin and Mia talk to themselves as they play, Janice discusses with their mothers that, as the children describe to themselves what they are doing or give themselves instructions, they are using their own language to guide their behavior. Parents' increased understanding of their child's progress stimulates their understanding, appreciation, and motivation to stimulate their child's development further.

From the beginning, children's language is meant to communicate. At the same time, young children learn to use language in private monologues to themselves to make sense of their everyday world and to help them attend to the task they are performing. In other words, young children's private speech is a tool for guiding and regulating self and problem solving.[10] Research indicates that these monologues are vastly different from dialogues. The book *Narratives from the Crib* reported the results of a study of the monologues of Emily and her dialogues with parents before bed.[11] These monologues and dialogues were tape-recorded for 15 months, between ages 21 and 36 months. Most striking was the contrast between monologue and dialogue speech. Emily's monologues were much richer and more varied than were her dialogues with her parents. In her monologues, Emily told stories of daily events that had happened or that she had been told were going to happen. She also recreated stories and created imaginary happenings. Some of her monologues were problem solving, sorting out her everyday world, and often were organized around daily events such as eating, sleeping, and dressing. Nelson, the book's editor, noted that Emily's monologues primarily served "the evident purpose of representing and sorting out her experience, using language to make sense."[12]

Most adults speak in simpler sentences and simpler vocabulary to children than they do with other adults. This pattern has been termed *motherese*.[13] Typical characteristics of motherese include short and grammatically simple wording, concrete vocabulary, and repeated phrases. As home visitors observe how parents' child-rearing interactions are promoting their child's language, they help the parents recognize these patterns.

Tracy: Mia [age 23 months] started talking at such an early age.

Janice: So many words and sentences. Tracy, I really believe that one of the reasons her language is so good is that there is a payoff for her. When she asks, you respond. You are the best motivation. That's wonderful.

Mia: [As the adults chat, Mia goes to her mother.] Tap, Mom?

Tracy: Hammer.

Mia: Go find it.

Tracy: I don't know where it is.

Janice: That is a perfect example. You don't correct her, but merely say the right word, "hammer."

Tracy: Yeah, she knows it goes tap, tap.

Janice explains that Tracy's comment is dependent upon what her child says: "When she asks, you respond." Tracy's response stimulates her daughter to talk more. In her interpretation of this mother's actions, Janice helps Tracy to understand how important she is in Mia's developing language.

Differences in timing of language development is normal.[14] Often girls' language develops earlier than boys'. Young children's speech contains immaturities typical of their age (e.g., errors in pronunciation), and this may be worrisome to parents. Parents frequently share these concerns with their home visitors. Parents may express a concern about what they call stuttering, but this is often normal dysfluency that many preschoolers experience as they learn language. Home visitors can help parents understand that their young children may sound like they are stuttering because their motor skills have not caught up with their thinking skills. The visitors can suggest that parents give their child time, that they try to ignore the stuttering until their child outgrows this normal dysfluency. As parents question and express concern about their young child's immature speech, Janice provides information and suggestions.

> Shelly: *I try to get Erin [age 29 months] to say words the right way. Is that stressful for her?*

> Janice: *Immature articulation is typical of children Erin's age. Let her go. At this age, your goal is communication. If she gets hung up on how words are said, communication won't flow as easily.*

> Shelly: *Rob's [Erin's father's] family goes crazy and are always correcting her.*

> Janice: *If someone is hung up about that, try and get her to say it for her without correcting, without making her repeat. You don't want to slow her down.*

In these conversations, parents learn what they can expect in typical child development and feel reassured that they are promoting their child's language. Home visitors can help parents pay attention to *what* their child is saying, not *how* they are saying it. They can help parents understand that their child learns to talk naturally, not from instruction.

LANGUAGE AND COMMUNICATION: AGES 2–5 YEARS

As toddlers approach age 2 years, their ability to understand speech increases significantly. They can understand 200–300 words as well as simple directions with prepositions—for example, "Put the cookie on the table." They can understand and respond to simple questions such as, "Where is your ball?" If they do not want to do something, they refuse by saying "no."

Listening is an important skill in language learning. Good listening does not simply emerge. Children learn to listen just as they learn to talk. As with talking, listening skills are learned gradually through everyday interactions with parents. Home visitors can help parents develop skills to help their energetic, active 2-year-olds maintain attention in listening. Respectful ways for parents to help their child learn to listen include the following:

- Keep your facial expression interesting.
- Vary your voice tone.

- Be sure to establish eye contact with your child before speaking.
- Squat down to your child's eye level so your child can easily look at you as you speak.
- When necessary, distract your child to gain attention, for example, suddenly whisper or sing a chant.

During their third year, children learn to understand most adult sentences. They can recognize and name themselves and other familiar people. They can understand and respond correctly to two related directions given at one time, for example, "Pick up your shoes and put them in your room." They can understand descriptive words such as "big," "heavy," and "fast."

Now young children can engage in extended simple conversations. By the time they are 2½ years old, they talk in three- and four-word sentences. They make simple requests, for example, "Open the door." They love singing songs such as "Jingle Bells" or "Happy Birthday." As children approach 3 years of age, they have a speaking vocabulary of 300 or more words. As they explore their everyday world, young children's developing language supports their thinking about this world. Language not only reflects what the child is thinking but also makes thinking possible.

Young children's simple sentences are creative yet also follow certain rules. Children begin using plurals, past tenses, and prepositions in a fairly predictable sequence. Similarly, initial use of questions and negatives follows a predictable progression. Examples are using "wh" words at the beginning of the sentence without the auxiliary verb, such as "When Mommy come home?," and omitting the auxiliary verb with a negative, such as "I no go." In addition, children express different meanings with the same sentence form. For example, the young child may say "Daddy hat" to connote "This is Daddy's hat" when she has picked up the hat from the floor. On another occasion, "Daddy hat" means "Daddy is putting my hat on me." Throughout the preschool years, vocabulary continues to increase and more complex sentence forms are learned.

In conversation, children as young as 2 years old change the form of their language according to the person with whom they are talking. A toddler will say "Gimme" as he grabs another toddler's cookie; but to his mother he might say "More juice." Research on children's conversations with younger children demonstrates that 3- to 5-year-olds are quite skilled at using simpler language when talking to younger children. These changes for the purpose of communicating better give clear evidence that very young children can adapt to another person's level: They recognize that other viewpoints exist.[15]

Once young children begin forming sentences, parents can incorporate spontaneous, incidental conversations in their interactions within daily routines, such as eating meals together, getting ready for bed, or riding in the car. Conversation includes joint attention and joint activity. In conversation, young children learn both speaker and listener roles. Conversation also involves taking turns. Parent–child interactions in early infancy and in games such as peek-a-boo promote turn taking, which prepares the way for later conversation. Home visitors can assist parents in understanding the value of conversation for promoting language, thinking, communication, and emerging literacy. They can help parents understand that because conversation symbolizes ideas, thoughts, and feelings, which in turn are grounded in experience, conversation promotes young children's thinking and reading readiness. Furthermore, as young children engage in conversation, they experience feelings of connectedness and shared enjoyment with their parents.

Not all parents know how to have conversations with very young children. Home visitors have many opportunities to model and discuss how to have extended conversations. On Janice's first home visit after Christmas, Erin's (age 33 months) new kitchen set was in the living room.

Janice: *This must be your most special Christmas present.*

Erin: *Yes. [She then picks up a frying pan and brings it to Janice.] A pan.*

Janice: *A frying pan.*

Erin: *And I have toy pots.*

Janice: *You have new toy pots?*

[Erin nods yes and then goes to Janice with her toy potholder glove on her hand.]

Janice: *Does that protect your hand?*

Erin: *No, it keeps my hand from getting hurt.*

Janice: *That's what we mean when we say "protect."*

As Erin speaks, Janice carefully listens. She asks Erin questions to encourage her to think and to continue talking. Janice has visited Erin and her parents since Erin's birth. Erin looks forward to Janice's visit; usually, upon Janice's arrival, she is eager to tell Janice stories. In turn, Janice replies in a manner to extend Erin's comments. Over the months and years, Janice has had many opportunities to share with Shelly the value of talking with her child. In turn, Shelly often shares with Janice her conversations with Erin and her delight in Erin's creative verbal constructions.

When parents engage in pretend-play with their young children, it provides a wonderful opportunity for promoting young children's language.

Cynthia puts toy pots and pans, dishes, and plastic food on the rug as she asks Willy's (age 21 months) mother, Sally, and grandmother, Donna, "Have you seen any pretend-play?"

Sally: *Not really.*

Donna: *He pretends to read and to talk on the phone.*

Cynthia: *Both are part of the beginning of pretend-play. Pretend-play would be a wonderful activity for you to do with Willy. Let's do a little today.*

As Cynthia gives herself and Sally a cup, she hands Willy a pitcher as she says to him, "Please pour some coffee for Mom and me." As Willy pretends to pour, Cynthia says to Sally, "See, he is pretending. You will see that he imitates what you are doing." Cynthia and Willy pretend to cook eggs for breakfast. She asks him for some juice and holds out her plastic glass, which Willy pretends to fill. She asks him, "Would you like some juice?"

Willy: *Like juice. [Cynthia pretends to pour juice for Willy.]*

Donna: *We used to think pretend-play was harmful to children.*

Cynthia: *It is important to use imagination. Pretending helps with Willy's language development. Pretend-play also helps with Willy's thinking and planning. He'll begin to pretend experiences from his everyday life.*

[Cynthia suggests that Willy wash and dry the dishes and invites Sally to help him, which she does.]

In this home visit, Cynthia has chosen a pretend-play activity, and she uses this activity to show Willy's mother and grandmother how they can promote Willy's language through playing with him. Sally thinks very concretely, so Cynthia provides developmental information directly related to the experiences that Sally is observing. On a subsequent visit, Sally describes how she and Willy have enjoyed pretending to go to the grocery store and cooking together.

Preschool children are active questioners. Questioning is an important way for young children to explore the world. When children ask questions based on what they see and wonder about, they have some control over their learning. They are actively searching for what they want to know. Through children's questions, adults can capture the inventiveness of children's thinking and explorations—for example, "Why do clouds move?" "Why do churches have steeples?" Home visitors can encourage parents to be active listeners and respectful responders to their child's questions. Visitors can model this active listening and can use a young child's question as an opportunity to extend their thinking—for example, "Why do you think the clouds move?"

EMERGING LITERACY

Just as communication and language learning are social activities, so too emerging literacy occurs within a social context—the everyday activities and interactions of parents and their infants and young children. This section uses the term *emerging literacy* to refer to the young child's awareness of print and its functions: Writing is used to express meaning, and the function of reading is to understand meaning. Studies indicate that reading is a process in which the reader draws on previously acquired learning to gain meaning from print.[16] Young children become ready for reading by looking at print in books and on signs and by writing and drawing.[17] Through these processes, they learn that written marks have meaning. Literacy development is gradual and is a part of the total communication process that includes listening, speaking, reading, and writing.[18]

The emotionally satisfying process of reading or reciting rhymes to babies while holding them close is the beginning of their emerging literacy. As the infant develops, storybook reading remains a powerful influence on the social development of the young child and parents. Additionally, the very young child learns that books are a source of enjoyment.

Young children have an easier time learning to read and write when they have experienced meaningful use of written language in their everyday lives. Early and frequent reading to young children can be one of the most important foundations in the growth of reading readiness. Emerging literacy includes listening to stories, reciting stories from memory, asking and answering questions about stories, and scribbling and other forms of drawing and writing. Many preschoolers spontaneously learn to read environmental print such as advertising logos, cereal boxes, and tee-shirts. When writing and drawing, young children experiment and developmentally proceed through exploratory motorial scribbling; purposeful scribbling that follows conventional writing patterns; mock writing; representational letters; inventive spelling; and, finally, conventional spelling and writing forms. This process of learning to write is an early phase in learning to read.

When infants are a few months old, home visitors can integrate story reading with picture books into each visit. With parents who have low literacy, Cynthia's home visits have a central focus on story reading.

Cynthia gives Willy (age 22 months) a picture book of farm animals as she says to him, "Willy, I have a really neat book here." Willy immediately takes the book and sits next to Cynthia, with the book open between his legs. Cynthia shows Willy how his and her fingers fit through the holes that are on each picture of each page. Willy's grandmother, Donna, asks him, "How does the cow go?" He replies, "Moo."

Willy then goes to Cynthia's bag as Cynthia asks him, "Do you think I have more books in here?" Willy affirmatively replies, "Uh-huh." Cynthia gives him a second book, and he sits down and turns the pages to look at the pictures.

Cynthia: [To Sally] He's changed his approach. Remember how he used to take the book and back into your lap? Now he turns the pages alone. See what he has learned about books?

Willy: Orange.

Cynthia: Did he say "Orange"?

Sally: He knows the color orange. He'll sit over there for the longest time. [Sally points to the shelf filled with picture books in the next room.]

[As the adults chat, Willy continues to look at his book. As he turns a page, his mother says, "pumpkin," which he repeats.]

Cynthia: When you say it, he repeats it back.

Willy: [To Cynthia] More.

Cynthia: You give me your book, and I'll give you another. [Willy gives Cynthia his book, and she gives him one that has pictures of trains.]

Cynthia: See how he listens. I tell him to bring me a book, and he brings it to me. He understands.

[Donna then tells Cynthia that the local store had a sale on children's books, and she bought six for Willy and three for his best friend.]

Cynthia: You bought a good variety, with good concepts to work on. Willy is using his language a lot more. And he's trying to respond to all my questions. It's good to ask him questions and then wait for his response. I can tell you both talk to him and read to him a lot.

Cynthia has been working with Sally and her son, Willy, for about 18 months. Sally left school in the eighth grade. She married at a young age, and she and her husband live with Donna, her husband's mother.

Given Cynthia's consistent pattern of modeling and encouraging conversation and story reading, early literacy is a central part of Willy's everyday life. Community libraries usually have a wide variety of high-quality children's books. These libraries can be a resource for low-income parents to get storybooks for daily use at home.

Infants and young children love these daily story reading rituals. Like Willy, young toddlers often enjoy looking at books themselves. Young children love hearing the same story over and over and soon can repeat it themselves. Parents often express surprise at how quickly their toddlers learn the stories and enjoy pretending to read as they tell the stories to themselves while looking at a book. These activities help the children learn the importance of written symbols. One of the parents with whom Janice works described this process.

> Evan loves the book you gave him. I read it over and over to him. His daddy reads it to him. And when nobody will read it to him, he just reads it himself—oh, just the pictures, but he knows every animal!

As infants grow older, they love singing, fingerplays, and nursery rhymes. Home visitors assist parents in understanding that their young child also needs numerous opportunities and time to draw and write and a caring adult to talk about these written expressions. Parents learn that having a variety of printed materials, along with a variety of paper and drawing and writing tools, available stimulates their young child's interest in reading and writing. Similarly, their child's understanding of the meaning of writing is enhanced if her or his everyday environment contains a great deal of written language, such as notes, recipes, grocery lists, newspapers and magazines, books, and so on, and the child sees her or his parents frequently reading and writing.

Often parents of preschoolers ask home visitors questions about stimulating their child's skill with the alphabet.

> Shelly: I have another question about reciting the ABCs. Is Erin [age 34 months] too young to get her to write them? She already knows how to write her name.

> Janice: Follow her lead on that. Don't push hard. She's now doing wonderful pictures. Creativity has to be expressed. When you tell her how to make letters, you are telling her how to do things correctly. . . . Let her write her scribbles and then you can ask her what it says and write down what she tells you. If she is strictly confined to making letters, it doesn't give her the chance to write on her own, and then say what it says, which is a significant step in her learning about the meaning of words. That is valuable creativity. She will do much more of it and is still getting her fine motor control.

As Janice works with Shelly, she helps Shelly understand developmentally appropriate writing and drawing activities and the importance of writing down what Erin says about her drawings.

Home visitors can help parents understand how they can promote emerging literacy throughout each day. Beyond reading stories to young children, families' everyday activities also can provide young children with meaningful experiences with written language. Young children see their parents write grocery lists and can suggest items to be included. As children make pictures and tell their parents about them, parents can write these dictations on their children's drawings. When another adult or older sibling reads these dictations on a child's drawings, the child experiences a powerful example of how meaningful letters are.

Home visitors can explain to parents that when they provide play experiences for their children, this play often fosters language, communication, and emerging literacy. For example, as children use words to substitute for objects, talk about what they are doing, and decide what roles they will play, this role-play fosters their language development. As the 3-year-old uses a long scarf tied around her waist to represent a skirt or uses a block for a telephone, she is using symbols—one thing is representing another. These early symbolic experiences help young children understand the symbolic nature of writing. Visitors also can encourage parents to provide toys with which children can refine their small-muscle coordination and eye–hand coordination, for example, puzzles, snap-together toys, crayons, and pencils. Developing this coordination assists the child's later ability to discriminate letters and words.

DIFFICULTIES AND DILEMMAS

In many parts of the United States, home visitors work with families whose first language is not the same as their own. The United States is a multicultural society. The preceding vignettes have depicted mainstream language usage. In reality, home visitors work with a wide diversity of families regarding ethnicity, family interaction patterns, and accompanying language usage. In their work with families, home visitors often need to adapt their approach to address unique family patterns. For example, home visitors working in Hispanic subcultures must be skilled in communicating in Spanish.

Another dilemma for home visitors can be working in homes in which parents do not spontaneously speak with their infants and young children and who themselves have minimal literacy. The home visitors learn to adapt their approach to address these patterns. Incorporating high-interest story reading into each visit provides parents with opportunities to see their infant's or young child's delight in this activity.

During the visit, home visitors can encourage parents to use picture books with their child and can leave several high-interest books for the parents to use between visits. Cynthia discussed how she uses books.

> Books are wonderful because what you can do with a book is to settle down. It settles you in the hope of a quiet time, even in families that seem chaotic. Often when I have more than one child, I'll start with a book. I'll read it to set the tone for the visit. And usually it is a pleasant time, for both the kids and their parents. With my one family that has about 18 children and two mothers living in one home, everyone joins me when I read. One of the things I do for these chaotic families is have things I always do, provide them with some routine. In the time that I am in their home, I try to bring some order. In that living room, for 10 minutes, if I can get everyone around me listening to that book I brought, that to me is powerful. And maybe they will pick up a book and sit down to read to their child and bring order.

A year after this conversation with Cynthia, the author interviewed Marquisha, one of the mothers Cynthia had been discussing. Marquisha has six children who, at the time, were between ages 3 and 21 years old. Marquisha described to the author how she has changed her parenting since she began working with Cynthia.

> Marquisha: I think working with Cynthia has made a lot of difference in the way I'm parenting my kids. Now I read to them. I used to read to them just every now and then. If they didn't seem interested, I would just go ahead and put the book down. Working with Cynthia, she helped me to get them interested, to wanting to sit them on my lap, and do it the fun way. I'll stop and let them try to read, you know, because they be wanting to read, too. So I stop and let them read a little. They don't know what they be reading, but they know the pictures real good. They learn the pictures, and it helps them learn the story.
>
> Carol: How often do you read to them?
>
> Marquisha: Now I read to them at least once a week. Before I read to them probably once a year.

Marquisha's oldest three children were between ages 18 and 21 years old. She described how her work with Cynthia helped her relationship with her older children.

> Marquisha: I can deal with my two older sons better now than what I could. I used to tell Cynthia all the time, "I cannot deal with my sons the way I can with my older daughter because she listens to me more." I just couldn't deal with my boys the way I wanted to.

Carol: *What do you think made the difference in terms of how you relate to the boys now as opposed to 4 years ago?*

Marquisha: *Talking, just talking. I used to talk to them, but mostly discipline talk. And listening to Cynthia talk to my oldest ones helped me understand what I was doing wrong. Now I just sit down and talk to them, or joke with them, something like that.*

Carol: *Like a good friend.*

Marquisha: *Yeah. I was doing that with my daughter, but I didn't realize that they needed it, too.*

Marquisha is the fourth of nine children in a low-income single-parent family. Previously, she had three brief experiences in general equivalency diploma (GED) programs. Her oldest brother is her only sibling with a high school diploma, which he received when in the military service. She was very proud that her two oldest children had received their GED certificates and that the third was working on it. When the author asked Marquisha what her dreams are for her 3-year-old daughter when her daughter turns 20, Marquisha replied as follows.

My dream for Tarina is to see her walk across the stage, which I have never gotten a chance to see. I want to see Tarina walk across the stage, do the things my oldest daughter or I didn't do. But most of all I would like to see her be able to make up her mind to want to do the . . . educational, everything . . . on her own. You know, because, in case if I'm not here, I would like to know that my daughter, that I left enough in her mind to motivate her to want to do everything that she want to do, you know, to succeed in life.

CONCLUSIONS

In their work together, parents and home visitors can interweave communication and language development into their discussions and activities. Parents enjoy sharing their young child's gains in language and appreciate having a friend with whom to share concerns. As home visitors observe and interact with child and parent, they listen, affirm, support, and reassure parents. They provide suggestions, information, and interpretations within the context of their observations, their activities, or parent concerns. As they become more aware of what to expect of their child, parents become more observant of their child's emerging communication and language. With knowledge and understanding, they can promote their young child's communication and language through their child rearing and provision of developmentally appropriate activities and experiences. Table 1 summarizes the developmental progression of language, communication, and emerging literacy and accompanying parenting strategies that can promote this developmental progression.

Table 1. Developmental progression of language, communication, and emerging literacy and accompanying parenting practices to promote this developmental progression

Developmental patterns	Parenting practices
Birth–3 months	
Watches parents' facial expressions change	Changes facial expression and voice during interactions with infant
Hears differences in sound and speech	Imitates infant's facial gestures and sounds
Has several different cries	Begins and responds to give-and-take vocal play with infant
Makes eye contact with parent when parent is talking	Sings and talks softly during routine activities
Shows pleasure by smiling and cooing	
4–10 months	
Uses vowels and consonants to babble	Repeats infant's sounds
Laughs and smiles in response to familiar persons	Describes what infant and self are doing during routine caregiving
Babbles rhythmically with sentence-like flow	Plays simple gesture games with infant (e.g., hide-and-seek with towel)
Playfully imitates nonspeech sounds (e.g., smacking lips, clicking tongue)	Reads simple picture books to infant
Understands regularly used individual words	Sings simple rhymes and songs to infant
Recognizes name and turns toward speaker	Encourages infant to respond to his or her name
Plays gesture games such as pat-a-cake	
Uses gesturing to ask for things	
Understands and responds to "no"	
Enjoys simple picture books	
10–15 months	
Understands simple and short sentences	Continues give-and-take vocal play with infant
Understands simple directions	Identifies infant's body parts and encourages infant to point to them
Enjoys picture books and simple story books	Sings simple rhymes, fingerplays, and stories
Imitates gestures like peek-a-boo	Reads simple storybooks
Waves bye-bye	Talks about what infant and self are doing
Says first words	Responds to infant's jargon talk as if infant is speaking words
Checks to see if parent is looking before exploring on own	
Strings sounds together in gibberish (jargon talk)	
16–24 months	
Has increased understanding of words, simple sentences, and simple directions	Plays simple interactive games like "chase me," telephone talk
Follows simple directions	Has simple give-and-take conversations with toddler during routine care

(continued)

Table 1. *(continued)*

Enjoys and understands simple songs, rhymes, and fingerplays
Uses "no" to protest
Uses "hi" and "bye" greetings
Uses jargon speech with state, command and questioning inflections
Refers to self by name
Names pictures, objects, body parts
Says two-word sentences
Makes simple verbal request (e.g., "More milk")

Extends toddler's speech
Sings simple rhymes, fingerplays, and songs
Reads familiar storybooks
Has toddler's eye contact before speaking
Actively listens and responds to toddler's talk
Encourages and participates in pretend-play with toddler

Ages 2–5

Understands and reponds to questions
Asks questions, especially about what child sees and experiences
Has large increase in vocabulary
Speaks in full sentences
Tells simple stories of immediate experiences
Enjoys songs, fingerplays, and storybooks
Enjoys using language in pretend-play, alone and with others
Has extended give-and-take conversations
Enjoys drawing and writing
Recognizes frequently seen words such as fast-food advertising

Has extended daily conversations with child
Actively listens and responds to child's talk
Responds to child's questions and invites child to continue talking
Asks child open-ended questions
Encourages and participates in pretend-play with child
Sings songs and fingerplays with child
Reads storybooks with child
Provides a variety of writing implements and paper for the child to use for drawing and writing

Routines, Rituals,
and Celebrations

Wee Willie Winkie rins through the town,
Upstairs and downstairs, in his nichtgown,
Tirlin' at the window, cryin' at the lock,
"Are the weans in their bed? for it's
now ten o'clock."
William Miller (1844)

This chapter focuses on the roles of two aspects of family life: 1) every-day family ritual and 2) special family celebrations and traditions. The term *ritual* as used in this chapter refers to the patterns of everyday routines that make up the shared lives of parents and their children. These include mundane practices such as eating, sleeping, bathing, or changing a diaper. It may seem odd to call such everyday happenings *rituals,* because they usually are not explicitly recognized or thought out by parents. But, in fact, the safe and predictable space that a child finds in these everyday patterns is very much like the familiar space created for adults by more traditional rituals such as religious services, holidays, or birthday celebrations. These more traditional rituals also play an impor-tant role in a child's life and as such deserve discussion. This chapter refers to these more formal or self-conscious traditions as *celebrations* to distinguish them from everyday ritual.

Rituals and celebrations are varied, and they function in the development of the parent–child relationship in a number of different ways.[1] The elements that go into making up ritual and celebration include

- Coordinated practices of family members' interaction patterns[2]
- Predictable, repeated patterns of experience over time
- A means of organizing daily life
- A means of regulating behavior
- An expression of a family's shared beliefs and values
- A means of giving each family member a sense of belonging
- A central element of each family member's sense of identity

Not every ritual or celebration has each of these elements, but the whole structure of ritual and celebration in which a young child lives serves these functions.

The development of parents and child occurs within and through their relationship, which consists of patterns of interaction. Predictable repeated settings for these child-rearing interactions are everyday rituals such as feeding, bathing, dressing, sleeping, diapering, and toileting. Over time, each daily ritual develops patterns of repeated, predictable parent action, child action, and parent–child interaction. These taken-for-granted daily rituals are the setting within which the infant and young child gain a sense of "who I am" (e.g., "I am a person sleeping in my bed, playing predictable peek-a-boo games during diaper changing, and eating dinner with my family"). Attachment bonds, feelings of security and self-worth, self-regulation and independence, language and communication, a sense of self, a sense of relatedness, and accompanying social skills all develop within these patterns of everyday rituals.

Principles of development, parenting, and home visiting approaches are relatively similar in each of these everyday rituals. This discussion examines three exemplar routines: 1) feeding and eating, 2) sleeping, and 3) toileting. The chapter also explores the special challenges that childhood illness presents to the patterns and rituals of everyday life and ways that these challenges can be met. Following the discussion on everyday rituals is a brief look at the role of more formal celebrations in family life. The chapter concludes with a discussion of some of the dilemmas and difficulties that home visitors experience with regard to everyday rituals and family celebrations.

EVERYDAY RITUALS

Sleep

Birth–3 Months Newborn infants have a sleep–wake rhythm that was established in utero.[3] Newborns often sleep 15–18 hours in 2- to 4-

hour stretches. Because the infant's central nervous system is immature, activities like feeding and sleeping occur at unpredictable times.[4] Newborns have about seven sleeping and waking periods during a 24-hour period.[5] How these cycles change into different patterns is partially dependent on individual infants' home environment. As parents learn their infant's different states of consciousness, they can begin to prolong their infant's alert states and encourage prolonged sleep states. In a responsive home environment, sleep–wake cycles become increasingly predictable.

An infant's temperament also influences sleep patterns. Very active infants, or infants who are very aware of sensations, are prone to waking during the night. In night sleep, periods of deep sleep (30–50 minutes) are followed by periods of light sleep, often termed rapid eye movement (REM) sleep. In deep sleep, newborns can shut out noises around them. During REM sleep, breathing is irregular and infants move about and are likely to cry out. Between these two cycles, infants often wake up.

Home visitors can help young parents learn that their infant's waking up in the middle of the night is normal. Usually at around age 3 months, infants can learn ways to keep themselves quiet and get themselves back into a deeper sleep. Different infants have different ways of self-comforting, such as finding their thumb, moving into a new position, or scooting to the corner of their crib. Most infants can settle themselves down. Infants' ability to soothe themselves—to self-calm—is an important first step in developing independence, which is an essential goal of development.[6] Home visitors can help parents understand the importance of their infant's learning to self-calm.

As Janice discusses the parent handout with Marta, Marta's 3-month-old infant lies on her back, sucking her thumb.

Janice: *It's good that Brianna is able to put her thumb in her mouth. Anything she'll do for herself, let her do it. Then, in the middle of the night, she won't need you. You can help her do for herself. When she awakens in the night, give her a couple of minutes to calm herself first—to get in the right position and find her thumb.*

Janice observes Brianna's ability to suck her thumb and thereby calm herself. She then helps Brianna's mother understand the importance of this self-calming skill and how she can help Brianna develop this ability.

Encouraging an infant to sleep throughout the night requires an agreed-upon commitment by everyone in the family, both parents and older siblings. To parents, especially those who want to hold and comfort their infant, these night awakenings can be very troubling. Home visitors can help new parents understand that it is their responsibility to calm their infants and put them to bed; however, it is the *infant's* task to fall asleep. When parents put their infant to sleep by rocking or breast feeding, infants then need their parents to help them to fall asleep when awakening during the night. In the following vignette, Janice assists a young mother in mastering this ability to let her infant learn to fall asleep.

Janice: *How is Jene sleeping?*

Natalie: *She doesn't sleep much during the day. At night, I rock her to sleep, and then she sleeps well, much better than Dvonne [Jene's 3-year-old brother] did as an infant. Dvonne didn't sleep through the night until he was 2¹/₂. He would cry whenever his pacifier fell out of his mouth.*

Janice: *This is the age to concentrate on Jene putting herself to sleep. Think about yourself. If I would fall asleep in my bed and awaken in the kitchen, I would not fall back to sleep. If she falls asleep in your arms and awakens in the bed, she'll expect you to rock her again.*

Natalie: *I probably cause more problems. I love to hold my babies when they go to sleep. I know it would be easier in the long run. With Dvonne, the minute he would cry, I would go in.*

Janice: *You can rock her, get her comfortable. But before she is asleep, put her in her bed. When she awakens and cries, let her go for 5 minutes for starters. I know it's harder with Dvonne in the room. Space the time: 5 minutes, then 10 minutes, and 15 minutes. It'll be hard to listen to her cry. Don't talk to her. She needs to realize this is not a social time. It will be helpful to you if she can go to sleep by herself and begin to develop independence.*

When Janice visits families with very young infants, she asks parents questions about sleeping and eating. These questions allow Janice to track the infant's developing skills at the same time that Janice also learns if parents need helpful information to make these everyday routines the setting for optimal development. Natalie had rocked her first child asleep for his first 18 months. Janice affirms Natalie's desire to rock Jene each evening but stresses that Jene needs to be put in bed prior to falling asleep. Jene needs to learn that her night routine is sleeping in her own bed. Most adults have had the experience of waking up and not being sure of where they are or having trouble going to sleep in a bed that is not their own. Janice helps Natalie understand this experience as she speaks of what it would be like for an adult to wake up in the kitchen. On her home visiting record, Janice makes a note to herself to remember to initiate discussion with Natalie on this issue during her following visits. Janice understands that this will be a major parenting change for Natalie and that Natalie will need her support in the coming months.

During the first three months, infants have cycles of eating and sleeping throughout the day and night. Home visitors need to tell some parents that they may have to help their 3- to 4-month-old infant learn that feeding is a day activity. Many parents believe that giving their infant food or a bottle assists in the infant's ability to sleep. Home visitors can tell parents that once their infant is 3 months old, the infant no longer needs to be fed at bedtime or during the night. Ferber warns, "If your child becomes accustomed to being fed at night, her system begins to regard nighttime sleep periods as only naps between feedings."[7] Infants sleep best when their digestive system is shut down for the night.

Some infants are colicky during their first 3 months. Colicky infants cry and cannot be soothed, especially in the late afternoon and evening. When a home visitor works with parents of a colicky infant, first the home visitor makes certain that the parents and physician have checked to see if there may be a physical reason for crying, such as a food allergy or obstructed bowel. Then the visitor works to reassure the parent. Fussy, crying periods can be a real threat to new parents, who may feel helpless and may blame themselves when not able to soothe their fussy infant. Usually, colic ends by the age of 3 months.

Ages 4–8 Months Between ages 4 and 8 months, infants continue to need a morning and afternoon nap. Most infants at this age easily accept naps. Home visitors can assist parents in understanding that providing a calm before-nap activity, such as rocking, cuddling, or soft lullabies, assists their child's ability to nap. Babies' brief naps when being held or in the car are poor-quality sleep and are not restorative, as is napping in their crib.[8] Infants who do not get enough sleep become overstimulated and irritable. Paradoxically, shortage of naps also seems to make going to sleep at night more difficult. The more tired infants are, the harder it is for them to fall asleep and stay asleep.

At this age, it is good to help infants to associate falling asleep with being in their own bed. In a previous vignette, Janice helped Natalie to understand how she could help her 3-month-old, Jene, fall asleep in her own bed. When Janice returned again, Jene was 5 months old, and her mother reported the following:

Natalie: *When it's time to go to bed, I lay her down, and she'll go to sleep.*

Janice: *That's great!*

Natalie: *Sometimes she'll cry for a second. And when she wakes up during the night, she begins talking to herself.*

Janice: *It's great that you have the patience to let her go back to sleep by herself.*

Whereas Natalie had rocked her first child to sleep nightly during his first 18 months, now, with help from her home visitor, Natalie allows her daughter to learn to put herself to sleep and calm herself when she awakens during the night. In response to the news, Janice expressed delight in Jene's new skills and affirmed Natalie's ability to nurture this skill.

By age 4 months, infants' nervous systems are mature enough to allow them to sleep 8–12 hours per night. Some infants need a calming routine so that they can relax enough to put themselves to sleep. Home visitors can help parents develop a regular bedtime routine, such as singing or reading stories, that is calming and nurturing. It is not too early for parents to begin reading simple stories. The body contact and even-tempoed voice tones of story reading provide one of the best calming and nurturant bedtime activities as well as preparing the way for later, when the child will start to develop skills that will lead to reading.

At around ages 7–8 months, infants' motor development makes significant leaps. Now infants are sitting up and crawling as they explore toys and other objects with their hands and mouths. With this burst of new skills and the accompanying exploration, infants may suddenly have difficulty calming down for naps and night sleeping. Home visitors can explain to parents how their infants' burst of motor skills is interfering with prior sleep patterns. They can encourage parents to be consistent and firm, with a predictable calming-before-sleep routine such as reading stories. Some parents may need to be reminded that, during the night, they may pat the infant or hum to their infant, but they need to make certain that night awakenings do not become social occasions; rather, it is their infant's task to go back to sleep.

A small proportion of infants enjoy head banging, head rolling (moving head from side to side when lying on one's back), or body rocking. These actions are soothing, rhythmic patterns of behavior that help infants fall asleep. These methods of self-calming are normal when they develop prior to age 18 months and disappear by around age 3 or 4.[9]

Ages 9–24 Months During this period, most children continue to nap. By ages 18–24 months, one nap per day usually is sufficient. With each new leap in development, sleep can become a challenge.

Developmental leaps occur at age 12 months and again at age 18 months. At around age 12 months, infants learn to walk and begin saying their first words. The excitement and the frustration of learning these new skills spill over into infants' and young toddlers' sleeping patterns. Now the infant can stand. Cruising around the crib seems a lot more fun than sleeping. An infant who has been sleeping through the night suddenly begins awakenings at night. Home visitors often can help parents see that these sleep changes are related to their young child's surges in development. Parents need to be firm with themselves and their infant to make certain that sleep remains the child's task. Some parents find it helpful to extend the length of bedtime routines, provide a lovey (see Chapter 4), sit by the infant, or pat the infant's back. But, once again, parents must make certain that night awakenings do not become playtimes.

Again at age 18 months, a new developmental leap occurs. Now the toddler is truly mobile, can speak in two- or three-word sentences, and can begin to enjoy pretend-play. It is easy at this stage for toddlers to get overexcited and therefore have difficulty settling into sleep. Once again, parents may need to be firm and may need to extend the bedtime routine to calm their toddler. Often stories after bathtime are a calm period of shared enjoyment that assists children in settling down for bedtime.

Ages 2–5 Years Two-year-olds usually need one afternoon nap. When parents arrange for their child's nap to end by 2:30 P.M. or 3:00 P.M., their child can be ready for bedtime in the early evening. At this age, many children talk themselves to sleep and, in this talk, often rehearse everything they have done during the day.[10]

By age 2, 3, or 4 years, night fears become common. Parents should respect their child's fears. New strategies such as leaving the child's bedroom door open, putting a light in the child's bedroom, and extending the bedtime ritual by adding a quiet snack or story often can be helpful. Home visitors can help parents learn that these night fears are normal and that they, as parents, can make sure their child knows they are available for support.

Children vary with regard to when they no longer need naps. Even though a preschooler does not sleep during the afternoon, it can be very helpful if the child has a brief period of rest. Young children who are comfortable going to bed at night can be comfortable in the afternoon looking at books or quietly playing with toys on their beds.

As preschoolers get older and develop self-care skills, it can be tempting for parents to omit bedtime rituals; however, attention to bedtime ritual remains very important. Preschoolers increasingly encounter new experiences and new people every day; thus, they thrive on predictability and the comfort of special bedtime moments with their parents. Usually, preschoolers know many of their stories, and they like to tell their favorite ones to their parents at bedtime. Evening storytime prior to the child's entering elementary school also strengthens the child's emerging literacy. Now that bedtime is a little later, a healthy snack or brief parent–child playtime can be added to the child's bedtime routine. These routines become rituals, and this continuity provides the young child with a sense of predictability, emotional security, belonging, and shared identity.

Feeding and Eating

Principles of parenting are similar for both eating and sleeping times. As the infant grows up, parents and child develop a predictable feeding ritual. Just as it is the task of the infant and toddler to fall asleep, so too it is the child's task to eat. The parent is responsible for what food is offered to the infant, and the infant is responsible for how much is eaten. As the child grows, a continuous push-and-pull develops between dependence—being fed—and independence—feeding oneself. The long-term goal is for young children to feed themselves and to enjoy eating and for mealtimes to be a social occasion for the family. The family mealtime routine becomes a ritual involving communication, connectedness, and shared identity and values.

Birth–3 Months During the infant's first few weeks, the newborn sets the feeding schedule. Newborns need support from their parents to master eating. At first, parents need to adjust their feeding to their infant's rhythm, and gradually they learn which cries mean hunger and which mean something else. By the time their infant is 6 weeks of age, parents usually can begin to work toward a regular feeding schedule, which usually is every 3–4 hours. As the infant grows, the number of feedings decreases until, at 20 weeks, four feedings a day are adequate.

The most important part of eating for the infant, other than nutrition, is to experience loving communication during feeding periods.[11] Home visitors can encourage parents to sing, rock, and hug their infant during feeding so that feeding can become a pleasurable time. During feeding, the infant–parent give-and-take interactions are like a dance, with the infant and parent responding to and influencing each other. Infants indicate that they are hungry, and their parents respond. The feeding process is infants' first experience in active engagement with their parents. These frequent exchanges are the beginning foundation of the development of attachment.

Feeding can be one of the first challenges for new parents, who may feel very insecure, especially if their infant is colicky. In these situations, home visitors can offer support and guidance that both affirms the parents and provides appropriate suggestions. In the following vignette, Karyn's 5-week-old has been colicky, and Janice assists Karyn.

Karyn tells Janice that Greg's pediatrician has given him formula with iron; however, she thinks it is the iron that is causing the colic. The pediatrician had explained that recent studies indicated that some developmental problems may stem from iron deficiency.

Janice: *This is one of the tricky things. In my position, visiting many families with infants, I hear so much different advice coming from pediatricians.*

[Karyn then tells Janice that her sister-in-law's pediatrician had given her different information.]

Janice: *That is one of the reasons you need confidence in yourself. "I have chosen this pediatrician, and I feel most comfortable with him." We add one qualification. You are your infant's mom. If the pediatrician says, "Don't worry," and you think differently, keep pushing with your pediatrician. How often does Greg eat?"*

Karyn: *Every 2 hours, but it can vary. At night, sometimes 8 hours, and last night, two 4-hour stretches.*

Janice: *These are helpful stretches for you.*

Karyn: *The pediatrician said no solid food for 4 months, but he seems to be never satisfied.*

Janice: *The reason is, his stomach is not ready. And it might make him gassy. His digestive system is not very developed. See if the no-iron makes a difference. Push your pediatrician on it. Ask him what is the critical period for the iron. Unless he has had a baby in his own home that is crying all the time, he may not understand.*

As a new mother, Karyn is ambivalent about the pediatrician's advice regarding iron. Janice supports Karyn and urges her to respect her own judgment—to recognize that she is the expert when it comes to knowing her son. Janice encourages Karyn to be assertive with the pediatrician and to know that his voice is merely one of many. As with sleep, Janice tracks Greg's feeding pattern. She gives Karyn developmental information so that Karyn can understand the basis for the pediatrician's directive regarding solid food. In the next few home visits, Janice continues to support Karyn: Her first topic of conversation with Karyn is feeding and Greg's colic. Karyn also knows that if she is feeling especially stressed, she can call Janice.

Ages 4–8 Months By age 4 months, most infants have a predictable schedule of feeding every 3–4 hours. Just as it is the task of infants and young children to fall asleep, so too it is the task of infants to control how much milk they drink. Parents are responsible for appropriate calm feeding times and for appropriate food, but it is the infant who regulates the amount taken. Home visitors can help parents understand these important divisions of responsibility. When feeding is a calm, predictable, positive, shared time between parent and infant, the foundation for healthy eating patterns is established.

Solid food usually is introduced at 6 months of age in the form of cereal with milk. Home visitors can help parents understand that the addition of solid food is a real transition for young infants. It can be problematic for young infants to learn to swallow solid food, to eat with a spoon, and to tolerate different textures. Infants are beginning to have increased eye–hand coordination, and they enjoy exploring with their hands. Thus, they enjoy batting about their bottles, pushing the spoon away, or putting their hands in their mouth to help suck their food down. Home visitors can describe these common behaviors that are typical of this transition, so that new parents can know what to expect and thus feel comfortable with these gradual changes within feeding patterns. When parents are confident, feeding times can be rituals with happy communication between parent and infant. Home visitors can encourage parents to introduce one solid food at a time so that they can learn if their infant has any allergies to certain foods. They also can tell parents to initially expect to see the new food in their infant's stool.

During these months, many infants begin teething. Teething may bother infants because of the swelling around the budding tooth, which feels like a foreign substance to the infant. Teething can cause discomfort and accompanying fussiness and sometimes lessens infants' appetite. To help soothe their infant's discomfort, parents can wipe their infant's gums with a wet cloth after the infant eats. This wiping cleans the plaque off the gums in the same way that brushing teeth does. Such suggestions from home visitors can be reassuring and helpful to young parents.

Karyn: *Everything goes in his mouth.*

Janice: *Are his gums swollen? [Karyn nods yes.] Do his gums seem to hurt him?*

Karyn: *I think so.*

Janice: *Dentists recommend washing babies' gums after they eat to get off the plaque. This helps the teething process and feels good—to have a soft damp terry cloth on one's gums. . . . Everything in his mouth, that's so good. He's so curious. And there is a connection between mouthing toys and eating later on. Greg is getting used to different textures in his mouth. It will be easier for him to have different kinds of table foods when he is older. Babies who are not used to lots of toys in their mouths will want only milk and mush.*

Karyn introduces two topics: teething and exploration through mouthing. Janice uses the topics Karyn introduced to provide helpful developmental and parenting information. Because Karyn has introduced the topics, she is more likely to hear Janice's information and decide to utilize it. Janice not only addresses ongoing issues such as teething but also helps Karyn have a long-range developmental perspective. Putting items in their mouths is not only the way curious infants learn but also the foundation for tolerating changing textures of food in the coming months and years. This information can help Karyn be at ease and understand the meaning and purpose of Greg's behavior patterns.

With increasing age, feedings become a playful exploration time for infants. With their increased eye–hand coordination, they explore new activities such as smearing food across their face and wanting to hold the spoon. Now parents need to allow additional time and have more patience while their infant eats. By the time infants are ages 7–8 months, they can grasp items and enjoy playing with their cup. When home visitors interpret the meaning of these new infant behaviors, they can assist parents in understanding that learning through exploration is as important to their infant as feeding and eating. These interpretations are especially important for very young or needy parents, who may see these exploratory actions as the infant's intentional attempts to upset the parent. When a parent understands that playful exploration during feeding is the normal way infants learn, the parent can allow more time for feeding and know that patience is necessary.

Ages 9–24 Months As infants and young toddlers' motor skills develop, so too does their interest in eating independently. If parents provide a variety of finger foods and a toddler cup as a part of each meal, they encourage their child to feed her- or himself. Often infants and young toddlers allow their parent to feed them while they also are feeding themselves with their hands. Feeding oneself is another independence skill to be mastered. Infants also may want to hold and tap their spoon, though they generally cannot use it properly until age 2 years.

As infants approach age 12 months, they can feed themselves chopped or mashed food and drink from a cup. This age often is a good time for parents to begin weaning the infant from the bottle or breast. Weaning can be a gradual process of replacing nipple feeding with other ways of eating and drinking. It begins as soon as parents introduce solid foods and drinking from a cup. Infants and young toddlers are so involved in these new experiences that they usually do not miss nipple feeding during meals. Breast or bottle feeding often can be reserved for early morning or late at night. As home visitors chat with parents, it remains important for them to track how feeding and eating are developing. When Greg is 9 months old, Janice asks his mother about eating.

Janice: *And he continues to like to eat and feed himself?*

Karyn: *Yes! Anything, even though he doesn't have but two teeth. He loves solid food.*

Janice: *It's important to pay attention to the baby's signals. It'll pay off in the coming months. It's not the teeth that help him chew. It's the jaw. He gets a lot of power from his gums.*

Janice continues to initiate conversation about everyday rituals in parenting an infant. In this brief exchange, Janice gives Karyn important developmental information so that Karyn can understand her infant's actions and tune in to the meaning of his actions.

Brazelton emphasized that "a rounded diet cannot be the goal for the second year."[12] This is the time during which independence and autonomy are dominant issues and toddlers become sensitive to adult demands about eating. Brazelton suggested that a minimal daily diet during the second and third year should include the following:

1. One pint of milk (16 ounces) or its equivalent in cheese, yogurt, or ice cream
2. 2 ounces of iron-containing protein (e.g., meat or an egg), or cereals fortified with iron
3. One ounce of orange juice or other fresh fruit
4. One multivitamin, which [can] cover for uneaten vegetables[13]

Because autonomy and negativism are a normal part of infants' development, eating times are the setting for toddlers to test newly discovered independence. Parents can expect toddlers to refuse to eat, spit food out, smash their food, or engage in other exploratory or testing behaviors during mealtimes. Home visitors can help parents understand that these new behaviors are normal parts of development and that parents need to be firm. They can assist parents in understanding that when toddlers lose interest in eating, parents should allow their toddlers to leave the table. Parents can tell their child that the meal is over *until* the next meal and that there will be no snacks. Once toddlers learn that there will be no food once they have left the table in the middle of a meal, they will learn appropriate eating behaviors.

Ages 2–5 Years By age 24 months, most toddlers can use a spoon and fork, although they occasionally prefer using their fingers. Toddlers usually continue to be messy when eating. Some young children are more sensitive to taste and smell and may react to foods more strongly than others do. Home visitors can reassure parents that it is common for preschoolers to be picky eaters; for example, they may not like things mixed together, such as pot roast with gravy or spaghetti with sauce. Young children are more sensitive to the textures and smells of food than are adults, but they outgrow this sensitivity. Parents' attitudes can make a difference. If parents themselves enjoy cooking and eating and provide a relaxed mealtime, their young children probably will adopt this attitude toward eating. Mealtime then can be a special family time of shared enjoyment—a time in which children know their parents are eager to chat with them and with each other. The predictable ritual of these daily meals nourishes children's emotional security and sense of belonging.

Even if parents are enthusiastic about eating, they may find it difficult to accept their young child's emerging independence and negativism. When a child leaves the table or refuses to eat, her or his parents can tell the child there is no more eating until the next meal. Like most young children, the child will learn quickly to remain at the table. Some parents believe that they will foster malnutrition if their young child misses a meal. Home visitors can give parents important information regarding their child's need for food. Often parents need reassurance that if their child ordinarily has a well-balanced diet, missing a meal will not matter. Janice's conversation with Tracy is illustrative.

> Janice has just arrived, and she and Tracy are chatting. Mia (age 28 months) begins fussing, and her mother asks her, "What do you want? Juice?"
>
> Mia: "I don't want juice!"
>
> [Tracy and Mia go to the kitchen and return with a small bowl of raisins and cereal for Mia.]
>
> Janice: It's good that you give her nutritious snacks. At this age, children often are picky.
>
> Tracy: She ate a good breakfast today, but last night she would not eat dinner.
>
> Janice: How did you feel about it?

Tracy: *I was frustrated. I tried to feed her, but she just didn't want any. So I just let it go. I tried everything.*

Janice: *Good, it is important to pay attention to the child's natural appetite—knowing, on the one hand, her behavior, and, on the other, she is not hungry. If we push, we are denying her own limits. The child should determine how much she eats.*

In this discussion, Janice affirmed Tracy's parenting. In addition, she gave Tracy developmental information to help Tracy learn the significance of her decision so that she could continue ignoring her child's pickiness and know that her child would be fine if she missed a meal.

It is important for children to develop the rhythm of eating meals when they are hungry, to stop eating when they are full, and to enjoy eating. Home visitors can help parents understand that there are liabilities when they use food for punishment or reward. When food is used as a reward for good behavior, young children learn to connect food with prizes rather than with hunger. When parents withdraw dessert as punishment, they unwittingly teach their child that there is good food and bad food.

Preschoolers enjoy helping their parents prepare meals. When children help cook food, they are more likely to eat it. When young children help set and clear the table and assist in simple cooking tasks, they are contributing members of the family. In these activities, they achieve a sense of belonging and pride in their new skills.

Our society has an ever-increasing number of working single parents and two-working-parent families for whom time is at a premium. With the accessibility of numerous fast-food restaurants, microwaveable dinners, and prepackaged foods, traditional food preparation and leisurely mealtimes may not be a given part of family life.

Rolanda and Carl Smith each have high-powered professional jobs. Carl takes their 3½-year-old son, Ben, to his child care program at 7:30 A.M., and Rolanda picks up Ben at 5:30 P.M. Ben was 36 months old the first time the Smiths' home visitor, Nina, visited them. Nina initiated a conversation about mealtimes.

Rolanda: *Well, in truth, we don't eat together as a family. Carl gets home an hour after Ben and I do, and he uses a couple hours to unwind— reading the paper, exercising on the treadmill, that kind of thing. So Ben and I eat simple meals together shortly after we arrive home. It's a pattern that just developed. We've never discussed it much.*

Carl: *You know, when we first got married, 8 years ago, I used to talk with Rolanda about how special it would be to have family dinners. My own father never returned home from his law office until after 8:00 in the evening, so I grew up without experiencing daily dinners with everyone.*

Nina: *It sounds like beginning a new pattern of eating together might be worth exploring together. Today many young working parents are developing a repertoire of simple meals, such as pasta, that they can manage to prepare after a long day at work. And, increasingly, grocery stores have prepared meats, such as rotisserie chicken, at reasonable prices. But the issue is not the type of food; rather, what is important is that children and their parents have time together each day. Every evening, dinner together can provide this shared time.*

Rolanda: *Now that I think of it, Carl and I hardly ever eat together. Dinners together would be important for our relationship, too.*

Given their high-pressured work, Carl and Rolanda had developed a daily pattern that excluded family dinners and had never thought much about it. When Nina introduced the topic, Carl and Rolanda quickly recognized what they and their son were missing. One month later, when Nina returned to visit the Smiths, Rolanda told Nina that her mother now picks up Ben from his day care on Wednesday and cares for him for several hours. Then she and Carl can take time to go out to dinner together, a pattern they maintained for 5 years prior to Ben's birth but did not continue. Rolanda explained that she and Carl plan to begin regular dinners with Ben, but that this shift was going to take time. Together Nina and Rolanda brainstormed possible easy meals and ways of preparing some meals during the weekend.

When they talk about eating and mealtimes, home visitors like Nina can help young parents understand the developmental significance of good eating habits and family mealtimes. They can talk about how family dinner rituals give each family member a sense of belonging and security. Nina and Rolanda did some problem solving as they discussed possibilities of weekend cooking for weekday dinners and munching on nutritious finger food like carrot sticks and celery with peanut butter instead of making time-consuming salads. Each person and each family have their own eating habits. For adults, eating is often a social occasion—for example, coffee breaks at work and going out to lunch. Home visitors can assist parents in making family meals a social occasion that includes their very young children.

Toilet Training

Just as it is the child's task to fall asleep and decide how much to eat, toilet training is also the child's accomplishment. Like sleeping and eating, the learning process initially involves parent and child working together. Likewise, learning independence is a central part of the toilet training process.

Unfortunately, many parents feel pressure to toilet train their toddler early. Grandparents may expect the child to toilet train as early as the parent had done as a child. Some preschools do not accept 2-year-olds unless they are toilet trained. Sometimes parents think of their child's early toilet training as a sign of their parental competence. There is no correct age for toilet training; however, most children are not ready until after their second birthday.[14]

Because many parents feel pressure and lack confidence in training their toddler, home visitors can assist by helping parents recognize when their child is really ready for toilet training. Experts agree that there are clear signs of readiness for toilet training. Lansky provided a summary of signs of readiness. The child

- Is aware of the "need to go" and shows it by facial expression or by telling the parent
- Can express and understand one-word statements, such as "wet," "dry," "potty," and "go"
- Demonstrates imitative behavior
- Dislikes wet or dirty diapers
- Is able to stay dry for at least 2 hours, or wakes up dry in the morning or after a nap
- Is able to pull pants up and down
- Is anxious to please
- Has a sense of social appropriateness (Wet pants can be an embarrassment.)
- Tells parent she or he is about to urinate
- Asks to use the potty chair or toilet[15]

Home visitors have an important role in helping parents understand that maturity of the child's gastrointestinal tract and central nervous system is necessary for a young child to be ready for toilet training. This maturity allows the child to know the sensations that come before a bowel movement or urination. Girls often are ready before boys, and children with older siblings may learn from them. Any time before age 4 is normal. Children most often gain bowel control before they have bladder control.

All young children need their parent's guidance in toilet training, and often home visitors can provide helpful suggestions. Parents learn to understand that toilet training takes a long time and that accidents are common. One aspect of toilet training is learning a new vocabulary. Home visitors can encourage parents to use whatever words are comfortable to them when they talk to their toddler about body parts and elimination. Portable potties allow young children to have their feet on the floor; with a potty, the child does not have to deal with a big noisy toilet that makes things disappear. It helps young children to see others using the toilet. When they begin the toilet-training process, parents can comment in a matter-of-fact manner when they see their child having a bowel movement. Parents can remind their child to use the potty, but it is the child's decision to use it. When the child does produce something, parents can enthusiastically praise their child and can leave it in the potty for their child to take pride in the accomplishment. Home visitors can encourage parents to avoid shaming or pressuring their child. Most young children cooperate because they find pleasure in pleasing their parents and in growing up.

Just as home visitor–parent discussions of feeding and sleeping behavior are important, toilet training is an important recurrent topic of discussion during toddlerhood. Janice and Shelly discussed toileting during Janice's visits when Erin was between 18 and 34 months of age. These discussions illustrate how home visitors can support, affirm, and guide young parents.

Janice and Erin (age 18 months) are rolling Erin's beach ball as Shelly says to Janice, "Erin is interested in the potty, especially since her older cousin is being toilet trained." Erin says "potty" and begins to pull down her pants. Shelly looks at Janice as she says, "Should I?" Janice responds, "Sure, if she is interested."

Erin and Shelly go to the bathroom. From the bathroom, Erin is heard to say, "Mamma?" Shelly replies, "Mamma sit down, too."

In a couple moments, Shelly and Erin return to the living room. Erin has her diaper and jeans off, and Shelly is carrying the potty, which she puts on the rug. With a small wad of paper in her hand, Erin sits on the potty.

Shelly tells Janice, "Rob and others say I should train her. I tell them she is not ready." Janice replies, "Good. But you are potty training because your child is interested. This is all a part of it."

Erin quickly loses interest in the potty and gets up. Shelly puts Erin's diaper and slacks on, and Erin and Janice return to playing ball.

Janice does not initiate the toilet-training topic until the child is 2 years old, the age that Janice thinks is appropriate for beginning the process. Janice explained, "By the time the child is 2 years, parents have learned that I prepare them for each step. If I bring it up earlier, they'll think it's time to start." When Shelly initiates the topic, Janice supports her because it is the child who first had interest in the task.

Janice has just arrived and Erin (age 23 months) has wheeled her doll carriage into the living room and begins showing Janice her dolls. Shelly suggests, "Tell Janice what we have been doing?" Shelly then whispers to Erin, who says, "Potty. I tinkle in the potty." Erin then bends over and puts her hand between her legs to pantomime as she says to Janice, "Wipe and then put it in the potty. Flush. It go—yeah!" Erin claps, and then continues, "Poo-poo too—baby one and big one, too."

Shelly tells Janice that, every single day for a week, Erin has used the toilet completely on her own initiative. Shelly states that she had no intention of starting toilet training this early and had not even bought any books about the topic. Recently, Erin was no longer going to the toilet every single day.

Janice responds, "It's great that you are so relaxed about it. Though children need our help, it is the child's decision to use the toilet." Erin then goes to Janice's toy bag and pulls out a book. The toileting topic ends.

Janice has three visits between Erin's 18th and 23rd months; however, Shelly does not initiate conversation about toilet training. When she does, Janice affirms Shelly's relaxed manner. Just as Janice encourages Shelly to maintain a relaxed manner and take her cues from her daughter, so too Janice takes her cues from Shelly when discussing the topic. If Shelly were not relaxed or were pressuring Erin, Janice would initiate the topic. During Janice's next two visits, Shelly briefly talks about toileting.

As Janice picks up her items, she asks Shelly, "Do you have any questions?"

Shelly: With regard to potty training, I'm not sure what to do—if it's okay for me to put diapers on Erin. Or would that be bad to be inconsistent?

Janice: Consistency is always best, but you need to follow Erin's lead. If she begins wetting, it's appropriate to return to the diapers.

Once again, Janice reminds Shelly that it is her daughter who decides when she will use the potty. When Janice visits the next month (Erin is age 25 months), Erin's father, Rob, also is part of the visit.

Rob: [To Shelly] Did you tell Janice that Erin is almost potty trained?

Shelly: I can't keep track of how often she is dry. And if she does have an accident, it's usually my fault—forgetting before we go out. Most of the time she says it herself.

Janice: *That's wonderful.*

Shelly: *I find we're reusing and reusing diapers. We use diapers when we leave the house. Like you suggested, I have been real relaxed.*

The previous conversation took place during the last visit before Janice's 3-month summer vacation. When Janice returns in the fall, Shelly gives her an update on Erin's toilet training.

Shelly: *If I would put her on the potty, she would just whine. She has very few accidents. I said to Rob, when she wants to go, she'll go. I put a calendar on the wall in the kitchen. Now I put up a star when she goes potty. I ask her if she wants a star, and she'll say "Yes" and go to the bathroom.*

Janice: *You're really smart. The decision must be Erin's.*

Three months later Shelly gives Janice another report.

Shelly: *Erin [age 34 months] seems to deal well with spontaneity. Like if we walk into the bathroom and she needs to go potty, it's fine. It works much better than when I suggest that we go to the bathroom.*

Janice: *You are really tuning in to her cues. This is another part of her growing autonomy. And you know what works and you use it. You have learned what causes confrontations.*

Just like the child's learning to walk or talk, toilet training progresses with stops and starts. Erin is dry for a few days; then she begins having accidents. Throughout these 7 months, Shelly keeps Janice informed of her daughter's toilet training. Janice supports and affirms Shelly's approach. Repeatedly, and in different ways, Janice maintains the theme that toilet training is the child's task, and parents need to remain relaxed. When toddlers experience pressure in toilet training, they may begin to retain their bowel movements. Holding back can lead to constipation.

Toilet training is another area in which young children need to become independent at their own speed. The process can be difficult for parents, who may think of toilet training as their responsibility. Children often are reluctant to follow their parents' timetable, and parents may feel that this resistance points to a failure in their parenting ability. Young children's reluctance may stem from parental pressure or from immaturity of their gastrointestinal tract or central nervous system. Home visitors can assist parents in this potentially problematic area by providing developmental information so that parents know what to expect from their child, as well as suggestions, support, and affirmation.

Patterns of Mutuality

Patterns of development and of parenting arise across these everyday routines of sleeping, feeding and eating, and toilet training. Each area involves child and parent working together; there is mutuality. In order for these patterns of mutuality to occur, parents learn to read the language of their child's behavior; for example, they learn to recognize the meaning of different cries, when to stand back, and when to nudge their child forward. Communication—nonverbal facial gestures, body posture and movement, and speaking—is integral to these everyday interactions in sleeping, feeding and eating, and toilet training.

Each of these areas involves the *child's* accomplishment: It is the child's task to learn to fall asleep, to decide how much to eat, and to use the toilet. As young children learn to feed themselves, put themselves to sleep, and use the toilet, they are developing increased independence. This process of growing independent is not always even. Development often occurs in bursts, such as the emergence of new motor or language skills. A burst in one area may lead to unevenness in another; for example, new motor skills may lead to overexcitement and accompanying difficulty in calming down to fall asleep.

As their child grows, parents learn that the different areas of their child's development are intertwined. As motor skills develop, infants can chew and swallow and begin to feed themselves. As their social-emotional and language skills develop, eating times can be pleasurable times of companionship. With increased language and cognitive skill, toddlers can understand and follow directions in sleeping, eating, and toilet-training activities. Because of the emotional bond with her or his parents, the young child is responsive and eager to please. Successes in these everyday rituals are major developmental accomplishments and become a part of the child's identity.

Predictability is central to each of these everyday rituals. Falling asleep becomes a natural part of everyday routine when there is a calm bedtime ritual. When family members regularly come together to eat, eating is enjoyable and the child feels a sense of connectedness. Regular reminders to use the potty become a part of the child's everyday routine until children can recognize their bodily signals for toileting. In time, the preschooler experiences a predictable rhythm—eating when hungry, sleeping when tired, and toileting according to bodily signals. It is not uncommon for everyday rituals to trigger parents' worry, anxiety, and insecurity. New parents may feel like a failure when their infant is colicky or when they think their child is not eating enough. Often parents love the process of putting their child to sleep, but then experience the frustration of nighttime awakenings with seemingly endless crying. Normal patterns of negativism lead to toddlers' refusal to eat or to nap. Within these experiences, new parents sometimes feel as if their sense of parenting competence is eroding.

Within everyday rituals, home visitors can provide valuable support, affirmation, developmental information, and suggestions to help young parents in their important and challenging parenting task. When home visitors prepare parents with information regarding what to expect from their growing infant and young child, parents can develop confidence in both their child's development and their ability to foster this development. As they observe parent and child behavior, visitors have the opportunity to interpret the developmental meaning of these actions and to support and affirm the parent. When a parent is feeling insecure or perplexed, home visitors' support and information may assist this parent's understanding of both child and self and thereby offer needed assistance.

CHILDHOOD ILLNESSES

Young children get sick quickly, but they cannot tell their parents what is wrong with them. Between ages 1 and 3 years, children average eight or nine illnesses a year.[16] Illnesses often make new parents feel anxious, even when illnesses are minor. Parents can be exhausted by the child's increased needs and by parents' own lack of sleep. Frequent illnesses include colds, nausea and vomiting, and diarrhea, which usually do not require antibiotics or other medicine. Parents can help their child best by letting the child build up an immunity to illness. Home visitors support and help parents of sick children when they provide clear guidelines. Visitors can explain that illness causes fussiness, interrupted sleep, and regression, no matter how skilled a parent may be. Furthermore, they can provide information and suggestions. For example, they can tell parents that clear fluids are important in order to prevent dehydration if a child has a fever or diarrhea. These common illnesses cause breaks in the family's predictable everyday routine. From a developmental perspective, home visitors can help parents understand that they and their child will develop important new rituals within the experience of illness.

Parents' care for their sick child is an intense personal and social experience for parent and child. A child's illnesses also are an important experience in social relatedness. When sick, the child's sense of self is changed and the child does not feel happy, energetic, or curious. When the child recovers, his or her sense of self is restored. During children's illnesses, parents' caregiving changes, too. They more readily accept irritability and make fewer demands on the child. They help reduce the child's discomfort and express empathy. Often the child's illness is contagious, so children may observe their siblings or parents go through similar experiences of illness. Then children can learn how to help in caring for someone else. Illness can be the setting for learning compassion, nurturance, and caring. Initially, when ill, the child experiences increased empathy and caring. When family members then become ill, the child can develop prosocial behavior such as empathy and assisting others.

Home visitors can make certain that parents have basic health and safety knowledge and resources; for example, they understand what is a medical emergency that needs immediate attention, they have phone numbers of a physician and of poison control center near every phone in the house, and they have in their home a good first-aid guide. Brazelton defined medical emergencies as those occasions when the child is unconscious, has obstructed breathing, or convulsions.[17] When children have fever or diarrhea, dehydration is a danger. It is common for children under age 3 to have high fever, because their body's regulatory system is immature. If children have more than six bowel movements a day or stop urinating, they are getting dehydrated. Not all new parents know this information; thus, it is important that home visitors explain the dangers of dehydration.

Middle-ear infections resulting from colds are quite common during infancy and toddlerhood. Fluid in the middle ear and a loss of hearing often accompany middle-ear infections. With frequent ear infections and accompanying hearing loss, a young child may have immature language skills. Janice is aware that infant Greg has had several ear infections (before Greg was 12 months old, he had outpatient surgery to put tubes in his ears to assist the fluid drainage); thus, she regularly initiates a discussion with Greg's mother about this topic.

Janice: *Has Greg continued to have ear infections? [Karyn nods yes.] When he has had ear infections, his hearing is not as good. If you notice a pattern that he is not responding to you, check with his pediatrician.*

[Janice proceeds with play activities with Greg and Karyn. Before she leaves, she returns to the earlier topic.]

Janice: *Even a couple of weeks after an ear infection, babies are not hearing as well. With ear infections, we encourage you to keep close track of his hearing. This can have a major impact on his language development.*

Because Janice has a strong commitment to relate to parents as a partner, she usually is not as directive as she is in this vignette. With experience, however, Janice has learned that many new parents do not know this ear infection information, which is crucial for Greg's healthy development.

Massage

Many parents also are not aware that a massage can help infants feel more comfortable during illness. In some countries, especially in Africa and Asia, infant massage is a common caregiving practice. In the United States, we are just learning that infant massage stimulates respiration, circulation, digestion, and elimination; promotes sleep; and relieves gas and colic.[18] Home visitors can share this information with parents and demonstrate the massaging process.

Allergies

Home visitors also need to consider possible allergies. Asthma and eczema usually are inherited allergies; thus, parents with a family history of these illnesses need to watch carefully for possible allergies in their young children. If asthma or eczema begins, parents need immediate help from their doctor because, if asthma or eczema is allowed to escalate, young children feel helpless and anxious, which can increase the severity of their illness.

If a young child's cold extends beyond 2 or 3 weeks and congestion seems endless, the cold infection may have developed into an allergic reaction. Over the past few months, when Janice has visited Tracy and her toddler, Maggie, Maggie has been congested. Janice helps Tracy understand the possibility of allergy.

Janice asks Tracy if Maggie (age 19 months) has a cold or if it seems to be allergies. (Maggie has had clear nasal drainage this morning, and her chest seems quite congested.)

Tracy: *Maggie has had a cold for a little over 3 weeks.*

Janice: *The allergy count has been very high this spring. It might be helpful to ask the pediatrician about possibilities of Maggie having allergies.*

Tracy: *I never really thought about allergies.*

Janice then explains that when one of her sons was quite young, he had allergic reactions in the spring. Tracy replied that she will ask the doctor and will begin to watch to see if being outdoors triggers Maggie's congestion. Janice then initiates play activities with Maggie and her older sister, Mia. Before leaving, she initiates a conversation about using a cold-water vaporizer to help Maggie's breathing. Tracy replies that occasionally she uses one to help Maggie's congestion. Janice replies, "My son's pediatrician warned me that the cold-water vaporizer builds up mold, which was one of the things Tom was allergic to. If Tom had a cold, the allergies would kick in and he would have an allergic reaction."

During this visit, Janice gave Tracy information about the possibility that Maggie's recurrent lingering colds and congestion might be due to allergic reactions. This was new information for Tracy. The younger the child is, the more successful allergy treatment can be. Once she had Maggie's allergies confirmed, Tracy could take prevention steps. She eliminated the stuffed animals, feather pillows, and throw rugs in Maggie's room. She was more quick to turn on the air conditioner, which would protect Maggie from some of the airborne allergens. She also began using antihistamines so that Maggie's breathing did not become obstructed. These steps prevented Maggie from having more symptoms.

Developmental Importance of Illness

Young parents, especially parents who find their child's illness a major intrusion into their complex work life, may not understand the developmental importance of their child's frequent illness. Working parents also feel the pull of conflicting demands when their child is sick: Do I earn a living or care for my child? Home visitors can offer developmental information and suggestions to help parents manage their child's illness as a natural part of growth and development—an experience that provides the child with significant learning about self and other and with development of prosocial behavior. In addition, the visitor can be aware of and sensitive to parents' feelings and concerns—for example, feelings of inadequacy in the face of illness, fear of their infant's fragility, or anger over the intrusiveness of this illness.

Times when young children are sick are intense interpersonal periods for parent and child. Children's illness is a time that can test parents' sense of competence and the children's sense of security. But when parents successfully nurse their child through illness, they gain a sense of competence and the child gains an increased sense of being cared for in a safe world.

FAMILY CELEBRATIONS AND TRADITIONS

Like everyday rituals, family celebrations and traditions involve predictable, repeated patterns of family interactions. These traditions give family members a sense of belonging and shared identity. Through celebrations and traditions, family members maintain shared beliefs and shared understanding of roles. Family traditions are regularly occurring events. Some are unique to the family, such as summer vacations, visits with extended families, and birthday parties. In some cases, the family traditions are part of a larger religious or national occasion, such as Christmas, Independence Day, Passover, or Martin Luther King, Jr.'s, birthday. Celebrations include rites of passage, such as baptisms, bar mitzvahs, weddings, and religious and national holidays. Family celebrations are connected to both the culture and the family's ethnic and religious roots.[19] Celebrations often involve symbols that will be important for the rest of the child's life. Families differ in the extent to which their traditions and celebrations are child centered and in the extent to which celebrations involve people beyond the immediate family. Past, present, and future are joined in these family traditions and celebrations. Traditions and celebrations provide connectedness and continuity.

In their relations with parents, home visitors have the opportunity to respect and honor each family's traditions and forms of celebration. Frequently, visits occur close to holiday seasons. Janice's visit during December illustrates.

> *Janice arrives at Natalie's home 1 week before Christmas. Dvonne (age 3¹/₂ years) greets her at the door and immediately shows her his Christmas tree. His mother, Natalie, suggests that Dvonne tell Janice where they got the tree, and he tells her that they cut it down at a tree farm. Natalie places Jene, Dvonne's little sister, on the rug in front of her. Dvonne excitedly tells Janice what he has asked Santa to bring him for Christmas.*
>
> *Janice: We ask Santa for what we think we want, but Santa has surprises, too. Santa also likes to have ideas.*
>
> *[As Janice speaks, Dvonne touches the ornaments and gestures for her to look at them.]*
>
> *Janice: You are being very careful with the ornaments. And the needles of the tree still feel sharp, so they can hurt your fingers.*
>
> *Dvonne: They feel sharp!*
>
> *[As Dvonne points to the ornaments for Janice to notice, she asks him if any are new for this year. They then have a brief conversation about which ornaments are new and which are old.]*

Janice has just arrived at Dvonne's home. She joins in the 3-year-old's excitement regarding the forthcoming holiday and engages in an extended conversation with him about his ornaments. By the time this exchange is completed, one fourth of the home visit time is consumed; but Janice understands that she must address the excitement of the holidays before Dvonne can settle down and let Janice also relate to his mother and baby sister. As Janice relates to Dvonne, she also models extended conversation and respect for his young mother, Natalie, who smiles as she observes and listens.

Holidays can be stressful for mothers of very young children. Mary is a young mother of two boys: Gary, age 4 years; and Paul, age 17 months. Mary's home visitor, Linnette, has worked with her since her older son was 6 months old; thus, Linnette understands that Mary tends to become anxious during holidays. When Linnette visits in late November, she tries to assist Mary.

Linnette: *It's getting into the Christmas season, a season that can be stressful for kids and for parents. Before decorating or shopping, it might be helpful for you and Stanley to sit down and see if you can make plans to lessen the stress. Other moms have tried things. One mom, she said that decorating the tree is a family thing. She doesn't have a formal meal that night, but puts out healthy finger foods that the kids like. The kids put ornaments on the low branches. Some moms involve the kids in baking cookies. Small kids love to play with cookie dough.*

Mary: *Our problem is we have 100 things to do. I took the kids to the mall to see Santa. We waited for an hour for him to show up. And then we waited for the picture taking. By the time the camera flashed, Gary was not smiling and Paul was crying.*

[By the time Mary had finished her story, she was chuckling.]

Linnette: *Lots of time we put stress upon ourselves. Afterwards, we can laugh about it. It's important to plan.*

Mary: *Like wrapping. I do it after they are in bed. And I find it a relaxing activity.*

Knowing that Mary can let holidays become stressful, Linnette begins a discussion of the forthcoming holiday. She speaks of strategies that other mothers use to help make the holiday a relaxing time for family activities. When home visitors strive to develop a partnership in their relations with parents, they find that using examples of other mothers is a helpful way of giving suggestions. Mary is comfortable enough to share a recent stressful experience and, with time, can laugh about it. The conversation ends as Mary reports a successful holiday experience. When Linnette visited Mary and her boys after Christmas, Mary eagerly shared holiday events – those that were pleasant and festive as well as those that were stressful. Linnette shared with the author as well that the level of stress decreased in each of the 3 years that Linnette visited Mary. Linnette's support, affirmation, and assistance no doubt helped.

Just as everyday rituals give young children a sense of connectedness and security, family celebrations and traditions offer each family member a sense of belonging and shared identity, both to that which is unique to the family and to the extended family and the larger culture. Home visitors can assist new parents in recognizing and understanding the value of these celebrations and traditions for their child and each family member's development. With very small children, parents may experience the task of creating these celebrations and traditions as additional tasks that are not easy to orchestrate and add unwanted stress. In these settings, the home visitor can offer needed support and suggestions.

DIFFICULTIES AND DILEMMAS

As home visitors strive to promote parents' ability to create and sustain healthy everyday rituals, celebrations, and traditions, they may encounter several difficulties. The first problem usually occurs in work with low-income families, because infants failing to thrive most often live in families of this environment. The second difficulty comes from the modern family's functioning in that the complexities of modern family life may create obstacles to providing predictable everyday rituals. Third, when parents are trying to bridge two family traditions, each containing unique patterns of everyday rituals, celebrations, and traditions, parents may find that the two patterns are not that easy to blend. Finally, home visitors may confront family problems that are unique to single parents or to a recently divorced family.

When home visitors work with low-income families with multiple problems, they need to watch for signs of poor growth and development in young infants and toddlers. These signs may be evidence of failure to thrive (FTT) syndrome, the medical term used to identify infants characterized by growth and development failure.[20] FTT is caused by malnourishment, which generally results from parents' inability to see and respond to their infant's needs. FTT is not an organic disease; rather, it is a descriptive phrase identifying infants and toddlers having growth failure. An FTT child is less than 2 years of age and most often is less than 6 months of age. Beyond failing to gain weight, these infants often have disrupted social-emotional development, delayed psychomotor development, and developmental retardation. Research has shown that malnourishment, especially during the first 6 months of life, can cause permanent brain damage. Infants hospitalized with FTT during their first year of life are likely to be cognitively slow during later years.[21] Children under 2 years of age who experience multiple risk factors such as poverty and low birth weight can be susceptible to FTT. Given the individual differences and fluidity of infant development, recognizing FTT early is one of the most important baseline responsibilities of home visitors.

People often see weight gain as concrete evidence of good parenting. When their infant or toddler is diagnosed with FTT, parents often respond defensively. No parents want to hear from others or admit to themselves that they are inadequate parents. Given this pattern, home visitors need to be sensitive when they work with parents of FTT infants and toddlers. Table 1 provides several guidelines for effective communication with parents of young children with FTT.

The second challenge is less life threatening but is also developmentally important. New family structures offer complexities that challenge our society's taken-for-granted notion of family life and threaten parents' ability to develop predictable daily rituals.[22] Home visitors need to be alert to these changes and develop flexibility in assisting parents in exploring new patterns of everyday rituals. As everyday family life in the United States becomes increasingly more complex, it becomes challenging for parents to provide predictable routines for their young children. It is increasingly rare for one parent to be a full-time homemaker. In 1996, only 9% of American families consisted of two parents with one parent at home full-time.[23] In 1992, 58% of American families with children under 6 years of age were single-parent families.[24] Current technology often merges family and work life. With car phones, personal computers, electronic mail, telefacsimile machines, and so on, technology allows adults to bring their work life into their home. Television and videotapes have become ready-made baby sitters. It is not uncommon for family members to have different daily schedules (e.g., older children engaged in sports or other after-school events, parents traveling out of town). These patterns often lead

Table 1. Guidelines for effective communication with parents of children with FTT

- Some parents do not express concern about their child's growth when the child is diagnosed with FTT. Communicating sensitivity to parents' sense of competence and at the same time helping parents recognize the needs of their child with FTT requires careful balancing of information.
- Taking time to learn parents' views of their child's condition is central to parents' trust of the professional.
- Professionals should expect many parents to give a medical explanation for their child's failure to gain weight.
- Professionals should expect some parents to disagree with the medical diagnosis of FTT, especially when they see their toddler running and climbing.
- It can be very helpful to focus on the future when discussing the child's condition with the parent. That is, parents can feel supported when a primary focus is how they can improve their child's growth and development.

Adapted from Sturm and Drofar (1992).

to disruption of families' daily rituals; for example, regular dinner times disappear because different family members are involved in their own tasks. No longer is shared family time a given. Family members, even spouses, share less and less of a common reality. As the home visitor and parents share in activities and conversations, the visitor can help parents recognize their young child's need for predictable, daily, shared family rituals. Once parents understand this need, the home visitor and parents can brainstorm strategies to make certain that these daily family rituals take place.

Home visitors also need to be alert to the complexities spouses experience in joining their separate family traditions, which not all couples think out thoroughly prior to marriage. Many people get married without realizing the challenge of uniting two different family traditions. Traditions such as celebrating a holiday or summer vacations may or may not be complementary. In addition, given the pluralistic nature of our society, beyond merging family traditions, many couples marry across race, ethnicity, and religion. For these couples, rituals take on added meaning because they must blend the traditions of not only two separate childhoods but also two racial, ethnic, or religious communities. Food for everyday mealtimes may not be a taken-for-granted part of one's day; rather, the couple may need to have mindful discussions about the different foods of their respective families. Initially, it may be helpful for menu planning and shopping to be a joint activity of planning and action. Some interreligious couples may need to make decisions regarding holidays, such as questions of celebrating Chanukah or Christmas. Parents often see their home visitor as a supportive person with whom they can talk through their decision making as they blend two family traditions.

For parents, divorce usually means grieving the loss of the complete family and giving up one's hopes, dreams, and expectations of having an intact family. Divorce is a stressful time that alters the custodial parent's social resources and disrupts many of their relationships that were intertwined with their former spouse.[25] When parents divorce, brothers and sisters often develop a close relationship because it seems they protect themselves and each other from the anxiety they feel in their parents' separation. In some families, the custodial parent unwittingly pushes the older child into a parenting role. For example, the mother may expect the older child to assume many responsibilities, some of which are inappropriate to the child's age. Alternatively, the mother, lonely for another adult, may begin to confide in the child and relate in ways beyond the child's social and emotional maturity. If home visitors sense that the older child is being "parentified," they can help single parents understand what is developmentally appropriate for the child's age. With the home visitor's support, most parents can understand that they need to change their expectations of the older child.

Given how stressful divorce can be for the custodial parent, it may be difficult to accept their young children's change in behavior. Most young children experience a lot of confusion and anxiety during their parents' divorce.[26] Although they probably are too young to express their feelings, young children often blame themselves for their parents' separation. It is important for parents to clearly and frequently state that their child is not the reason why they are separating. Some young children may feel deserted by the noncustodial parent, and these feelings may spark aggression or other behavior problems. Divorce and separation can be a confusing, painful, and anxious time for young children. As a result, they may regress to lower developmental levels (e.g., by beginning to stutter, wetting their beds at night). When home visitors describe these possible feelings and behavior changes in a matter-of-fact way, they help parents understand that their child's behavior is normal, is to be expected, and is a transitional response to significant, abrupt changes in their daily life.

Parents in the midst of a divorce also experience confusion, pain, and anxiety. Home visitors can offer parents their attention, support, and guidance. Many single parents feel isolated, especially when living far from their extended family.[27] In these situations, home visitors can help the parent connect to informal support systems, such as a local singles group or a child care cooperative. Parents may have no experience in seeking help and may need their home visitor's support and encouragement to understand that to seek assistance can be part of healthy adulthood.

CONCLUSIONS

This chapter discussed families' everyday routines; childhood illness and how illness disrupts taken-for-granted daily patterns of family life; and traditional family rituals, called *celebrations* to distinguish them from everyday rituals. Rituals consist of repeated, predictable patterns of interaction among family members that give each family member shared beliefs and values and a sense of belonging and identity. For young children, everyday rituals of eating, sleeping, diapering, and toilet training are the settings for developmental growth. Although this discussion of daily rituals may seem very detailed, it is in the detail that the quality of parent–child interaction has an impact on the child's development and sense of self. Initially, daily rituals of eating and going to sleep allow for the child's biological regulation. Intertwined with the interactions in these rituals is regulation of the child's emotion. Development in all areas (e.g., a sense of self, a sense of relatedness, language and communication, an understanding of the world) occurs within parent–child interaction during everyday rituals.

The chapter also discussed two related areas, frequent childhood illnesses and family celebrations. Frequent childhood illnesses can disrupt everyday interactions and can lead to both parents' and children's feelings of insecurity. At the same time, illness can be a setting for enriched social relatedness between family members and young children's learning of nurturance and caring. Regularly occurring family celebrations reflect both unique family beliefs and values and those of the surrounding culture. These celebrations provide family members with a sense of belonging and shared identity.

8

Play, Learning, and Development

Child, how happy you are sitting in the dust, playing with a broken twig all the
morning!
I smile at your play with that little bit of a broken twig.
I am busy with my accounts, adding up figures by the hour.
Perhaps you glance at me and think, "What a stupid game to spoil your morning
with!"
Child, I have forgotten the art of being absorbed in sticks and mud-pies.
I seek out costly playthings, and gather lumps of gold and silver.
With whatever you find you create your glad games. I spend both my time and my
strength over things I can never obtain.
In my frail canoe I struggle to cross the sea of desire, and forget that I too am
playing a game.
                    Rabindranath Tagore (1958, p. 48)

Play is infants' and young children's primary task. Play is the main way
through which they learn and develop. Infants and young children love
to play because play is intrinsically motivating; that is, children play for
the enjoyment and satisfaction of the activity itself. It is through play
that infants and young children understand and gain mastery of their
bodies, and it is the way they master their experiences in their everyday
world. Unlike adults, who leave their everyday work so they can play
for relaxation, young children's primary way of learning is through
play; play is children's work.[1]

Infants and young children are by nature curious. In their play, they explore spontaneously. First, they examine their own bodies and then the surrounding world, persons, and things. Young children learn through imaginative and active play, which involves people and objects. As they play, they create and make something entirely new. After she described the many steps a young child needs to pursue understanding of how the telephone works, Margaret Mead observed, "This is the creative moment. The child, like Alexander Graham Bell, has just created the telephone—suddenly, from all the little bits and pieces of slowly understood meanings, the idea of telephone has come up."[2] To explore, to understand, to master, to create—these are some of the central meanings and purposes of infants' and young children's play. According to Piaget, young children gain knowledge and understanding through their actions; that is, each child individually constructs knowledge through action.[3]

Play occurs within infants' and young children's everyday relationships with their parents. Parents make a difference in their child's play in how they interact with their child, interaction that occurs not only during play times but also within everyday routines such as diapering and feeding. The quality of parent–child interaction is pivotal to the infant's and young child's ability to play. The discussion of the role of the parent and of additional meanings and purposes of play in this chapter unfolds as it tracks the developmental progression of play and the home visitor's role in promoting optimal child and parent development.

INFANT PLAY: BIRTH–12 MONTHS

As their parents playfully interact with them, infants experience approval, connectedness, and shared delight. These interactions often are very brief; for example, a mother moves her eyes and mouth in a certain way when her infant smiles, or she responds with similar sounds when her infant coos.[4] These 1- to 2-second exchanges are the beginning of everyday patterns of playful parent–infant exchanges. Even when they do not interact directly with their infant, parents are a stabilizing presence. That is, they give their infant a sense of security: "If I need something, my parent is available." As infants develop, parents need to continue being active play partners and to tune in to their child's interests, ideas, and feelings. Often communication is achieved through gestures; for example, a parent quickly lifts the infant's arms up to indicate surprise.

Infants' Abilities to Interact Socially

Infants are born with the distinct feelings of joy, distress, disgust, and surprise. In addition, infants are born with biological readiness for social interaction. From the start, infants are able to begin and end social interactions with others. *Affect*, the term for feeling and emotion in developmental literature, is central to the infant's experiences of relating to others. From their earliest moments, infants' experiences are governed by what is pleasurable and unpleasurable. Newborns can begin and end interactions with others. For example, they can focus on their mother's face as she speaks or turn away from their mother. Young infants playfully explore their bodies, beginning with their mouth and hand, and their parents' bodies. A great deal of parents' interaction with their very young infant involves meeting the infant's biological needs: dressing, bathing, feeding, and diapering. During these tasks, skilled parents take time to talk, smile, and cuddle with their infant. As they care for their infants, they can play with them by touching, holding, imitating, and playing simple peek-a-boo games.[5] A variety of behaviors that parents just do automatically seem to be instinctive.[6] For example, parents in virtually all cultures give exaggerated hellos and imitate their infant's facial and vocal expressions.

Beginning at birth, infants prefer to look at people's faces. By age 8 weeks, they smile, give more direct eye contact, vocalize socially, and are more responsive. Now there are longer periods of wakefulness. Active interest in toys and people increases, with its accompanying learning and development. For example, when a father comes to his 3-month-old daughter lying in her crib, she smiles, kicks her legs, and moves her arms excitedly. Mutual, shared involvement and attention between baby and parent are essential for the infant's healthy development. These shared interactions provide mutual pleasure and a sense of connectedness. Parents and infants communicate by facial and vocal expressions and by the quality of movement, such as how the parent picks up, cuddles, or soothes the infant. Parents and their infants develop patterns of interaction that become highly ritualized; that is, parents approach their infant, respond to their infant's awakening, and smile and coo in a similar manner each day.[7] These playful routines are the same for every parent and infant, yet the particular interactions are unique. In time, parents learn how much activity and which forms of sensation and communication their baby enjoys most. Is it sound? Touch? Sight? Movement?

Exploratory Play

During the first year, infants' play is primarily exploratory because they investigate their bodies, objects in their everyday environments, and other people. As they play, infants discover what does and does not fit into their mouth and what does and does not feel good. Infants first learn to bring objects to their mouth and explore them with their lips and tongue, and shortly after that they bring objects before their eyes to look at. With increased motor coordination, they turn small objects about, bang them, and continue to put them in their mouth. Moving, touching, and making sounds are basic components of these play activities. Parents' responses are crucial to the development of these infant exploratory actions. Parents have the opportunity to encourage play, and this encouragement is communicated by their positive response to their infant's play; for example, parents can imitate their infant's facial expressions or body movements.

Not all new parents understand that, beginning at birth, their infant is capable of actively relating to them and that their interactions with their infant are essential for the infant's optimal development. Thus, it helps when home visitors share this developmental information and make certain that parents understand the developmental significance of their active involvement with their infant. Home visitors can model, praise, and encourage these daily patterns of interaction, as demonstrated by the following vignette.

> Karyn holds her son Greg (age 4 months) as Janice softly speaks to him: "You're looking right at me. You have very good eye contact." Greg begins cooing, and Janice repeats the same sounds. Janice continues, "You're used to having someone talk to you. I can tell. You are a good talker, and that's the best news! I'd never get any work done if I were your mommy."

This is Janice's second home visit since Greg's birth, and she can observe that this mother and infant interact frequently. As she relates to Greg, Janice both models imitation of Greg's vocalizations and affirms Karyn's talking with her son. Karyn asks Janice what would be good toys to buy for Greg.

> Janice: Small things that he can get a hold of—the kinds of things I see you have. Bright things—things he can get a grasp of—things that make different kinds of sounds—a variety of different kinds of stimulation to explore. Small kitchen items such as measuring spoons are good as toys.

> Janice moves the ring rattle out of Greg's view, and Greg does not follow it. Janice comments, "Notice how out of sight still is out of mind." She then puts a rattle in Greg's hand, and he puts it in his mouth.

> Janice: That's babies' primary way of exploring. It makes sense, for feeding is so important, and the mouth is the first body part that really works for them.

Janice stresses that exploration is the primary way young infants play. Within the context of Karyn's questions and Greg's actions, Janice gives developmental information: Greg is too young to track objects when they are removed from his sight, and his mouth is still his primary tool for exploration. Karyn tells Janice that each night Greg's daddy has extended play with him for a couple hours and that lots of this play involves moving him about and pretend-wrestling.

Janice: *For Greg, that's real learning, playing together with Dad. And it's great that dads have different play patterns than some moms have.*

Janice returns to Karyn's home when Greg is 5, 7, and 9 months old. Each time, she brings a tub of small assorted kitchen items and toys. As the months progress, Greg continues to make developmental strides. As she and Karyn observe Greg's play, Janice identifies new areas of learning and development. Within the context of Greg's play, she chats with Karyn, giving her developmental information, suggestions, and interpretations of the meaning of Greg's actions that she and his mother are observing.

Greg (age 5¹/₂ months), supported by his mother, is seated on the rug. Janice puts a tub of infant toys next to Greg, who looks into the tub.

Janice: *It's important for you to watch to see how he reacts to containers. As he gets older and has eye–hand coordination, he'll immediately dump [the tub].*

Karyn: *He used to just look at his toys; now he grabs.*

Janice: *Isn't that neat! It's hard for him to reach in [the tub]. I'm allowing a little bit of frustration, for frustration now helps him deal with frustration later. [Janice gives Greg a rattle, and he puts it in his mouth.] Straight to my mouth. Greg, that's what we want to see. It doesn't mean he's hungry, but exploring.*

Karyn: *His favorite toys are the small ones.*

Janice: *Developmentally, it's very predictable what kinds of toys a baby likes. He likes small things because he can hold them and can get them to his mouth.*

Janice spontaneously expresses delight in Greg's actions and helps Karyn see meaning in her son's play. Janice explains that Greg's eye–hand coordination soon will allow him to dump things. As she and Karyn watch Greg's approach to the tub of toys, Janice helps Karyn anticipate steps in her son's development and understand the important role of motor development in her son's play. As she also had observed when Greg was 4 months old, Janice again calls attention to how Greg is learning by exploring objects with his mouth. After she leaves Karyn and Greg, Janice writes down what Greg did with these toys so that she can identify changes in the next visit.

Six weeks later, Janice returns to visit Karyn and Greg. She helps Karyn recognize and understand her son's new gains in motor development, and she affirms Karyn's keen observation of her son.

Janice gives Greg (age 7 months) a tub of toys, and he reaches in the tub and pulls out a roll-toy.

Janice: *Last time he didn't get anything from the tub; now he's getting his hand right in there. That's really good. [Greg tips the tub, and all of the small-infant toys fall out.] He's much more secure in the sitting position.*

Karyn: *The last week or so.*

Janice: *Your mommy watches close and knows when you've changed. He handles that toy very well. Notice he takes it in both hands and has lots more freedom with his fingers. He turns it over and turns it back. [Greg drops a toy, which rolls to his side, and he turns to find it.] You lost it. And he remembered where it was. That's very significant. He dropped and looked for it. This is something to watch for. [Greg rolls over on his stomach and reaches for a toy.] You can see how motor development and curiosity are hooked together.*

As Greg explores the small objects in the tub, Janice helps his mother see how his actions point to gains in his fine motor skill. Janice links curiosity with motor development to help Karyn understand the manner in which her infant learns through play.

Janice returns when Greg is 9 months old and once again gives him a tub of toys. As Greg plays with the toys, Janice again comments on Greg's actions and how these actions point to Greg's developmental progress.

Karyn: *Dad has asked me to ask you what can he do with Greg besides playing and reading books.*

Janice: *That is really the way an infant learns in all areas of development. For Greg, that's real learning—playing together. Suggest [to Greg's dad] that he mimic what Greg is doing. Mimicking extends his attention span, affirms his play, and invites him to continue [the play].*

Karyn: *He plays with Greg about 3 hours each night.*

Janice's first home visit with Karyn and her husband, Joe, was during Karyn's third trimester of pregnancy. Joe clearly is very involved in parenting. Joe also wants to use this home visiting program to assist in his parenting. In turn, Janice acknowledges that Joe is a central player in his son's development and gives a helpful suggestion.

Beginning at around age 6 months, parents and their infants enjoy playing motion sequence games, such as pat-a-cake and peek-a-boo. Parents often invent new games as their infant grows older. For example, when an infant hits two blocks together, the parent makes a popping sound as she claps; and the sequence is repeated. Beyond the shared enjoyment and connectedness the infant feels in these experiences, these patterned, turn-taking games anticipate the young child's learning to take turns.

Infants usually begin to creep and crawl around 8–10 months of age. Movement offers new ways to explore, and suddenly the infant is cruising or crawling in every possible direction. Travel offers infants new perspectives, new discoveries within their everyday world. Now infants can explore all sides of the living room couch and, with practice, can learn to pull themselves to an upright position. This is the time for home visitors to remind parents that they need to make certain that they have child-proofed their home (e.g., put gates on open stairways, put safety latches on low kitchen cupboards that contain cleaning supplies, put plugs on electrical outlets).

TODDLER PLAY: AGES 12–30 MONTHS

The most striking characteristics of toddlers are their interest in movement, their curiosity, and their strong attempts to be independent. At first, simply walking and climbing are totally absorbing. With movement, toddlers realize they can be independent of their parents. Yet, at the same time, toddlers have strong security needs of attachment and accompanying feelings of dependence. As they explore their newly found skills in movement and their newly found upright world, toddlers struggle with the ambivalent feelings of independence and dependence. Much of toddlers' play centers around this ambivalence because it is at the core of the toddler's striving to form his or her own identity. When toddlers begin games of give-and-take with their parents, it is as if they are exploring what is "yours" and "mine." As they become more sure-footed and begin to run, in hide-and-seek games, toddlers explore whether the parent knows where they are.

Nancy (age 24 months) and Ricky (age 22 months) have been playing in the sandbox, and Ricky's mother, Jean, is seated with them. The children leave the sandbox and run into the garage to hide from Jean. Jean goes to a large tree near the sandbox and calls out, "Where are you? Nancy and Ricky, where are you?" The children laugh gleefully and look out at Jean.

Jean asks the children, "You can't find me?" Jean then walks behind the tree, and the children run toward her. As the children come to the tree, Jean walks around the tree so they can't catch her as she says playfully, "Where's Nancy and Ricky? Where are you?" The children giggle as they run around the tree with Jean. When they catch her, they race to the garage as they yell, "We hide!"

In their spirited hide-and-seek play with Jean, these toddlers are experimenting with their strong feelings of separation and independence. In these games, toddlers learn turn taking and cooperation.

Movement, Simple Pretend-Play, and Continued Exploration

Playing alone, toddlers enjoy dumping and filling containers repeatedly or piling blocks and then knocking them down. These seemingly endless play sequences give the toddler practice in fine motor skill development and eye–hand coordination. In this exploratory play, they are learning about cause and effect: how their own actions have an effect on objects. As they initiate play with toddlers, home visitors provide everyday play experiences and use these experiences to assist parents in understanding the meaning of their toddler's play.

As she shakes the cans, Cynthia places two cans, each containing plastic poker chips, on the rug next to Cassandra (age 14 months). As she gives the cans to Cassandra, Cynthia says to Cassandra's mother, Samantha, "Let's see how she plays with these toys."

Cassandra throws a chip, and Cynthia says, "She found a new way to play with this." Samantha puts a chip into the can as she says to her daughter, "Can you do that?" Cynthia asks, "Mommy made a different sound, didn't she?" Samantha then helps her daughter by supporting one can as Cassandra dumps the chips from one can into the other.

Cynthia: *That's neat, the way you put your hand under hers and allow her to do it but help her a little bit. [Cassandra puts her hand in the can and shakes the chips.] Now we're making some new noises.*

As she dumps out the chips, Samantha says to her daughter, "Let's try it again." Cassandra puts the chips into the can and looks up to her mother, who nods affirmatively. Cassandra continues the task.

Cynthia: *Just with a look, you gave her encouragement to do it. You gave her that go ahead to do it, and she did. See how this finger is coming together with that? [Cynthia demonstrates the pincer grasp with her hand.] That is called the pincer grasp. The pincer grasp is developing and is really important because you have to have the pincer to be able to write. Another thing, this is good for using her eyes with her hands. In order to pick them up and put them back in the can, she is building eye–hand coordination, which is another skill needed in writing. [As Cynthia talks to Samantha, Cassandra dumps and fills the can with chips.] Lots of time we think this is fun, and we don't recognize it's learning, too.*

As she watches Samantha assist Cassandra in this new task, Cynthia tells Samantha the importance of what her toddler is doing. She also helps this mother understand how this type of play fosters Cassandra's pincer grasping and eye–hand coordination—basic skills needed for writing.

At age 12 or 13 months, toddlers begin to say their first words. As they gain increased skill in speaking and understanding language, toddlers love naming games. Just as they love to explore their hands and feet as young infants, so, too, toddlers love to name the parts of their bodies, name pictures in books, and name objects in the world about them. This is a period in which toddlers love spontaneous, impromptu games with adults, especially when their bodies are involved.

Jeff (age 18 months) brings the basket of plastic Easter eggs to Sally, his family child care provider. Jeff puts a half-egg on Sally's nose as he says, "Nose."

Sally: On my nose! I'm going to put a purple on Jeff's nose.

As Sally holds the egg over Jeff's nose, he laughs gleefully. Sally then says to Jeff, "And I can make it a hat," as she puts her half-egg on top of her head. Sally puts two more half-eggs on her head as she says, "Three hats." The hats fall off, and Jeff laughs. Jeff then puts a half-egg on his head as he says, "Hat."

Jeff has initiated a simple pretend game, and Sally is skilled in entering into his play as a play partner. Sally imitates Jeff, who in turn imitates Sally, a common play pattern among young toddlers and adults. Sally encourages and extends Jeff's language—"on my nose"—and takes the play one step further as she puts the egg on her head. In his play, Jeff practices his language and experiences shared enjoyment and connectedness.

Often an adult can support and extend a toddler's play without being a full participant. In the next vignette, the family child care provider, Jean, is folding clothes in the room where three toddlers, Nancy, Ricky, and Jason, play.

Nancy (age 19 months) gets on the school bus and rides past Jean as she says, "Beep, beep." Jean asks her, "Where is your horn?" Nancy then makes the horn sound of the school bus.

Jean: *Picking up the kids from school? Got any kids?*

Nancy: *Pick up.*

Jean: *Picking up the kids.*

Jean reaches down to the floor, picks up a play person, and hands it to Nancy as she says, "Here is one." Jason (age 28 months) then sees another play person across the room and gives it to Nancy as he says, "Here's another people. I find one." Nancy then rides off as she says, "Go school."

While folding laundry, Jean skillfully provides guidance to these young children's play. Nancy has taken the lead, and Jean enters into the play and extends it. Like Sally, as she role-plays with Nancy, Jean promotes her language as she repeats and extends Nancy's spontaneous comments.

In their work with parents, home visitors can help parents understand that play is the means by which their toddler is learning and that they can significantly influence their toddler's play and accompanying learning and development. When parents understand the meaning of their toddler's playful explorations, independent actions, and negative responses, they will not see these actions as mere signs of the so-called terrible twos. Instead, they can strive to provide a setting that encourages developmental progress within clear limits. Shelly and Rob, who have had a home visitor since Shelly's third trimester, explained this type of learning.

Shelly: *It helps to know that these things are going to occur, and what Erin (age 26 months) is doing now is good. This is good that she wants to play with the knobs on the stereo. You know, most people would just say "No," and slap their children's hands. But we knew that was just a way for Erin to investigate things. Instead of correcting her for something that wasn't really going to hurt, we let her do it. And she doesn't play with anybody's knobs when we go to their house. We didn't have to stand there and yell "No!" to her. Because we knew that these things were going to pass, and that this was good for her to investigate things. Just those little things that we knew ahead of time, I think, helped us prepare for each step."*

Rob: *Yes, knowing what's coming up when you see her do something. Knowing "Hey, this is a stage that this child is going through." And you should pick up on it and work with it rather than put her on a leash!*

Toddlers seem to spend most of their day experimenting. They climb into cupboards, twirl to music, scatter their food about their highchair tray, and splash vigorously in the bathtub. Objects in their everyday world become toys, and their approach to experiences is playful during dressing, eating, and bathing, as well as during "legitimate" playtimes. Home visitors can assist parents in understanding that their toddler's exploration, experimentation, and testing is their way of knowing and learning. In order to assist parents in seeing and understanding this dominant approach of their toddlers, Janice brings a "curiosity bag" filled with "beautiful junk" for the toddler to explore.

Janice puts a cloth toy bag on the floor as she says to Mia (age 24 months), "Here is a whole bag for you to explore." Mia sits down and begins to pull items out of the bag as Janice comments to Tracy, "This is basically a bag of junk. It's important to continue to give Mia the opportunity to explore and to be creative."

Tracy: When Mia is downstairs with me, when I am doing laundry, she is always finding things. Anything that is new and different. And she's always asking me, "What's this, Mommy?"

Mia has pulled a toy plastic milk bottle out of the bag and begins to shake it. Janice helps Mia begin to open the lid, and Mia finishes opening it and dumps a play person on the floor. She then goes into the bag and removes a car as she says, "Ooooh, car." She puts the play person in the car as Janice comments, "Sure, he can ride in the car." Mia responds, "I too big." Tracy affirms, "You are too big to ride in that car."

In each of her visits, Janice emphasizes that Mia is learning as she actively explores her everyday environment. Bringing a bag of everyday "beautiful junk" for Mia to explore helps Tracy observe how her toddler is learning as well as how to take the toddler's point of view toward objects in her home. As Mia investigates the items, Janice assists Mia, and her actions are powerful models for Mia's mother, Tracy.

As Mia looks through the bag, Janice comments to Tracy, "Children all have their own style with this bag. Mia is so precise—looking and deciding what she wants. When you think about how her exploring has changed—initially everything went right into her mouth. Now she explores things with her hands and eyes."

Mia takes a small cosmetic bag but has difficulty unzipping it. Her mother says, "Bring it here, and I'll hold it so that you can unzip it." Mia does as her mother has directed. Janice comments, "It is good that you structure the job so that she could do it herself." Mia unzips the bag and removes a small play figure that she identifies as "Cookie Monster."

As Tracy assists her daughter, Janice affirms the manner in which Tracy enables Mia to succeed at a task. With her bag of "beautiful junk," Janice models encouragement and uses Mia's play to help

Tracy understand how her toddler's curiosity, exploration, and learning are progressing.

Quality of the Home Environment

Janice also helps parents understand that the quality of their home environment makes a difference in their child's play. Home settings that promote play include

- A relaxed atmosphere with minimal adult directives
- Adequate and safe space
- A variety of objects and toys that promote active participation and creative construction

As Janice brings everyday objects and simple toys to use during her home visits, she helps parents understand the value of play activities that invite construction, foster eye–hand and fine motor coordination, and encourage imagination and self-expression. Some toys encourage early role-play, for example, dishes, pots, and pans; dolls; and blocks and toy trucks.

Role-Play

Toddlers begin not only to speak in words but also to role-play—two actions that give evidence that toddlers can think symbolically; that is, they can represent actions, objects, and people in their minds. In pretend-play, toddlers begin to use meanings other than those usually attached to objects or actions. For example, they feed their toy dog with a cup, or a stick becomes a horse to ride. Usually, the role-play centers around simple themes of everyday home experiences.[8] In these role-play sequences, toddlers replay their familial activities, explore their related feelings and reactions to those experiences, and gain mastery of these feelings. For example, as a child rigorously washes his doll's hair, he is gaining control of his feelings when his own hair is being washed. Home visitors can help parents understand the value of role playing. During their home visits, they can initiate role-play activities with the toddler and encourage parents to join in the play.

> Home visitor Winneta has placed a checkered tablecloth and assorted plastic dishes, utensils, and plastic food on the tablecloth. She suggests to Jayla (age 25 months) that they are having a picnic. Jayla brings a toy hamburger in a bun to Winneta, who says, "Let me have a bite. Mmmmm . . . real good." Jayla then brings her mother, Sheryll, a hamburger and sits next to her as she pretends to eat a hot dog and

potato chips. Sheryll tells Winneta that in the same fashion that Jayla is pretending to eat her hot dog without a bun, with real hot dogs, Jayla never eats a bun.

Winneta: *She brings her real world into her pretend-play. That's very important. Pretend-play helps understanding of her real world.*

Sheryll: *My husband plays this with Jayla in her kitchen in her bedroom.*

Winneta: *Super!*

Sheryll describes how, the previous night, Jayla had taken the dust pan and broom and pretended to sweep and then put everything away. Winneta responds, "I encourage you to let her continue to role-play. By acting out her experiences, she better understands her feelings about these experiences."

Winneta, Sheryll, and Jayla enjoy an extended role-play sequence during Winneta's home visit. Winneta affirms the role-play that Jayla's dad has with her. Winneta helps Sheryll understand that role playing is an important way for Jayla to understand her everyday experiences.

Jayla's dad works a split-shift work schedule and often is part of Winneta's home visits. In fact, he came home at the end of the visit just described and read a story to his daughter. Winneta is very committed to involving both parents in her home visits. She explained her perspective to the author as follows.

I feel each parent has their own style. And they both bring equally important techniques. Maybe dad might be real interactive and playful and like to do motor things, whereas mom might like to do more calming things, reading things. I try to tell parents they are both equally important, and their roles are very important even though they are different.

Encouraging Parents to Play with Their Child

An important goal in home visiting is to encourage parents to be partners in play with their young child. As parents enter into their child's play, their child feels affirmed, feels a sense of connectedness, and has an invitation to express herself imaginatively and constructively.[9] Many home visitors can play skillfully with a very young child and have constructive conversations with the parents about the child's development and their parenting. Commitment and ability to stimulate parents as play partners is a skill that home visitors develop with experience and professional guidance. The following home visit illustrates this process.

During her home visit, Janice places a box of about 50 small, colored wooden blocks on the floor next to Erin (age 30 months). Once the blocks are on the rug, Erin immediately begins to build a simple structure. Janice then makes the same structure as she says to Erin's mother, Shelly, "One thing I really like to do with blocks is to follow the child's lead." Shelly asks, "You mean imitate?" Janice nods yes. Erin then lines up several blocks and puts a second row on top of the first. Janice duplicates the pattern as she says to Erin, "That's a neat building you're making. Is mine like yours?" Erin smiles and says, "Yeah."

Janice then suggests, "Let's let Mommy build. You build and Mommy can copy." As Erin begins a new block structure, her mother duplicates it as she says, "Look at mine! It's just like yours." Erin smiles and claps enthusiastically. As Erin and her mother continue building, Janice comments, "One of the nice things with blocks, it gives you the opportunity to follow her lead. Children need to be the leader." Shelly reflects, "I never thought about that. I don't imitate her, even when we color together."

Janice first demonstrates how Erin likes Janice's mirroring her block building. Shelly then clearly enjoys following her child's lead—a first experience in her parenting. Several days after this home visit, Janice talked about her rationale for involving parents in play activities with their toddler.

It's a goal for almost every visit to involve the parent and child together in a play activity. And I definitely involve the parent more when the child is a little older than when there is an infant. I ordinarily initiate the activity with the child so that I have the opportunity for modeling, because I think modeling is an important aspect of what we do. But then I always like to say, "Give Mom a turn," or "Let's let Mom do it now," or "We can all do it together." The easy ones are the blocks where the parent mirrors what the child has built. It's also pretty easy to do with dishes. Playdough is really easy. If you have an activity built around the child exploring something, then you have the parent back off. But even then, I will try to reserve time for a book for mom and her child to read together.

When parents learn to be active participants in their child's play, home visitors can talk about the specific meaning and purpose of this type of parent involvement for their child's development. For example, a parent's active involvement as a play partner gives his or her child a sense of connectedness and self-worth. The parent is promoting her or his child's ability to maintain focus—an essential readiness skill for school success.

PRESCHOOL PLAY:
AGES 30 MONTHS–5 YEARS

During the preschool years, children achieve mastery in play, especially in imaginative constructions and dramatic role-play. Play often stimulates problem solving, for example, figuring out, "How can I prevent the wall of my block building from falling down?"[10] In role-play, children can represent real and imagined experiences (e.g., pretending to build an apartment building, being a Halloween witch, putting out a fire). In this role-play, children express themselves creatively and feel a sense of power because they are in control of their play. In these experiences, children develop an increased sense of competence and self-worth. As home visitors provide these types of play activities for young children, they can help parents understand the developmental meaning and purpose of these experiences.

As young children act out roles, their play is process-oriented; that is, the activity is pleasurable in and of itself, and no product is needed. For children ages 30 months–4 years, play themes remain mostly about family situations; however, role-play sequences become more elaborate and extended. Pretend roles are fluid and shifting: One minute the child is a sister; the next, a mother. These young children have not firmly separated reality and fantasy; thus, they dislike being the baby. Because a major task of young children is still separation and identity formation, it is not surprising that they most often choose to be the mother.

Most noticeable in preschoolers' play is their delight and complete absorption in role-play sequences. In the following vignette, Amos has had his third birthday the previous week and has started a child care program this week. He engages in a brief role-play sequence in the housekeeping area with his teacher, Dana.

> Amos sets the table and calls to Dana, who is seated at the nearby puzzle table, "Dana, I'll give you some coffee and lunch." Dana comes to the table and says, "Good, I like that a lot." She pretends to eat. Amos tells Dana, "Now I'll make you a birthday cake." He takes a plate to Dana, and they sing "Happy Birthday." Then Amos hands Dana a physician's kit as he says, "Now this is your present." Clapping her hands, Dana replies, "Oh, I love it. Thank you. But now I have to go home. Thanks for the party."
>
> Amos turns to Dana as he tells her, "Now it's closing time." He takes Dana's hand as Dana asks him, "Now where are we going?" Amos replies, "We're going home. Dana questions, "Are you my Daddy?"

Amos replies, very seriously, "Yes. And we need to use the seat belts so it won't be dangerous." Amos and Dana then leave the housekeeping area hand-in-hand.

Amos's teacher, Dana, is a full participant in Amos's play, and this role gives Amos respect and a feeling of connectedness. Amos is the leader of the play sequence, and, as leader, he is able to act out his everyday world at home and have it affirmed by Dana. Within the play, Amos is creative and enters into conversation that is grounded in his reality. In his first week away from home, Amos is able to experience that the child care program is a setting where adults understand and value him.

Development of Abstract Thinking and Pretend-Play

Role-play of 4- and 5-year-olds no longer centers only around family themes. Children at this age have a firmer sense of self, can better separate fantasy and reality, and thus know they are pretending. Ghost, monster, and other themes of aggression often surface and give the children experiences in mastering their fears. Because children can now use one object to represent another in pretend-play, this representation indicates that the child's thinking is moving from the concrete to the abstract.[11] As their representation and language skills develop, children's need for realistic objects to communicate symbolic meaning is lessened. With age and pretend-play experience, they learn to represent imagined objects without using anything concrete. The following role-play sequences of children this age in the playground of their child care center illustrate this point.

Four boys are pretending that the large horizontal concrete pipe is a haunted house. Dan sits on top of the west opening, and J.T. sits on the opposite side. Rob pretends to be a bat and continually makes bat movements with his arms as he runs from one end of the pipe to the other. Chris whispers the magic word to J.T. before he enters the pipe. Chris is a ghost who makes "whoooo" sounds as he moves about the pipe.

Jana and Treeva have just entered the playground and run to the child care center sign, which they pretend is a restaurant sign. Jana asks, "What do you want?" Treeva replies, "An ice cream cone." Jana pretends to give one to Treeva, who leaves the area as she pretends to lick the cone. Annie comes to the area and Jana asks, "What do you want?" Annie answers, "Cherry pie." Jana responds, "We have only chocolate pie. Do you want some?" Annie nods yes, and Jana pretends to give her some. As Annie leaves, Jana says to herself, "All the children are gone now." Before leaving the area, she calls out loudly, "Anybody want food or drinks?"

As older preschoolers gain greater understanding of both happenings at home and in their community, adults can provide props for children to role-play sequences beyond their home. Family child care provider Jean has structured a post office for her son Ricky (age 4 years, 1 month) and another child, Nancy (4 years, 3 months).

Jean has made a mailbox from a cardboard box, and she has small church offering envelopes for the children to use for their letters. She suggests to Ricky and Nancy that they each get a crayon or a pen and paper and write a letter. As she puts the envelopes on the table in front of the mailbox, Jean says, "Here's our envelopes. Whenever you get your letter done, you can get an envelope. You need to get a big storybook to write on."

Jean gives the children small pieces of paper to write on as she says, "I'm not the one who will write. I am the post officer. I have some stamps [stickers]. Who are you going to write to?" Ricky replies, "To George Washington." Nancy replies, "To my Mommy" (who is in the hospital). Ricky brings his mother his paper and asks her to write George Washington on it, which she does. Nancy then asks her to write her mother's name, which Jean does. Both children then make pictures on their papers, fold them, get envelopes, and carefully put their papers into the envelopes. Ricky tells his mother, "I'm folding mine good." Jean nods yes. Both Ricky and Nancy then get stamps and put them on their envelopes, and then place them inside the box.

Jean has sequenced the tasks clearly for these young children. Each child writes three letters, and, as they make pictures, they tell Janice about the pictures and to whom they are writing. The children remain focused on the task for approximately 30 minutes. This simple role-play activity offers opportunities for fine motor and eye–hand coordination, creativity, and oral communication. Together, Nancy and Ricky experience shared enjoyment in the task. Smilansky's research demonstrated how children's dramatic role-play with other children helps children learn to communicate and take the perspective of others.[12] Role-play demands joint decision making, such as which child will play which role and what the action will be. In this play, children experience how other children act out being a mother, father, or sibling.

In a home visiting program for families with young children, visitors need to initiate brief play sequences during each of their visits. Janice explained how she tries to help parents understand the meaning of learning and play.

One way I think our program is important is pointing out to parents that play is important. That when the child is young and trying to do a puzzle or shape sorter, I can talk about that as a way of learning and problem solving for the young child. And I compare a task to how things are going to be different when she gets a little older. Yes, we look at it as maybe just play, but it is very serious problem solving for the child. And I try and help the parent to appreciate that when a child is experimenting and exploring, when they are trying a multitude of the things that they do, when they are pretending, doing private talk, it isn't just silly little play activities. It is something that is very valuable in the total scope of preparing them for the different kind of learning that will happen when they get to the first or sixth grade, and they are sitting at a desk in the classroom. It is all learning, and it just is a different method. It is both serious and necessary for the young child.

Play sequences in Janice's home visit (described next) illustrate how she stimulates children's learning through play. As the children play, Janice helps parents understand that, in their play, these young children are learning about relationships. When Erin is 33 months old, Janice provides a matching game for her.

Janice places an assortment of vehicles and play people on the rug. Then she makes a long line, about 4 feet long, with red yarn on the living room rug. She suggests to Erin, "Let's see if we can make a parade." She puts a fire truck with a toy fire officer on the front end of the yarn as she asks, "Can you find another fire truck?" Erin searches and exclaims gleefully, "I found one!" There is a play fire officer in the truck. Janice asks, "Can you find a fire officer to match?" Erin finds the fire officer and says, "I found one!" Erin then picks up a race car driver doll and puts it into the car. Following Janice's suggestions, she finds the second race car, puts it behind the first, and puts the driver in each seat.

Janice: *Which car will go next?*

Erin: *[Picks up the police car and puts it behind the race cars] How about this one?*

Janice: *A police car—how about a driver for it?*

Erin: *I can't find one.*

Janice: *I think she's behind the horse.*

Janice tells Erin's parents, Rob and Shelly, "That's a great way to reinforce prepositions, such as 'behind,' as she is playing." Erin continues making the parade for several more minutes. As she plays, Janice and Erin explore "next to," "in front of," and other spatial relationships. Janice explains to Rob and Shelly that matching is an important premath relationship skill.

When Erin's toy parade is completed, Janice initiates a second matching game. This game uses pictures of *Sesame Street* characters. As they play, Janice explains to Rob and Shelly that first young children learn with concrete objects, then with objects and pictures, and then with pictures alone. The fourth step involves letters and numbers. After this visit, Janice described her intent in introducing these games.

My goal is to help parents see that their child is able to pick out things that are alike, to see similarities and differences. And most young children do it spontaneously as they explore. I want parents to be aware of that. It helps me talk about the young child's intellectual development. And I guess what's fun about it is that a child does it spontaneously, and the parent begins to notice what they are doing. . . . And the second game gives me a chance to help parents see the difference between using objects, touching and manipulating them, to see things that are alike as opposed to using pictures that are alike. This progression I don't get to with every child, but Erin is very quick. It depends on how they handle the objects in the first game as to whether I pull out the cards.

Toys and Materials to Promote Creative Self-Expression

When parents provide pencils, pens, crayons, felt markers, paint, chalk, playdough, and clay, these materials invite young children to explore and express themselves creatively.[13] Before age 3, children's drawings primarily consist of scribbling. The activity initially is a motor activity. As children begin to think symbolically and develop motor control and eye–hand coordination, they make representative drawings. When children draw and make something uniquely their own, they feel good about themselves and feel a sense of competency. These also are tools that provide enjoyable releasing experiences.

Construction toys such as blocks and snap-together toys invite another rich medium for imaginative construction. During the preschool years, these constructions become representational (e.g., building a house, a train, a school). Whether the activity involves creative art or manipulative toys, the child experiences initiative and mastery. There are no rules to follow. In this play, the children also learn about spatial relations such as size, shape, and form.

DIFFICULTIES AND DILEMMAS

Some family patterns trigger difficulties for the home visitor eager to assist parents in understanding how young children learn through their everyday play. One of the most common activities of family life—television viewing habits—can be one of the most problematic for the home visitor.

Other challenging family patterns with which a home visitor comes into contact include those parents 1) who did not themselves learn how to play as children, 2) whose primary focus is assisting their young child's academic learning, and 3) whose style is very directive.

Television Viewing Habits

Increasingly, television and videotape viewing takes the place of young children's active learning through play. It is important for home visitors to be knowledgeable about the impact of television and videos on children's play. Dilemmas include both the excessive amount of television watching and the content of children's commercial television programming. As of 1990, children 3–6 years of age watched an average of 4–6 hours of television each day; for children from low-income families, the hours increased by 50%.[14]

By age 18, the average American child has watched 7 years of television. With deregulation of children's commercial television programs in 1984, television shows and toys could be marketed together for the first time. The dominant theme of both television and the related toys is violence. Within 3 years after deregulation, the number of war toys (e.g., Power Rangers) increased by 600%. As a result, we are seeing changes in children's play. Preschool teachers report that, in much of their play, children imitate television characters, resulting in marked increases in violence and aggression. Young children are feeling power through their television toys. Young children always have played war games; but, in the past, children chose the content of the war play and used their imagination as they invented heroes and enemies. Currently, children's war games most often are imitations of television programming. When watching television dominates how children play, creatively acting out one's everyday experience and gaining mastery over these experiences often is no longer the dominant theme in children's play.

Home visitors have many opportunities to talk about the impact of television in their conversations with parents. They can help parents understand the meaning and purpose of active learning through play and the distinction between imitations of television characters and creative role-play. They can suggest that parents watch television with their child. As they watch, parents can discuss with their child what is being viewed or can choose to monitor the programming as being developmentally inappropriate. Unfortunately, parents frequently use television and videos as baby sitters, that is, as times when their child is occupied and the parents can be doing something else in a different part of their home.

In spite of these cautions about television, home visitors need to be respectful of family patterns. In many American homes, television is on during a large part of the day; in some homes, it is on all the time. Thus, this topic demands sensitivity and skill. The home visitor should maintain respect for family patterns and, at the same time, responsibly provide developmental information regarding the impact of television on young children's development. For example, as a child engages in role-play with her home visitor, the visitor can explain to the child's parents that today this type of role-play is decreasing as the time that young children spend watching violent cartoons on television is on the rise. Many children imitate the violent television cartoons rather than role-playing their everyday life. Use of television remains the parent's decision; however, the home visitor has provided appropriate information regarding its developmental impact.

Parents Who Have Difficulty Playing with Their Children

A further challenge that home visitors may face involves parents who do not enjoy or know how to play with their infant or young child. When home visitors are working with parents of very young children, it is important for them to see whether the parents enjoy playing with their infant and toddler. A parent who does not enjoy playing probably does not know how to play. Parents reared in a troubled family may not have extensive joyful childhood play memories to draw upon in their relations with their infant. Spontaneity and having fun is not a given among all parents. Janice spoke with the author regarding this issue as follows:

Janice: *Some mothers really don't know how to play with their baby. They know how to do something for their baby, like change her diapers. They may know how to make their baby laugh. They know how to ask their baby questions. But they just don't seem to catch on as to how to play. It's as if they need to be taught. Once a parent is able to enjoy observing her infant and home visitor play together, then the home visitor can go a step further and invite the parent to join in the play.*

This one mom I'm thinking about, I'd invite her on the floor. She'd come down sometimes, but not all the time. We'd do something, and then she'd be back up on her chair, just being apart from, instead of a part of, the activity. That is something that for me as a home visitor has evolved over time, in that I'm better at encouraging parents now than I used to be. But there are just some parents that just won't do it.

Carol: *Do you think there are different reasons for the resistance, such as some parents are afraid they'll look silly or others might be too shy?*

Janice: *I think there's a certain amount of distance that some parents always may have with their children, and they see their role as a directive role and a caretaker, as opposed to a playmate. Getting them to even see themselves as a playmate and then to act that out is real difficult. It's as if they fear they are losing ground in maintaining the respect they want. They fear the authority and response will somehow get muffled.*

For these parents, home visitors first have to engage in play with the infant or young child and help the parent see and understand the meaning of this play. Once a trusting relationship between home visitor and parent is firmly established, then the home visitor can encourage the parent to enter into the play. It is through concrete experiences in play with their child that parents can begin to enjoy and value these experiences and then provide them for their child on their own.

Parents Who Do Not Appreciate the Learning Value of Play

In addition to not enjoying play with their children, many parents may not value play as the primary way their young child learns. Rather, many are eager for their child to excel in more structured learning. One parent remarked that she was more interested that her child "learn his 1-2-3s and A-B-Cs." In fact, 2-, 3-, and 4-year-olds can learn to recognize numbers and letters. This is rote learning, however, without understanding of the meaning of the symbols. For example, many 3-year-olds can count to 10 and recognize numerals; however, they often do not grasp the concept of what *three* actually means or the concepts of *more than* and *less than*. At first, parents may see their home visitor as their child's teacher, and their expectations are for this person to focus on helping their child's academic learning. One of the home visitor's first challenges is to help these parents to understand the developmental importance of play as their child's primary means of learning. To do this, the home visitor can use a strategy similar to that which was discussed with parents who do not know how to play. Once home visitors have established a trusting relationship with parents, they can encourage the parents to enter into play with their child. It is important to have open-ended materials such as a tub of birdseed or beans or playdough for sensory play. These activities have no rules. The parents can experience their child's delight, and the home visitor can explain the developmental value of the play.

Directive Parents

Some parents are very directive in their interactions with their young child. These parents often are anxious that their child perform in the right manner. Given this concern, it is very difficult for these parents to allow their infants or young children to first explore a toy in their own way. When a home visitor recognizes that a parent has such parenting patterns, she needs to explain concretely the meaning and purpose of exploration. As the infant or young child does explore, the visitor can tell the parent specifically what the child is learning. Janice discussed how she has learned to relate to directive parents during home visits.

When I first began doing home visits, I had a low-functioning mother. Each visit, she would take over the toy and play with it herself. Then she would show her child every step of what she was supposed to do. I didn't feel secure enough to jump in and say anything.

Then I physically got in the mom's way. And then I would put the toy far away from the mom, and then engage her in conversation so that her baby first could explore. With experience, I got better with that—better with talking with the mom who could not let her child explore. When I saw that a mom was overly directive, I started my chatter immediately. I would put a toy down and say, "Let's watch and see what she does with this."

Janice described how she blocked this mother's intrusion into her baby's play. Her blocking is successful only because she is skilled in establishing a relationship with this mother—a relationship that allows, over time, the mother to hear and integrate new developmental information and parenting strategies.

Directive moms get real embarrassed when their child turns a toy upside down. They are quick to say to the child, "No, that's not the way you're supposed to play with it." Again, I'll be quick to add, "Isn't it wonderful that she wants to explore it from every angle?" I'll also make comments that babies could teach manufacturers many ways that toys could be used.

Janice ties her comments to the baby's actions. Her comments both affirm baby and parent and inform the parent. The parents' learning is experiential; it is grounded in their baby's actions, which Janice observes and interprets.

I'll tell moms another reason why it is helpful for a child to explore a toy is that it'll extend the time a child plays with a toy, and moms always need time. And finally, I'll suggest that in exploring, the child will get more mileage out of the toy. Then when a directive mom will let her baby explore, even for half a minute, I'll say, "It's so great the way you let Joey explore!" If an older sibling is part of the visit, I'll talk to mom through the sibling, as I tell him to let his sister first explore.

Janice does not specifically address parents' directive style. Rather, in each visit, she provides play experiences in which she can affirm the baby's exploratory learning, interpret the developmental purpose of this learning, and affirm both baby and parents. Janice is secure in the knowledge that, once she has established a trusting relationship with a parent, over time, the parent will learn experientially to value the baby's manner of learning.

Strategies suggested above can assist home visitors when they work with difficult family situations. At the same time, there are situations in which a family rejects all of a home visitor's approaches. In other words, in some situations with some families, home visiting just does not work. Given these potential difficulties, home visiting programs need to provide home visitors with a working climate of support and guidance from peers, mentors, and administrators.

CONCLUSIONS

From infancy through early childhood, play remains the primary method of learning and development. Parents of infants and young children can provide a relaxed atmosphere, space, and interactions that promote and encourage play, learning, and development. In turn, home visitors can help parents develop understanding and skill to promote their infant's and young child's learning and development through play.

This chapter described how infants and young children by nature are curious and spontaneously explore and experiment as they relate to people and to objects. The activity of exploring and experimenting is pleasurable in and of itself; it is intrinsically motivating. As infants and young children explore and experiment, they are playing, which is their primary way of learning. In their play with objects and with people, they often are creative and express themselves imaginatively.

This chapter illustrated and discussed the many ways that home visitors can promote parents' understanding and skill in promoting their child's play. They provide developmental information so that parents can understand the meaning and purposes of their child's play and can anticipate future developmental gains. It is natural that parents may take for granted routine activities such as diapering, dressing, and feeding. Thus, home visitors can be very helpful in discussing how these routine activities are a wonderful setting for playful parent–child interactions. When home visitors observe playful, spontaneous parent–child interactions, they can affirm the parents' actions and describe the meaning of what they are seeing in terms of the young child's learning and development. When they bring small objects and toys with which infants and young children can play, home visitors can help parents see how their child is developing new understanding and skills through their play. Home visitors can provide play activities in which they can encourage parents to be active participants and, in this participation, learn how being a play partner benefits their child.

9

Siblings

I was the eldest of five children. But I have very few memories of my early childhood in which my brother does not play a part. I remember my second birthday party and I remember spoiling my new red shoes by going out in the snow that winter. Then in spring Richard was born, and very soon Margaret and Richard were expected to do everything together.

We used to have our supper together, wearing white nightclothes (with feet) and eating cereal or, on Sunday night, browies made of dried remains of Saturday's Boston browis bread and baked beans soaked in hot milk. We were taught to sing the same songs together until it became obvious that while Richard's voice was true and clear, I had no voice at all. We even were dressed alike in blue coats with brass buttons and round stiff berets, and I passionately wanted a hat, embroidered hat that a young aunt had left behind. Richard was my little brother. He was valiant in my defense, standing in front of me and proclaiming, "You let my sister be!"

Margaret Mead (1972, p. 61)

Relationships with siblings endure longer than any other. The sibling bond offers feelings of intimacy, support, and belonging. The strength of the sibling bond is indicated by the way people use the terms *brother* and *sister* in religious groups, sororities, fraternities, unions, and service clubs. Communities have "big brother" programs in which men "adopt" boys from single-parent families. Some African Americans frequently greet nonrelatives as "brother" or "sister" or refer to each other in conversation as "brother" or "sister," with or without the person's name.

The childhood history siblings share allows them to understand one another's strengths and vulnerabilities more fully than they can understand such personality traits among people outside of the family. Within this shared history, siblings can provide a lifelong support system and a source of honest feedback, as well as shared responsibilities in caring for sick and aging parents.

The sibling bond also contains rivalry and conflict. Although quarrels among siblings are normal, many children in the same family spend a large portion of their childhood playing and positively relating with each other. Research indicates that siblings as young as 3 years old can skillfully understand their younger siblings' acts and feelings and can adapt their speaking to accommodate their younger brother's or sister's developmental level.[1]

Once parents have a second child, they encounter unexpected new experiences that can challenge their sense of competence as parents, change their image of family life, and evoke memories of their own childhood struggles. This chapter discusses themes that emerge in families with multiple children. These themes include

1. Preparation for the new infant
2. Parental expectations and comparisons
3. Parents relating differently to their children
4. Children's perceptions of these differences
5. Sibling's patterns of relating together, including conflicts and rivalry

The discussion reviews how home visitors can support and affirm parents and their children and provides helpful developmental information, interpretation, and suggested parenting approaches. The chapter also explores the skills needed for home visitors to balance their involvement with parents and more than one child.

PREPARATION FOR THE NEW INFANT

Sometimes parents worry that if they have another child, the older child will suffer because the new baby will distract them from their relationship with their older child. These feelings are strongest before the birth of the second child, because the first child has had the parents' exclusive attention. Not surprisingly, the first child may resent the sibling's intrusion and may fear parents' loss of love more than might middle children. But adjusting to a new sibling also offers new learning opportunities. Brazelton stated that there is no ideal time for having a second child. He claimed that once parents "can handle another, the first child can handle one, too."[2] In contrast, throughout his book, White stressed that the ideal spacing of children is a minimum of 3 years, because rivalry and resentment are more problematic for first children younger than 3 years old.[3]

The addition of a new child to the family brings significant changes to the older child's everyday life, changes that begin in the months leading up to the birth of the child. It is normal for pregnant women to turn inward and subtly withdraw from their family. Older children notice these changes. Thus, it is helpful for parents to discuss the baby's pending arrival, beginning in early pregnancy, as if the pregnancy were a natural event in the family's development.

Home visitors can offer parents needed support and guidance during this important transition period of family life. As they help parents prepare their first child for the arrival of their new baby, home visitors can help parents know that their concerns are normal. The following conversation between Janice and Shelly is illustrative.

Shelly is in her second month of pregnancy. She tells Janice that her daughter, Erin (age 32 months), thinks she is having the baby.

Janice: *Let it go.*

Shelly: *She says, "I'm going to have one and you, too, but not Daddy. He doesn't have milk."*

Janice: *Erin wants to be like you.*

Shelly: *I'm concerned because she is with me so much. I'm getting Rob to do more with her, like wash her hair.*

Janice: *You are going to see her really growing up in the next several months—around 3 years.*

Shelly: *Everybody tells me we're going to have so many problems when there's a new baby.*

Janice: *It's always an adjustment. And it's always hardest with the first child. The second child is used to sharing attention when another child comes.*

Shelly: *We've never even spent a night away from Erin.*

Janice: *My three children are just about the same distance apart. I remember how well my first was able to entertain himself. Erin also is very skilled at that.*

Shelly: *Now I think I'll be more worried than Erin. Erin probably will be fine.*

Janice: As long as you know there's an adjustment—that nothing is wrong—as long as you are really sensitive to what she is needing. You and Rob are wonderful parents, and you'll continue to be. We'll talk about it more.

Shelly: It's hard to imagine having another one, hard to think it is possible that you can split the time and have the same feelings for the second one.

Janice: You'll experience a whole range of new feelings. I can't even describe the excitement of seeing the two children together. You'll wonder at it—at Erin's sensitivity and at the baby's response.

In the 34 months that Janice and Shelly have known each other, they have developed a close personal relationship. Shelly feels comfortable sharing her worries with Janice. In turn, Janice offers reassurance: She reminds Shelly of her daughter's strengths and that Erin will develop new skills in the coming months. She compares Erin's strength to that of the oldest of her own three children and thereby lets Shelly know that she has had similar experiences. Janice is able to interpret the meaning of Erin's behavior. She acknowledges that the new baby will be an adjustment for all family members; at the same time, she affirms Shelly's and Rob's parenting skills.

Two months after the previous conversation took place, Shelly shares with Janice what she has learned when she attended two parent meetings that focused on siblings. She reports that Rob has arranged time for activities just for Erin and himself, and she sees them becoming much closer. Shelly describes her plans for rearranging the space in their small home, and Janice replies, "A lot will fall into place. Probably you're better off to let Erin have the same space that she is used to. So much else will be new for her."

As the months progress, Shelly tells Janice about the plans she and Rob are making together and about how they are involving Erin in preparations for the new baby. Over time, Shelly shows more confidence in both Erin's and her own ability to adjust to the birth of her new baby. Janice's visits have offered needed support, reassurance, and guidance during this significant transition in this family's everyday life.

BIRTH OF THE ADDITIONAL BABY

As discussed previously, the birth of a new baby sparks older siblings' fear of losing their parents' love. Because older children go through so many changes in their moment-to-moment experiences, once the new baby arrives, it is normal for these children to feel a large sense of loss. Parents' feelings about their older child change after the new baby's birth. Parents often expect more grown-up behavior, yet they find that suddenly their older child begins acting in babyish ways (e.g., suddenly asking for a bottle, having toileting accidents). Home visitors can reassure parents that it is normal for their older child to regress. Visitors can suggest to parents possible new patterns of family life in which the older child can participate. For example, parents can create ways in which their older child can help with baby care. Visitors can call attention to the skills that the older child has but the baby does not; in doing so, visitors affirm the older child. Visitors also can help parents reassure the older child of their love by setting aside a few moments each day to be with only the older child. Just as they helped parents know what to expect with their first child, home visitors can give information regarding expectations of older siblings' behavior.

> *Natalie's 3-month-old, Jene, has just fallen asleep in Natalie's arms. Dvonne (3¹/₂ years old) is playing in the back yard.*
>
> *Natalie: Now he is doing very well. It's helpful that he can enjoy playing outside without me.*
>
> *Janice: It's nice that he feels that way about his new sister. It indicates what a close relationship you two have. His ability to go play outdoors by himself says good things about your relationship with him. And Dvonne still is in a period of adjustment. His life has changed dramatically and will continue to change, like when she becomes mobile. And he'll sense she is getting more attention because of her doing new things, and how [he has] to adjust again and again.*

The first few months can be a relatively easy adjustment for the older sibling because the new infant sleeps a great deal. Janice is helping Natalie understand that, as her daughter matures, Dvonne will begin to experience more intrusion from his sibling. At the same time, Janice gives a clear affirmation to Natalie regarding her role in her son's healthy adjustment and independence.

In her relations with older children, Janice repeatedly affirms the first child in relation to the younger sibling. For example, when Maggie began crawling at age 8 months, Janice told Maggie's 26-month-old sister, Mia, "Look at Maggie crawl! Did you show her how to do that? I bet you showed her all you could do, and she thought, 'Look at my big sister.'" When Dvonne's 4-month-old sister began fussing, Janice said, "Your sister is saying, 'I want to play with you.'" Home visitors often bring special toys for the older child. When Janice begins visiting

Marta's second child, Brianna, she brings Brianna's 3-year-old brother, Antoine, a wooden train set. As Janice and Marta chat with Brianna on the floor in the living room, Antoine puts together the train set in the adjoining kitchen. When Antoine joins Janice and Mary, Janice affirms him (e.g., "Only Antoine can play with tiny things, for Antoine is old enough to understand. Brianna [age 4 months] is still too little.").

Once another child is born, home visitors usually try to divide their attention between the children. If the home visitor has been working with the family since the first child's infancy, the parents have been exposed to the developmental information on infancy. Often parents maintain their focus on the oldest child, because the behaviors of the oldest child are new to the parent. It can be challenging for home visitors to reintroduce infant material in a meaningful and nonrepetitious manner. Sometimes home visitors can interpret the infants' behavior for the older sibling. Then the home visitor is both involving the older sibling in the home visit and providing information for the parent.

> When Janice arrives at Tracy's home, Maggie (age 8 months) is a bit uneasy. Janice explains to Mia (age 26 months), "Maggie knows someone strange is in my house. When Janice and Carol come, Maggie is not sure yet—they are not Mia, Mommy, or Daddy. She knows she loves Mia, Mommy, and Daddy. She's not sure of those new people."

Janice both involves the older sibling, Maggie, in the home visit and provides information for Tracy, their mother.

PARENT EXPECTATIONS AND COMPARISONS

Every parent has images of what or how they would like their child to be. These images are central to parents' expectations. Tracy's comments are a poignant example.

> When Maggie comes, I want Mia to be as old as I want her to be. I have to remind myself that she is still a baby.

Parental expectations can be powerful influences on their own behavior and their children's behavior. As noted earlier, after the birth of a new baby, parents may expect competency from their oldest child while the child is acting like a baby. When their older child behaves immaturely, parents may respond in anger. This anger is not a response simply to their child, but to the difference in unstated expectations and the child's action. When visitors help parents say their expectation out loud, parents often see that they are being unrealistic.

Parents unwittingly have different expectations for each of their children. These expectations stem from factors that are unique for different children and parents. Sometimes more is expected from first children and from sons.[4] Sometimes the first child sets the standard for younger siblings. Although the second child develops differently, parents may set their expectations according to the development of their first child. When parental expectations are not met, parents sometimes feel overwhelmed and inadequate. Often the child senses these feelings. Shelly's comments to her home visitor are illustrative.

Shelly: I remember the parent meetings on siblings and the leader saying that the first-born always knows the rules. We would never let Erin get by with what her younger brother does.

Janice: And she wouldn't try.

A central way in which we know and understand objects, persons, and events is by making comparisons with other objects, persons, and events in our lives. It is normal for parents to compare their children. As parents make these comparisons in conversations with home visitors, home visitors can let parents know that their comparisons and accompanying feelings are normal. Home visitors can talk about how even though all children progress through similar developmental phases, the timing and speed of development varies for each child. Similarly, visitors can show that each child has a different personality and temperament. Home visitors can assist parents to understand that their children are more different from each other than the same. Talking about these differences is natural; but comparisons become problematic when they are judgmental, that is, when one child is deemed good or bad but is just different from his or her sibling.

Often the home visitor can make an interpretive comment to help parents understand their different children's behavior and development.

Natalie: When Jene [age 3 months] is in her crib, I hear her making noises as she sucks her fists.

Janice: How wonderful, by herself, the best possible way.

Natalie: Dvonne needed the pacifier to drop off to sleep. And he'd cry whenever it fell out of his mouth. He still needs his pacifier when going to bed.

Janice: She doesn't need it, for she can calm herself without it.

Natalie: She's such a good baby. Dvonne didn't sleep through the night until he was 3.

Janice: Each child is born with a different temperament; that is, different babies have different manners of sleeping, different levels of activity, and *different ways of responding to their parents. It seems as if your children each have a different temperament.*

Natalie: *That's helpful. I keep talking of Jene being a good baby, but I don't mean that Dvonne is bad.*

As Natalie spontaneously compared her two children, she unwittingly thought of her second baby as the good baby, in contrast to Dvonne. She might unwittingly communicate these judgments to Dvonne. Janice introduces the idea that each infant is born with a unique temperament that is expressed in different ways of relating to others and different levels of activity, and Natalie begins to understand that her children's differences are not a matter of good versus bad.

When Janice returns home after the visit, she writes a note on the home visit form to remember to continue the comparison topic on future visits in order to make certain that Natalie understands temperament and comparisons. As the months progress, Natalie continues to make comparisons of her children, but in a new manner. She compares Jene and Dvonne, but nonjudgmentally. For example, when Jene is 6 months old, Natalie describes how Dvonne, when a baby, seemed to manage well when different people beyond his parents were present; however, Jene seems to need to have her mother at her side. In response, Janice is able to explain that this is the age when infants learn to be very aware of different people who are not their parents, and she notes that every child follows a different path in relating to others.

VALUING EACH CHILD
AS SPECIAL

Studies provide convincing evidence that siblings not only are different from each other but also do not experience family life in the same way.[5] Faber and Mazlish noted that, although it is natural for parents to strive to treat their children equally, in reality, parents unwittingly treat each of their children quite differently.[6] Children are sensitive not only to how their parents treat them but also to how their parents treat their siblings. Just as it is normal for parents to compare their children, children also compare their parents' treatment of themselves as opposed to their siblings. In contrast to popular opinion, studies indicate that there is no straightforward relationship between a child's birth order and how the child is treated by parents or by siblings.[7] In reality, siblings do not need to be treated equally by their parents. Rather, each child needs to feel that parents treat them uniquely, that their parents value each of them as special.

As home visitors help parents to be good observers of their infant and his or her older siblings and to gain information on the meaning of their children's actions and development, visitors play an important role in assisting parents to recognize the specialness of each child. When home visitors are relating to the older sibling, they often can model for the parent ways to affirm the older siblings in relation to their younger sibling. For example, they can invite the older child to give the younger one a toy. The following excerpts from two of Janice's home visits are illustrative.

> As Mia (age 21 months) plays at the side of her mother, Tracy, Tracy and Janice discuss Mia's increased vocabulary and ability to express her needs verbally. Janice comments to Mia, "You're teaching Maggie [age 3 months] to talk, too—all those good sounds."

> Janice has put on the floor two 10-inch-high cylindrical canisters, each with a circular hole on the lid. Janice empties one canister and dumps out an array of small film cans. Maggie (age 12 months) takes a canister and immediately puts it into her mouth. Mia (age 30 months) skillfully puts the film cans into the canisters' circular hole. Janice says to her, "It helps Maggie to learn when you play with what she does. Good, right there in the hole of the can. And Maggie is watching everything you do." Mia smiles proudly as she continues the task.

Janice's comments help Mia feel she is special. When Janice praises Mia's ability to do things better than Maggie, Janice helps to counteract Mia's inevitable ambivalent or jealous feelings. As Tracy observes the way Janice helps Mia feel good, how Mia really helps her baby sister learn, Tracy learns to affirm Mia herself in a more powerful way than she would have if Janice had just made a verbal suggestion. Tracy has not only a clear example but also the concrete results to observe— Maggie's delight.

In an interview, Tracy spoke of the pleasure she gets when she observes Janice and her children.

> Tracy: I like the fact that when she does come into my home, she directly interacts with the kids rather than just sitting down and just talking to me.

> Carol: What part of the home visit do you find most enjoyable?

> Tracy: Actually, just watching how my kids respond to what Janice is asking them to do. It's exciting to see that they can do what she asks them to do. . . . And every time Janice leaves, she tells me, "You are doing a wonderful job." And it makes me feel real good for somebody to come and tell me I am doing so good, and my kids are developing so good.

Mia was born 2 years after Tracy and her husband graduated from high school. Janice's ability to involve Tracy's children in play activities and to discuss how their behavior points to their development helps this young mother recognize her children's strengths. She can believe Janice's verbal praise of her children because she has repeatedly observed her children succeed with Janice. And these repeated experiences allow Tracy to integrate Janice's verbal praise of Tracy as a mother.

SIBLING RELATIONSHIPS

Fighting among siblings is normal. Although some parents focus on the fighting, most siblings also spend a lot of time playing together and interacting with each other in many different ways. For example, siblings do family chores together, walk to school together, join in games with neighborhood friends together, and simply play with each other for hours without fighting. In their hours together, siblings experience a wide range of feelings, both positive and negative. They experience shared interest, affection, caring, and nurturance, as well as jealousy, irritation, control, conflict, and rivalry. The sibling relationship changes as the children's developmental levels change and as each child is able to both enjoy a sibling and be frustrated by a sibling in new ways. Each sibling relationship is unique to each individual child.[8] That is, each child may experience his or her relationship to a brother or sister quite differently than does the brother or sister. For example, a younger child may view her sister as a good friend with whom she loves to play, whereas the older sister may view the little one as bothersome and intrusive.

The age and developmental level of children are big factors in the ease with which siblings interact with each other. The most psychologically dangerous period is toddlerhood because, when a sibling is born, the toddler is at the age when fears of losing parents' love and being replaced are most upsetting.[9] A 3- to 6-year-old can better understand parents' explanations about the new baby and is more skilled at maintaining focus on play and play alone. When the youngest child is a toddler, the toddler frequently disrupts the older sibling's play because exploring is the toddler's natural way of relating to the world. Usually, toddlers do not understand their intrusiveness. Because older children can better understand their parents, parents may expect them to be more generous with their younger sibling than is fair or developmentally appropriate. In this case, visitors can make sure that the parents understand what they expect of each child and can help parents to test whether their expectations are realistic.

Personality and temperament also influence the way in which siblings interact with each other. An older child's temperamental style and personality influence the child's ability to accept a new baby and later affects how he or she responds to a toddler sibling's intrusions. For example, an even-tempered toddler can be more accepting and patient than a more active, easily frustrated toddler.

Home visitors can assist parents in helping their children get along in many different ways. Earlier this chapter discussed how Janice modeled skill in affirming the older child's skill level in contrast to the younger sibling and in giving the older child small tasks to help her younger sibling. As the second baby develops, Janice asks if the children are playing together more, and the parents often enjoy in sharing small sequences of their children's play.

> Tracy: It's fun to see how Maggie [age 18 months] follows along with Mia [age 36 months] with purses, dolls, stuff like that. The other night they were playing with a whiffle ball in their bedroom. Mia was trying to get Maggie to play catch, and Maggie was laughing so hard. In the next room, Dave and I chuckled as we listened to them.

> Janice: Now that she is 3, Mia is getting better and better playing with Maggie. Three-year-olds understand more.

Janice frames these questions positively, and, in turn, parents like to describe their children playing together. Janice's frequent questions help parents become good observers of their children's play together. Seeing over time how Janice enjoys their children, the parents will spontaneously share when their children enjoy each other, for example, when an infant begins to enjoy watching her brother's play or when an older sibling spontaneously assists his younger brother.

> Natalie: Dvonne [3½ years] will get down on the floor with Jene [age 4 months] and tell her to say "Dada" or say "Mama." He plays with her like that.

> Janice: Wonderful. A study I recently read showed that when the first child gets involved with the baby, it makes a difference in the second child's language development. It's going to help.

Janice takes pleasure in listening to Natalie talk about her children. She also provides developmental information to help Natalie understand the value of her son's interactions with Jene. As the months progress, this kind of exchange between Janice and Natalie becomes a natural part of the home visit.

Sibling Rivalry and Fighting

It is inevitable that brothers and sisters will be jealous and competitive with each other and will fight. When parents are able to stay out of their children's fights, children have a chance to learn to work out problems together. Letting their children fight without interfering is difficult for most parents. It is natural for parents' images of being a good parent to be threatened when their children fight. When parents do become involved in their children's fights, fighting can become a setting for children to manipulate their parents (e.g., by convincing the parent who is at fault or what a punishment should be).

Home visitors can help parents understand that their children's fights are normal. They also can help parents see these fights as an opportunity for their children to learn social skills, especially conflict resolution skills. Faber and Mazlish as well as Galinsky and David provided helpful suggestions for parents to respond to their children's fighting.[10] If one child is dominating the other or if one child has an unfair advantage, however, visitors can help the parents to intervene in a constructive way. Parents can learn when it is most reasonable to withdraw (e.g., when their children are simply bickering) or when to intervene (e.g., to separate children when a situation is potentially dangerous). Most important, home visitors can provide helpful suggestions for parents to assist their children in learning how to negotiate. For example, the parent can allow each child to state his or her feelings and intentions, or, if a child is quite young, the parent can interpret the younger child's feelings and intentions for the older sibling. Then the parent can help the children figure out solutions to the problems. As home visitors help parents learn to talk about their young children's feelings and intentions, some parents are having their first experience in recognizing and talking about feeling and intentions. When that happens, parents are learning the same significant social skills as their children. Parents and children are developing increased ability to recognize the perspective of the other as well as their own feelings and motivations.

PARENTS AND SIBLINGS: BALANCING THE HOME VISITOR'S INTERACTION

When there are two or more mobile children plus their parent in the interactions of a home visit, the home visitor's job becomes more difficult. The visitor's task may be most challenging when the older child is still a toddler because the toddler may not be mature enough to focus on solitary play activities for an extended time while the home visitor focuses on the infant. As home visitors develop their skills, they learn the art of introducing activities that invite extended involvement for both children. Janice demonstrates remarkable talent in orchestrating the sustained involvement of Maggie and Mia, siblings with 18 months' difference in age.

Janice removes from her bag a box filled with several dozen colored 2-inch-diameter circular plastic chips, each with one, two, or five holes in the center. She also removes two cardboard and two plastic canisters, each with a slot on the lid. As she puts the toys on the rug, she says to Mia (age 33 months) and Maggie (age 15 months), "I brought these today. There's enough so that everybody can play." Mia immediately takes some chips and places them into one of the holes of the canister as she says, "It's like a bank to put money in." Janice answers, "You are right. It's like a bank to put money in." Meanwhile, Maggie is using alternate hands to put chips into a canister that does not have a top. Mia puts two chips into a slot at the same time, and Janice says, "Mia, you did that fast, putting two in at the same time, wow!" As she watches Maggie open and shut the cigar box containing the chips, Janice says, "Close the box, open the box, close the box." Maggie then places a chip through a large slot of another canister. Janice exclaims, "Good Maggie, you put it right through the slot!" As Mia watches, she says, "Yeah, Maggie."

Both children stay involved in extended play. Given Janice's repeated affirmation of Mia, Mia is able to enthusiastically praise her younger sister. As Maggie and Mia play, Janice repeatedly describes the children's play. These descriptions affirm the children's involvement, help them recognize their own successes, and model powerful ways for Tracy to help her children feel their self-worth.

Maggie continues to busily dump several chips into a can and then dump them out and begin the process again. (Both children have remained focused in play for 15 minutes.)

Janice places a 12-cup muffin tin on the floor, and Mia slowly places one chip into each of the muffin tin cups as Janice says with each placement, "One, one, one," and so on. Mia then begins placing a second disk into each of the cups as Janice comments, "One more makes two."

When Mia seems to tire of filling the muffin tin, Janice gives her a string with a knot on its end and suggests, "Do you think we could put some of these on the string?" Janice holds up two red chips, one with one hole and one with five holes. She asks Mia which chip looks like the one on the string, and Mia picks the chip with the one hole and puts it on the string. They continue this game until Mia has about 10 chips on the string. Janice comments, "Good, you know all of them that have just one hole."

As Mia and Janice play together, Maggie continues to play with the canisters and chips. Janice asks Tracy if Mia understands "two," and Tracy shrugs as she says, "Try it." Janice suggests to Mia that they can string the two-hole chips and shows her how she can put the string in each of the holes as if she were sewing. Mia then successfully chooses the two-hole chips and puts the string through them. Janice then holds up the string as she says, "Look how nice it is. Maggie, isn't it nice what your sister has made? The ones are on the bottom and the twos are on the top." As Janice speaks, Mia smiles.

Janice then removes two large metal spoons from her bag and shows Maggie how she can tap the bottom of the canister with the spoon. Maggie seems to enjoy this tapping action. She alternately taps the plastic and the metal bottom of the canisters as Janice comments, "Different sounds. The plastic one is not like this one, is it?" Maggie nods her head.

During these activities, each child is able to maintain sustained interest in the same toys. With each child, Janice plays several roles — observing, affirming, clarifying, structuring, and extending the children's action as well as interpreting their actions for the children's mother. These are roles typical of Janice's work with one child and parent, but they are made more complex with two small children who are 18 months apart in age.

As the children play, Janice extends and structures new uses of simple materials. She integrates learning into the children's play. (See Chapter 8 for a fuller discussion of learning through play.) Her descriptive comments help these young children learn important concepts. For example, she comments about sameness versus difference of sound and spatial relationships of the one- and two-hole disks on the string. Janice explained her approach as follows.

I think all of that helps parents to see how children's play is legitimate learning. And many times I can say in a visit a statement that I heard Burton White say in a training session several years ago, that this is just as serious learning as any child is doing in school. It's neat to see the parents' reaction to that. They'll grin or say, "Oh, really!" It just makes what the child does seem important to the parents, and it is important.

Although she usually has a general idea of the children's play involvement, Janice also improvises. In a conversation with the author after this visit, Janice commented:

I have to admit, I just thought of that on the spot. I knew that, in the visit, I wanted to differentiate the task for Mia and still follow her lead. And once she started threading, I thought this is the time we can start talking about numbers and help her mom realize that she can be aware of those kinds of things. And I thought, "Oh, that's going to work. I can do it some more."

Janice always has some activity plans before beginning a home visit. She chooses activities that are somewhat open-ended so that she can be flexible in use of materials. This flexibility is especially important when more than one child is present because unpredictable occurrences are more likely during the home visit. Beyond having materials, the home visitor constantly observes, interprets, and evaluates ongoing happenings. This internal dialogue, which sometimes is only in the home visitor's mind but which often is what the home visitor is saying aloud, allows the home visitor to shift gears when appropriate. Knowing that relationship is more important in promoting development than any specific activity gives the home visitor the security to be flexible.

In some situations, the home visitor has not worked previously with the family's older children, who are present during the visitor's work with parents and the young child or children. Because the home visiting experience is new, it is not unusual for the older children to be more demanding of attention. For these families, home visitors need to provide play activities specifically geared for the older children and to be prepared to devote some time to them.

DIFFICULTIES AND DILEMMAS

Each home visitor has a caseload of families of varying size and varying patterns of relationships. When focusing on siblings, there are two identifiable problem areas that may provoke challenges for the home visitor. First, parents may be carrying into their interactions with their own children their unresolved childhood sibling conflicts or other unpleasant sibling experiences that left emotional scars. A second difficult area involves making home visits in families with several children present.

Ever since Cain asked, "Am I my brother's keeper?," it has been clear that there is tension in sibling relationships. When they are extremely problematic, parents may carry their childhood feelings into their own parenting. For example, they may feel helpless and out of control when their children tease each other or fight because these sibling behaviors trigger the parents' own feelings from their negative childhood experiences of living in a family with continual conflict. Other parents live with feelings of being less competent than their siblings or of being left out, and these feelings are carried into their interactions with their own children. When these parenting dynamics are operating, the home visitor's role takes on new dimensions. First, skilled home visitors learn to recognize these parent–child dynamics. Once they recognize the dynamics, home visitors need to decide whether this issue can be addressed in the visitor's work with the parents or whether the family needs a referral to a mental health specialist or other resource.

The home visitor's task can become very challenging when she or he visits homes where there are many children. Sometimes all the children are within one large family; at other times, two different families are living in the same home. To have a successful home visit, the home visitor must be flexible and skilled in working with people of various ages. In these situations, the home visitor often does not know how many people will be present during the visit. Some home visitors go prepared with materials or activity ideas for each of the age ranges. Others choose activities that all different ages can enjoy. Cynthia works with several low-income families in which several children are always involved in her home visits. Cynthia shared her approach during these visits.

It's not as hard as it sounds. You just need to have a couple of good books. Books are wonderful because what you can do with a book is settle down. It settles you in hopes of a quiet time. Lots of time, if I have more than one child, I'll start out with a book and read it just to set the tone—a pleasant time.

The hardest thing is working with two babies. If you have a toddler and a small baby, that is a high level of difficulty because their attention span is real short. So the baby has to have lots of different activities, lots of things to do. Toddlers demand a lot of attention in that respect. Sometimes I think they get the bulk, and, in that case, I may actually plan a time when I know that child is napping so I can spend more time with the baby. And you can have some material for each child. So if you get the kids involved in that, then you have time to play with the other child and to work with mom.

Especially when siblings and parents seem to have difficulty with managing the kids, I like to do activities where everybody can play, regardless of their age. Then what you can show mom is yes, this 6-month-old can play lotto. And it's a time for mom to hold the baby. Let the baby hold the cards while mom is still interacting with the 4-year-old and doing the matching. And the baby wants to eat a card, and that's okay because it's cardboard.

The home where I went the other day, I had a 3-year-old, a 4-year-old, an 8-year-old, a 7- and 9-year-old, and a 13-month old, and we all played lotto. Everybody had a card. They took turns. The older kids I used to be the callers and they took turns calling. The 18-month-old got to walk around holding the cards and stacking them because he had extra cards. You can take one activity and make it apply to all the kids because that is what families do. Families don't get up in the morning and say, "Oh, well, you are 12 months old, so you are going to do this activity. Okay, George, you are 15 years old," and so forth. Families do what they have to do and everybody participates, and they all have a place. That's pretty much what I do with siblings.

Cynthia is skilled in involving all children in home visits, regardless of their age. She understands that if she is not successful in this task, parents will not gain much from her work with them, because, as she states so clearly, "That's what families do" (i.e., participate in similar activities, regardless of the age span of family members).

CONCLUSIONS

The birth of additional children brings new family dynamics for both parents and their first child. Both parents and their first child experience the push and pull of feelings, some of which are new and uncomfortable. Parents may experience unexpected changes in the feelings and expectations for their older child; challenges in their sense of parental competence; and unanticipated feelings, which may evoke their own childhood struggles as siblings. The older child's everyday predictability vanishes with the arrival of a new baby, and feelings of loss abound. During this transition period of a family, home visitors can listen, affirm both the parents and their children, and provide developmental information and suggestions as needed.

This chapter discussed common patterns of parenting more than one child, for example, having different expectations for each child, unwittingly comparing children, and relating to each child differently. We have seen how home visitors can assist parents to compare their children nonjudgmentally and value each child as unique and special.

This chapter also examined how sibling relationships involve a complex web of interactions that cross over a wide range of feelings— from admiration, intimacy, support, and belonging to jealousy, competition, and rivalry. Each child's unique temperamental style and personality influence the nature of her or his relationships with siblings. Their interactions with each other change with changes in their age and developmental level. Fighting usually is a normal part of this relationship; however, the fighting may be quite problematic to the children's parents. Home visitors can help parents understand the different ways their children interact with each other. When parents are uneasy with their children's fighting, home visitors can give helpful developmental information and, when appropriate, assistance in gaining skill in conflict resolution.

Home visitors who work with families who have more than one child are working in a complex web of relationships—relationships between children, between parents and their children, and between the home visitor and all family members. An essential skill in these situations is the home visitor's ability to orchestrate sustained involvement of young siblings and simultaneously maintain interactions with their parents.

There are two challenges embedded in the home visitor's work with families with more than child. First, home visitors need to develop awareness of when parents are bringing unresolved pain from childhood memories of their own siblings into their current parenting and when these parents may need assistance beyond the expertise of a home visitor. Second, the balancing of one's interactions in homes with many children during a home visit demands great care and skill.

III

Person and Profession

Personal History and Professional Competence

Every life has its own significance. This lies in a context of meaning in which every moment that can be remembered has an intrinsic value and, yet, in the context of memory, it also has a relation to the meaning of the whole. The significance of an individual existence is quite unique and so cannot be fathomed by knowledge; yet, in its way, like of Leibniz's monads, it represents the historical universe.

William Dilthey (1910/1961, pp. 88–89)

Throughout this volume, it is clear that who the home visitor is as a person plays a large part in each visitor's approach. Home visitors' commitment, perspective, values, decision making, and patterns of relating all have roots in their unique personal history. In other words, in home visiting, personal and professional identity are intertwined.[1]

The previous nine chapters presented observations of how these home visitors conduct home visits. This chapter first explores how these two women see their home visiting work as part of the meaning and purpose they find in their lives, how they have grown professionally, and what resources have promoted that professional growth. The next section discusses the interaction between their personal histories and their home visiting. There is no formula to predict or explain the way that a person's life history influences who that person is today. Nevertheless, a very important way in which a person's past interacts with the present is in the process of remembering, retelling, and actively integrating her or his personal history because when we retell a past event, we also interpret it and make it our own. (Think about the stories you retell the most often and how the retelling informs you of the importance, both about who you were at the time and what life was like then and who you are now and what life currently means to you.) These stories help us to reflect on who we are, both in our relationships with others and in our understanding of ourselves.[2] Thus, although there is no formula for the process through which someone's personal life history influences her or his professional life, by presenting two life histories as told by Janice and Cynthia as they reflected on their own experiences, perhaps this chapter can provide a window into this process.

In order to learn how home visitors' professional work is connected with their childhood and present personal life as adults, the author conducted life history interviews with Janice and Cynthia, the two exemplar home visitors discussed in this book. Janice and Cynthia each told the author in four different interviews about their childhoods and adult lives.[3] They began by telling the author about their early childhood and family. As they progressed beyond their stories of early childhood, their stories expanded to include extended family, friends, schooling, religion, and community. Later they described their adult personal lives and career paths, from their first jobs to their current work.[4] Throughout the interviews, the author occasionally asked a question either to clarify or to extend their description.

Prior to these interviews, the author had observed and discussed Janice's home visits with her for 4 years. The author had known Cynthia also for 4 years and worked with her in the author's role as action researcher for 18 months. In working together with Janice and Cynthia, the author had many lengthy conversations and several interviews with both women. So, by the time Janice and Cynthia sat down for life history interviews with the author, all knew each other quite well.[5] The interviews, structured by these women's remembrances and by their understanding of their personal and professional lives, were informal. As they told the author about their life experiences, the author felt the freedom to ask questions or to comment on similar experiences in her own life.

The personal and professional histories of Janice and Cynthia should not be regarded as case studies or blueprints. Rather, the chapter presents the voices of Janice and Cynthia as they reflect on their own development as persons and professionals for readers to use as a resource to think about how this sort of reflection and development works. In considering how these home visitors reflected on their histories and integrated them into their work, the reader is challenged to think about how this process works, both in the home visiting profession in general and in the reader's own professional development.

Janice's and Cynthia's self-portrayals begin with each woman's description of her home visiting work. First, she identifies the personal meaning and purpose she finds in her work with parents and their infants and young children. Second, she describes her growth in understanding and skill. Third, she discusses what has helped her to grow professionally. Janice's and Cynthia's reflections capture some of the ways that home visiting can be meaningful, that home visitors can grow over time, and that resources available for professional development can play a role in the home visiting process. There is no single way in which home visitors find meaning in their work, grow as professionals, or use the available resources for professional development. But reading the stories of Janice and Cynthia can provide a range of possibilities and can indicate how one's work and resources can be *actively* and *reflectively* used.

Not all competent professionals grew up in families in which parents had strong family values and gave their children consistent, loving care. Prior to doing the life history interviews with Janice and Cynthia, the author was unaware that each woman had had a healthy, happy childhood family life, though their families are quite different from each other. Therefore, the chapter closes with a conversation with another home visitor, Karen, who uses her recognition and resolution of her painful childhood as building blocks for her professional competence.

JANICE DISCUSSES
HER HOME VISITING WORK

Personal Meaningfulness of Home Visiting

The strength and happiness of Janice's childhood family life and commitment to her husband and children are themes that blend into her home visiting work. The strongest passions in her personal life are school, babies, and parenting. Home visiting blends these passions.[6]

PAT [Parents as Teachers] has given me something in my life that I love to do. I knew all along with my own babies that I really loved that stage of development. And it gives me a chance to renew that joy for myself.[7] Work is just fun. It gives me a lift every time I do it. Yes, I get frustrated when things aren't going well with a child. But every situation, and I truly mean this, every child, every situation, there will be parts of the visit that I truly enjoy. There has not been a child, not a parent that I have ever worked with—

and I've had some pretty difficult situations—that I've not been able to say, "This is good, that's good, or whatever," because it is there, and I truly enjoy little children. Part of the joy is being with very young children who aren't tainted yet. It helps me to keep a more positive outlook on the rest of my life. It helps me stay happy. When other things are sort of bearing down, I have this picture of Erin in my head, doing something especially darling. It helps alleviate other stresses in my life.

I also am intrigued with child development. Intellectually, I find it very fascinating to learn about something in a course, to read about something in a book, and go into a home and see it happen right there in front of my eyes. I truly enjoy education, and being able to convey this knowledge is just fun. I mean, I liked it when I was a classroom teacher; but doing one-on-one adult education and having a baby to play with at the same time— what could be better for somebody that loves to teach, but not in a formal classroom manner?

Home visiting continues themes integral to Janice's personal life history and counterbalances stresses that she encounters. She loves home visiting because it is sheer fun for her. Furthermore, this enjoyment can balance those parts of her life that can be stressful. Since she was a young child, Janice has used her intellect in being an active learner. She always has loved teaching. Child development stimulates her intellect, and working with parents continues her love of teaching.

Janice also knows that she is making a difference in people's lives, that her work has meaning beyond just herself.

I love the process. You definitely can see results from the information you convey. You get feedback from the parents and from the child. You know it's good. You know that you are making a difference. I think most people like to see results from their work. If you can see that in another human being, that's really valuable.

The author has observed Janice working with young parents and their babies and young children for 4 years. The author can better understand her home visiting style now that she and Janice have completed four life history interviews. The author often has been impressed by Janice's ease and very soft manner as she relates to a baby and parent, her spontaneous and genuine delight in a child's action, and her openness when she shares her own parenting experiences.

Professional Development Over Time

Since she first began home visiting, Janice has enjoyed her work. At the same time, she is aware of the many changes in her professional development over the course of 10 years.

I'm getting better at it now that I am aware of more detail and better at understanding development. I understand the significance of certain parts of development better, and thus I can convey this better. And my increase in child development knowledge has helped me, especially where development is not progressing quite normally. I am better at seeing subtle things that indicate progress, and I can suggest activities that will help that progress. I know it's going to make a difference because, with experience, I've seen it.

I don't think my basic approach has changed. From the very beginning, I have conducted my home visits in a very integrated way rather than thinking about specific things I was supposed to accomplish. I was never lesson plan–oriented. I always knew there was certain information that I needed to convey, but I didn't have an outline in my head as to how that hour was going to go. I always used the child's action to talk about development—that when I would see the child do something I would point that out. Because, from the beginning, I had learned how important it is to hook information to something that is important to the parent. Certainly, the baby is very important to the parent. If I can hook developmental information to what we both see as being significant, something they might not have even noticed, this will help a mom appreciate her child's development. I've always taught development that way.

The third place my developmental knowledge has changed is in understanding premature babies. The in-service training that I have gotten through Parents as Teachers made all the difference in the world in my ability to provide meaningful service to families with premature babies. It's incredible how much preemies are on their own timetable. And working with families of preemies for 3 full years has given me increased understanding to share with other families.

Also, in the beginning, I thought I had to take a zillion activities because, if something didn't work, I wanted to be sure to have something else to do. I don't take so much stuff anymore, because I realize that no matter how much I bring, the child will go through all of it anyway. When they get through all of it, they'll go do their own thing or bring their own toys and we'll play with that. So, since that's going to happen anyway, I might as well not have so much stuff. Also, the other advantage is the child will focus more and spend more time with an appropriate activity or two that I now bring. The game is no longer "Let's go through the bag." The game is "Let's really do this activity." I'm also better at tuning into each child's tempo, and that is different for each child and different for each age.

And finally, my relationships with parents have changed. I think my relationships with parents always have been pretty solid. It certainly is better with families that I have a chance to spend the full 3 years with. And there always are certain families where it's going to click and certain families where it's not going to click as well.

I know my families are comfortable with me, and I'm not really sure why. I know I always would enjoy staying longer, and I always feel like they would like to have me stay longer. But I don't. I stick to a schedule because I know realistically that's what it needs to be for them and for me.

I guess the difference has been sort of in the general comfort level as far as I feel like I don't have anything to prove. The confidence I have in my own ability to do this job sort of takes any pretense away. And I am much more comfortable with silence than I used to be.[8] I used to feel like I needed to talk all the time. Now I realize that the parent can be comfortable and I can be comfortable just watching the child play and waiting for something to happen that we can talk about. It used to be that I couldn't do that. It would just be too scary. But now I can do it.

The pattern that definitely has changed is the way I respond to parents' questions. It's typical for parents to ask questions about their child's behavior and how to manage this behavior. It used to be that if a parent asked me a question, I thought I had to answer it. Now I usually will remember to say, "What have you tried?" They'll talk about what they have tried, and I'll say, "What else have you tried?" And, in this manner, I let the answer come from the parents instead of from me. Often I can say to them, "That's really a good idea. Just stick with it and give it more time." That's so much more powerful than my saying an answer. And sometimes I'll expand on their idea and give them something to read.

In her 10 years as home visitor, Janice has gained new professional knowledge, skill, and understanding of herself. Gaining increased knowledge in child development and in understanding premature infants, for example, has helped Janice's skill in observing and interpreting behavior and in giving information to parents. The process of doing home visits over time has led to improved skill. For example, Janice's visits no longer involve a series of activities; instead, the child can have extended focus in only one or two activities and Janice can be more involved with the parent as well as the child. Janice described how her increased self-confidence has allowed her to slow down. She is comfortable with silence as she and the parent watch the infant play. These observations can be the basis of helping the parents understand the developmental meaning of their infant's actions and what to expect next. Being comfortable with herself, she no longer feels she has to answer each parent's question; rather, a question can be the basis for helping parents problem-solve on their own.

Resources for Professional Development

Each home visitor has a different way of knowing and a different way of learning. Janice spoke clearly about what she thinks has helped her most over the course of her career. In the chapter on professional development (Chapter 3), Janice described how sharing her work with colleagues has helped her. She also spoke of how helpful the regularly scheduled PAT in-service sessions have been for her in terms of deepening her knowledge base and of process.

> I have had the opportunity to hear some well-known professionals in the field of early childhood, and several really have impacted how I work, one of them being T. Berry Brazelton. Brazelton gave me a new view of infants. Initially, I was thinking much more along the cognitive line that we had learned from Burton White, who intrigued me also. But when I heard Brazelton talk about the things that infants could do and the relationships between infants and their parents, it was a new understanding for me. It opened many new avenues of thought in terms of how I work with parents and help them understand their baby.
>
> Very early in my career I heard Sally Provence talk about the importance of building rapport with a family, beginning with your phone call, and the importance of sharing enough of yourself with parents so that they understand who you are as a person and that you really do share some common ground.
>
> I'm a firm believer that professionals should access every opportunity to learn from leading authorities in the field.[9] It's not good enough to have one person on the staff go hear somebody and bring back their notes. If you're really going to get it, you've got to hear somebody yourself. I think the reason for this is in the work that we're doing, we are doing person-to-person work, not book-to-person work. And to see how experts who are experts in engaging people can engage me on a personal level means that, if I am going to access any of their skills, I have to experience it.

Given her keen intellect and love of learning, Janice actively engages in new learning that national experts provide. She gains new ways of thinking and new skills in the same way that the parents with whom she works learn from her.

As previously discussed, home visiting is a craft, and professional growth occurs best through doing and reflecting on that doing. Janice described how she has always been self-reflective.

> A lot of my reflection probably is just part of my growing. I always think about situations that have occurred in my own parenting experience with my own three children. I would think about things and wonder if I could do it better the next time if a similar instance occurred or do it better the next time with my younger child. That's the kind of person I am.

As a child, Janice's family's daily conversations at dinner and before bedtime were the anchor point of each day. These times in which family members reflected together on daily happenings seem to parallel Janice's ease in being self-reflective about her work and parenting.

As discussed in Chapter 1, Janice maintains boundaries in her work and thereby recognizes when she does not have the expertise to work with some of the problems a parent may share. In these situations, she offers empathic listening and support to parents. Just as she gives to parents, Janice's husband listens and supports her when she feels frustrated in her work.

> I talk to my husband about situations that I find frustrating in my job. Sometimes when you're talking about frustrations you don't need anybody to give you answers. You just need somebody to sit there and nod their head and give you a hug. It is a skill or an art to be able to shield yourself, given the burdens of the job, because parents sometimes share more than you wish they would share. And if you are a sensitive person, and I am very sensitive, it's hard to just listen and walk away from it. I do listen and I do walk away from it. But I can't get it out of my head as quickly as I wish I could. And that's because it's the kind of job where if you don't have some way to take care of yourself and somebody who will listen, it's too stressful.

Janice talked about the work she did together with the author and about how it influenced her home visiting.

> The kind of observation of my work you did when you would go into a home with me was very helpful. You would go into a home with me and, with the parents' permission, write down everything that was said during a home visit, and then we'd go back over what you had written. I know I became more aware of giving interpretive comments of the developmental meaning of a child's action once you pointed this out to me. And then I was able to work toward giving interpretive comments more frequently.
>
> But also it was the time that I could take privately to read through what had occurred during the home visit. It helped me to appreciate what really had gone on. A home visitor doesn't remember everything that she has said or a parent has said. For example, it certainly helped me to appreciate the necessity to wrap up before I leave the home so that the parent really will have a parting thought. Over the course of the hour, she may not have realized, because so much goes on. Our program is now teaching coordinators how to do what you have done.

Janice ended her discussion of influences on her work by returning to her own parenting.

> There is always professional development that makes you do your job well, but I think there also is a very personal development that makes you do your job well. I think a lot of why I enjoy the work I do and why I have

confidence in myself doing this job is because I really enjoyed my own motherhood. I enjoyed my children as babies. I enjoyed them as toddlers, young children, and the teen years that always are a new challenge. And now I enjoy them as young adults. I look at my children and see how successful they are in their relationships with other people and how successful they've been in school. It gives me the confidence in this job to think, "Yeah, I think I did a pretty good job as a mother. My children are really great."

So it gives me the confidence to talk about some of these child-rearing issues in a very sincere way. I'm not just talking about it because I've read it in a book. I'm talking about it because I've experienced it in my own life, and the results have been positive. Because I have the personal experience, I think that makes me more credible.

A give-and-take mutuality seems to characterize Janice's parenting and her work life. Just as her parenting influences her home visiting, so too her home visiting work influences her parenting. Four years before doing these life history interviews, Janice told the author how working as a home visitor helped her parenting of teenagers.

PAT helps me keep a focus on development, even though my children are older. It helps me structure my thinking about my children in terms of their development. And the parenting techniques I talk about with the mothers of little ones, I find I really use with my teenagers, only adjust up a little. And when I go to parenting workshops at the high school, I hear them saying the same kinds of things that I am telling parents of toddlers. And I can say to the parents of my babies that these are techniques that you will use all the way through your parenting, because you do.

Janice's personal style makes the interplay between her own parenting and home visiting possible. She is quite self-reflective about all her experiences and tends to approach both family and her professional experiences in a thinking manner.

JANICE'S PERSONAL AND PROFESSIONAL HISTORY

Childhood Family

Janice grew up in Nathan, a middle-class suburb of a large midwestern city, Centerville. She was the older of two daughters in a family where children and adults were very close, within both her nuclear and extended families. Janice described her childhood family life as being routine, predictable, and traditional.

My dad went to work at the same time every morning and got home at 5:15 every single night. Mother cooked, cleaned, and dusted the furniture every day. Dinner was the same time every night, mashed potatoes every night. We'd sit around the table and everyone would share happenings of the day. In the summer, conversation would happen again around 10:00 P.M. Everybody would be back out in the kitchen talking again. Lots of sharing about things going on in other families, families within our family, job stories and Navy stories from Dad. And we were very active in the church. Dad was on the vestry, so I guess there'd be stories about church activity. . . . Just lots of conversation.

And every Sunday, like clockwork, after church we went to my father's mother's house—a ritual. She was my only grandparent. We would always have the same dinners. Even now when I walk into anybody's house and smell pot roast, immediately I think of Sundays walking into my grandmother's house after church. After dinner was over, we would clear the table, do the dishes, and spend the day together. That was Sunday, a family day.

Predictable daily routines, lengthy daily family conversations, and gatherings of extended family each Sunday anchored Janice with a firm sense of connectedness and security.

When Janice was 7 years old, her parents adopted a baby girl. Janice described her sister as follows.

We weren't playmates, but I spent a lot of time with her because I loved the way she laughed. I just had fun playing with her, even though it wasn't playmate kind of play. She was my baby sister. She was bright and creative, but she never really could accept the success that I had in school and felt like she always was trying to be my sister instead of being herself. She was much more resistant to authority. As a teenager, Sherry had a different peer culture than I did—1965 versus 1958. She was incredibly rebellious, and my parents did not know how to deal with it. They had some very difficult times. Bottom line is Sherry moved out. She moved to Oregon and has maintained her distance ever since.

As a child, Janice never questioned her parents' love and adoration for their daughters.

I always had the strong feeling that my parents really adored us. They always spoke to us in a very respectful way. I don't remember any harsh words. I don't remember being punished. We just always understood what was expected.

Shared time with extended family was an important part of Janice's childhood. Her mother was one of seven children, and her father had a twin brother. Everyone lived in Centerville. Each year Janice and her family had holiday and birthday celebrations with her mother's siblings, their spouses, and children.

> *This was a family that truly knew how to have fun, and that probably gave me my sense of family. As I was growing up, we always had family birthday parties for every cousin's birthday, every single year. And there were very large holiday parties that were family-oriented and fun. They had quite wonderful parties because everybody loved music and sang all the time. That's my memory of what it was like to grow up in this family. We'd sing, dance, and party in the front room. And lots of just playing the old-time parlor games like the pig in the parlor. That's the context in which I grew up.*

Janice shared that she had been sorry that her own children did not have the same kind of extended family experiences, with "lots of laughing, lots of playing, and the old-time parlor games." At the same time, as a full-time homemaker, she could create much of her own family patterns and parenting parallel to her childhood family life. Her children had predictable routines and shared time among family members, just as Janice had had as a child. After she gave birth to her first child, she was a full-time homemaker for 17 years.

> *I never will understand how some people can buy into what I see as a very narrow view of what it means to be a woman. I think that there is too much setting aside the whole concept of motherhood and marriage. My view of it is that it's so much career, and that is your obligation to yourself to head out in a career. That negates what for me is a very important part of my life. My experience has been that you can have both. I think you can have a rewarding professional experience, take time out for a rewarding family experience, and come back at another stage in your life and have a rewarding professional experience, I think doing that has helped my family be more stable.*
>
> *I remained home for 17 years without objection. Granted, that's the way I grew up, and that may be more difficult for young women now. I'm not so sure of that, because I think we don't take a realistic view of how important parenthood is. One of my objections to the feminist movement is the whole emphasis on moving away from what the children need, from what the family needs.*

Schooling

Citizens in Janice's childhood community of Nathan were part of the first-generation postwar middle class in the United States. Nathan residents valued education, and parents expected that their children would gain more education than they had and in turn be successfully employed. Janice spoke of her love of school and how early schooling had influenced her choice of career in teaching.

Janice: *I loved school. It was just my favorite place to be, my favorite thing to do. I can remember every single teacher I had in grade school. Those grade school teachers—I can remember stories from every single year.*

Carol: *What do you mean, stories?*

Janice: *Things stick in my mind. Like in kindergarten—all the way through school, I was tall. In kindergarten, I was always in the back row. At the tables, I was in the back row. It frustrated me that we always were learning to write other people's names, and I never got to write my name. That's just the way they taught. They'd demonstrate one person's name on the chalkboard, and everybody would practice over and over and over again. The fact that my name was Janice didn't matter. We all learned to write Mary.*

I had the same teacher for first and second grade. She was wonderful. She absolutely was the person who made me want to become a teacher. She had a wonderful sense of humor and was so much fun to be with. I loved learning.

As Janice talked about her schooling, her detailed description of each of her elementary school teachers some 30–40 years later was amazing. Two teachers, the one who taught first and second grade and her sixth-grade teacher, became models who triggered her lifelong love of education. Both her teachers and her parents had high expectations of her, and she excelled throughout her schooling.[10]

In high school, Janice was in accelerated classes, and she continued to love all aspects of school.

Nathan at that time was considered one of the better districts, and my high school education was excellent. People really valued education. Everybody was expected to work. Everybody was expected to do well. Everybody was expected to learn. I was very well prepared for college.

I was editor of the high school newspaper. I drove my mother crazy because of the hours I kept. I always was very busy because I was incredibly active in all kinds of things in high school. I did tons of term papers in high school and had lots of homework—burning the midnight oil.

Janice also spoke of having fine teachers at Johnson University, and, once again, she loved school. Only the education classes were dull. They were taught by "uninteresting people," she said. She lived at home.

Janice: *It never entered my head to go anyplace other than Johnson University. I knew how special it was. I was the first person in my family or my extended family who graduated from college.*

She graduated Phi Beta Kappa and looked forward to returning to the classroom as a primary teacher.

Friendships

Janice's life revolves around relationships. As a child, she experienced family-like intimacy with close friends. During her childhood, Janice had several special friends, several of whom remain her friends.

> At my last high school reunion, which was the 25th year, or was it 30? We had a group of people from my elementary school at the same table. Several of us still are friends, and several of us were the key people who put together the high school reunion. Suzi is my closest friend, since first grade.

Janice also spoke of creative play with friends in the neighborhood.

> Two little girls close to my age lived across the street until I was about 10. We used to play together all the time, and we usually played things like office or school. And we played movie stars and dress-up. TV and that kind of stuff just wasn't in my life. We had to create our own fun, and it was a very happy time.

Religion

Religion has played a significant role in Janice's childhood and adult life.

> My grandmother Mawie on my dad's side was very, very religious, very faithful. We are Episcopalian. I grew up going to Sunday school every single Sunday. I taught Sunday school for years, through high school and college. I think I mentioned earlier that, after church, we would go to my grandmother's, so that ritual of Sunday was very important.
>
> I started going to church again regularly when we came back to Centerville and returned to church where we absolutely fell in love with the minister. He was both very warm and very humorous. We started going back there every single Sunday. My children were reared going to church every Sunday.

Janice clearly holds faith to be important.[11] She spoke of the influence of having a pastor who could translate religion meaningfully for her.

Janice's grandmother Mawie was her model in religious faith. Mawie had a leadership role in the church in a time when it was rare for women to be leaders. Janice described how Mawie had regular prayers that she recited to give her strength. When Janice was a child, Mawie always told her, "When you can't figure something out, pray about it." Janice told me that now she feels like she has a very personal relationship with God. "In difficult times in my life, I really will say. 'I can't handle this. Please help me.' And I gain the strength to deal with the situation."

Marriage, Work, and Parenting

Janice met her husband when they both were sophomores at Johnson University; she got married and started a new job shortly after graduation.

> When I met Joe, I fell for him so fast. He was serious about his studies, an engineering major. And he was very good to me. We went together 3 years and decided we would get married. He was very kind, always treated me well. We never quarreled. I perceived him as very much like my father. He treated me similarly.
>
> When we married, we moved to Northton, where Joe was in graduate school. We had a wonderful life in Northton. I got a job in the wealthiest suburb on the South shore, Bentley. I taught first grade, and I felt like I had died and gone to heaven. I had a wonderful class, flexibility, good support, and many new friends, other young teachers. I loved teaching!

Janice has been able to continue her love of teaching as she works with parents of infants and young children in home visiting.

In October of Janice's second year of teaching at Bentley, she learned that she was pregnant. Because she had been taking oral contraceptives, the pregnancy was a total surprise to her and Joe.

> The news was like a lightning bolt.[12] I was devastated. I could not imagine it. I was the one teaching, with my husband in graduate school. This is not the way my life was planned. When I told Joe, he couldn't believe it either. We couldn't even be excited about it at first, because we were so stunned. It never even dawned on me that I would go back to work after this baby was born.[13] My baby was due the middle of March. And the pregnancy put Joe on the fast track. He finished his Ph.D. 3 years after graduating from college.

Janice's life was a planned life, carefully planned by her parents and by Joe and herself. Having a baby was not planned. Once Janice integrated this dramatic life-cycle change, her teaching plans were put aside so that she could give total devotion to parenting.

In April of that year, Janice gave birth to a baby boy named Brett. One year later Joe received his Ph.D. degree, and they returned to Centerville. They moved to a suburb adjacent to Janice's childhood home, where her parents still lived. When Brett was 4 years old, Janice gave birth to another son and then, 3 years later, another son. She loved being a homemaker. She returned to her childhood schooling and church interests by becoming very active in her children's schools and teaching Sunday school. Janice felt continuity between her own family and her childhood family life.

Janice has worked half-time for 5 years and full-time for 5 years for Parents as Teachers. She always has been hard-working and thinks nothing of working a full day and then spending the evening at one of her children's concerts or sporting events. During the weekend, she sometimes cares for her two grandchildren, who live 5 minutes from her home.

CYNTHIA DISCUSSES HER HOME VISITING WORK

Personal Meaningfulness of Home Visiting

Cynthia described to the author how her home visiting work has been meaningful to her.

> Cynthia: I think it's meaningful work. Again, it's not something I consciously chose to do. I think we follow a path that feels comfortable to us. Not that it isn't challenging and frustrating at times. But, for the most part, when I go into a home and sit down and talk to people, I feel comfortable.
>
> And I can use my intellect, although it may not seem that way to someone on the outside looking in. I get to use it with the family as I am watching the dynamics and helping people process, and I reflect on what I've done and how I've done it, why I've done it. I do a lot of that. I will leave a home visit, and I can tell by my spirits how that home visit went. Sometimes I fly high out of a home visit. I feel like I made some progress with this person; it was a good experience for both of us. I like to think that the adult and child I leave feel the same way—high. This was a good thing that just happened.
>
> Then there are others that I leave and I feel like the slug of the earth. It just didn't go well. I didn't say the right thing. I should have known better. I missed this. So, I know by how my spirit is soaring as to how that visit went. I could leave it at that, or I can take the time—I even do it as I'm driving or as I go out walking. I'll replay the visit in my head. I can almost repeat it verbatim. I remember the look the mom shot the kid or the kid shot the mom. I'll just play it in my head; and I'll think, "Well, what if I'd done this or what if I'd done that?" Again, the chance to sit and talk to other people who do this kind of work is so important. We never get enough of that.
>
> The other thing I want to say about why this work is meaningful to me is because I've made the statement that I go in and have things to offer, and people take from me what they need or are ready to take. I think the same of myself. I take from the people I work with on an everyday basis. I take things for myself. For example, I take your knowledge. I take your ability to synthesize and to look at things from a different perspective, and I make that my own. I play with it. You have given me a new way to look at things.

It may be something as simple as the way someone has arranged flowers in a vase, but it catches my eye and I may use it in my own home. It may be a phrase, the way they put their words together, and I like the way that sounds and it becomes my own.

So I get stuff from my home visits, from my interactions with people. It may be a way of correcting the child. I've watched a mom just touch a certain part of the baby's hair to caress, and I've actually gone home and done it with my child. There is a reciprocity. I think there has to be that reciprocity. You have to have an understanding that this is not a one-way street. I'm not just going into a home just to do things with people. I am going into homes to have a relationship. They give me as much as I give them.

Carol: *Can you give an example?*

Cynthia: *I have taken exact words, verbatim from another home visitor, from Janice, words that I read from one of your home visit observances, her explanation of language. I now use it. It's mine. I can't create everything, so I take things from people. My home visits still look very different from Janice's, even though we may have several phrases in which we use the exact same words.*

I know I make a difference, and parents will tell me that. It's taking the time to sit back and think about it—to think about what that person was like 3 years ago, to be able to do the Denver for the child and see that the child is growing, is developmentally appropriate. Maybe it's not the way you want it, but it could have been worse. What has been consistently the most difficult for me is not being able to find the key or not being there when that person needs me.

Professional Development Over Time

For the past 5 years, Cynthia has worked as a home visitor with primarily low-income, at-risk families. This is her first home visiting position. Cynthia sees home visiting as deepening the level of her involvement with low-income families. She also is aware of her increased level of knowledge and skill. She described how she has grown in her home visiting role.

Cynthia: *When I started home visiting, I had been working in the early childhood field about 12 years. I had some experience working with parents, but not in the home setting. When I first went on home visits, I would talk to parents about their children; my visit was child-focused. The PAT curriculum, the manual, says this is your lesson and this is what you are going to do. I really didn't deal that much with the parents. It was more the child and how the child felt and how the child was developing. With time,* and especially with the kind of families I work with, I still focus on the child and talk about the child; but I'm much more aware of the relationship between the parent and child, and the parent as a person, and how that person deals with everyday life. Some new home visitors actually will sit there and almost read from the lessons. But as you go and develop your skill and become more knowledgeable of development and of the many different ways to promote development, you merely use the written materials to reinforce information with the parent. It's such an interesting profession. You are privy to a person's innermost life. You get to see where they live, what possessions they have, how they arrange them, how they arrange their life. Then you watch their interactions with their baby. When I think about that, I get a little afraid sometimes.

Carol: Afraid in what way?

Cynthia: Well, because it's that person's private world. I don't want to invade that private world, and I don't want to be an intrusion into someone's private world. I guess that's where the balance is.

Carol: Maybe it's being cautious.

Cynthia: Maybe, but I tend to think of caution as negative. I don't mean fear like, "Oh, my gosh, what am I going to do? or "I'm going to be hurt" or that kind of thing, but just that I'm very aware that this is a person's private life that I'm seeing. I want the person I'm talking with to know that I value their privacy, that I understand that what they are sharing with me is private. Actually, it is a gift when somebody shares something that is private.

Cynthia spoke very specifically about how she has changed her approach with increased experience in home visiting.

Cynthia: My visits have changed over the years. When I first started, I was concerned about how I'd do with the child. You know, would the child respond to me? Would I be able to get the child to play? Over time, I realize that my job isn't to play with the child, but to involve the parent with the child so that there's more interaction. Then I'm able to talk with the parent about how the parent interacts with the child.

When I first started home visiting, I spent more time playing with the child. The play would end, and we'd go to the next section of the lessons, which is review what we've been talking about. It was much more step A, step B, step C, step D. Now it melds together, though I do try to summarize at the end, summarize important things to remember.

I still play with the child and often do model. Not just model. I play with the child because it is fun. And through that play, the parent is more likely to want to participate because it is fun. And if it looks like fun and sounds fun, then it must be fun. I found that most parents want to play with their kids, but they may not be sure exactly how to do it.

So, if we can spend 20 minutes where everybody is having fun and the parent feels successful and the child is having a good time and parent and child are interacting, then I'll physically back off. We all will be sitting on the floor, and the parent, child, and I will be playing. Then I'll back out of the play so that the parent and child are playing together. Then I can observe and can give the parent feedback on what's going on, on what they are doing.

I use the written materials—the parent handouts—to help parents see what they already know how to do because I'll observe them as they play with their child. Toward the end of the visit, when I summarize, I'll say, "Here are the handouts for language development. Look here, your child already is doing these things. We heard him today. Then I'll summarize, "Remember when he said 'Ba ba?' He is using those sounds. Then when you responded to him, that is one of the most important things you can do. It says it right here." I relate the written material back to what has happened in our visit. That's been part of my growth. I wasn't able to do that at first. It makes the parent feel good: "I must be a good parent if I can do these things."

When I first started home visiting, I relied on those written materials. I thought it was all in the manual. I felt that if I just read it long enough and memorized it, I'd know every answer to any question any parent would ask me. Now there are all kinds of questions I can't answer. I don't know why that child sleeps 12 hours and then he's awake 2 and then sleeps 8 more. I don't have definite answers for all these things, and that's okay. I'm much more comfortable saying to a parent, "Well, I'm not really sure. What do you think?," instead of feeling that I have to give the answer. They just need some help pulling it out or taking a look at it from a different point of view. Now I'm more aware of what I don't know, and I'm comfortable with that. I used to feel that I alone was responsible for this child's development. Now I'm comfortable with knowing that "No, I'm not totally responsible. What I'm responsible for is supplying information and being there, and interaction with the parent and the child." But it's not my responsibility to make sure that child develops in a certain way. That's the parents' responsibility.

And I have grown in my ability to accept that not all people want my service; not all people are ready to accept it. There are homes I'll never get in.[14] There are homes I'll get in once and never be invited back. There are other homes I can be in all the time but never get past a certain point. I really believe that people take from me what they need, not what I want to *give them. When I first started, I thought I had things to give them and they needed to take them. Now I feel I have things to offer, and they'll take what they need, what they're able to take at that time. That's what I've learned. Patience is a virtue, one that I've never had.*

Carol: *Patience with your families or with yourself?*

Cynthia: *Patience with everything. I've learned that when you're working with families over time, changes flow and changes may never come. Giving parents time to be able to do things and giving myself time and knowing that if something doesn't happen tomorrow, that's okay. It may happen the next day, and I've learned to wait for that next day.*

Like Janice, when she first began home visiting, Cynthia focused primarily on the baby or young child. The author was not surprised to hear each woman describe her initial inclination to focus on the children, because these two women had years of prior experience with babies and young children. With time, Cynthia learned that the greatest gift she could give the parents was to involve them in play with their children and to help them to see the meaning and purpose of this involvement. Cynthia really enjoys playing with little ones, and she skillfully generates this pleasure in parents as she invites them to play. Initially in her approach, she moved from one step to another as she followed the lesson plan. Now, like Janice, she has an integrated approach. She involves parents and baby, and she shares developmental information and interpretation in terms of the baby's and parents' actions. She also integrates the parent handouts—the written materials. As she summarizes the visits, she notes what the parent and baby did that directly relates to the written materials. Cynthia has learned that she cannot be all things to all people, that parents take what they are able to take from her, and she can be at peace knowing some families will reject her services.

Resources for Professional Development

Cynthia has been working in the field of early intervention for almost 20 years. She feels that, during her first few jobs, she developed skills by "dealing with the task at hand and learning by trial and error." The author asked her if, over the years, other people or experiences have influenced her professional development.[15]

Cynthia: *A person who has been influential in my work was one of my professors at graduate school. Every time we moved, there were new courses needed for certification, or I even had to repeat a course. When I* arrived at Dr. Frank's office at the University of Alabama, I learned that they were going to take away all the hours I had completed at the University of Florida. I sat crying in his office. He made three phone calls, and they made some exceptions for me and wrote a special program for me. It wasn't that he did me the favor, but that he cared. I had been in so many colleges at that point where nobody wanted to listen to my story, nobody really cared: Just give me your money and go to class and abide by these state rules. This man was different. The thing I always remember about Dr. Frank was when you walked in that door and he was terribly busy, he took time to listen to what you had to say and responded as a human being. I think he was as pleased as I was when I finally got my master's. For years after I left there, I sent him a poinsettia every Christmas.

He taught me to slow down and to listen to people and to see people as people, not as a means to an end. That's what I took from that man. It's so easy when you get busy and caught up in things to look at the people you work with as a way to get the job done, rather than a person, a human being with hopes and dreams and problems at home. I think we forget that too often. It helps me to be more compassionate, to remember to stop and say to my Even Start home visitor, Terry, "How is Lori doing? How's the toilet training going?," rather than, "Do you have the report done that I need?" Dr. Frank helped me learn to relate to people as people rather than just co-workers. The truth is, a lot of people have influenced me. I've always been one to sit back, watch, and observe. I take things from others and put them into my own repertoire. But as far as influencing me, I can tell you exactly what Dr. Frank gave to me, his gift to me.

Carol: Cynthia, since you have begun home visiting, do you have anybody with whom you can discuss your work?

Cynthia: Yes, in that respect, I have a lot of support. I can share with Margaret [director of the district's early education], with Dan [the clinical psychologist who regularly works with staff], and being able to talk to you has been helpful. I do have people to talk to about certain things. I'm the kind of person who pretty much needs to talk about something to figure it out.[16] I process by talking. And my husband, Bob, knows that about me. As I said before, Bob calms me down. And especially when I'm struggling with supervision issues, he helps me process and think things through. Mostly, he listens to me. I spent a lot of years pretending I could handle anything. Now I am able to say I have a problem. That's my personal development and growth. Many things have contributed to that. The people I've mentioned, different books I've read, and being able to sit and talk about the work with families we do with other home visitors, who often encounter similar problems.

Relationships always have been at the center of Cynthia's life, in childhood and in her work. Not surprisingly, she sees her professional development emerging through relationships with significant people. Cynthia has learned that she need not always excel, need not have all the answers, and, in fact, can be comfortable with problems. She knows she needs individuals with whom she can talk about her work. She feels fortunate to have several colleagues, as well as her husband, Bob, who listen and offer supportive feedback.

CYNTHIA'S PERSONAL AND PROFESSIONAL HISTORY

Childhood Family

Cynthia, like Janice, grew up in a very close nuclear and extended family. The daily life of this family of seven children did not proceed "like clockwork," however. They lived in a small rural town, Florence, 1 hour from the closest metropolitan area. Cynthia's father owned a bar in town, and her mother was a full-time homemaker until Cynthia was 9 years old. Then her mother taught Spanish in the town's high school. Cynthia is the fifth of seven children.

> Cynthia: I was the start of the second family. My mom had me at 40 and 2 more by the time she was 43. My oldest sister was 17 when I was born. I was raised in an extended family.

> Carol: A nuclear family that seemed extended.

> Cynthia: Right. But we also had grandmas and grandpas. We lived in this huge house. First my mother's mother lived with our family, when I was very young. And I also grew up with my mother's father living in our home. And there always was a new baby in our family. And as a teen, I had a lot of experience with young children. I did a lot of taking care of them. That's pretty much how I grew up—in a litter.

Cynthia grew up in a family that loved babies and chose a career path continuing her early love of babies and small children. Family celebrations with singing, laughter, and game playing were a central part of her childhood. Whereas Janice's family rituals stayed about the same, Cynthia's daily family life and celebrations always changed.

> Holidays always were celebrated with food, decoration, and ceremony. We were raised Catholic, so Christmas and Easter especially were religious holidays, but also fun holidays. Who was there as a family always changed because of the differences in ages and who was and wasn't

available at that time. The celebrations always included a lot of food, a lot of noise, a lot of laughter, playing games, and a lot of music. My older sisters both played the piano, had good voices, and sang.

Although her parents did not finish college, they valued learning and they instilled that value in their seven children.

Reading was extremely important. My mother read to us from the time we were babies, and my father read to us from about ages 6–12. He'd take the three of us—the little ones. Every night after dinner, for a half hour, he'd read nonfiction to us. He had a love of history. I remember all the presidents' lives. He'd read those children's books to us. It was just such a nice, special time.

My mom and dad had such a love of learning. They both were very determined that all of us would grow up well educated and go to college. I always knew—that was the expectation, that you will go to college. And you will do well in school. You had no choice. And that's what we did.

Beyond a love of learning, Cynthia's parents "had a love of their fellow man," she said. Cynthia explained:

They displayed this love in different ways for different things that were important to them. I remember when I had my mom as a teacher. She was so understanding of these other kids, especially the ones having difficulty. And when Mom died last summer, about 10 of her high school students from about 30 years ago came to the funeral. They loved her. Mom cared about people, understood people, and took time for them.

My dad displayed caring for other people in an entirely different way. He was the local pawn shop. When someone was in trouble, he'd bail them out of jail and pay for it. If someone didn't have money, they'd bring him their TV and he'd give them 20 bucks and keep it until they could pay him back. In their own way, both Mom and Dad were very generous people. I grew up with that tolerance of other cultures right from the start. It just always was there, that you are accepting of people who are a little bit different or have different ideas. You don't have to agree with them. But that doesn't have anything to do with the respect you feel for them as a person.

As I listened to Cynthia describe her parents' tolerance, understanding, and assistance to people, I reflected on how these themes are central to Cynthia's work as a home visitor and coordinator of Even Start, a program serving very-low-income families. Although the individual members living in Cynthia's family might have changed, the patterns of her family's daily life were consistent. Dinnertime was one of these consistent patterns.

At dinnertime, everyone was expected to be there. You knew you had to be home at a certain time for dinner. Then you had conversation. Sometimes you had arguments because my mom and dad had such different opinions politically. So we would listen and learn both sides. Mom was a Democrat, and dad was a Republican. They would have lively arguments.

Dinner was a time of discussion. My dad might come home with a story from the bar. They were always interesting stories. We learned a lot about human nature and the kinds of things that can happen in families. You recapped your day, what was going on, or what was important. It wasn't so much a time of planning what was going to happen next as a time to be together.

Cynthia grew up in a small town, and Janice grew up in a large metropolitan area. As young children, dinnertime for both involved daily extended conversation about ideas and happenings of family members. As children, both women found a sense of security and connectedness in these daily rituals; yet there were substantive differences between the two families. Janice experienced very predictable, conservative thinking within her family's daily dinner that always involved the same four family members. Cynthia experienced lively arguments and a wide range of perspective taking as she ate with an ever-changing family constellation.

Cynthia had two brothers and four sisters.

My mom was pregnant a very short time after she had me and then pregnant again. Karen was a sophomore in high school when I was born. The first 3 years of my life she pretty much took care of me. In our family, the older kids always bore responsibility for the younger kids. I got to do all kinds of things that most very young babies don't get to do. I hung out with a teenager, so it was great fun.

We all grew up at a very young age with family responsibility. The daily chores of cooking and cleaning with a very large family take a lot of time and organization. At 8, I started doing the laundry with my older sister for our weekly responsibility. I couldn't go to the movies until I had washed the floors on Saturday morning. Everybody had their jobs.

We used to do all kinds of things we weren't supposed to do. Like one time we tried to persuade my little sister Annie that there really was a tooth fairy. My sister Liz, who is 5 years older than I am, dressed me up like a fairy, and I went out on a narrow ledge outside Annie's window and tried to convince this kid that I was the tooth fairy. She was maybe 3, and I wasn't very old. She took one look and said, "Oh, that's just Cynthia." I was dancing two stories up on a ledge, and I shouldn't have been doing that.

We did all kinds of things. We'd sneak out at midnight. My older sister would go swimming in the lake in the moonlight, and she'd take me. I was

3 years old. They'd swim, and I'd sit on the edge and watch. It was wonderful. Then, when the second litter grew up, we'd sneak out of the house while everybody was sleeping and go down to the lake and swim.

For Cynthia, risk taking was just what you did as a child. As an adult, Cynthia continues to be comfortable with taking risks. At the same time, she sometimes feels fearful.

Cynthia: *In my work, I have pursued different kinds of positions with more responsibility and a chance to do things in a different way. I have actively sought positions and pushed myself. And sometimes there is risk involved. At the time, I'm thinking, "You don't want to do that." But there's something inside me that makes me do it. I just do it anyway. Until now. Now I've gotten to the point where I don't think I have to run around taking chances anymore to know who or what I am.*

Carol: *When you go on home visits in dangerous neighborhoods, do you have the frightening feelings that you remember having as child?*

Cynthia: *No. It's funny that I don't because I've thought that I probably should. Why am I not afraid? I know some people who work in dangerous neighborhoods are very afraid, and some just won't do it. Maybe it's just stupidity. I feel safe. No, I'm not stupid about it. I feel aware that there could be danger. I don't go to these neighborhoods at night or after 3:00 P.M.*

Carol: *Well, you seem to have had a childhood, beginning at 3 years, involving risk taking.*

Cynthia: *That's probably true, though I've never thought about it much.*

Cynthia described her mother as being a very strong woman who had great influence on her own life. She poignantly described her mother's gifts and how she influenced her own development.

I was crazy about my dad, but I lost him at 19. I said to my son the other night, "I only knew my dad 19 years." I looked at him and said, "You're 13 years old already. I only knew my dad 19 years. That's only 6 more years." But I knew my mom 41 years. So I had more time to know her as a person. I never knew my dad as a person like I grew to know my mother.

My mother had a formidable strength. Yes, she was bossy, and everybody was half afraid of her. But she had love and compassion. I think of her love of life, her sheer delight in a bite of a peach. She would just howl with laughter at things her kids said. No one entertained her more than her own children. She absolutely loved being with them. She waited for the minute we would walk in the door to tell her a story. She would give you her undivided attention at the moment to hear your story. Then she would make sure that everybody else knew about our accomplishments.

And her love of learning. I was able to watch the different things she could do and realize that, while your talents are gifts, they also have to be nurtured and take work. She helped me understand that. It doesn't just happen; you have to work to develop your talents.

And she worked hard throughout her life. She worked hard at learning. I mean, even up to the bitter end, she played Scrabble and wanted to win. Half-blind, she would get this big magnifying glass to be able to study the dictionary to learn new words to beat May Kabias. They had a Scrabble club. Up to her last day, she still was trying to learn new words to beat May Kabias.

And she never lost her love of gardening. She watched birds. She taught me to appreciate nature. When I was growing up, I hated pulling those weeds. I would cry, "You can't make me go out in that garden." But you know, that taught me something, too. It taught me that you can bring order to the chaos of weeds. I took great pleasure in how it looked when I was done, when I got all those weeds removed. I learned the names of the plants, and I knew how to take care of them because I spent a lot of time out there with Mom. That has become important in my life. I need my time in my garden.

Although the author observed and interviewed Cynthia for only 18 months, as she listened to Cynthia describe her mother, the author reflected on how the descriptions matched what she knew of Cynthia. During several meetings, the author listened to Cynthia tell stories of a 39-year-old Even Start mother who lived with her sister and their 12 children and 4 grandchildren in a home bordering on chaos; and the author sensed her caring and compassion. One Friday, during a break from interviewing, she told the author that she was looking forward to a day of gardening on Saturday. She shared with the author the pleasure she gets in the unusual names of her irises.

Schooling

Cynthia attended a Catholic elementary school and a public high school. She described school as being very easy for her. Throughout her childhood, close friendships and time with her large family occupied her far more than did school. There was nothing remarkable about school. It was just something she did, and she did not have to work hard to get all A's. Cynthia did not describe her elementary schooling; she began with high school.

I remember my high school years as just a lot of fun. School wasn't hard for me at all. I started working my sophomore year in high school at a pizza place. I worked one or two nights during the week and on the weekend. That gave me spending money, my clothes money, things like that. I never had to work really hard. I learned things quickly.

Cynthia has a keen intellect that her parents nourished by reading to her from the time she was a baby and by engaging in extended daily conversations and debate at dinner. As I listened to her brief description of school, I thought of how much more stimulating her life at home had been than at school. I also reflected on the stark contrast between Cynthia's and Janice's schooling experiences. Cynthia's small-town elementary and high schools were unexceptional, and she sailed through with ease. Janice's teachers had higher expectations, and she worked very hard to excel.

Given her family's decreased income, Cynthia could not choose which college to attend, and her courses in college seemed as unremarkable to her as her experiences in grade school and high school.

I wanted to go to the main state university, but we couldn't afford it. I didn't want to go into education. Everyone else in my family was a teacher, and I didn't want to be a teacher. But, at the time, my dad gave me no choice. If he sent me to the main state university, then my younger brother and sister couldn't go to school, because there wouldn't be enough money. They had three kids to try to get through college, and all of us were going to be in college a year or two together. Dad said that he wanted me to go to Western, and he wanted me to take a teacher ed scholarship because women need that.[17]

Friendships

Cynthia continues contact with her close friends of early childhood and adolescence, friends with whom she shared many happy hours of playful abandon.

I was just talking to one of my childhood friends two nights ago. Her mother is in the hospital, dying. It made me think back to my first memory of Lane Kabias. We were both in diapers and were crawling under a dining room table, one of those gate-leg tables where the sides come down. When I think about Lane, that's the first image that comes to me. Our mothers were dear friends. They were gardener friends and avant garde in this small town. What the moms had in common was that tolerance of what is different. Lane and I have remained friends. Lane now lives in Chicago, and we talk to each other a couple times a year. She was one of my dearest friends.

Already in high school, Cynthia's actions seemed to mirror her parents' tolerance of difference.

Even though I came from a big family, I always had friends at school. I had friends from pretty much all walks. I had West-Ender friends who were the kids on the wrong side of the track. I didn't really hang around with them, because I didn't drink and that kind of thing. But I was respectful of them, and they knew it. I would help them with schoolwork.

Jean Bath became one of my best friends. She was loud and obnoxious and totally hysterical. Jean and I stayed friends through all the years, and I lost her 2 years ago when she died at the age of 38 of pancreatitis. She was one of my best and dearest friends.

Another good friend was Rose Matthews. She also became my friend in high school, and we ended up at the same college. We were kind of like a rat pack, Jean, Rose, and I. Rose continues to be a good friend of mine. I see her probably two or three times a year, whenever I go back to Florence.

All the friends I have mentioned spent hours at my house. Our home was the hangout. Poor Mom and Dad—how they could stand it, I'll never know. I mean, we were the last of seven kids. Our home was across the street from the pizza place where I worked. So we'd close the pizza place, and everyone would come over to my house. Mom and Dad must have been deaf by that point. We would stay up 'til 1:00, 2:00, or 4:00 in the morning. I remember my high school years as lots of fun.

Throughout childhood and adolescence Cynthia was immersed in a caring and loving web of relationships. Her parents modeled caring and compassion in their personal and work life; teenage siblings were primary caregivers when she was very little; and lifelong childhood friends are remembered within a circle of love and caring.[18]

Religion

Cynthia was raised Catholic and attended a Catholic grade school in Florence.

Cynthia: *In grade school, I spent a lot of time in religion class. I went to church every day. My parents were quite active in the church. I loved the old Latin Mass and the symbolism and incense. The mysticism was to me more prevalent then, because you didn't understand the Latin. It's like it was shrouded in a mystery, and to me that made more sense. So, when I think of religion and church, those are the things come to my mind.*

Carol: *Symbols, images, and mystery.*

Cynthia: *Yes. And the celebrations. The Catholic Church is great for celebrations. The priests dress up in fancy vestments. They use incense. I think that's important in my life—celebrations in my life. And the religious celebration matched my family life. We carried it into the home. Growing up, religion had a strong influence.*

Carol: And sin?

Cynthia: And sin—oh, yes, mortal sin. I was scared to death. I remember growing up scared to death they'd catch me doing something awful. And you know, interestingly, I still have that need to confess. I don't actually go to confession anymore. But if I do something I think is wrong, I have to tell somebody. I still have that ingrained in me. Once I confess, I'm fine.

I do have a strong faith in God. My belief in God has influenced my life. In fact, today I had a conversation with one of our Even Start mothers who has been very depressed. We talked about how hard it is when you're depressed to keep moving forward. I said, "You know, I don't look at this as the only part of my life. I really do believe that something comes after this. And that makes daily life, the troubles, and ins and outs not quite so difficult. They are difficult. But this is just a piece of it, not the whole shebang. If I mess this up, there's still something else out there. I think of life as a dress rehearsal for who knows what comes next. I think that for me that makes a difference, and it helps me put things in perspective." She looked at me and nodded.

I've chosen to work with people in a certain way, and I think that probably the way I was raised and my beliefs in a caring and nurturing God probably influence the kind of work I do.

Carol: Do you and Bob continue the Catholicism of your childhood?

Cynthia: I hate to say this, but I don't like to give up my Sunday morning. But I never miss a Christmas or Easter. Being Catholic is great because as long as you go Christmas and Easter, you've got it made. I've never missed. I have a foot in the door.

Cynthia has a strong faith in a tolerant, caring, nurturant God. She is very clear that she strives to continue to be tolerant and caring in her professional life. Her religion has a sense of mystery, symbolism, images, and celebration that Cynthia embraces. Like Janice, she gains strength through her religion, but in a different way. Janice spoke of God giving her strength through prayer in difficult times; Cynthia spoke of trust in an afterlife helping her come to terms with difficulties.

Marriage, Work, and Parenting

Cynthia and her husband, Bob, both grew up in Florence. Bob's brother was Cynthia's classmate, and she knew him well. Bob is 4½ years older than Cynthia. She did not actually meet him until she was in college and he was in the U.S. Naval Academy.

Bob would come back home for basketball games. Our brothers played on the same team. We met at one of the games and began dating. I graduated from college in December, and we married in February.

When we were first married, we moved very frequently. First, he was stationed in Texas; then the Navy moved him to Germany for 3 years. So we ended up in this little tiny Navy base. Here I was, 21 years old, an officer's wife. Bob was a junior officer, and we were thrown in with older people. I came from a generation that was burning bras and wearing blue jeans. The military was still old guard. Officer's wives were to wear gloves and hats and go to teas. The wives seldom worked. It was awful!

The only job I could find was teaching 4-year-olds. I had no idea how to teach 4-year-olds or what a preschool curriculum looked like. So I flew by the seat of my pants. I did enjoy this; but even at that time, I knew I didn't want a steady diet of teaching preschool. Actually, I've never wanted a steady diet of classroom teaching in any shape or form. For me, it's too confining, too limiting. But I do have a genuine affection for children, and I realized that. The other thing it made me realize is how families impact development.[19] I began that realization in that base nursery. There were so many little kids whose parents were young and poor. I got interested right then in the family and how the family works and how to help kids with early intervention.

Cynthia's interest in young children, family, and early intervention for children at risk began with her first position. Yet Cynthia speaks of classroom teaching as being "too confining, too limiting." As the author listened to Cynthia describe classroom teaching as too confining, her feelings made sense. Cynthia also described to the author the ever-changing daily pattern of her childhood family life and her love of impromptu fun and excitement. In contrast, Janice felt totally fulfilled teaching first grade in a small, very wealthy suburb.

After 3 years in Germany, Bob and Cynthia moved to Florida, where they stayed for 10 months.

Cynthia: *That's where I taught Spanish in an inner-city high school to Cubans, which probably started my risk taking and living dangerously, because it was crazy. At that time, teachers were getting beat up in the hallways. I was about 25 years old, looked 12, wore jeans and platform shoes to school. So I would blend in and look like one of my kids. It also was scary because I hadn't used my Spanish for 3 years, and I had to teach first-year Spanish through fourth-year Spanish.*

Carol: *A new environment, like Germany, but with a lot more risk taking. And you were able to do well?*

Cynthia: Well, yes. But, by that time, Bob decided that he didn't have much of a career in the Navy, with me as his wife. I mean, that was really part of the decision.

Carol: I'm not sure I understand.

Cynthia: Well, at that time, the wife was expected to have parties, not a career, and to kowtow. That isn't the only reason for Bob's decision, but it was clear to both of us that I was not going to be just an officer's wife; I wanted a career also. I had one tell me that it was my duty to rub elbows with the big brass. I told him something like "If I could find somebody to watch his kid," because I worked at the nursery, that I'd be there. Otherwise, Bob was perfectly capable of rubbing elbows on his own.

Cynthia was a woman in her early twenties whose life experience prior to moving overseas had been growing up in a small town and graduating from a rural state university. Yet Cynthia knew who she was and felt secure in her values and competence, so she could refuse to act in a manner that she thought violated her temperament and basic principles. As the author listened to Cynthia describing her determination to remain true to her self, I reflected on her secure, loving childhood that allowed her to know who she was.

Bob and Cynthia then moved to New Jersey, where Bob worked in a chemical company and Cynthia found a position in Head Start.

Cynthia: Head Start was the only job offered me. I was a home visitor for special needs children. My caseload included Puerto Rican families, so I got to use my Spanish. I learned very quickly about families and family dynamics and child development. And then there was an opportunity to move up. So I interviewed and got the job. But then we moved again. Bob's company moved him from New Jersey to their plant in New Mexico.

We were in New Mexico for about 3 years. Again, I worked for Head Start. They hired me as their handicap coordinator. I coordinated services for special needs kids. I could use my Spanish with the large Mexican population. Head Start hired me, even though I was pregnant.

I liked that job. I did that until our son was born; then I went back on a part-time basis. Then I decided I needed to get my master's, so I also started going to the state university. I decided to major in early education. I completed 6 hours, and then we moved again.

We returned to Florida, and I didn't work for the first 18 months. I went to school and was a full-time mommy and didn't do real well with it. All my classes did not transfer, so I had to take the same classes again.

Carol: Cynthia, given your dislike of the classroom, having to repeat education classes, and our culture's negative stereotype of education, how have you dealt with this?

Cynthia: I have real mixed feelings. Part of me wholeheartedly agrees that our education system doesn't, for the most part, educate very well. I have experienced it firsthand. I've been in a lot of different schools. Not that I've been in the best schools, but I've hit enough of them that I worry about the level of education in this country. Especially now that our son is in school, I see that he is getting even less than I did. But I have been in education now for so long. Most of the people in education that I have met truly care about kids and want to be good at what they do, and work hard to do that.

In every state I have lived, I have to take their courses to be certified, and it has been such a waste of time and money. I should have three Ph.D.'s by now. I've gone to school all but 2 years of my adult life, and I'm 42. When I moved here, I had to take six classes to get state certification, and I already had a master's."

Carol: Did the teacher education courses you have taken over the years make a difference or influence you, either in terms of knowledge or skill?

Cynthia: In my undergraduate work. They just threw in 20 hours of education at the very end, and that didn't help a bit. I would say that mostly what has helped over the years has been teacher training on the job. Once you have a position, you seek information. The one thing my teacher training did supply was some resources, some books that I have used. I doubt it really had much impact on how I think or how I do things.

During their first 10 years or marriage, Cynthia and Bob lived in six very different communities in the United States and Germany. In each area, Cynthia was able to get an early childhood position working with low-income families. She often was in an administrative role where she could be independent and creative. The positions seemed to match her personal style. Each involved young children and families, and in each she could make a contribution. As a reflective, bright young woman, Cynthia was able to develop skills on the job through what she termed *trial and error.*

Combining Career and Family   After her son, Andrew, was born, Cynthia worked half-time. When Andrew was in first grade, Cynthia began working full-time, and she always had the summers off. Unlike Janice, Cynthia never considered being a full-time homemaker. Combining career and family was not easy.

It's been difficult. I remember standing on a stranger's doorstep and knocking on that door to ask this stranger, asking if she'd watch my baby, who was about a year old. And it just struck me, I'm going to ask a total *stranger to watch my baby! I couldn't do it. I went home and told Bob, "We've got to figure something else out." And eventually we found a neighbor who we knew. I remember getting in my car at the end of the day with utter terror in my heart that I would get to that baby sitter's, and my baby wouldn't be okay. We didn't have car phones then. Now I really like my car phone because when I'm stuck in traffic, I can call my son.*

He answers the phone, and I know he's okay. I really sympathize with working moms because I've experienced that fear myself, and it's awful. It's also something I chose to do in spite of its being awful. I chose to work and didn't necessarily have to. Financially, we probably could have made it.

I have given up opportunities to do things as far as my career that I'll never get back. But I chose to do that because I wasn't willing to give up the time with my child. I don't regret that, but I mourn it sometimes. I wish I'd had the chance to do whatever I wanted to do. Parenting is important to me. I understand that awful feeling of having to leave your child day after day. I'm a working mother. I have been all along. It's an important piece of me to be able to work and contribute and use my skills. But I also bear the guilt of leaving my kid.

Parenting and relationships are central themes in Janice's and Cynthia's personal histories. Both women are exceptionally competent home visitors, but they are quite different in many ways. Each woman also has a unique personal history. Both women loved and respected their mothers, though their mothers were very different models. Janice's mother was a quiet, even-tempered homemaker with two daughters. Cynthia's mother was a strong, talented woman who loved lively arguments with her husband; had a passion for writing, poetry, and gardening; and taught school when three of her seven children were under age 10. Janice's husband changed employers only once in the first 27 years of their marriage, while Cynthia's husband's career brought seven moves in 15 years.

For 7 years, Cynthia lived 2 hours from her hometown of Florence. Thus, she often could spend weekends with her mother, with whom she remained close through out her adult life. Cynthia's mother died 1 year prior to Cynthia's interviews with the author, who asked Cynthia if she thought her parenting of Andrew resembled the parenting she received from her mother and father.[20]

Sure, I think it has. At the same time, I made conscious choices not to do some of the things my parents did; but it doesn't always work, such as not lecturing, not yelling. I grew up in a yelling family. So I've had to really work not to do that. I am trying to control myself. But when I'm tired, I feel myself slipping into those old patterns. They are hard to break.

I think the positives I have provided for my child are things I grew up with, a strong sense of routine. My mom was a drill sergeant. You did this, and you made sure this happened. Even though she drove me nuts, I also could count on it. It was there. And the feeling that you are special, that you are important in this world, that you can do things in the world. I feel that all that came from my mom and dad. And the love of reading. The importance of education. The expectation that you will do well. There's no question about it. And with Andrew, I've maintained this stance.

But the difference between my childhood and Andrew's is that he can tell me. He will say to me, "I think you care too much about that. Who cares if I get a B on that? It's okay, Mom. It's okay if I get a B." I wouldn't have dared to say that to my parents.

Cynthia grew up with clear parental expectations of excellence, and she continues this theme in her parenting. In spite of family members coming and going in her childhood home, it was a place of daily ritual and routine like Cynthia provides for Andrew.

Cynthia explained the difference between her husband's temperament and personal style and her own, and how he has assisted her personally and professionally.

Bob calms me down. He keeps my feet on the ground. He's very pragmatic and is excellent with people issues. When I'm struggling with how to deal with a supervising issue, he's helpful. He listens to me, helps me process and think it through. He nurtures our son in a way you often don't see in men. He's the one who will put Andrew's vitamin out in the morning. I don't even think about it half the time. He'll take Andrew to the Dairy Queen at 9:00 at night, but I'll tell him to wait until tomorrow.

He gives a lot. He's a very calm man. He doesn't get upset about things, but he doesn't express himself. He stifles his emotions, whereas I wear him out screaming sometimes. I think there are times he'd love to just shut me up, just as there are times I would love to make him mad, to see him rant and rave. But he knows me, and I know him. He's known me for 20 years, and he loves me. Bob listens to me. I guess I'm the kind of person who pretty much needs to talk about something to figure it out. I process by talking, and so he knows that about me. We go on walks at night, and he lets me talk.

Like Cynthia's parents, Cynthia and Bob have significant temperamental and personal style differences. But, as with Cynthia's parents, both lead lives where caring, compassion, and tolerance are dominant themes.

The themes of connectedness and relationships have been central throughout Cynthia's career.[21] During the last 5 years, these themes have become even more dominant in her home visiting work. Between the spring of 1990 and the fall of 1993, Cynthia was a home visitor. In the fall of 1993, she became an Even Start Coordinator. The Even Start program serves approximately 40 low-income families. Beyond administering the program, Cynthia continues to do home visiting with approximately six families.

CHILDHOOD PAIN
TO PROFESSIONAL COMPETENCE

Unlike Janice and Cynthia, many home visitors do not have happy childhood memories. In fact, some may have grown up in very troubled families. But just because someone's childhood family was troubled, it does not mean that he or she cannot be a competent home visitor. Often, in coming to terms with their own pain, home visitors gain a sensitivity to others and find insights into their own lives that can be a resource when they help others. They may understand and be more sensitive because they do not take anything for granted.

Adults carrying pain from their childhood may have achieved resolution in different ways. For example, some adults may come to terms with their childhood pain through reading about ideas and concepts. This process may be varied. Some read novels, biographies and autobiographies, histories, or therapeutic literature; some become well educated in one specific field of knowledge and practice. Other people may learn alternative attitudes, values, and behavior from those outside their family—for example, by spending time with families of childhood friends or by learning from older adults who are role models. Some use psychotherapy to come to terms with their troubled childhood.

Whatever means home visitors use to grow, it is important that they understand that each individual must find her or his own path. For example, an adult abused as a child may find in God the parent she wished for; her client's path, however, must be the client's own, and the client may not find resolution in a religious faith like that of the home visitor. The answers a home visitor finds to deal with childhood pain may or may not work for another.

Because relationship is central to the process of home visiting, it is common for work with some families to trigger the visitor's own childhood pain. When this happens, home visitors may respond unwittingly more to what has been triggered by their own history than by the needs of the children and parents they are serving. Karen is a home visitor who serves low-income families. As a child, Karen had a very angry mother who directed much of her anger toward Karen. Karen's description of her work with a family illustrates how home visitors' sometimes painful memories can be triggered.

Karen: One mother is a real challenge to me in lots of ways and probably the family that comes closest to my situation when I was growing up. The mother is trying hard, but she has a lot of problems. People have said that she was mentally ill, and she probably still is. She has had some counseling and therapy in the past, but not presently.

She is very negative with her daughter, who recently turned 3. This mom had a really rough time when she was young. And she has become very angry and hardened because of it. She is a very rude person. The mother is treating her daughter, I assume, the way she was treated. She is not one who is easy to like. And what I had as a child was a very angry mother."

Carol: So when you are sitting in her living room, Karen, what is going through your mind?

Karen: I really have to detach from it. But when I leave, it hits me. When I get away, the feelings start coming back. I have been this little girl. I identify with what is going on with the little girl. That is tough for me.

Carol: Has there been anyone in the program with whom you can talk about this family?

Karen: Yes, when Dan [the program consultant, a clinical psychologist] was at our team meeting, I found that I ended up needing to say some things about what was going on in that family. When I spoke, I didn't realize it was kind of rolling around in me. I just talked about what was going on in a visit one day, and how that little girl was being affected. And I was very angry. Dan told me that I was blaming the mom, which I was.

At the time, it felt terrible for a professional to say that to me. Dan said, "You can't work with this family if you are blaming the mom and putting guilt on her." I sat back and thought. "Well, she needs to be blamed because she is wrong." That was one of the best things that has happened. Because putting blame was exactly what I was doing, and it was getting in the way of things. I stepped back and thought, "I need to be there for this mom and this little girl, and see how we can work with this to make things different." Because the mother has told me several times that she doesn't want things to be the way they are. She doesn't want her daughter to be afraid of her.

And, in my next visit, I told this mom that she can change things, that she can make a difference, and I believed it as I told her. I told her that it is very hopeful to see somebody with a daughter this young who has had some problems and is saying, "I don't want to do this." I encourage her and tell her she can change and make it different, that she doesn't have to keep doing things the way she had been. I feel that when I first told her that, that's when we really connected. I think she holds on to that hopeful talk.

Carol: *And you, too?*

Karen: *Yeah, we both do. So I don't know what is going to happen. She is very difficult to talk with, and she can be very rude. But I work hard to find something positive. For example, she told me that sometimes she puts on music and has this dance with her little girl. And I told her that's a great thing to do, and maybe you can do this when you recognize that you are getting angry.*

When Karen was able to discuss happenings with this family with her team, the team leader interpreted her actions and gave her a new understanding, not just of the family, but of her response to this family. Once Karen recognized that she was angry and was blaming the mother, she understood how nonproductive her approach was. She then became proactive and spoke directly to this mother about knowing that the mother could change. Karen's clear statement of hope became the beginning of a new phase in their relationship, a relationship that continues to be difficult, but one in which Karen knows she can help make a difference.

It always is important for home visitors to strive to recognize their vulnerabilities, that is, to be alert for experiences that may trigger unresolved childhood issues. For Karen, being with an unstable mother who raged at her 3-year-old rekindled the feelings of Karen's own childhood memories of her mother. With the help of supervision, Karen was able to step back and ask herself what was happening. Once she recognized her vulnerability, Karen could move forward and approach the mother differently.

Home visitors cannot assume that resolutions they have found in their own lives will fit the parents with whom they work. For example, the home visitor who has achieved resolution of childhood pain by becoming well versed in a particular area may experience vulnerability when she works with a parent or child experiencing pain similar to that of her own childhood. The home visitor may respond intellectually as she strives to problem-solve with the parent. Her intellectual approach may protect herself but may miss where the parent or child is emotionally.

Although parents may look forward to the home visitor's visit, the visitor may dread it because it is too similar to her own childhood past. For example, one home visitor, Anna, has a sister who has Down syndrome. Anna's mother had told her many years ago that God sends special blessings and that children with Down syndrome are the chosen recipients of God's love because they remain as little children who are fit for the kingdom of God. In this religious view, resenting her sister was sinful. As a child, Anna felt anger at her sister's interference, at her mother's preoccupation with her sister, and later at having to remain at home to be with her sister because she could not be alone. She felt guilty about having all these feelings because to her they indicated a lack of faith in God's wisdom.

Now Anna works with a couple who are coming to terms with their 1-year-old with Down syndrome. The parents are angry that they do not have a perfect child. They feel cheated because they had waited so long for this child and had dreamed of a perfect child. After amniocentesis showed that his child would have Down syndrome, the father had wanted his wife to have an abortion. The mother briefly considered this idea but then could not bring herself to do it. She is unable to clearly state religious or philosophical reasons for her choice, however. These parents' conflict over the abortion continues: The father still thinks he was right even as he begins to bond with his daughter. The mother's anger at his request for abortion continues to be strong, even though she knows her child is not the one she had dreamed of having. In this complex network of emotions, Anna discovered that she was having difficulty with these parents' conflicts because she wanted the answers to seem as simple to these parents as they seemed for her own mother. At the same time, she had trouble separating the parents' resentment toward their child from the resentment she once felt toward her sister. Discussions with other home visitors or Anna's supervisor may help Anna to examine her feelings about working with this family.

Not all home visitors actively work toward ensuring that their own personal history does not confuse them as they relate to the visit. Even if a home visitor is sensitive to this possibility, sometimes it takes an outsider to identify the dynamics. Given this complexity in home visiting relationships, supervision becomes very important in assisting home visitors' skills in self-reflection and relating to families.[22]

CONCLUSIONS

This chapter portrayed rather fully the life histories of two home visitors, Janice and Cynthia, and how they see their home visiting work as giving meaning to their lives and how their personal histories are intertwined with their home visiting. Each woman's home visiting grows out of her childhood history. Relationships with family and friends with whom they continue to connect were central to their childhood and are the core of their home visiting work. As an adult, each woman has strong commitments rooted in her childhood. Janice's adult life expresses a strong commitment to education and her family; Cynthia's, to helping others and to her family. Each woman's early life was situated in an environment—neighborhood, community, and society—that had an impact on her development. Nathan was a suburb that valued education highly, a dominant theme in Janice's life. Although Cynthia's family valued education highly, their small rural community did not challenge her educationally; rather, schoolwork was just something she did as a child. Coming from a conservative family and community and being 10 years older than Cynthia, Janice did not consider continuing to work after she had her first child. In contrast, it never dawned on Cynthia to remain home for an extended time once she had her child.

Each person has her or his own values, attitudes, beliefs, and ways of relating to others. These patterns are rooted in personal history, a history in which childhood relationships are intertwined with present patterns. When the home visitor experiences strong emotions before or after a visit or feels confused or conflicted when she is there, it sometimes helps to ask if the drama being played out in the family or with the family and herself is similar to a drama the home visitor has experienced in her own family. For example, Karen discovered that her blaming of the mother of a 3-year-old was in reality her reexperiencing her own mother's behavior when she was 3 years old. Just as a home visitor's problem often is a response to her own childhood, a person's strength is also part of a childhood pattern. When she shared her childhood history with me, Cynthia discovered that her ability to move in and out of dangerous neighborhoods is not too different from the risks she and her siblings took as very young children.

Both Karen and Cynthia were able to see these connections between current struggles at work and personal history as they talked it over with another person. For Karen, it was the team facilitator; for Cynthia, it was the author as an interviewer doing research. Most people understand themselves best when they are reflecting on their experiences with someone else. That is why peer support and supervision are central dynamics for promoting high-quality home visiting.

Home visiting is a new profession. Builders know what they need to construct a house. When she or he goes to work, a teacher knows what the day's plans are. In contrast, home visitors never know what to expect as they enter a family's home. As in Janice's and Cynthia's work with families, home visiting can be rewarding work; simultaneously, it can be very difficult and untidy.

Central to the home visiting process is the evolving relationship between home visitor and child and parent; development of both parent and child occurs through and within these relationships. The process is different for each family and can be known only as the relationships evolve over time and they develop mutuality in their collaborative work together. The child and parent develop in relationship to each other. Parents develop in their relationships with their home visitor, and the home visitor develops in relation to her or his personal history, to the families she or he visits, and to her or his professional peers and supervisors.

Appendix
Resources for Home Visitors

Children's Play

Biber, B. (1984). *Early education and psychological development.* New Haven, CT: Yale University Press.

Bruner, J.S., Jolly, A., & Sylva, K. (Eds.). (1976). *Play: Its role in development and evolution.* New York: Basic Books.

Carlsson-Paige, N., & Levin, D.E. (1990). *Who's calling the shots? How to respond effectively to children's fascination with war play and war toys.* Philadelphia: New Society.

Erikson, E. (1950). *Childhood and society.* New York: Norton.

Fein, G., & Rivkin, M. (Eds.). *The young child at play: Vol. 4. Reviews of research.* Washington, DC: National Association for the Education of Young Children.

Galinsky, E., & David, J. (1988). *The preschool years: Family strategies that work—from experts and parents.* New York: Ballantine Books.

Greenspan, S.N., & Greenspan, N.T. (1989). *The essential partnership: How parents and children can meet the emotional challenges of infancy and childhood.* New York: Penguin Books.

Cultural Diversity

Garcia, E.E. (1994). Addressing the challenges of diversity. In S.L. Kagan & B. Weissbourd (Eds.), *Putting families first: America's family support movement and the challenge of change* (pp. 243–275). San Francisco: Jossey-Bass.

Mallory, B.L., & New, R.S. (1994). *Diversity and developmentally appropriate practices: Challenges for early childhood education.* New York: Teachers College Press.

Nai-Lin Chang, H., & Pulido, D. (1994). The critical importance of cultural and linguistic continuity for infants and toddlers. *Zero to Three, 3*(2), 13–17.

Phillips, C.B. (1995). Culture: A process that empowers. In J.R. Lally (Ed.), *Infant/toddler caregiving: A guide to culturally sensitive care.* Sacramento: California State Department of Education.

Polk, C. (1994). Therapeutic work with African-American families. *Zero to Three, 3*(2), 9–11.

Early Risk

Cicchetti, D., & Lynch, M. (1993). Toward an ecological/transactional model of community violence and child maltreatment: Consequences for children's development. *Psychiatry, 56,* 95–118.

Garbarino, J. (1990). The human ecology of early risk. In S.J. Meisels & J.P. Shonkoff (Eds.), *Handbook of early childhood intervention* (pp. 78–96). New York: Cambridge University Press.

Garbarino, J., Dubrow, N., Kestelny, K., & Pardo, C. (1992). *Children in danger: Coping with the consequences of community violence.* San Francisco: Jossey-Bass.

Goodman, S.H., Radke-Yarrow, M., & Teti, D. (1993). Maternal depression as a context for child rearing. *Zero to Three, 13*(5), 10–16.

Helfer, R., & Kempe, C.H. (1976). *Child abuse and neglect: The family and the community.* Cambridge, MA: Ballinger.

Kempe, C.H., & Helfer, R. (1980). *The battered child.* Chicago: University of Chicago Press.

Klein, N.K., & Campbell, P. (1990). Preparing personnel to serve at-risk and disabled infants, toddlers, and preschoolers. In S.J. Meisels & J.P. Shonkoff (Eds.), *Handbook of early childhood intervention* (pp. 679–699). New York: Cambridge University Press.

Main, M., & Goldwyn, R. (1984). Predicting rejections of her infant from mother's representation of her own experience: Implications for the abused–abusing intergenerational cycle. *Child Abuse & Neglect, 8,* 203–217.

Olds, D.L. (1980). Improving formal services for mothers and children. In J. Garbarino & S.H. Stocking (Eds.), *Protecting children from abuse and neglect* (pp. 173–197). San Francisco: Jossey-Bass.

Richters, J., & Martinex, P. (1993). The NIMH community violence project: Children as victims and witnesses to violence. *Psychiatry, 56,* 7–21.

Sugar, M. (1992). Toddler's traumatic memories. *Infant Mental Health Journal, 13*(3), 245–251.

Everyday Routines and Rituals

Feeding, Eating, and Sleeping

Brazelton, T.B. (1992). *Touchpoints: The essential reference. Your child's emotional and behavioral development.* Reading, MA: Addison-Wesley.

Ferber, R. (1985). *Solve your child's sleep problems.* New York: Simon & Schuster.

Jones, S. (1992). *Crying baby, sleepless nights: Why your baby is crying and what you can do about it.* Boston: Harvard Common Press.

Pediatric Nutrition Practice Group. (1992). *Quality assurance criteria for pediatric nutrition conditions: A model.* Chicago: American Dietetic Association.

Satter, E. (1983). *Child of mine: Feeding with love and good sense.* New York: Bell.

Satter, E. (1992). The feeding relationship. *Zero to Three, 12*(5), 1–9.

Weissbluth, M. (1987). *Healthy sleep habits, happy child.* New York: Fawcett.

Toilet Training

Brazelton, T.B. (1992). *Touchpoints: The essential reference. Your child's emotional and behavioral development.* Reading, MA: Addison-Wesley.

Cole, J. (1983). *Parents' book of toilet training.* New York: Ballantine Books.

Lansky, V. (1984). *Toilet training.* New York: Bantam Books.

Welford, H. (1987). *Toilet-training and bed-wetting: A practical guide for today's parents.* Rochester, VT: Thorsons.

Toilet Training Books to Be Read Aloud to Children

Allison, A. (1984). *Toddler's potty book.* Los Angeles: Price, Stern, Sloan.
Frankel, A. (1986). *Once upon a potty.* New York: Barron's.

Family Ritual: Celebration and Tradition

Lieberman, S. (1984). *Let's celebrate: Creating new family traditions.* New York: Putnam.
Wolin, S.F., & Bennet, L.A. (1984). Family ritual. *Family Process, 23,* 401–420.

Guidance and Discipline

Clewett, A.S. (1988). Guidance and discipline: Teaching young children appropriate behavior. *Young Children, 43*(4), 26–36.
Gartrell, D. (1987). Punishment or guidance? *Young Children, 42*(3), 55–60.
Gordon, T. (1989). *Discipline that works: Promoting self-discipline in children.* New York: Penguin Books.
Greenberg. P. (1988). Avoiding "me against you" discipline. *Young Children, 44*(1), 24–29
Honig, A.S. (1985). Compliance, control, and discipline. *Young Children, 40*(2), 50–58.
Miller, C.S. (1984). Building self-control: Discipline for young children. *Young Children, 39*(7), 15–19.
Snyder, M., Snyder, R., & Sndyer, R., Jr. (1980). *The young child as person: Toward the development of healthy conscience.* New York: Human Sciences Press.
Soderman, A.K. (1985). Dealing with difficult young children: Strategies for teachers and parents. *Young Children, 40*(5), 15–20.

Home Visiting

Bromwich, R. (1981). *Working with parents and infants: An interactional approach.* Austin, TX: PRO-ED.
Burch, P., Palanki, A., & Thompson, S. (1994). *Home visiting.* Boston: Institute for Responsive Education.
Cochran, M., Dean, C., Dill, M.F., & Woolever, F. (1984). *Empowering families: Home visiting and building clusters.* Ithaca, NY: Cornell University Family Matters Project.
Doan-Sapon, M.A., Wollenburg, K., Campbell, A., & Portage Project Staff. (1993). *Growing: Birth to three.* Portage, WI: Portage Project.
Harvard Family Research Project. (1995). *Raising our future: Families, schools, and communities joining together.* Cambridge, MA: Harvard Graduate School of Education.
Johnson, E.G., Strickland, C.S., & Thompson, S. (1993). *Home visiting: A tool kit for quilting.* Boston: League of Schools Reaching Out, Institute for Responsive Education.
Klass, C.S., Pettinelli, D., & Wilson, M. (1993). Home visiting: Buiding a bridge between home and school. *Equity and Choice, 10*(10), 52–56.

Morra, L.G. (1990). *Home visiting: A promising early intervention strategy for at-risk families.* Report to the Chairman, Subcommittee on Labor, Health and Human Services, Education, and Related Agencies, Committee on Appropriations, U.S. Senate. Washington, DC: General Accounting Office.

Parents as Teachers. (1993). *Parents as Teachers program planning and implementation guide.* St. Louis: University of Missouri.

Wasik, B.H., Bryant, D.M., & Lyons, C.M. (1990). *Home visiting: Procedures for helping families.* Newbury Park, CA: Sage Publications.

Illness

Brazelton, T.B. (1992). *Touchpoints: The essential reference. Your child's emotional and behavioral development.* Reading, MA: Addison-Wesley.

Dawson, P. (1992). Should the field of early child and family intervention address failure to thrive? *Zero to Three, 12*(5), 10–14.

Parmelle, A.H., Jr. (1993). Children's illnesses and normal behavioral development: The role of caregivers. *Zero to Three, 13*(4), 1–8.

Sturm, L., & Drotar, D. (1992). Communication strategies for working with parents of infants who fail to thrive. *Zero to Three, 12*(5), 25–28.

Villarreal, S.F., McKinney, L., & Quackenbush, M. (1992). *Handle with care: Helping children prenatally exposed to drugs and alcohol.* Santa Cruz, CA: ETR Associates.

Infant and Toddler Development and Caregiving

Bernstein, M.H., & Bornstein, H.G. (1995). Caregivers' responsiveness and cognitive development in infants and toddlers: Theory and research. In P.L. Mangione (Ed.), *Infant/toddler caregiving: A guide to cognitive development and learning.* Sacramento: California State Department of Education.

Brazelton, T.B. (1974). *Toddlers and parents: A declaration of independence.* New York: Dell.

Brazelton, T.B. (1983). *Infants and mothers: Differences in development.* New York: Dell.

Brazelton, T.B., & Cramer, B.G. (1990). *The earliest relationship: Parents, infants, and the drama of early attachment.* Reading, MA: Addison-Wesley.

Chess, S., & Thomas, A. (1987). *Know your child: An authoritative guide for today's parents.* New York: Basic Books.

Field, T. (1995). Supporting cognitive development through interactions with young infants. In P.L. Mangione (Ed.), *Infant/toddler caregiving: A guide to cognitive development and learning.* Sacramento: California State Department of Education.

Lally, J.R. (1995). Discovery in infancy: How and what infants learn. In P.L. Mangione (Ed.), *Infant/toddler caregiving: A guide to cognitive development and learning.* Sacremento: California State Department of Education.

Lieberman, A.F. (1993). *The emotional life of the toddler.* New York: Free Press.

Language, Communication, and Emerging Literacy

Barclay, K., Benelli, C., & Curtis, A. (1995). Literacy begins at birth: What caregivers can learn from parents of children who read early. *Young Children, 50*(4), 24–28.

Bates, E., O'Connell, B., & Shore, C. (1987). Language and communication in infancy. In J.D. Osofsky (Ed.), *Handbook of infant development* (2nd ed., pp. 149–203). New York: John Wiley & Sons.

Bruner, J. (1985). *Child's talk: Learning to use the language.* New York: Norton.

Devine, M. (1991). *Baby talk: The art of communicating with infants and toddlers.* New York: Plenum.

Dole, J.D., Duffy, G.G., Roehler, L.R., & Pearson, P.D. (1991). Moving from old to the new: Research on reading comprehension instruction. *Review of Educational Research, 61*(2), 239–264.

Fields, M.V., & Lee, D. (1994). *Let's begin reading right: A developmental approach to beginning literacy.* Columbus, OH: Charles E. Merrill.

Galinsky, E., & David, J. (1988). *The preschool years: Family strategies that work— from experts and parents.* New York: Ballantine Books.

Heath, S.B. (1983). *Way with words: Language, life, and works in communities and classrooms.* New York: Cambridge University Press.

Lee, P. (1989). Is the young child egocentric or sociocentric? *Teachers College Record, 90*(3), 279–291.

Mahoney, B., & Powell, A. (1988). Modifying parent–child interaction: Enhancing the development of handicapped children. *Journal of Special Education, 22*(1), 82–96.

McCartney, K., & Robeson, W.W. (1992). Emergence of communication: Words, grammar, and first conversations. In J.R. Lally, P.L. Mangione, & C.L. Young-Hold (Eds.), *Infant/toddler caregiving: A guide to language development and communication.* Sacramento: California State Department of Education.

Nelson, K. (1973). Structure and strategy in learning to talk [Entire issue]. *Monographs of the Society for Research in Child Development, 38*(149).

Nelson, K. (Ed.). (1989). *Narratives from the crib.* Cambridge, MA: Harvard University Press.

Sach, J. (1992). Emergence of communication: Earliest signs. In J.R. Lally, P.L. Mangione, & C.L. Young-Hold (Eds.), *Infant/toddler caregiving: A guide to language development and communication.* Sacramento: California State Department of Education.

Shatz, M. (1994). *A toddler's life: From personal narrative to professional insight.* New York: Oxford University Press.

Thal, D.J. (1992). Emergence of communication: Give and take between adult and child. In J.R. Lally, P.L. Mangione, & C.L. Young-Hold (Eds.), *Infant/toddler caregiving: A guide to language development and communication.* Sacramento: California State Department of Education.

White, B. (1985). *The first three years of life.* Englewood Cliffs, NJ: Prentice Hall.

Home Visitors' Professional Development

Almonte, B.E. (1994). Professionalization as culture change: Issues for infant/ family community workers and their supervisors. *Zero to Three, 15*(2), 18–23.

Fenichel, E. (1991). Learning through supervision and mentorship to support the development of infants, toddlers and their families. *Zero to Three, 12*(2), 1–8.

Sexuality Education

Bernstein, A. (1977). *The flight of the stork.* New York: Delacorte Press.

Brick, P., Davis, N., Fischel, M., Lupo, T., Marshall, J., & MacVicae, A. (1989). *Bodies, birth and babies: Sexuality and education in early childhood programs.* Hackensack, NJ: Planned Parenthood, Center for Family Life Education.

Calderone, M., & Johnson, E. (1988). *The family book about sexuality.* New York: Harper & Row.

Calderone, M., & Rame, J. (1982). *Talking with your child about sex.* New York: Ballantine Books.

Gordon, S., & Gordon, J. (1982). *Did the sun shine before you were born?* New York: Ed-U Press.

Gordon, S., & Gordon, J. (1983). *Raising a child conservatively in a sexually permissive world.* New York: Simon & Schuster.

Siblings

Dunn, J., & Plomin, R. (1990). *Separate lives: Why siblings are so different.* New York: Basic Books.

Faber, A., & Mazlish, E. (1987). *Siblings without rivalry: How to help your children live together so you can live too.* New York: Norton.

Galinsky, E., & J. David. (1988). *The preschool years: Family strategies that work—from experts and parents.* New York: Ballantine Books.

Television

Carlsson-Paige, N., & Levin, D.E. (1990). *Who's calling the shots? How to respond effectively to children's fascination with war play and war toys.* Philadelphia: New Society.

Levin, D.E., & Carlsson-Paige. (1994). Developmentally appropriate television: Putting children first. *Young Children, 49*(5), 38–44.

Endnotes

Preface

1. Current literature uses the term *ecological* to describe the reciprocal relationship between people and their environment. Bronfenbrenner, Garbarino, and Cochran have each conducted extensive research on the interplay of child and parent development and multiple levels of environment—personal, community, and national. Bronfenbrenner, 1979; Cochran, Larner, Riley, Gunnarsson, & Henderson, 1990; Garbarino, 1992; Garbarino, Dubrow, Kostelny, & Pardo, 1992.

2. Klass, 1986, pp. 99–117.

3. Klass, 1985.

4. Klass, 1990.

5. In acknowledging the reciprocal relationship between my personal history and my professional and research perspective, I am following the tradition of field workers such as Mills, Rabinow, and Whyte. Mills, 1959; Rabinow, 1977; Whyte, 1943.

Introduction

1. Lazar and Darlington provided an overview of early intervention programs of the 1960s and 1970s and of accompanying research on these programs. Lazar & Darlington, 1982.

2. Weissbourd provided a provocative overview of traditional parent education and a history of the development of family support programs. Weissbourd, 1987.

3. Greenblatt provided an overview of the initiation of child care programs and Head Start in the United States. Greenblatt, 1979. Schlossman offered an historical overview of the emergence of parent education. Schlossman, 1976.

4. Varying dimensions of home visiting and different types of programming were discussed in Behrman, 1993.

5. Philosophical literature calls our ability to understand another and ourselves through another's lived experience *intersubjectivity.* Mutual understanding is possible because of our shared experience and manner of expression (i.e., language). Dilthey, 1961; Habermas, 1971.

6. Garcia provided an extensive overview of at-risk families in the United States and the challenges to professionals working with these families. Garcia, 1994.

7. The April/May 1995 issue of *Zero to Three* was devoted to descriptions of family support programs serving rural families of young children across the United States. Fenichel, E. (1995, April/May). *Zero to Three* [entire issue], *15*(5).

Chapter 1

1. Bronfenbrenner discussed this type of reciprocal two-person relationship as a primary dyad. In primary dyads, two persons coordinate their activities with each other within a mutuality of positive feeling. This mutuality motivates young children to engage in progressively more complex patterns of interaction and increasingly complex learning processes. Bronfenbrenner wrote that the primary dyad continues to exist for both participants even when they are not physically together. Bronfenbrenner, 1979, pp. 56–66.

2. Garbarino wrote poignantly of how parenting "depends in large measure on the character and quality of the social environment in which we bear and raise our children" (p. xv). Garbarino identified and discussed the array of relationships connecting the child, family, and social environment and how these relationships influence parent and child development. Garbarino, 1992.

3. A large proportion of community-based home visiting programs use paraprofessional home visitors. Musick and Stott identified dilemmas of paraprofessional helping and explored new methods of educating these individuals. Musick & Stott, 1993, pp. 651–657.

4. Weissbourd provided a provocative overview of traditional parent education and a history of the development of family support programs. Weissbourd, 1987, pp. 38–56. Weissbourd also discussed the emergence of the current family resource movement in Weissbourd, 1994, pp. 28–48. In his historical overview of the first 32 years of parent education in America, Schlossman described U.S. public policy with regard to new knowledge in the behavioral sciences. He also found parallels between parent education of the 1960s and the origin of the parent education movement in the late 19th and early 20th centuries. Schlossman, 1976, pp. 436–467.

5. Pawl, 1995, p. x.

6. Freeman described how many families organize around problems. Problems can have useful purposes and can organize family members in a way

that allows members to feel connected to the problem. For example, a child's problem can provide a focus and stabilize a marital relationship. Freeman, 1992.

7. Weiss argued that home visiting programs are a "necessary but not sufficient" service to at-risk families with multiple problems. Parents whose multiple complicated problems are so great that they interfere with the parents' attention to their child often are beyond a home visiting program that does not provide broader social services. Weiss, 1993, pp. 113–128. Schorr provided detailed descriptions of successful intervention and prevention programs for at-risk families and discussed the approaches needed to "break the cycle of disadvantage." L. Schorr & D. Schorr, 1988.

8. In a discussion of a home visiting program for families at risk with children from birth to 3 years, Bromwich indicated that the reciprocal positive feelings of parent educators and home visitors was strongly related to the effectiveness of their program's intervention. Bromwich, 1981.

9. Wasik, Bryant, and Lyons provided an overview of characteristics of teenage parents and effective home visiting approaches for working with such families. Wasik, Bryant, & Lyons, 1990, pp. 193–199. Since 1978, the Prenatal/Early Infancy Project has provided nurse home visiting to new teen mothers and their infants. The program has been helpful in improving mothers' and infants' health and has assisted them in using community resources. The program resulted in a decrease in second pregnancies and an increase in mothers' finishing school and gaining employment. Olds, 1981, pp. 173–197.

   McDonough has spent many years guiding low-income teenage parents in Chicago. McDonough first forms a positive alliance with the parent. She uses educational and behavioral psychology to improve mothers' parenting. Her work always focuses on expanding the parent's strength. After parent and child play together, McDonough and parent watch the videotape of this play sequence. McDonough picks out a positive strength and elaborates on it. Once the positive alliance is formed and the parent can recognize her strengths, the parent often begins talking about her own difficulties nondefensively. McDonough, 1993, pp. 414–426.

10. Beeghly and Tronick reviewed the compromising main effects of drugs such as prenatal cocaine abuse on infant behavior and development. Beeghly & Tronick, 1994, pp. 158–175.

11. Zuckerman & Brazelton, 1994, pp. 81–82.

12. The National Council on Alcoholism and Drug Dependence, Inc. (NCADD), and the March of Dimes provide fact sheets with information and references on alcoholism and drug addidction. Contact NCADD, 12 West 21st Street, New York, NY 10010, or March of Dimes, 1275 Mamaroneck Avenue, White Plains, NY 10605.

Chapter 2

1. Bruner discussed how language is the way we "sort out our thoughts about things" (p. 72). He wrote that narratives, or stories, give meaning to experience. If we want to understand people, Bruner claimed, we need to understand the ways in which people construct their world in narrative. Bruner, 1986, pp. 44–78.

   Anderson wrote that, in talking, we are not only informing others but also forming ourselves. "When one expresses oneself one is in the process of realizing one's identity." Anderson, 1992, p. 89.

2. Penn discussed how concepts of the future and concepts of change are one. She wrote of the power that families have by imagining new solutions in the future and thus facilitating change. Penn, 1985.

3. Wasik, Bryant, and Lyons discussed their problem-solving model of home visiting. They identified seven stages of problem solving: defining problems, selecting goals, generating alternatives, considering consequences, decision making, implementation, and evaluation. Wasik, Bryant, & Lyons, 1990, pp. 139–146.

4. Bronfenbrenner explained primary dyads as two-person relationships in which people are engaged in a joint activity. Bronfenbrenner claimed that, once two people participate in a joint activity, they are likely to develop positive feelings toward each other and engage in mutuality. Joint activity, mutuality, and positive feelings promote the young child's learning and development. Bronfenbrenner, 1979, pp. 56–60.

5. Greenspan urged parents of young children to spend 30 minutes each day in "floor time" with their child. Greenspan suggested that parents follow their child's lead so that the child can set the emotional tone of the play and can feel both affirmed and connected. Greenspan & Greenspan, 1989, p. 29.

6. Garbarino described the primary threat to the modern world as the "weakening of traditional sources of social pluralism—a wide range of people and groups surrounding the family which shared basic commitment to the family." Garbarino, 1992, p. 313.

7. Bronfenbrenner, 1979, pp. 209–236; Cochran, Larner, Riley, Gunnarsson, & Henderson, 1990.

8. Stern found that a mother of a newborn needs a supporting matrix that serves two functions: 1) physical protection of the mother from the everyday maintenance of family life and 2) a maternal supportive expert force educating the mother on "how to do it," validating and modeling what motherhood is. Stern noted that fathers can fulfill the first function but only "experts," women who have been there before, can fulfill the second function. Stern, 1994.

9. Bronfenbrenner and Neville discussed how the emotional attachment and complexity of the young child and the child's caregiver relationship is

enhanced by the other adults who assist, encourage, nurture, and affirm the caregiver. Bronfenbrenner & Neville, 1994, p. 14.

10. Wasik, Bryant, & Lyons, 1990, pp. 69–90.

11. O'Hearn Family Outreach Project Members, 1995.

12. Home visitors learn the Parents as Teachers curriculum when they attend a 1-week training institute sponsored by the Parents as Teachers National Center, 10176 Corporate Square Drive, Suite 230, St. Louis, MO 63132. Home visitors can purchase the Portage Project curriculum through the Portage Project, 626 East Slifer Street, Portage, WI 53901.

13. Garcia provided a demographic overview of the United States's diversity and the vulnerable populations within this diversity. He identified standards for effective services and recommended qualities of professionals working with these populations. Garcia, 1994.

14. Garbarino found that, given their lack of employment and impoverished neighborhoods, people with low incomes often have minimal informal support systems. He called such support systems the "staff of life in childrearing." Garbarino, 1992, p. 313.

15. Smith & Wells, 1990.

16. Ibid.

17. Weiss, 1993.

Chapter 3

1. Schon discussed "indeterminate zones of practice" (p. 6), that is, indeterminate, uncertain, and unique situations that are central to professional practice and cannot be handled solely by applying knowledge or strategies stemming from traditional professional knowledge. Schon argued that at the core of competency in these indeterminate zones of practice is artistry, a kind of knowing in action. Conditions needed for professional development, then, become learning by doing, with access to coaches, who help increase home visitors' skills by reflection on practice. Schon, 1987, pp. 3–4.

2. Fenichel, of the National Center for Clinical Infant Programs (NCCIP) Work Group on Supervision and Mentorship, emphasized that increased understanding of one's own emotional responses in home visiting is a central aspect of professional development:

   By attending to her own affective experience, the worker may be able to learn more about what children and families are feeling. As the supervisee's own emotional responses are acknowledged and respected, she may become increasingly able to acknowledge, respect, and respond sensitively to the

emotional experiences and expressions of infants, toddlers, families and col-
leagues. (Fenichel, 1992, p. 5)

3. Larner & Halpern, 1992; Musick & Stott, 1993.

4. Bruner, 1986; Dewey, 1916; Rogers, 1969.

5. Mead, 1934, pp. 135–226.

6. In Holly's report of an interview study of 60 teachers in the United States
   and England, she noted that what teachers consider most important is the
   time to discuss with colleagues and connecting professional development
   content with their everyday teaching. Holly, 1989.

7. Norton, 1994.

8. Cochran and colleagues compared how networks function in African
   American and Caucasian families in the United States as well as families in
   Sweden, Wales, and Germany. Cochran, Larner, Riley, Gunnarsson, &
   Henderson, 1990.

9. Gilligan, 1982; Gilligan & Brown, 1992; Loevinger, 1976.

10. Smith, Wigginton, Hocking, & Jones, 1991.

11. Zero to Three National Center for Clinical Infant Programs is an inter-
    disciplinary organization of researchers, theorists, and practitioners work-
    ing with infants, toddlers, and their families. A primary goal of Zero to
    Three is to promote the continued education of professionals in this field.
    The organization publishes a bimonthly bulletin, *Zero to Three*. See Fen-
    ichel, 1992.

12. Bertacchi & Coplon, 1989; Gilkerson & Young-Hold, 1991; Shanok, 1991.

13. Bertacchi & Stott, 1992.

Chapter 4

1. Greenspan, 1992; Sameroff & Emde, 1989; Stern, 1985.

2. Sroufe, 1989.

3. Winnicott, 1965, p. 39.

4. Emde, 1989; Stern, 1985, pp. 26–33.

5. Greenspan described six developmental levels from birth to 5 years.
   Greenspan's developmental levels provide indicators of observable behavior that point to the infant's and young child's increased emotional and

behavioral capacities. Greenspan, 1992. Greenspan's developmental levels occur within the same age levels that Stern described as changes in sense of self. Whereas Greenspan's levels are behavioral, Stern's levels point to internal experiences. Stern, 1985, pp. 26–33.

6. Sammons, 1989, pp. 10–11.

7. Villarreal, McKinney, & Quackenbush, 1992, pp. 103–112.

8. Chess & Thomas, 1987.

9. Stern discussed how the behavior of newborns gives evidence of four qualities of sense of self: self-agency, self-coherence, inner affectivity, and self-continuity. These qualities describe experiences that are integrated. Stern, 1985, pp. 70–94.

10. Stern called this cross-modal transfer of information *amodal perception*. Infants experience a correspondence across vision and touch and across hearing and vision. For example, when a 3–week-old blindfolded infant sucks a specifically shaped pacifier, and two differently shaped pacifiers are placed in front of the infant, the infant will look more at the pacifier he or she sucked; thus, touch and vision are joined. This cross-modal transfer allows the newborn to experience self-coherence. Stern, 1985, pp. 47–54.

11. Emde, 1989.

12. Emde, 1989, p. 37.

13. Brazelton & Cramer, 1990, p. 98.

14. Bowlby introduced the concept of *internal working models (IWM)*, memories of interactions with one's parent, as a way of explaining how the infant's sense of self emerges from relationships with parents. Bowlby, 1969, 1973.
    Stern stated that many of an infant's specific memories of similar interactions with a parent become organized into a generalized memory, which he termed *remembered interactions generalized (RIGS)*. Stern, 1985, pp. 97–99, 114–119.

15. Ainsworth and Bowlby identified infant behaviors such as crying, cooing, smiling, and clinging as *proximity-seeking*—bringing the caregiver into closer contact. Bowlby explained that these infant proximity-seeking behaviors are essential for survival. Ethological studies of animal social life support Bowlby's biological explanation for infant attachment behavior. Ainsworth, Blehar, Waters, & Wall, 1978. *Bonding* is used in the psychological literature to refer to a mother's maternal sensitive period, shortly after birth. Bowlby, 1969, 1973. There is some research evidence to suggest a maternal sensitive period immediately following delivery. Klaus & Kennell, 1976. *Attachment* refers to the parent–infant relationship that develops progressively throughout the infant's first year. There also is some research evidence to suggest that, for fathers, early contact also helps to

create a stronger initial bond between fathers and their infants. Park & Tinsley, 1981.

16. Infant specialists term these parent responses *contingent responsiveness* — the parent is emotionally available to the infant, and thus the infant's behavior sparks the parent's response. Brazelton & Cramer, 1990, pp. 123–124.

17. Stern and his colleagues in Geneva, Switzerland, conducted microanalytic interviews with mothers, who were asked to recall what they felt, thought, and did during an interaction with their infant. The mothers' experiences involved not only their interactions but also their past and future representations. Stern noted, "The mother, in the parenting situation, is necessarily operating in at least two subjective spaces: the behavior interaction and her representational life." Stern, 1995, p. 52; see also Bennett, Lefcourt, Haft, Nachman, & Stern, 1994.

18. Stern stated that the developmental leap at ages 7–9 months is a new sphere of relatedness, termed *intersubjective relatedness*. That is, infants discover that their parents also have inner states of experience and that these inner states are shareable (i.e., intersubjective). A new form of experiencing connectedness emerges. Stern identified three states of intersubjectivity, or shared mental states: *shared joint attention, shared intention,* and *shared affective states.* Stern, 1985, pp. 128–133.

19. Emde, 1989, p. 43.

20. Stern, 1984, pp. 3–4. Stern termed this interactive process *affect attunement.* Stern used the term *vitality* to describe how feeling qualities are communicated. Vitality "is captured in such terms as exploding, surging, fading, fleeting" (p. 11). Stern suggested dance and music as examples of vitality changes. Vitality in this sense can be thought of as the quality of feeling being expressed. Different experiences may be joined as long as they share the same quality of feeling that Stern calls vitality. For example, the infant joins a parent's soothing by voice and by touch, because each have the same quality. As these experiences are joined by the same quality of feeling, young infants experience their empathic responsiveness and thus experience communication.

21. Erikson, 1950, pp. 72–80.

22. Tronick, Cohn, & Shea, 1986, p. 12.

23. Winnicott called attention to objects to which young children become passionately attached and called such objects *transitional objects.* Winnicott, 1971, pp. 1–25. Brazelton termed these objects *loveys.* Brazelton, 1992, pp. 171–172.

24. Greenspan and Greenspan discussed how playing as a partner can influence the emotional development of one's infant and young child. The Greenspans emphasized the importance of the infant's active discovery

and parents' following their infant's lead in play. Greenspan & Greenspan, 1989.

25. Stern called this developmental leap of toddlers *the sense of verbal self.* Stern emphasized that the young child's learning to speak creates "a new type of 'being-with,' between adult and child . . . the infant and mother create a being-with experience using verbal symbols—a sharing of mutually created meanings about their personal experience." Stern, 1985, p. 172.

26. Erikson, 1950, pp. 80–85.

27. Beeghly and Cichetti examined the impact of low social status and child maltreatment on 30–month-olds' emergent self–other understanding. This research provided evidence that these children had signficantly less language that reflected their internal states and understanding of self and other. Beeghly & Cichetti, 1994.

28. Howes's 3–year study of toddlers' peer relationships in child care programs indicated that very young children, when given the opportunity, can develop a range of social skills. In the early toddler period, young children demonstrated abilities in give-and-take reciprocal roles as they played with each other. These children were ages 16–33 months at the outset of Howes's study. As they engaged in social pretend-play in the late toddler period, the children skillfully communicated with one another. Those most socially competent formed friendships that remained stable over the years. Howes, 1988.

29. Stern stated that this developmental leap is marked by young children's ability to narrate their own life stories. Stern claimed that this narrative ability is universal across cultures, innate, and no different from walking and talking. Stern stressed that the importance of this new developmental leap is that narratives are "a dynamic laboratory in which the child is constantly working on who he is, defining, redefining who he is, and constantly updating." Stern, 1991. Greenspan described the 36–month-old's ability to "create logical bridges" between different emotional ideas (i.e., "Hit bad guy because he did bad thing."). Greenspan, 1993.

30. Piaget called this lack of perspective-taking *egocentrism.* Piaget, 1969, p. 32.

31. Lee, 1989.

32. Cauley & Tyler, 1989.

33. Erikson, 1950, pp. 90–92.

34. Baumrind, 1972, 1973.

35. Goodman, Radke-Yarrow, & Teti, 1993.

36. Fraiberg, 1980; Fraiberg, Adelson, & Shapiro, 1975. The literature on child battering provides evidence that a mother's childhood experience of her

own mother as rejecting is related to her own rejection of her infant. Main, Kaplan, & Cassidy, 1989.

37. Greenspan, 1992.

38. Osofsky's research indicated that the homicide rate in 1993 for males 15–24 years old was 22 per 100,000 in the United States. All other Western industrialized nations had five homicides or less for this age group. In the United States, African Americans committed 85 homicides per 100,000; Caucasians committed 11.5 per 100,000, more than twice the rate of any other Western industrialized nation. Osofsky, 1993.

39. Osofsky, Wewers, Hann, & Fick, 1993; Terr, 1991; Zeenah, 1993/1994.

Chapter 5

1. *Random House Dictionary,* 1973, p. 409.

2. Galinsky & David, 1988, p. 7.

3. Honig, 1985.

4. Brazelton, 1992, p. 254.

5. *Random House Dictionary,* 1973, p. 628.

6. Vygotsky described the social nature of young children's learning and development. Vygotsky said that the adult guides the young child by providing a zone of proximal development. Vygotsky explained that the zone of proximal development "is the distance between the actual developmental level as determined by independent problem solving and the level of potential development as determined through problem solving under adult guidance or in collaboration with more capable peers." Vygotsky, 1978, p. 86.

7. Thomas & Chess, 1977.

8. Chess & Thomas, 1987, p. 56.

9. Brazelton & Cramer, 1990, p. 123.

10. Stern, 1985, pp. 220–223.

11. Mahler, Pine, & Berman, 1975.

12. Stern spoke of narratives as a "dynamic laboratory in which the child is constantly working on who he is, defining, redefining who he is . . . constantly updating." In other words, now the young child can view him- or herself, and, in narratives, this view is constantly changing. Stern, 1991.

13. The Snyders explained how adults can enter into young children's experiences; assist them in understanding intentions and feelings; and, in this process, enable the development of young children's conscience. Compelling vignettes illustrated this process by depicting adults' skillful interactions with preschool-age children. Snyder, Snyder, & Snyder, 1980.

Chapter 6

1. Bates, O'Connell, & Shore, 1987, pp. 151–169.

2. Heath, 1983, pp. 73–148.

3. Stern, 1995, pp. 59–78.

4. Stern, 1977, p. 74.

5. Bates, O'Connell, & Shore, 1987, pp. 151–169.

6. Devine provided a practical guide for parents to understand developmental milestones in their infant's and toddler's language and communication development as well as parenting activities to foster this development. Devine, 1991.

7. Mahoney and colleagues have developed the Transactional Intervention Program (TRIP), for children from birth to 3 years old who have disabilities. TRIP promotes parents' communication and offers an approach to playing with their young children. Turn taking and interactive matching are two instructional strategies used in this program. Mahoney & Powell, 1988. Using a mental health perspective, Greenspan does similar work with parents of very young children. Greenspan termed the give-and-take interaction as *opening and closing circles*. Greenspan, 1992.

8. Emde, 1989, p. 45.

9. Nelson, 1973.

10. Berk & Winsler, 1995, pp. 34–49.

11. Nelson, 1989.

12. Ibid. p. 16.

13. Schachter & Strange, 1982.

14. Bates emphasized that between birth and age 3 years is the window of maximum opportunity for neural development and maximum plasticity for language development. Bates, 1994.

15. Lee, 1989.

16. Dole, Duffy, Gerald, Roehler, & Pearons, 1991.

17. Fields and Spangler provided a thorough overview of a developmental approach to emerging literacy and a holistic approach to extending reading and writing skills. Fields & Spangler, 1994.

18. Heath, 1983, pp. 190–235.

Chapter 7

1. Wolin & Bennett, 1984.

2. Reiss, 1989.

3. Brazelton, 1992, p. 381.

4. Weissbluth, 1987, pp. 84–87.

5. Ferber, 1985, p. 32.

6. Sammons, 1989; see also Chapter 4.

7. Ferber, 1985, p. 82.

8. Weissbluth, 1987, p. 119.

9. Ferber, 1985, p. 196.

10. Essays in the book, *Narratives from the Crib,* discussed a 2–year study of monologues of a child between ages 15 and 23 months as she was going to sleep. The reports showed that monologues have greater complexity than the child's dialogues with her parents just prior to sleeping. The study found these monologues helped the child to understand her daily experience. Nelson, 1989.

11. Satter, 1992, pp. 1–2.

12. Brazelton, 1992, p. 141.

13. Ibid.

14. Ibid. p. 190.

15. Lansky, 1984, p. 9.

16. Parmelee, 1993, p. 3.

17. Brazelton, 1992, p. 313.

18. Field, 1993, p. 8.

19. Wolin & Bennett, 1984, pp. 413–417.

20. Dawson, 1992, p. 20.

21. Ibid. p. 21.

22. Gergen, 1991.

23. *1996 World Almanac & Book of Facts,* p. 961.

24. Department of Labor, 1992.

25. Walters discussed the potential liabilities, myths, images, realities, and potential strengths that characterize single-parent families headed by a female. Walters, 1988.

26. Brazelton provided guidance for parents in helping their child to adjust to divorce. Brazelton, 1992, pp. 261–268. Galinsky and David discussed common assumptions parents may have about their children's experience in separation and divorce and suggested strategies for parents to help children in this difficult time. Galinsky & David, 1988, pp. 291–310.

27. Garbarino warned that, even when single parents have excellent parenting skills, their children may experience an insufficient number and range of adult relationships, adult roles, and adult–child activities. Garbarino, 1992, p. 39.

Chapter 8

1. Erikson, 1950, p. 222.

2. Mead, 1962, p. 7.

3. Piaget, 1963.

4. Stern explained the developmental significance of these microevents: "To the extent that these interactions are purely social with no other goal in mind, they consist of mutual microregulation of affect and activation. . . . They are the basic step of an interaction regulatory process." Stern, 1995, p. 63.

5. Bruner & Sherwood, 1976.

6. Emde, 1989, p. 3.

7. Erikson, 1977, pp. 85–92.

8. Erikson wrote that "dramatic play in childhood provides the infantile form of the human propensity to create model situations in which aspects of the

past are re-lived, the present represented and renewed, and the future anticipated." Ibid. p. 44.

9. The role of parent as active participant in young children's play is a relatively new insight among developmental and early education theorists and researchers. Historically, developmental theory promoted adult roles as providers of settings, observers, and periodic participants in children's play who participate as the explicit need arises, for example, to implement a rule in conflict situations. Since the mid-1980s, theory and research across the mental health and educational fields has emphasized the developmental value of adults' active role in young children's play. Greenspan and Greenspan provided a convincing discussion of how parents' active engagement as play partners with their infant and young child enhances their child's social and emotional self. Greenspan & Greenspan, 1989.

10. Duckworth, 1972.

11. Piaget, 1962.

12. Smilansky, 1968.

13. Biber, 1984.

14. Carlsson-Paige & Levin, 1990.

Chapter 9

1. Dunn & Kendrick, 1982; Lee, 1989.

2. Brazelton, 1992, p. 199.

3. White, 1985.

4. Galinsky, 1987, p. 187.

5. Dunn & Plomin, 1990.

6. Faber & Mazlish, 1987, p. 99.

7. Dunn & Plomin, 1990, pp. 283–284.

8. Dunn and Plomin provided autobiographical and biographical materials of famous people to illustrate remarkable differences in the affection, interest, control, and dominance of brothers and sisters, differences not linked to birth order. Dunn & Plomin, 1990, p. 90.

9. Lieberman discussed the difficulties that toddlers have when displaced by a new baby. Lieberman, 1993, pp. 165–168.

10. Faber & Mazlish, 1987, pp. 162–176; Galinsky & David, 1988, pp. 284–288.

Chapter 10

1. Since the mid-1980s, there has been a growing literature analyzing the relationship of teachers' careers and their childhood history and adult personal life. E.g., Ball & Goodson, 1985; Goodson, 1992; Nias, 1989; Raymond, Butt, & Townsend, 1992; Smith, Kleine, Prunty, & Dwyer, 1986.

2. Anderson, 1991; Bruner, 1986; White & Epston, 1990.

3. Bruner described a person's story, or narrative, of her or his life as being a cognitive act of thought involving not only memory but also interpretation. A narrative is a construction in the present. Narratives of past experiences are shaped by experiences and understandings that have occurred since the remembered experience. They also are shaped by anticipations of future experience. Past, present, and future each play a role in the composition of a narrative, and the narrative unites the three. Bruner, 1987, pp. 13–15. This perspective on time was discussed by William Dilthey and his student, George Herbert Mead. Dilthey, 1961; Mead, 1934.

4. Clandinin and Connelly wrote that personal experience methods are focused on four areas: inward (i.e., thoughts, feelings, values, attitudes), outward (i.e., the environmental context), and backward and forward (i.e., past, present, and future). Clandinin & Connelly, 1994, p. 417. Sociologist Mills argued for the integration of biography, history, and social structure. Mills, 1959. The philosopher Dilthey spoke of one's life preserving "the relation between the outer and something inner, which is the meaning of that life." Dilthey asserted that biography cannot capture this relation without including the sociocultural context of that period. Dilthey, 1961, p. 91.

5. Sociological research in the 1980s and 1990s emphasizes the central role of the relationship of researcher to participant. Denzin discussed how writing a biography involves both subjective and intersubjective understanding of experiences, both of the person studied and of oneself. In other words, understanding is an intersubjective hermeneutic process. Denzin, 1989.

6. Nias emphasized the personal nature of teaching. Following George Herbert Mead's understanding of the inescapably social nature of self, Nias emphasized how teachers' assumptions, passions, and schemata are rooted in experiences from birth. It follows that many of a teacher's satisfactions are tied to the teacher's identity and sense of self. Nias, 1989.

7. Noddings identified *joy* as the basic human emotion experienced within relatedness and the fulfillment a person experiences when caring for others. Noddings, 1984, pp. 6–7.

8. Schon discussed those fields, such as teaching, in which the worker is a craftsperson, an artist; thus, most of the learning is in the doing. In these professions, framing problems and improvising are essential components of the professional's practice. Schon, 1987, p. 13.

9. Jackson wrote about teachers' development through prolonged reflection on teaching from different perspectives: "The goal is to articulate and broaden the context." Jackson, 1992, p. 73.

10. Bruner argued that most learning is a "sharing of culture. It is not just that the child must make his knowledge his own, but that he must make it his own in a community of those who share his sense of belonging to a culture." Bruner, 1986, p. 127.

11. Butt, Raymond, McCure, and Yamagishi discussed the powerful interaction of person and private and public contexts over time and how this interplay affects a teacher's personal and professional life. Butt, Raymond, McCure, & Yamagishi, 1992, p. 62.

12. Literature on personal biography describes times in a person's life cycle termed *critical incidents, turning points,* or *epiphanies.* These critical incidents are key events in a person's life around which pivotal decisions are made, which in turn lead the person in specific directions. Critical incidents may be extrinsic, such as a historical event like the Vietnam War, or intrinsic, like an unexpected pregnancy. E.g., Denzin, 1989, pp. 69–71; Measor, 1985.

13. Bruner stated that experience and memory of experience are powerfully structured by deeply internalized cultural *notions,* which he termed *folk psychology.* He argued that we can interpret meaning only if we situate that meaning in the larger cultural context in which specific meanings are created. Bruner, 1990.

14. Seligman and Pawl discussed four broad categories of obstacles they have experienced when they do therapeutic work in the homes of parents experiencing multiple difficulties. The categories include socioeconomic and sociocultural variables, prior experience with professionals and social agencies, the family situation, and personal history and psychology. Seligman & Pawl, 1984.

15. Schon explained the artistry of good coaching and the importance of coaches "who initiate students into the 'traditions of the calling' and help them, by 'the right kind of telling,' to see in their own behavior and in their own way what they need most to see." Schon, 1987, p. 17.

16. Nias argued that crucial to a teacher's identity are reference groups that help one by offering support in defining the value, meaning, and understanding of one's work. Nias, 1992, pp. 115–116.

17. Bruner discussed how meaning and symbols are public and communal rather than private and individual. He argued that to understand a person is to locate that person in a cultural and historical time and place. Bruner, 1990, pp. 11–65.

18. Noddings argued that "ethical caring depends not upon rule or principle but upon the development of an ideal self . . . in congruence with one's best remembrance of caring and being cared for." Noddings, 1984, p. 940.

19. Rogers argued that significant learning is acquired through experiencing practical problems. Rogers, 1969, pp. 158–162.

20. Beginning with Freud, therapy literature discusses the transference of adults' replication of childhood relationships with parents in their relationships with their own children or spouse or with other significant people. E.g., Basch, 1980; Fraiberg, 1980; Kerr & Bowen, 1988.

21. Beginning with her classic work, *In a Different Voice*, Gilligan's research explores women's psychological development. Gilligan argues that women have different views of self and morality and different ways of understanding and experiencing relationships than do men. Women see relationships as webs of connectedness, whereas men think in terms of images of hierarchy. Men view morality in terms of the logic of justice, whereas women's view is in terms of the ethic of care. Gilligan, 1982.

22. Shanok discussed the supervisory relationship as the context within which to learn by reflection with a confidante with whom one feels secure enough to expose one's vulnerabilities. Shanok, 1991.

References

Ainsworth, M.D.S., Blehar, M.C., Waters, E., & Wall, S. (1978). *Patterns of attachment*. Hillsdale, NJ: Lawrence Erlbaum Associates.

Anderson, T. (Ed.). (1991). *The reflecting team: Dialogues and dialogues about the dialogue*. New York: Norton.

Anderson, T. (1992). Relationship, language and pre-understanding in the reflecting process. *Family Therapy, 12*(2), 87–91.

Ball, S.J., & Goodson, I.F. (1985). *Teachers' lives and careers*. London: Falmer Press.

Barrie, J.M. (1911). *Peter Pan*. London: Penguin Books.

Basch, M.F. (1980). *Doing psychotherapy*. New York: Basic Books.

Bates, E. (1994, December). *Normal and abnormal variation in early language development*. Paper presented at the Frontiers of Infancy Research, ZERO to THREE/National Center for Clinical Infant Programs' 9th National Training Institute, Dallas.

Bates, E., O'Connell, B., & Shore, C. (1987). Language and communication in infancy. In J.D. Osofsky (Ed.), *Handbook of infant development* (2nd ed., pp. 149–203). New York: John Wiley & Sons.

Baumrind, D. (1972). Socialization and instrumental competence in young children. In W.W. Hartup (Ed.), *The young child: Reviews of research* (Vol. 2, pp. 202–224). Washington, DC: National Association for the Education of Young Children.

Baumrind, D. (1973). The development of instrumental competence through socialization. In A.D. Pick (Ed.), *Minnesota Symposium on Child Psychology* (Vol. 7). Minneapolis: University of Minnesota Press.

Beeghly, M., & Cichetti, D. (1994). Child maltreatment, attachment, and the self system: Emergence of an internal state of toddlers at high social risk. *Development and Psychopathology, 6*(1), 5–30.

Beeghly, M., & Tronick, E.Z. (1994). Effects of prenatal exposure to cocaine in early infancy: Toxic effects on the process of mutual regulation. *Infant Mental Health Journal, 15*(2), 158–175.

Behrman, R.E. (Ed.). (1993). *Home visiting: The future of our children*. Los Altos, CA: Center for the Future of Children, David and Lucille Packard Foundation.

Bennett, S., Lefcourt, I.S., Haft, W., Nachman, P., & Stern, D.N. (1994). The activation of material representations. *Infant Mental Health Journal, 15*(4), 336–347.

Berk, L.E., & Winsler, A. (1995). *Scaffolding children's learning: Vygotsky and early childhood education*. Washington, DC: National Association for the Education of Young Children.

Bertacchi, J., & Coplon, C. (1989). The professional use of self in prevention. *Zero to Three, 11*(4), 1–7.

Bertacchi, J., & Scott, F.M. (1991). A seminar for supervisors in infant/family programs: Growing versus paying more for staying the same. In E. Fenichel (Ed.), *Learning through supervision and mentorship to support the development of infants, toddlers, and their families: A source book* (pp. 132–140). Washington, DC: ZERO TO THREE/National Center for Clinical Infant Programs.

Biber, B. (1984). Drawing as expression of thinking and feeling. In B. Biber (Ed.), *Early education and psychological development* (pp. 155–186). New Haven, CT: Yale University Press.

Bowlby, J. (1969). *Attachment and loss: Vol. 1. Attachment.* New York: Basic Books.

Bowlby, J. (1973). *Attachment and loss: Vol. 2. Separation, anxiety, and anger.* New York: Basic Books.

Brazelton, T.B. (1992). *Touchpoints: The essential reference. Your child's emotional and behavioral development.* Reading, MA: Addison-Wesley.

Brazelton, T.B., & Cramer, B.G. (1990). *The earliest relationship: Parents, infants, and the drama of early attachment.* Reading, MA: Addison-Wesley.

Bromwich, R. (1981). *Working with parents and infants: An interactional approach.* Austin, TX: PRO-ED.

Bronfenbrenner, U. (1979). *The ecology of human development: Experiments by nature and design.* Cambridge, MA: Harvard University Press.

Bronfenbrenner, U., & Neville, P.R. (1994). America's children and families: An international perspective. In S.L. Kagan & B. Weissbourd (Eds.), *Putting families first: America's family support movement and the challenge of change* (pp. 3–27). San Francisco: Jossey-Bass.

Bruner, J.S. (1986). *Actual minds, possible worlds.* Cambridge, MA: Harvard University Press.

Bruner, J.S. (1987). Life as narrative. *Social Research, 54*(1), 11–32.

Bruner, J.S. (1990). *Acts of meaning.* Cambridge, MA: Harvard University Press.

Bruner, J.S., & Sherwood, V. (1976). Peekaboo and the learning of rule structures. In J.S. Bruner, A. Jolly, & K. Sylva (Eds.), *Play: Its role in development and evolution* (pp. 268–276). New York: Basic Books.

Buber, M. (1958). *I and thou.* New York: Charles Schribner's Sons. (Original work published 1923)

Butt, R., Raymond, D., McCure, G., & Yamagishi, L. (1992). Collective autobiography and the teacher's voice. In I.F. Goodson (Ed.), *Studying teachers' lives* (pp. 51–98). New York: Teachers College Press.

Carlsson-Paige, N. (1994). Developmentally appropriate television: Putting children first. *Young Children, 49*(5), 38–44.

Carlsson-Paige, N., & Levin, D.E. (1990). *Who's calling the shots? How to respond effectively to children's fascination with war play and war toys.* Philadelphia: New Society.

Cauley, K., & Tyler, B. (1989). The relationship of self concept to prosocial behavior in children. *Early Childhood Research Quarterly, 4,* 51–60.

Chess, S., & Thomas, A. (1987). *Know your child: An authoritative guide for today's parents.* New York: Basic Books.

Clandinin, D.J., & Connelly, F.M. (1994). Personal experience methods. In N.K. Denzin & Y.S. Lincoln (Eds.), *Handbook of qualitative research* (pp. 113–127). Thousand Oaks, CA: Sage Publications.

Cochran, M., Larner, M., Riley, D., Gunnarsson, L., & Henderson, L.R., Jr. (1990). *Extending families: The social networks of parents and their children.* New York: Cambridge University Press.

Dawson, P. (1992). Should the field of early child and family intervention address failure to thrive? *Zero to Three, 12*(5), 20–23.

Denzin, N.K. (1989). *Interpretive biography.* Newbury Park, CA: Sage Publications.

Devine, M. (1991). *Baby talk: The art of communicating with infants and toddlers.* New York: Plenum.

Dewey, J. (1916). *Democracy and education.* New York: Macmillan.

Dilthey, W. (1961). *Patter and meaning in history: Thoughts on history and society.* New York: Harper & Row. (Edited by H.P. Rickman from Volume VII of Dilthey's collected works, written in 1910)

Dole, J.D., Duffy, G.G., Roehler, L.R., & Pearson, P.D. (1991). Moving from old to the new: Research on reading comprehension instruction. *Review of Educational Research, 61*(2), 239–264.

Duckworth, E. (1972). The having of wonderful ideas. *Harvard Educational Review, 42*(2), 217–231.

Dunn, J., & Kendrick, C. (1982). *Siblings: Love, envy, and understanding.* Cambridge, MA: Harvard University Press.

Dunn, J., & Plomin, R. (1990). *Separate lives: Why siblings are so different.* New York: Basic Books.

Einstein, A., & Infeld, L. (1966). *The evolution of physics.* New York: Simon & Schuster. (Original work published 1938)

Emde, R.N. (1989). The infant's relationship experience: Developmental and affective aspects. In A.J. Sameroff & R.N. Emde (Eds.), *Relationship disturbances in early childhood: A developmental approach* (pp. 33–51). New York: Basic Books.

Erikson, E. (1950). *Childhood and society.* New York: Norton.

Erikson, E. (1977). *Toys and reasons: Stages in the ritualization of experience.* New York: Norton.

Faber, A., & Mazlish, E. (1987). *Siblings without rivalry: How to help your children live together so you can live too.* New York: Norton.

Fenichel, E. (1992). Learning through supervision and mentorship. In E. Fenichel (Ed.), *Learning through supervision and mentorship to support the development of infants, toddlers, and their families: A source book* (pp. 1–8). Washington, DC: ZERO TO THREE/National Center for Clinical Infant Programs.

Ferber, R. (1985). *Solve your child's sleep problems.* New York: Simon & Schuster.

Field, T. (1993). Infant massage. *Zero to Three, 14*(2), 8–12.

Fields, M.V., & Spangler, K.L. (1994). *Let's begin reading right: Developmentally appropriate beginning literacy.* Riverside, NJ: Macmillan.

Fraiberg, S.H. (1980). *Clinical studies in infant mental health: The first year in life.* New York: Basic Books.

Fraiberg, S.H., Adelson, E., & Shapiro, V. (1975). Ghosts in the nursery: A psychoanalytic approach to the problems of impaired mother--infant relationships. *Journal of American Academy of Child Psychiatry, 14,* 378–421.

Freeman, D.S. (1992). *Family therapy with couples.* Northvale, NJ: Jason Aronson.

Galinsky, E. (1987). *The six stages of parenthood.* Reading, MA: Addison-Wesley.

Galinsky, E., & David, J. (1988). *The preschool years: Family strategies that work—from experts and parents*. New York: Ballantine Books.

Garbarino, J. (1992). *Children and families in the social environment*. New York: Aldine de Gruyter.

Garbarino, J., Dubrow, N., Kostelny, K., & Pardo, C. (1992). *Children in danger: Coping with the consequences of community violence*. San Francisco: Jossey-Bass.

Garcia, E.E. (1994). Addressing the challenges of diversity. In S. Kagan & B. Weissbourd (Eds.), *Putting families first: America's family support movement and the challenge of change* (pp. 243–275). San Francisco: Jossey-Bass.

Gergen, K.J. (1991). *The saturated family*. New York: Basic Books.

Gilkerson, L., & Young-Hold, C.L. (1991). Supervision and the management of programs serving infants, toddlers, and families. In E. Fenichel (Ed.), *Learning through supervision and mentorship to support the development of infants, toddlers, and their families: A source book* (pp. 113–119). Washington, DC: ZERO TO THREE/National Center for Clinical Infant Programs.

Gilligan, C. (1982). *In a different voice: Psychological theory and women's development*. Cambridge, MA: Harvard University Press.

Gilligan, C., & Brown, L.M. (1992). *Meeting at the crossroads: Women's psychology and girls' development*. Cambridge, MA: Harvard University Press.

Goodman, S.H., Radke-Yarrow, M., & Teti, D. (1993). Maternal depression as a context for child rearing. *Zero to Three, 13*(5), 10–16.

Goodson, I.F. (Ed.). (1992). *Studying teachers' lives*. New York: Teachers College Press.

Greenblatt, B. (1979). *Responsibility for child care*. San Francisco: Jossey-Bass.

Greenspan, S. (1992). *Infancy and early childhood: The practice of clinical assessment and intervention with emotional and developmental challenges*. Madison, CT: International Universities Press.

Greenspan, S. (1993, December). *Toward a new vision for the developmental assessment of infants and young children*. Paper presented at the plenary session of the National Center for Clinical Infant Programs' Eighth Biennial Training Institute, Washington, DC.

Greenspan, S., & Greenspan, N.T. (1989). *The essential partnership: How parents and children can meet the emotional challenges of infancy and childhood*. New York: Penguin Books.

Habermas, J. (1971). *Knowledge and human interests*. Boston: Beacon Press. (Original work published 1960)

Heath, S.B. (1983). *Ways with words: Language, life, and works in communities and classrooms*. New York: Cambridge University Press.

Holly, M.L. (1989). Teacher professional development: Perceptions and practices in the USA and England. In M.L. Holly & C.S. McLoughlin (Eds.), *Perspectives on teacher professional development* (pp. 172–203). London: Falmer Press.

Honig, A.S. (1985). Compliance, control, and discipline. *Young Children, 40*, 50–58.

Howes, C. (1988). Peer interaction of young chidlren [Special issue]. *Monographs of the Society for Research in Child Development, 53*(1).

Jackson, P.W. (1992). Helping teachers develop. In A. Hargreaves & M.G.B. Fullan (Eds.), *Understanding teacher development*. New York: Teachers College Press.

Kerr, M.E., & Bowen, M. (1988). *Family evaluation: An approach based on Brown theory.* New York: Norton.

Klass, C.S. (1985). *A profile of caregiving: Life history interviews of family day care providers.* Paper presented at the American Education Research Association Annual Meeting, New Orleans.

Klass, C.S. (1986). *The autonomous child: Day care and the transmission of values.* London: Falmer Press.

Klass, C.S. (1990). *Anatomy of the personal visit: A case study of the Missouri Parents as Teachers program.* St. Louis, MO: Missouri Parents as Teachers National Center.

Klaus, H.M., & Kennell, J.H. (1976). *Maternal-infant bonding.* St. Louis, MO: C.V. Mosby.

Lansky, V. (1984). *Toilet training.* New York: Bantam Books.

Larner, M., & Halpern, T. (1991). Lay home visiting programs: Strengths, tensions, and challenges. In E. Fenichel (Ed.), *Learning through supervision and mentorship to support the development of infants, toddlers, and their families: A sourcebook* (pp. 91–99). Washington, DC: ZERO TO THREE/National Center for Clinical Infant Programs.

Lazar, I., & Darlington, R. (1982). Lasting effects of early education: A report from the Consortium for Longitudinal Studies, *Monographs of the Society for Research in Child Development, 47*(2, Serial No. 195), 2–3.

Lee, P. (1989). Is the young child egocentric or sociocentric? *Teacher's College Record, 19*(3), 379–391.

Lieberman, A.F. (1993). *The emotional life of the toddler.* New York: Free Press.

Loevinger, J. (1976). *Ego development.* San Francisco: Jossey-Bass.

Mahler, M.S., Pine, F., & Berman, A. (1975). *The psychological birth of the human infant: Symbiosis and individuation.* New York: Basic Books.

Mahoney, G., & Powell, A. (1988). Modifying parent–child interaction: Enhancing the development of handicapped children. *Journal of Special Education, 22*(1), 82–96.

Main, M., Kaplan, N., & Cassidy, J. (1989). Security in infancy, childhood, and adulthood: A move to the level of representation. In I. Bretherton & E. Waters (Eds.), Growing points in attachment theory and research. *Monographs of the Society for Research in Child Development, 50,* 66–106.

McDonough, S.C. (1993). Interaction guidance: Understanding and treating early infant caregiver relationships. In C.H. Zeenah, Jr. (Ed.), *Handbook of infant mental health* (pp. 414–426). New York: Guilford Press.

Mead, G.H. (1934). *Mind, self, and society from the standpoint of a social behaviorist* (Vol. 1). Chicago: University of Chicago Press.

Mead, M. (1962). *A creative life for your children* (Children's Bureau Headliner Series, No. 1). Washington, DC: U.S. Department of Health, Education, and Welfare.

Mead, M. (1972). *Blackberry winter.* New York: Simon & Schuster.

Measor, L. (1985). Critical incidents in the classroom: Identities, choices, and careers. In S.J. Ball & I.F. Goodson (Eds.), *Teachers' lives and careers* (pp. 61–77). London: Falmer Press.

Mills, C.W. (1959). *The sociological imagination.* New York: Oxford University Press.

Musick, J.S., & Stott, F.M. (1993). Paraprofessionals, parenting, and child development: Understanding the problems and seeking solutions. In S.J.

Meisels & J.P. Shonkoff (Eds.), *Handbook of early childhood intervention* (pp. 651–667). New York: Cambridge University Press.

Nelson, K. (1973). Structure and strategy in learning to talk [Entire issue]. *Monographs of the Society for Research in Child Development, 38*(149).

Nelson, K. (Ed.). (1989). *Narratives from the crib.* Cambridge, MA: Harvard University Press.

Nias, J. (1989). Teaching and the self. In M.L. Holly & C.S. McLoughlin (Eds.), *Perspectives on teacher professional development* (pp. 155–171). London: Falmer Press.

Nias, J. (1992). Reference groups in primary teaching: Talking, listening, and identity. In S.J. Ball & I.F. Goodson (Ed.), *Teachers' lives and careers* (pp. 105–119). New York: Teachers College Perss.

Noddings, N. (1984). *Caring: A feminine approach to ethics and moral education.* Berkeley: University of California Press.

Norton, D.G. (1994). Education for professionals in family support. In S.L. Kagan & B. Weissbourd (Eds.), *Putting families first: America's family support movement and the challenge of change* (pp. 401–440). San Francisco: Jossey-Bass.

O'Hearn Family Outreach Project Members. (1995). When families lead: The Patrick O'Hearn Family Outreach Project. In A. Palanki & P. Burch (Eds.), *In our hands: A multi-site parent-teacher action research project* (pp. 117–134) Boston: Center on Families, Communities, Schools & Children's Learning.

Olds, D.L. (1980). Improving formal services for mothers and children. In J. Garbarino & S.H. Stocking (Eds.), *Protecting children from abuse and neglect* (pp. 173–197). San Francisco: Jossey-Bass.

Osofsky, J. (1993). *Working with infants, toddlers, and caregivers exposed to violence. Tales from two cities: Boston and New Orleans.* Paper presented at ZERO TO THREE/National Center for Clinical Infant Programs Eighth Biennial Training Institute, Washington, DC.

Osofsky, J.D., Wewers, S., Hann, D.M., & Fick, A. (1993). Chronic community violence: What is happening to our children? *Psychiatry, 25,* 306–331.

Parents as Teachers National Center. (1993). *Parents as Teachers planning & implementation guide.* St. Louis, MO: Author.

Park, R.D., & Tinsley, B.R. (1981). The father's role in infancy: Determinants of involvement in caregiving and play. In M.E. Lamb (Ed.), *The role of father in child development.* New York: John Wiley & Sons.

Parmelee, A.H., Jr. (1993). Children's illnesses and normal behavioral development: The role of caregivers. *Zero to Three, 13*(4), 1–9.

Pawl, J.H. (1995). The therapeutic relationship as human connection: Being held in another's mind. *Zero to Three, 15*(4), 1–5.

Penn, P. (1985). Feed-forward: Future questions, future maps. *Family Process, 24*(3), 299–310.

Piaget, J. (1962). *Play, dreams and imitation in childhood.* New York: Norton.

Piaget, J. (1963). *The origins of intelligence in children.* New York: Norton. (Original work published 1952)

Piaget, J. (1969). *The language and thought of the child.* New York: Meridian Books.

Rabinow, R. (1977). *Reflections on field work in Morocco.* Berkeley: University of California Press.

Random House Dictionary of the English Language (Unabridged). (1973). New York: Random House.

Raymond, D., Butt, B., & Townsend, D. (1992). Contexts for teacher development: Insights from teachers' stories. In A. Hargreaves & M.D. Fullan (Eds.),

Understanding teacher development (pp. 143–161). New York: Teachers College Press.

Reiss, D. (1989). The represented and practicing family: Contrasting visions of family continuity. In A.J. Sameroff & R.N. Emde (Eds.), *Relationship disturbances in early childhood: A developmental approach* (pp. 191–220). New York: Basic Books.

Rogers, C.R. (1969). *Freedom to learn.* Columbus, OH: Charles E. Merrill.

Saint Augustine. (1961). *Confessions* (R.S. Pine-Coffin, trans.). New York: Penguin Books. (Written c. 396–397)

Sameroff, A.J., & Emde, R.N. (Eds.). (1989). *Relationship disturbances in early childhood: A developmental approach.* New York: Basic Books.

Sammons, W.A.H. (1989). *The self-calmed baby: Teach your infant to calm itself—and curb crying, fussing, and sleeplessness.* New York: St. Martin's Press.

Satter, E. (1992). The feeding relationship. *Zero to Three, 12*(5), 1–9.

Schachter, F.F., & Strage, A.A. (1982). Adults' talk and children's language development. In S.G. Moore & C.R. Cooper (Eds.), *The young child: Reviews of research: Vol.3.* Washington, DC: National Association for the Education of Young Children.

Schlossman, S.L. (1976). Before home start: Notes toward a history of parent education in America, 1897–1929. *Harvard Educational Review, 46*(3), 436–467.

Schon, D.A. (1987). *Educating the reflective practitioner: Toward a new design for teacher and learning in the professions.* San Francisco: Jossey-Bass.

Schorr, L.B., & Schorr, D. (1988). *Within our reach: Breaking the cycle of disadvantage.* New York: Anchor/Doubleday.

Seligman, S.P., & Pawl, J.H. (1984). Impediments to the formation of the working alliance in infant–parent psychotherapy. In J.D. Call, E. Galenson, & R.L. Tyson (Eds.), *Frontiers of infant psychiatry* (Vol. II, pp. 232–237). New York: Basic Books.

Shanok, R.S. (1991). The supervisory relationship: Integrator, resource, and guide. *ZERO TO THREE/National Center for Clinical Infant Programs, 12*(2), 16–19.

Smilansky, S. (1968). *The effects of socio-dramatic play on disadvantaged preschool children.* New York: John Wiley & Sons.

Smith, H., Wigginton, E., Hocking, K., & Jones, R.E. (1991). Foxfire teacher networks. In A. Lieberman & L. Miller (Eds.), *Staff development for education in the '90s: New demands, new realities, new perspectives* (pp. 193–220). New York: Teachers College Press.

Smith, L.M., Kleine, P.F., Prunty, J.P., & Dwyer, D.C. (1986). *Educational innovators: Then and now.* London: Falmer Press.

Smith, L.M., & Wells, W.M. (1990). *Difficult to reach, maintain and help urban families in PAT: Issues, dilemmas, strategies, and resolutions in parent education* (Final report submitted to the Smith Richardson Foundation). St. Louis, MO: Washington University.

Snyder, M., Synder, R., & Snyder, R., Jr. (1980). *The young child as person: Toward the development of healthy conscience.* New York: Human Sciences Press.

Sroufe, L.A. (1989). Relationships, self, and individual adaptation. In A.J. Sameroff & R.N. Emde (Eds.), *Relationship disturbances in early childhood: A developmental approach* (pp. 97–124). New York: Basic Books.

Stern, D.N. (1977). *The first relationship: Infant and mother.* Cambridge, MA: Harvard University Press.

Stern, D.N. (1984). Affect attunement. In J. Call, E. Galenson, & R.L. Tyson (Eds.), *Frontiers of infant psychiatry* (Vol. II, pp. 3–14). New York: Basic Books.

Stern, D.N. (1985). *The interpersonal world of the infant: A view from psychoanalysis and developmental psychology.* New York: Basic Books.

Stern, D. (1991, April). *Infant observation and the formation of psychic structure.* Paper presented at the Institute for Psychoanalysis Conference, Erikson Institute & Institute for Psychoanalysis, Chicago.

Stern, D.N. (1994). *The world of infant research and adult psychotherapy.* Paper presented at the Eighth Annual Cape Cod Summer Symposia, Eastham, MA.

Stern, D.N. (1995). *The motherhood constellation: A unified view of parent-infant psychotherapy.* New York: Basic Books.

Sturm, L., & Drotar, D. (1992). Communication strategies for working with parents of infants who fail to thrive. *Zero to Three, 12*(5), 25–28.

Tagore, R. (1958). *Collected poems and plays.* New York: Macmillan.

Terr, L.C. (1991). Childhood traumas: An outline and overview. *American Journal of Psychiatry, 148,* 10–20.

Thomas, A., & Chess, S. (1977). *Temperament and development.* New York: Brunner/Mazel.

Tronick, E.Z., Cohn, J., & Shea, E. (1986). The transfer of affect between mothers and infants. In T.B. Brazelton & M.W. Yogman (Eds.), *Affective development in infancy* (pp. 11–25). Norwood, NJ: Ablex.

Twain, M. (1947). *The adventures of Huckleberry Finn.* Cleveland, OH: World Publishing. (Original published 1885)

Villarreal, S.F., McKinney, L., & Quackenbush, M. (1992). *Handle with care: Helping children prenatally exposed to drugs and alcohol.* Santa Cruz, CA: ETR Associates.

Vygotsky, L.S. (1978). *Mind in society: The development of higher psychological process.* (M. Cole, V. John-Steiner, S. Scribner, & E. Souberman, Eds. & Trans.). Cambridge, MA: Harvard University Press.

Walters, M. (1988). Single-parent, female-headed households. In M. Walters, B. Carter, P. Papp, & O. Silverstein (Eds.), *The invisible web: Gender patterns in family relationships* (pp. 289–332). New York: Guilford Press.

Wasik, B.H., Bryant, D.M., & Lyons, C.M. (1990). *Home visiting: Procedures for helping families.* Newbury Park, CA: Sage Publications.

Weiss, H.B. (1993). Home visits: Necessary but not sufficient. In R.E. Behrman (Ed.), *The future of children* (pp. 113–128). Los Altos, CA: Center for the Future of Children, David and Lucille Packard Foundation.

Weissbluth, M. (1987). *Healthy sleep habits, happy child.* New York: Fawcett.

Weissbourd, B. (1987). A brief history of family support programs. In S.L. Kagan, D.P. Powell, B. Weissbourd, & E.F. Zigler (Eds.), *America's family support programs* (pp. 38–56). New Haven, CT: Yale University Press.

Weissbourd, B. (1994). The evolution of the family resource movement. In S.L. Kagan & B. Weissbourd (Eds.), *Putting families first: America's family support movement and the challenge of change* (pp. 28–48). San Francisco: Jossey-Bass.

White, B. (1985). *The first three years of life.* Englewood Cliffs, NJ: Prentice Hall.

White, M., & Epston, D. (1990). *Narrative means to therapeutic ends.* New York: Norton.

Whyte, W.F. (1943). *Street corner society: The structure of an Italian slum.* Chicago: University of Chicago Press.

Winnicott, D. (1965). *The maturational processes and the facilitating environment.* New York: International Universities Press.

Winnicott, D. (1971). *Playing and reality.* New York: Basic Books.

Wolin, S.J., & Bennet, L.A. (1984). Family rituals. *Family Process, 23,* 402–420.

World Almanac Books. (1996). *1996 World Almanac & Book of Facts.* New York: Author.

Zeenah, C.H. (1993/1994). The assessment and treatment of infants and toddlers exposed to violence. *Zero to Three, 14*(3), 29–37.

Zuckerman, B., & Brazelton, T.B. (1994). Strategies for a family-supportive child health care system. In S. Kagan & B. Weissbourd (Eds.), *Putting families first: America's family support movement and the challenge of change* (pp. 73–92). San Francisco: Jossey-Bass.

Index

Page references followed by "f" or "t" indicate figures or tables, respectively.

Accessibility, 76
Action research, 4
Addiction, 36
Administrators, 105
Adult development, 97–99
Affect, 223
    regulation, 116–117
Affirmation of parents and child,
        28–29, 45, 46
Aggression, 158, 161*t*, 240
    see also Violence
Alcoholics Anonymous, 63
Alcoholism, 37
    see also Substance abuse
Allergies, 211–212
Alternative suggestion to
        misbehavior, 157–158
Asthma, 211
Attachment, 117–119
Attention, 119
Authority, 13
Autonomy, 122–123, 155, 200

Babbling, 168
Barrie, J.M., 111
Behavior
    misbehavior, 153–156
    negative, 151–152
    parenting competence and,
        209
    prosocial, 132–133, 210
    regression in, 249
Birth weight, 215
Biting, 150

Body image, 127
Bonding, 117–119
Books, 181–183, 185
Brain damage, 215
Bruner, Jerome, 87
Buber, Martin, 11

Celebrations, 189–190, 212–215, 218
Change
    in adult development, 97
    in children's play, 240
    divorce and, 98
    infants, parents, and, 192–193
    social, 141–142, 216
Child development, 94, 163*t*
    abstract thinking, pretend-play
        and, 236–239
    ages 7–18 months, 119–124
    ages 19 months–3 years, 124
    ages 3–5 years, 130–134
    birth–6 months, 113–119
    communication and language in,
        165–166
    illness and, 212
    information and parents, 48–50
    parents and, 186–187
    play and, 221–222, 233, 242
    rituals and, 208–209
    sense of self and, 111–129,
        138*t*
    sibling relationships, 254–255
    toilet training and, 204
    see also Infants; Language
        development; Toddlers

Children
abuse and neglect, 69–70
adjusting to additional siblings, 246–250
child-rearing strategies and, 133–134
divorce and, 217–218
home visitors' shared delight in, 28–29
illnesses of, 209–212
parental comparison of siblings, 250–252
parents' interaction with, 55–57
parents' play and, 221–222, 233
stranger anxiety in, 121–122
substance abuse and, 36–37
valuing, 252–254
violence and, 136–137
see also Families
Communication, 40–59, 165–166, 187t–188t, 208
ages 10–15 months, 171–174
ages 16–24 months, 174–177
ages 2–5 years, 177–181
birth–10 months, 167–171
during feeding periods, 196
play and, 222–223, 237
Communities
agencies, 99–100
social supports in, 62–63
violence in, 136–137
Confidentiality, 68–69
Conscience development, 160
Consequences, 154
Cultural diversity, 71–84, 96–100, 184, 217

Depression, 134–135
Dewey, John, 85, 87
Dilthey, William, 265
Discipline, 141–142, 163t
ages 8–17 months, 147–151
ages 18–36 months, 151–157
ages 3–5 years, 157–160
birth–8 months, 142–147
developmental approach in, 142–143
methods of, 160–161, 163t
Divorce, 98–99, 217–218
Drug abuse, see Substance abuse

Ear infections, 210–211
Eating, 198–202, 215
Ecological approach, 95–96
Eczema, 211
Education, 87–101
of administrators, 105–106
of home visitor, 275–277, 289–290
of parent, 16
teenage parent, 34
Einstein, Albert, 39
Emerging literacy, see Literacy
Emotional availability, 146
Erikson Institute, 105
Ethical issues, 68–70
Even Start, 5

Failure to thrive (FTT) syndrome, 215, 216t
Families
American, 216
at-risk, 96–97
celebrations and traditions, 212–215
chaotic, 78–83
cultural diversity within, 217
difficulties with, 78–83
dinners, 202–203
divorced, single-parent, and blended, 98–99
extended, 60–62
of home visitor, 271–272, 275, 285–289, 295–298, 298–301
individualizing across, 41–43, 88–89
large, 260
low-income, 74–77, 215
home visiting with, 260–261
television and, 240
systems and life cycle, 97–99
see also Children; Parents
Fears, 156–157, 195
see also Stranger anxiety
Feeding, 198–202
Fetal alcohol syndrome (FAS), 36
Fighting, 256
Foxfire Teacher Networks, 101
Friendships, 277, 290–291
Frustration tolerance, 144

Gender identity, 125–126
Gestures, 171
see also Communication

Ghosts in the nursery, 135
Grandparents, 30–33, 41, 60–62, 204
Guidance, 142–143, 163*t*
   ages 8–17 months, 147–151
   ages 18–36 months, 151–157
   ages 3–5 years, 157–160
   birth–8 months, 142–147

Hall, G. Stanley, 3
Holidays, 213–214
Holophrase, 174
Home environment, 18, 154–155, 232
Home visiting
   assumptions about, 5–6
   cultural diversity and, 72–74
   expectations regarding, 12–15
   history of, 2–3
   across large geographic areas, 101
   as new profession, 302
   personal meaningfulness of,
      267–268, 279–280
   primary purpose of, 39
Home visitors
   education of, 275–277, 289–290
   expectations of, 12–15
   friendships of, 277, 290–291
   interaction with children, 57–59,
      256–259
   interaction with large and extended
      families, 60–62, 260
   interaction with parents, 55–57,
      256–259
   models of, 4
   parent affirmation and, 28–29,
      45–47
   parent involvement and, 54–55
   parent relationship with, 11–12,
      25–28, 43–45, 50–52, 82–83
      teenage, 25–28
   personal history of, 265–267, 275,
      285–289, 298–301
   personal life of, 23–25, 278–279,
      292–295, 295–298
   philosophy and principles to guide,
      89–90
   problem solving and, 53–54
   professional development of,
      85–87, 105
   program agenda for, 12, 15–16
   religion of, 277, 291–292
   roles of, 12, 16–18

Illness, 209–212
Independence, 122–123, 151, 155, 200,
   207–208
Infants
   communication, 167–174, 187*t*
   feeding, 198–202
   massage and, 211
   parents' needs and, 144–145
   play, 221–222, 223–227,
      241–242
   with prenatal exposure to
      substance abuse, 114*t*–115*t*
   preparation for new, 246
   sleep and, 190–195
   social interaction and, 222–223
   temperament of, 115–117, 145–147, 191
Infeld, Leopold, 39
Intention, shared, 119

Jargon, 171–174

Kinaesthetic understanding, 127

Language development, 165–166,
   187*t*–188*t*
   ages 10–15 months, 171–174
   ages 16–24 months, 174–177
   ages 2–5 years, 177–181
   birth–10 months, 167–171
   emerging literacy, 181–184,
      187*t*–188*t*
   play and, 184, 238
   receptive language, 170
   see also Child development
Legal issues, 68–70
Lesson plans, 65–66
Libraries, 183
Life histories, 265–266
Limit setting, 147, 150*t*, 155
Listening
   active, 27
   empathic, 44–45
Literacy
   emerging, 181–184, 187*t*–188*t*
   of parents, 184
Loveys, 121

Malnourishment, 215
Management, 66–68

Massage, 211
Materials, 67–68
Maternal depression, 134–135
Mead, Margaret, 222, 245
Medical emergency, 210
Miller, William, 189
Mobility
  of families, 76
  of toddlers, 150
Modeling, 4, 47–48
Motherese, 176
Motor development, 226
Movement, 228–232

Negativism, 151–152, 200, 209
Networks
  with community agencies, 63–65,
    99–100
  within neighborhood, 62–63
  promoting social, 59–60

Obedience, 147
Observation, 45–47

Parents
  affect regulation and, 116–117
  affirmation of, 28–29, 45–47
  authoritative, authoritarian, and
    permissive, 133–134
  bonding, 117–119
  challenges of working with, 34–37
  child development and, 138t,
    186–187
  communication with toddlers and
    preschoolers, 174–181,
    187t–188t
  developmental information and,
    48–50
  directive, 242–244
  divorce of, 217–218
  expectations
    regarding children, 250–252
    regarding home visits, 12–15
  home visitor as, 273
  illness and, 209–212
  infant communication with,
    167–174, 187t
  infant needs and, 144–145
  interaction with children, 134, 222

  interaction with home visitor,
    55–57
  involvement in play, 54–55
  literacy and, 184
  personal problems of, 134–135
  play and, 123–124, 233–234,
    240–242
  problem solving and, 53–54
  reactions of, 18–20
  regulation by, 124
  relationship with home visitor, 43
    forming, 13–20
    progression of, 20–25
    reciprocal positive feelings in,
      25–28
  responsiveness of, 119–120
  roles of, 12, 16–18
  siblings and, 256–259
  single, 98–99, 134–135
  strengths of, 23
  teenage, 29–34
  television and, 240–241
  unresolved childhood sibling
    conflicts of, 259–260, 300–301
  violence and, 136–137
  see also Discipline; Families;
    Guidance
Parents as Teachers Program (PAT), 3,
  5, 65
Physical punishment, 160–161, 161t
Piaget, Jean, 222
Play, 128, 221–222
  abstract thinking and, 236–239
  ages 30 months–5 years, 235–239
  ages 12–30 months, 227–234
  birth–12 months, 222–227
  directive parents and, 242–244
  exploratory, 223–232, 242–244
  home visiting and, 238–239,
    256–259
  parallel, 129
  pretend-play, 228
  role-play, 157, 184, 232–233,
    235–239, 241
  television and, 240
  value of, 242
Portage Project, 65
Poverty, 74–77, 215
Praise, 161–162
Pregnancy, 247
Prenatal/Early Infancy Project, 65

Preschoolers
  books and, 181–183, 185
  play and, 235–239
  problem solving and, 158–160
  questioning and, 180–181
  sexual curiosity, aggression, and, 158
  sleep and, 195–196
  toilet training and, 203–207
Problem solving, 53–54, 158–160
Professional competence, 265–267
  childhood pain and, 298–301
Professional conferences, 92–93
Professional development, 268–270, 270–273, 280–283, 283–285
Program agenda, 12, 15–16, 65–66

Questioning, 52–53, 180–181

Rapid eye movement (REM) sleep, 191
Record keeping, 68
Recruitment, 76
Regulation disorder, 135
Religion, 277, 291–292
Research, 4
Rewards, 161, 202
Rites of passage, 213
Rituals, 189–190, 190–209, 208–209, 209, 218
Rogers, Carl, 87
Role-play, 128, 157, 184, 241
  preschoolers and, 235–239
  toddlers and, 232–233
Rural, 101

Safety, 77–78, 78t, 149, 149t, 227
St. Augustine, 165
Self, sense of, 111–112, 138t
  ages 7–18 months, 119–124
  ages 19 months–3 years, 124–129
  ages 3–5 years, 130–134
  birth–6 months, 113–119
Self-calming, 113–114, 114t–115t, 121, 191
Self-control, 160
Self-esteem, 133–134
Self-expression, 239
Seminars, 92–93

Settlement houses, 2–3
Sexuality, 126–127, 127–128, 131–132, 158
Shared intention, 119
Shared joint attention, 119
Siblings, 245–246
  differential treatment of, 254
  parents and, 256–259
  relationships of, 254–256
  rivalry, 249–250, 256
Sleep, 190–195
Social change, 141–142
Social class, 74–78
Social development, 128–129, 131–133
Social referencing, 147, 171
Social supports, *see* Networks
Staff meetings, 94–95, 100
Stranger anxiety, 121–122
  see also Fears
Substance abuse, 36–37, 114, 114t–115t
Supervision, 102–105

Tagore, Rabindranath, 221
Talk, parallel and jargon, 173–174
Team meetings, 90–92
Technology, 216
  see also Television
Teething, 198–199
Television, 127, 158, 239–241
  see also Technology
Temperament, 115–117, 145–147, 191
Temper tantrums, 152–153
Time management, 66, 202–203
Time-out, 153–154
Toddlers, 151–157
  eating, 198–202
  guidance and discipline of, 147–151, 150t
  parents playing with, 241–242
  play, 227–234
  sleep and, 194–196
  toilet training and, 203–207
Toilet training, 203–207
Toys, 239
Traditions, 212–215
Trust, 120–121
Twain, Mark, 141

Values, 141–142
Videotapes, 240

Violence, 142
  community, 136–137
  physical punishment and,
    160–161, 161*t*
  television and, 158, 240

Women, Infants, and Children
  (WIC) program, 63

Word combination, 174–177
Workplace supports, 62–63
Workshops, 92–93
Writing, 181, 183–184

ZERO TO THREE/National Center
  for Infants, Toddlers, and
  Families, 102, 105